CRISIS

CRISIS

THE LAST YEAR OF THE CARTER PRESIDENCY

HAMILTON JORDAN

MICHAEL JOSEPH
LONDON

First published in Great Britain by Michael Joseph Ltd
44 Bedford Square, London WC1
1982

All photographs not otherwise credited are courtesy of the
Carter Presidential Materials Project.

ISBN 0 7181 2248 8

Printed by Hollen Street Press, Slough, Berkshire
Bound by Hunter & Foulis, Edinburgh

For Ad and Doffy

Introduction

"1980 was pure hell—the Kennedy challenge, Afghanistan, having to put the SALT Treaty on the shelf, the recession, Ronald Reagan, and the hostages . . . always the hostages! It was one crisis after another."

Jimmy Carter said this to me on January 22, 1981, when we were on our way back to Georgia from Wiesbaden, West Germany, where the former President had greeted the fifty-two Americans who had just been set free by Iranian terrorists.

My responsibilities in the Carter White House were varied, but as 1980 approached, my thoughts and efforts became increasingly concentrated on a single objective: the re-election of President Carter. A series of unexpected events pushed me to center stage in the drama that featured the hostages.

This is my story of the last year of the Carter Presidency, a year in which I learned a lot about America, about the world, and about myself.

To tell my story, I relied heavily on the following sources:

1. *My Own Records*. From the time that I became formally involved in the foreign policy processes of the Carter Administration (January 1978), I kept careful notes of weekly foreign policy breakfasts, intelligence briefings, and other meetings in which major issues were discussed and decided. When I became directly involved, in December 1979, in moving the former Shah of Iran to Panama, and later in secret negotiations with the Khomeini government, I kept meticulous notes of every meeting, telephone call, and conversation on that subject, often writing on the backs of memos and notepads. When I traveled, I often wrote "trip reports," recording not only the substance of the meetings but also conversations and anecdotes that conveyed the flavor of those encounters. My personal records, now stored in the Federal Archives, were available to me in writing this book.

2. *Official Documents*. For the portions of the book that relate to President Carter's campaigns, I relied on records stored at his office in Atlanta. To reconstruct the substance and details of the negotiations for the release of the hostages, I had access to and relied heavily upon the official documents and records—cables, memcons (memoranda of conversations), and transcripts of meetings—that were part of the Administration's files stored at the Federal Archives. These voluminous records recap very precisely the telephone calls, meetings, and negotiating sessions.

3. *Eleanor's Diary*. My secretary, Eleanor Connors, kept a personal diary for me. It is a lively account of whom I saw and talked with each day, laced with her own thoughts, feelings, and descriptions of persons, meetings, and events. Eleanor's diary was extremely helpful to me in recalling both major events and anecdotes that I hope give some life and humanness to this story. Most important, her diary helped me to recall and rediscover my own feelings from that long and difficult year.

4. *Interviews*. In reconstructing this story, we interviewed more than ninety individuals who were directly involved in its

various aspects. Over two-thirds of the interviews were conducted in person, tape recorded, and transcribed. The average interview lasted about an hour and a half, although sessions with many of the principals extended for as long as four or five hours. Twenty of the interviews were made by telephone. I personally conducted more than forty interviews. The others were conducted by Elizabeth Gibson and Tom Laney, two able Emory University graduate students who served as the researchers for this project.

The three of us traveled all over the country and the world, trying to reconstruct the history of that last year. I went to France to talk with Dr. Georges Flandrin, the prominent French oncologist who was the Shah's physician for eight years. Dr. Flandrin made the original diagnosis of the Shah's cancer, and traveled secretly to Iran every few weeks for six years in order to treat the Shah. Dr. Flandrin was helpful in providing me with a better understanding of the interaction of politics and medicine.

I went all the way to Montreux, Switzerland, on the promise of an interview with Ardeshir Zahedi, the Shah's son-in-law and the suave Ambassador to the United States during those last critical years. After I arrived, Zahedi refused to see me.

I spent five hours with William Sullivan, the U.S. Ambassador to Iran from 1977 to early 1979, and a critic of our policies. Sullivan provided a different perspective on our policies and actions in Iran.

Through third parties, we were also able to interview certain Iranians who played important roles in the U.S.-Iran crisis. These persons for obvious reasons agreed to be interviewed only if their anonymity could be protected. Others in the present U.S. government have made the same request.

The only people who consistently refused to be interviewed were the friends, business associates, and family of the late Shah of Iran. Their logic, as expressed by Bob Armao, who served on the Shah's staff, was that "no one associated with Carter could write a fair book." In responding to my request for an interview, Princess Ashraf, the late Shah's twin sister, wrote, "As you say, you and I view this period of history from very different perspectives, and our opinions of policies and decisions differ as well.

Under these circumstances I see no useful purpose to be served by an interview. I will be very interested to see whether the result of your efforts will indeed be the accurate story of what happened." Princess Ashraf systematically prevented me from talking with persons in the employ of the Pahlavi family.

Denied access to the Shah's family and associates, I was left to rely on notes from my meetings with him as well as on the recollections of the group of Panamanians who worked for him during the four months that he lived on Contadora Island. We spoke with the Shah's butler, his secretary, his wife's tennis instructor, and others who observed him at close range during his exile in Panama. These persons liked the Shah and his family, and their remembrances of him were largely sympathetic.

To help appreciate and understand the Shah's own attitudes and feelings about this period of his life, I read two books: the Shah's *Answer to History*, completed on his deathbed, and *Faces in a Mirror*, by Princess Ashraf. Both books support the theme that Jimmy Carter alone was responsible for the Iranian Revolution and its aftermath.

The following are the persons, with their roles, who were interviewed in conjunction with my research on this book:

RAFI AHMED, chef de cabinet to UN Secretary General Kurt Waldheim

CECIL ANDRUS, Secretary of the Interior

COLONEL MIMS AULTMAN, doctor, Gorgas U.S. Army Hospital, Panama

COLONEL CHARLES BECKWITH, Commander of Delta Force, which attempted to rescue the American hostages in Tehran

CHRISTIAN BOURGUET, French lawyer and human rights activist; intermediary during the secret negotiations

HAROLD BROWN, Secretary of Defense

EDWARD BRUNNER, Chief of Political Division Number Two, Government of Switzerland

ZBIGNIEW BRZEZINSKI, National Security Advisor

LANDON BUTLER, deputy to Hamilton Jordan

PATRICK CADDELL, Carter pollster and adviser

MIKE CARDOZO, former deputy to White House Counsel Lloyd
   Cutler
JIMMY CARTER, President of the United States
ROSALYNN CARTER, First Lady
WARREN CHRISTOPHER, Deputy Secretary of State
SUSAN CLOUGH, personal secretary to President Carter
ELEANOR CONNORS, secretary to Hamilton Jordan
PETER CONSTABLE, member of Secretary of State Vance's staff
RICHARD COTTAM, University of Pittsburgh professor and Iran
   expert
LLOYD CUTLER, legal counsel to President Carter
TOM DONILON, Carter convention manager and campaign
   adviser
TIM FINCHEM, key Carter-Mondale campaign strategist
DR. GEORGES FLANDRIN, French doctor and personal
   physician to the Shah
JIM FREE, White House Congressional staff member and
   Southern coordinator of the Carter-Mondale campaign
DR. CARLOS GARCIA, Panamanian physician and close friend of
   General Omar Torrijos
FRANÇOIS GIULIANI, press spokesman for former UN Secretary
   General Kurt Waldheim
RORY GONZALES, Panamanian businessman; friend of and
   adviser to General Omar Torrijos
BECKY HENDRIX, assistant to media adviser Jerry Rafshoon
RICK HERTZBERG, speechwriter for President Carter
DR. JEANE HESTER, American oncologist who traveled to
   Panama to treat the Shah
RICK HUTCHESON, staff secretary to President Carter
WADE ISHIMOTO, Delta Force member
JIM JOHNSON, staff member and adviser to Vice President
   Mondale
GENERAL DAVID JONES, Chairman of Joint Chiefs of Staff
CHARLES KIRBO, Georgia lawyer and close friend of President
   Carter
TIM KRAFT, Carter-Mondale campaign manager
SHELDON KRYS, State Department official responsible for
   liaison with hostages' families; also in charge of return of
   former hostages

BRUCE LAINGEN, U.S. chargé d'affaires in Iran and senior
    American hostage

GABRIEL LEWIS, Panamanian Ambassador to the United States
    and close friend of General Omar Torrijos

ROBERT LIPSHUTZ, legal counsel to the President

MADELINE McBEAN, personal assistant to Rosalynn Carter

SERGEANT JOSÉ DE JESÚS (CHU-CHU) MARTÍNEZ, bodyguard to
    General Omar Torrijos

PAUL MASELIN, assistant to pollster Patrick Caddell

TONY MAY, Panamanian tennis pro and instructor to the Shah's
    wife

WILLIAM MILLER, Secretary of the Treasury

DICK MOE, Chief of Staff to Vice President Mondale

WALTER MONDALE, Vice President of the United States

FRANK MOORE, Assistant for Congressional Affairs to the
    President

AMBLER MOSS, U.S. Ambassador to Panama

FRANZ MUHEIM, Swiss diplomat

EDMUND MUSKIE, Secretary of State

DAVID NEWSOM, Deputy Under Secretary of State

COLONEL MANUEL ANTONIO NORIEGA, Panamanian officer in
    charge of the Shah's security in Panama

STEVE POLLAK, lawyer to Hamilton Jordan for drug charges

JODY POWELL, press secretary to President Carter

HENRY PRECHT, head of Iran Working Group, in charge of
    efforts to win release of the hostages

JERRY RAFSHOON, media adviser to President Carter

ARNIE RAPHEL, member of Secretary of State Vance's staff

DR. ADAN RIOS, Panamanian physician in charge of the Shah's
    medical care

DAVID RUBENSTEIN, Deputy Assistant to the President for
    Domestic Policy

MARCEL SALIMAN, Panamanian political adviser to General
    Omar Torrijos

PIERRE SALINGER, ABC correspondent who covered the
    hostage crisis and produced a documentary on it

HAL SAUNDERS, Assistant Secretary of State for Near Eastern
    and South Asian Affairs

CHARLES SCHULTZE, Chairman, Council of Economic Advisers

WILLIAM SCHWARTZ, U.S. Ambassador to the Bahamas during the Shah's stay there

LIEUTENANT COLONEL CHARLES SCOTT, Army officer and hostage

CAROLYN SHIELDS, assistant to Jody Powell

TIM SMITH, Carter-Mondale legal counsel and strategist

JOSÉ SOSA, general manager of Contadora Island, Panama

BOB STRAUSS, chairman of Carter-Mondale re-election campaign

WILLIAM SULLIVAN, U.S. Ambassador to Iran

GENERAL OMAR TORRIJOS, Panamanian leader

STANSFIELD TURNER, Director of Central Intelligence

RALPH TURSI, manager of Contadora Island hotel and casino

CRISTÓBAL VALENCIA, Panamanian valet to the Shah

CYRUS VANCE, Secretary of State

STEPHANIE VAN REIGERSBERG, State Department interpreter

DALYS VARGAS, Panamanian secretary to the Shah

HECTOR VILLALON, Argentinian businessman living in France; intermediary in secret hostage negotiations

KURT WALDHEIM, Secretary General of the United Nations

JACK WATSON, White House Chief of Staff

SARAH WEDDINGTON, Assistant to the President

ANNE WEXLER, Assistant to the President

PHIL WISE, appointments secretary to the President

My grateful thanks also to the following people:

President Jim Laney and Emory University for providing me a stimulating environment in which to research, reflect, and write.

My colleagues at Emory, particularly Dean Jim Waits and Dr. Dan Carter, both of whom read my book at an early stage and offered important criticism and advice; and my friends at Woodruff Library, Emory University, for their support and help.

Dr. Richard Hammonds, a physician and my friend, who reviewed our medical research on the Shah's illness and wisely guided me away from making value judgments about his treatment. Richard also read my manuscript at an early stage and offered good advice.

The staff at the Jimmy Carter Presidential Archives in Atlanta, for their cooperation.

Andrea Reed, for her help in the preparation of the final manuscript.

Tom Laney, who was involved in the research phase and gave me good advice about what *Crisis* should and should not be.

Sheri Feldman Cerny and Elizabeth Gibson. This book was a team effort, and would not have been possible without them. Sheri managed my Emory office and organized the research for this book, giving along the way her very human touch to my writing. Elizabeth was initially a researcher and later worked at my side as my "Georgia editor" and critic, devoting herself totally to this book.

Bob Malina and Bruce Bodner, my lawyers and friends, who represented me and introduced me to Putnam's Senior Editor Faith Sale.

Putnam's President Peter Israel and Publisher Phyllis Grann, who gave me the opportunity to write this book; Bob Tabian, Subsidiary Rights Director, for his good efforts on my behalf; Gypsy da Silva and Fred Sawyer, who toiled over every word and phrase; and Maura Walsh, my editor's assistant, who was able to solve any problem.

Putnam's gave me the support that a new writer needs, but most of all it gave me Faith—Faith Sale, my editor, who guided me in developing the idea of *Crisis* and prodded me along the way to be true to that idea. Without Faith's encouragement, friendship, and constant advice, and her belief in that idea, this book could never have been written.

Hamilton Jordan
Lawrenceville, Georgia

It was 11:40 A.M. In a few short minutes, Ronald Reagan would be sworn in as President of the United States. And, much more important to me, Jimmy Carter would no longer be President. After more than a year, there was still a chance we could get the hostages out of Iran in twenty minutes.

The Situation Room, on the ground floor of the White House, has the best communications facilities in the world. I had phones pressed against both ears, and my eyes darted from the clock on one wall to the television set, showing the Reagan inauguration, mounted on the opposite wall. With me was Captain Gary Sick, a member of the National Security staff at the White House, who specialized in the Middle East. Eleanor Connors, my secretary for the past four years, and Gerald Rafshoon, the President's media adviser and my good friend, were there too, waiting to ride with me to Andrews Air Base, where Air Force One was standing by to take Citizen Jimmy Carter and the rest of us home to Georgia.

One of the phones connected Gary and me to President Carter in the limousine that was carrying him and the President-elect to the Inaugural ceremonies at the Capitol. The other phone connected us to an intelligence officer who was monitoring the Tehran airport and two Algerian planes on the runway. Earlier, the intelligence officer had reported that the hostages were on the two planes, headed for Algiers. Now the voice on the phone said, "The planes have been told to taxi to the end of the runway." *My God*, I thought, *maybe they'll take off before noon.*

We were obsessed with having the hostages leave Iran during Carter's Presidency. At the end of fourteen months of frustration and disappointment, Jimmy Carter deserved one last, sweet moment: to announce that the hostages had been released.

The White House operator came back on the phone. "Mr. Jordan, the President wants you."

"Any news, Ham?" Carter asked.

"No, sir. The reports are that they're actually in the planes and on the runway. It could be any minute now."

"That's what you and Gary told me five minutes ago!" he snapped.

"That's what they're telling us."

The President said he had instructed his personal aide, Phil Wise, to notify him the minute they took off; the Secret Service could pass him a note on the platform, he explained.

As usual, Jimmy Carter was a couple of steps ahead of the rest of us. I could just imagine it: *Reagan is taking the oath of office while a very conspicuous Carter aide rushes down the Inaugural platform to hand Carter a note. Carter smiles broadly, walks up to the Justice who is about to administer the Presidential oath to Reagan, and says, "Excuse me, Governor Reagan—I have an announcement to make."* This pleasant thought was interrupted as the television showed the President and the President-elect arriving at the Capitol.

"Any news, gentlemen?" I asked into the red phone.

"No, sir, Mr. Jordan. We'll let you know the second we hear

anything. By the way, all of us here would like the President to know that we're pulling for him on this thing."

"Thanks. I'll sure pass that on."

"Hamilton," Eleanor nagged, "you've got to go. We were supposed to be out of the White House before the President left. The Reagan people are moving in right now. It'll look *terrible* for you to still be here."

"Ellie," I replied, "I don't care *how* it looks—I'm staying on this damn phone until either the hostages take off or Ronald Reagan takes the oath of office!"

The President came back on the open line. He was calling from inside the Capitol Building and told me that they were about to go out to begin the ceremony. He asked in a quiet voice if there was any news. I checked once again with the intelligence officer: still nothing.

I watched the two couples walk out onto the Inaugural platform. Reagan paused and waved; Carter seemed to be forcing a smile. Applause thundered across the Capitol grounds. The Carters and Reagans walked down the platform and took their seats. It was high noon, and the dreaded ceremony began. A beaming George Bush took the oath of office as Vice President.

"That's the last time we'll ever see *him*," Rafshoon quipped.

Then the Chief Justice and Governor Reagan rose and walked to the podium. Reagan raised his right hand and began: "I do solemnly swear that I will faithfully execute . . ."

I had a sinking feeling in my stomach. The television camera flashed to Carter. His eyes were closed; I wondered if he was sleeping or praying. He looked pale, wrinkled, and very tired. I clung to the phones, waiting for the message that did not come.

"So help me God," Reagan said, completing the oath.

It was over. The deed was done. Ronald Reagan was President of the United States, Jimmy Carter was not, and the hostages were still waiting in the planes on the runway in Tehran. . . .

November 4, 1979 (Sunday)

I left Washington on Friday to spend the weekend on the eastern shore of Maryland at the home of Nate Landow, a successful Maryland businessman and a friend of the President's. Tim Smith, legal counsel and strategist for the campaign, and Tim Finchem, the campaign treasurer, went with me. We hoped to make some key decisions away from the rush and bustle of events at the White House.

Sunday was certain to be a big day for us. The much-talked-about Roger Mudd interview with Ted Kennedy would be aired. It was an hour-long special during prime time. CBS had bumped its other lucrative programs for a political interview—a sure sign that it was going to be newsworthy. The network was promoting the event heavily, leaking the text to certain reporters and columnists. Several friends in the White House press corps had pulled me aside or called to tell me that the program was a political disaster for Kennedy.

We spent much of the weekend anticipating the show. Our goal was to review the campaign budget for key states, but time and again some reference or joke was made about the Kennedy interview. Could it be possible that the CBS special was as bad for Kennedy as the advance stories suggested?

About 4:30 A.M. the phone in my room rang. It took me a minute to recall where I was. I grappled in the dark, and on what must have been the tenth ring, managed to answer it.

"Mr. Jordan, this is the duty officer in the Situation Room," the voice on the other end said. "We wanted to advise you that the American Embassy in Tehran has been overrun by demonstrators and the American personnel are believed to be held in captivity."

"My God," I said. "Are there any injuries? Was anyone killed?"

"Not that we know of, Mr. Jordan—but we really don't have complete information. We'll keep you informed."

I asked if the President had been notified and was told that

Secretary of State Vance had called him earlier from the Operations Center at the State Department.

I lay in bed thinking about what I had just heard. This could mean war with Iran. And what would it do to the campaign?

The phone rang again. It was Phil Wise, Carter's appointments secretary, who was always with the President, calling from Camp David. Had I heard the news from Iran? I told him that I had just been called and hadn't had much time to think about it, but obviously the President needed to stay on top of things.

"Don't forget," I said, "the press will be looking at this in the context of the campaign. It'll be over in a few hours, but it could provide a nice contrast between Carter and our friend from Massachusetts in how to handle a crisis."

Wise asked if I thought the President should rush back to Washington. I suggested that he wait a few hours. I reminded him that when the same embassy was overrun the previous February, hostages had been taken but then released several hours later when the Iranian government intervened. This, I told Phil, would end the same way.

I was awakened again at 6:15 by another call from the Situation Room. Nothing had changed in Tehran. The State Department was in direct contact with personnel at the embassy and also with Chief of Mission Bruce Laingen, who was at the Iranian Foreign Ministry when the embassy was seized. The fact that we were talking directly to the people being held seemed to me to be a positive sign. *It takes time to work these things out*, I thought to myself, and went back to sleep.

Later in the morning I got up and jogged on a narrow dirt road that meandered beside the quiet waters of the eastern shore. We all had breakfast together and I told about the calls during the night. Everyone agreed that what was going on in Tehran sounded bad and that the Iranians were crazy. They hoped that public attention wouldn't be deflected from the weaknesses of the Kennedy program. "They'll be released before tonight," I predicted confidently.

We were all eager to see how the press was going to play the Kennedy story in the Sunday papers, and I volunteered to drive about fifteen miles into Easton, Maryland, to buy *The Washington Post* and the *Star*. Both papers carried articles by political columnists who had seen the Mudd interview. It was going to be even bigger than I had anticipated. I had seen the same thing happen in 1976 to Jimmy Carter. First the media play an active role in building a candidate, then they seem to delight in tearing him down. And now it was Ted Kennedy's turn.

Although he hadn't announced, there was no question that Kennedy was running. I had thought for over a year that he would challenge us. From studying the 1976 Reagan challenge to President Gerald Ford, I determined that Ford had made one big mistake: his people had spent the entire year trying to persuade Reagan not to run instead of raising money and organizing. Consequently, when the challenge came, the Ford campaign was unprepared. I urged that we use the early part of 1979 to get ready; if Ted Kennedy saw tangible evidence of Carter's determination and political strength, he might be dissuaded from running.

I believed that Kennedy's decision would be based simply and only on whether or not he thought he could win. Consequently, Carter's best stance was to keep on with the nation's business. We would ask him to devote more of his time to campaign politics, but being a good Chief Executive was the best politics of all.

Many at the White House disagreed with me, believing that the way to keep Kennedy out of the race was for the President to adopt more of Kennedy's domestic agenda, particularly his costly and impractical national health insurance program. They also thought that the President should try to make Ted Kennedy his friend and invite him more often to White House functions. Carter wouldn't hear of it. "I'm willing to treat him as an important senator," he said, "but not as the only senator." He wasn't bothered at all by the prospect of a Kennedy challenge. When a Democratic congressman asked what he would do if Kennedy ran, Carter replied, "I'll whip his ass!"

We began to organize for the nomination fight in January. The Kennedy challenge unfolded with repeated denials of candidacy, contradicted by widely reported meetings at the Kennedy compound and calls to political leaders around the country. By September, formal announcement or no, we were certain that Kennedy was running.

I was hoping to see Kennedy do himself in now, in the Mudd interview. And I was discouraged to learn that the other networks were offering big draws opposite the CBS program—one of them had the blockbuster movie *Jaws*. *The biggest political story of the year*, I thought, *and everybody's going to be watching mechanical sharks eating swimmers instead of Roger Mudd eating Ted Kennedy alive*. I wanted everyone to see what I saw: the Kennedy legend reduced to a bumbling, inarticulate man. Others watching with me were shocked by both his poor responses to the Chappaquiddick questions and the devastating film showing the clearly marked road that Kennedy claimed not to have seen that fateful night when he turned onto the beach road and drove off the bridge. But for me the greatest shock came when the Senator was asked why he was running for President.

He started out, in a halting, rambling, almost incoherent way, to mouth a series of clichés and half sentences. Senator Kennedy did not have an answer. And that, to me, was the most revealing moment in the interview. He was running because he wanted to be President. That was not such an unusual motive, but most aspirants figure out some way to disguise it better.

I could hardly contain my pleasure. The public-opinion polls were turning back in Carter's favor, and the Mudd interview would be reverberating throughout the political community. Maybe Kennedy would get the message at last and drop out.

November 5, 1979 (Monday)

But all I heard on the car radio as I drove back from the eastern shore in the morning were news reports from Tehran. I arrived at the White House just in time for the 7:30 preliminary to the daily senior staff meeting. An hour before the actual meeting, deputies reporting to the daily senior staff members got together to outline

the issues and specific problems that would constitute the agenda
for the 8:30 meeting, which I presided over.

Starting at 8:30, the senior staff members, sitting around the
large mahogany table in the Roosevelt Room, reported to me one
by one. Phil Wise would provide details on the President's schedule, and Frank Moore, Congressional liaison, would give a report
on activities in Congress. Presidential Assistant Anne Wexler
often described her office's attempts to muster support among
constituent groups for Carter's policies and legislative proposals.
Jody Powell would usually review topical stories in the news and
try to achieve a consensus on how the press office should handle
them. At 10:00 A.M. a small group of us—including Vice President Mondale, Domestic Adviser Stu Eizenstat, Frank Moore,
Jody Powell, and I—would meet with the President in the Oval
Office to review the earlier sessions and to discuss matters on his
mind.

Everyone at today's meeting was feeling pretty cheerful after
the Ted Kennedy fiasco. "It was terrible," someone said. "Fatal,"
someone else offered. We all snickered.

Then the question of the hostages was raised. "Don't forget," I
said, "this same thing happened last February. We're talking to
our diplomats at the embassy and Foreign Minister Ibrahim Yazdi
and Prime Minister Mehdi Bazargan at the Foreign Ministry. As
soon as the government gets its act together, they'll free our
people."

November 6, 1979 (Tuesday)

I received the usual 6:00 A.M. wake-up call from the operator on
my White House line at my apartment in northwest Washington,
got up, and made myself a cup of coffee. I glanced over my daily
schedule, which Eleanor summarized and slipped into my coat
pocket at the end of every working day.

The debate between President Carter and Senator Kennedy

(scheduled for January in Iowa) was going to be announced that day. It would be the first head-to-head contest between the two men. We were still the underdogs in the race, but Carter pollster Pat Caddell had been reporting for several weeks that the race was tightening, and a *Time* magazine survey had shown that Kennedy's lead over Carter had plummeted from 30 points to 10 points in less than eight weeks.

It's amazing, I thought. *A sitting President is the long shot in the fight for the nomination of his own party*. Of course Carter had always been a long shot. The first time I met him was in 1966, when he was a candidate for Governor of Georgia. It was the summer of my junior year at the University of Georgia, and a friend had dragged me along to be a warm body at an Elks Club luncheon. Carter's speech was halting, his voice so soft that I had to strain to hear him. He rambled on with apparent uncertainty for about ten minutes. I was thoroughly unimpressed. But when he started taking questions from the floor and answering them directly and thoughtfully for nearly an hour, I realized that this was a man of considerable intelligence who had a commonsense approach to Georgia's problems. He struck me as different from the other Georgia politicians, and I became intrigued by the idea of his candidacy.

When I got home, I wrote him a long letter telling him I had worked in Governor Carl Sanders's campaign, exaggerating my involvement and offering to help him in my hometown of Albany, Georgia. Several days later, on the Fourth of July, the phone rang at six in the morning. My father scolded the caller before he said, "Hamilton, it's for you." It was Jimmy Carter, offering me a job in his campaign. Barely awake, I mumbled that I already had a full-time job spraying mosquitoes in a federal program. Carter laughed and said that he was going to have a tough time getting elected if people like me couldn't choose between mosquitoes and him.

I accepted and several hours later was on a bus to Atlanta, entertaining visions of high-level strategy sessions and crucial campaign decisions. Shortly after my arrival, I found myself driving candidate Carter in a Fourth of July parade down Peachtree Street in a big convertible. No one in the crowd paid much attention to our car or our candidate, and by the end of my first day, I thought perhaps I should have stuck with the mosquitoes.

But as Jimmy Carter and his family crisscrossed the state, shaking hands and meeting voters, we gradually came to believe he could win. So it was doubly difficult to accept defeat when Lester Maddox, Georgia's segregationist clown, edged him out of the race by a few thousand votes. Carter departed abruptly for Plains as soon as the outcome was clear.

A couple of weeks later, Jimmy Carter called me at home and apologized for leaving that sad election night without thanking me. I told him that it had been an honor to work for him and that he had run a good campaign. "I'm tired of people saying that I ran a good campaign," he complained. "It wasn't good enough—because I lost. I never intend to lose another election."

When members of my family and several friends from the campaign received hand-addressed Christmas cards from Jimmy and Rosalynn later that year, I knew that defeat had only stimulated him to greater efforts.

After graduation and a stint doing refugee relocation in Vietnam for a voluntary organization, I went to Plains. I wasn't surprised to learn that Jimmy Carter was planning another race for Governor—this time against Carl Sanders, the very popular former Governor, who was considered a shoo-in. I argued that Carter should run for Lieutenant Governor and lay the groundwork for 1974. He smiled, shook his head, and said that he wasn't interested: "I'm going to run for Governor if I don't get but two votes, mine and Rosalynn's." I found his confidence contagious and said I would help him: "You'll get at least three votes."

Jimmy Carter won that time and hadn't lost an election since. But none of them had been easy—and this one against Ted Kennedy wouldn't be, either.

The fact that Teddy Kennedy had decided to challenge the President would distract us from dealing with some of the country's problems, and would create divisions in the party, but it was just a matter of time until Kennedy dropped out of the race.

If we could dispense with our opponent quickly and soundly, it might restore some of the lost glow to Carter's Presidency. In any case, it would allow us. to devote more attention to national priorities.

I switched my television from station to station, hoping to find some good news on the hostages—with our embassy out of business, this was the best way to keep informed. For the last two days I had been calling the Situation Room for updates, but all they could give me were news reports. The three major networks were reporting from the front of the American compound in Tehran, so I didn't have to hear the same thing from the Situation Room as well.

One network reported that the moderate government of Prime Minister Bazargan had resigned in protest over the seizure of the hostages. It was Bazargan who had engineered the release of the American personnel when our embassy was overrun in February, and the State Department had been in contact with him since Sunday, hoping he could do it again. We had no embassy left and now there was no government. *Who in the hell are we going to deal with?* I thought.

The phone rang again. It was Phil Wise—the President wanted me at an eight-o'clock meeting in the Cabinet Room. I asked what it was about.

"Iran," Wise replied.

I called the White House garage and ordered my car to come immediately. The gray Chrysler compact was outside my apartment by the time I finished dressing and got downstairs. The Sergeant opened the back door. As usual, the morning papers—*The New York Times* and *The Washington Post*—lay on the back seat. The hostage story dominated the papers, too. As I had feared, the Kennedy interview had almost vanished from sight, destined to remain a "Washington story," discussed among the lobbyists and political operatives at cocktail parties and chic Georgetown restaurants, but never to permeate the consciousness of the average American voter. Although the campaign and the interview were covered in both papers, even the political columnists had turned their attention to Tehran. Would this be Carter's Mayagüez or Vietnam?

As the car turned off Pennsylvania Avenue and started through the White House gates, I saw the bright lights and the "newsies": the three networks were doing standups—live broadcasts from the White House lawn for their morning news programs—and the other press corps regulars, huddled under the portico, shielding themselves from the cold wind, were watching for clues as to what was happening on the inside. They almost never turned out en masse this early; it was a sure sign that the hostage problem was turning into a full-fledged crisis.

The Sergeant asked, "Do you want to be dropped in the middle of that mess?"

I had him pull around to the back gate, where I could slip in without having to dodge the cameras and the questions. I barely had time to drop off my briefcase at my office. Eleanor walked with me down the hall toward the Cabinet Room, reminding me of calls that had to be returned, staff members who wanted to see me, and last-minute changes in my daily schedule. When I hired Eleanor Connors I had no doubt about her abilities—she had worked under Presidents Kennedy, Johnson, Nixon, and Ford—and her loyalty was beyond question. The one thing I did worry about at first was whether such a gentle woman could handle the pressures of my office. Eleanor's looks turned out to be deceiving. She was under five feet tall, with a soft voice in keeping with her size, but she stood at her desk like a giant cobra, coiled and always ready to protect me from the hundreds of calls from persons in and out of government who were determined to lay their problems or needs on my desk. She had finished filling me in by the time we reached the Oval Office. I walked past it to the Cabinet Room, where only the President could conduct business.

A long, rectangular room, lined on one side with French doors that look out on the Rose Garden and on the other with two doors that lead back to the main White House offices, the Cabinet Room is separated from the Oval Office by the small room where Presidential guests wait before entering the Oval Office. A large mahogany table runs the length of the room, and each brown leather chair around it contains a small bronze plate with the namè of the Cabinet Secretary who sits there. Cabinet officers take their chairs with them when they leave the government.

The President's chair, slightly taller than the others, is at the middle of the table; the rest are arranged in the historical order of the creation of the Cabinet offices.

Traditionally, each President selects the portraits of his favorite Presidents to hang in the Cabinet Room. President Carter had chosen Jefferson for his wisdom, Abraham Lincoln for his compassion, and Harry Truman for his courage.

Vice President Fritz Mondale, Secretary of Defense Harold Brown, National Security Advisor Zbigniew Brzezinski, Press Secretary Jody Powell, Secretary of State Cyrus Vance, Gary Sick, and David Newsom from the State Department had already assembled, waiting for the President. Vance was bringing them up-to-date on developments in Iran, while Navy stewards in blue blazers bearing the Presidential seal moved from chair to chair, quietly serving coffee.

At 8:00 A.M. sharp, the President entered, walking briskly and carrying a notepad and a stack of cables. He didn't speak as he took his seat. Then, turning to Vance on his immediate left, he asked for a report on the hostages.

Harold Brown scribbled on his notepad and slipped it across the table to me: "I am waiting for the President to say 'I told you so.'"

And I was, too. For it was less than three weeks ago, at our regular foreign policy breakfast in the same room with the same group of people, that Carter had made a reluctant decision to allow the former Shah of Iran to come to the United States for medical treatment.

We had talked about the Shah in this room many times over the past year.

By November 1978, it was obvious that his regime could not survive, and this presented the President with a real dilemma. Iran provided oil to the industrial West and separated the Soviet Union from the Persian Gulf and the oil states; the United States had an enormous stake in keeping it stable and independent. Now that stability was threatened by a seventy-nine-year-old religious fanatic, the Ayatollah Khomeini, who was in Paris orchestrating the opposition to the Shah.

The Shah had obviously lost the support of his people, but the

President hoped that a coalition of the moderate opponents might be formed. But, as long as the Shah remained in Iran and clung to the false hope that he might be magically saved by the United States, his presence in Iran provided a rallying point for the Khomeini forces and worked against the chances that the moderate group could take power.

Finally, in a conversation with Ambassador Sullivan in early January 1979, the Shah decided to leave Iran and travel to the United States.

The Shah's close American friends, including Nelson Rockefeller, went to work trying to find an American residence fit for a king and his family. Sunnylands, the luxurious California estate of diplomat-businessman Walter Annenberg, was made available for the Shah.

Then came a call from President Sadat inviting the Shah to visit Egypt, where he would be received with full honors. Flattered, the Shah felt he couldn't reject the invitation and postponed his trip to the United States. Furthermore, he apparently did not want to give his enemies the satisfaction of seeing him flee to America, confirming allegations that he was a "U.S. puppet."

The Shah was also convinced by people in his entourage (particularly Ambassador to the U.S. Ardeshir Zahedi) that Khomeini might fall quickly and therefore he should stay near Iran so he could return, as he had in 1953 with the active help of the CIA.

The Shah traveled first to Egypt and then to Morocco. Dispirited and bitter, he spent most of his time listening to news reports from Tehran on his shortwave radio. The widespread chaos and sharp drop in oil production made it look as if Khomeini's days might indeed be numbered.

And while the Khomeini government faltered, it did not fall. By February, the Shah had renewed his interest in coming to the U.S. and was prepared to make an official request.

By this time, the Administration's attitude had changed. Neither President Carter nor Secretary Vance wanted him to come. The Ayatollah Khomeini had returned in triumph to Tehran and clearly had the support of the Iranian people. For better or worse, the Khomeini government was a fact of life, and the United States now had a stake in trying to build relations with the new government.

The chances of doing that seemed good. Mehdi Bazargan, a lifetime opponent of the Shah and an educated, secular man, had been asked to serve as Prime Minister while a committee studied the question of how to organize the Islamic Republic. The appointment of Bazargan was encouraging: Khomeini had turned to a person with governmental and political experience to manage the affairs of state. Maybe Khomeini would do what he had said from exile: once the Islamic Republic was formed, he would return to the religious center in Qom, content to be the spiritual leader of his people.

Certainly, many, many problems had to be worked out between the United States and Iran. Relations would not be what they had been, but it was clearly in the interests of the United States to try. And, as Secretary of State Vance said to the President, whatever chance existed for establishing relations with the new government would surely be destroyed if the Shah came to the States. For the supporters of Khomeini, the return of the young Shah a quarter of a century earlier with the help of the CIA was a dark day in Persian history: the Moslem nation exploited by the godless West.

Brzezinski, however, argued forcefully for allowing the Shah to come to the States. "It is unlikely we can build a relationship with Iran," he said, "until things there have sorted themselves out. But it would be a sign of weakness not to allow the Shah to come to the States to live. If we turned our backs on the fallen Shah, it would be a signal to the world that the U.S. is a fair-weather friend."

The President and Secretary Vance saw it differently. "As long as there is a country where the Shah can live safely and comfortably," the President reasoned, "it makes no sense to bring him here and destroy whatever slim chance we have of rebuilding a relationship with Iran. It boils down to a choice between the Shah's preferences as to where he lives and the interests of our country."

But Carter did not want to embarrass the Shah, nor did he want to have to reject the request, so he instructed Vance to send a suitable emissary to Morocco to sit down with the Shah and explain the problem. The emissary would not have to tell him not to come, but could hint strongly that it was not a good time for him to make such a request. Under Secretary of State David Newsom contacted David Rockefeller and former Secretary of State Henry Kissinger, both of whom were close friends of the Shah and could easily convey the President's message.

Rockefeller was irritated by Newsom's request and would have no part of it, feeling strongly that the United States owed the Shah safe asylum. Kissinger said he resented being asked to represent a view that he disagreed with. At that point, a former intelligence agent who had been stationed in Iran and who knew the Shah was recruited.

The Shah, a proud man, listened to the message and said sternly, "I have no desire to go where I am not welcome." He added, "I am thankful for my true friends—President Sadat and King Hassan."

But even Hassan, King of Morocco, turned on the Shah, making it known, however nicely, that it was time for him to move on. The Shah's odyssey continued. With David Rockefeller's help, he moved to the Bahamas. Then, under alleged pressure from the British, the Bahamian government let him know that he had to leave; after Henry Kissinger's direct intervention with President López Portillo, the Shah was permitted to travel on a tourist visa to Mexico, where he settled into a relaxed life at Cuernavaca.

But the friends of the Shah had not given up trying to bring him to this country. Their argument was simple: How could the United States turn its back on a good and trusted ally? What would it say to our other friends and allies in the world if the Shah were not welcome in the United States after so many years of steadfast support? Through the spring and summer, Kissinger and Rockefeller mentioned it in numerous phone calls to the State Department and the White House. Kissinger openly expressed his disgust with the Administration's failure to provide asylum for the Shah to political friends and members of the press, saying, "A man who for thirty-seven years was a friend of the United States should not be treated like a Flying Dutchman who cannot find a port of call."

So, periodically, sparked by a call from Rockefeller or Kissinger or a note from John McCloy (a friend of Vance's whose law firm represented the Shah), the subject would be raised at our Friday-morning breakfasts—usually by Zbig. And time and again, the President would cite the greater interests of the United States with respect to the new government.

Later, it would be charged that Kissinger and Rockefeller had pressured the President into admitting the Shah. This was not true. The President deeply resented the pressure, and if anything it was counterproductive.

But when Secretary Vance brought it up on October 19, it was in a different context. Joseph Reed, a key member of Rockefeller's staff, had called David Newsom on October 6 to inform him that the Shah was seriously ill and might require medical treatment in the United States. Newsom agreed to pass along the information, but advised Reed that a "substantial medical case" would have to be made before the government of the United States would agree to allow him in. Ten days later, Reed revealed that the Shah had been secretly treated for cancer for over seven years and that he was in critical condition in Mexico. He was in the care of Dr. Benjamin Kean, a prominent New York pathologist recommended to him by David Rockefeller's staff; Dr. Kean was urging that the Shah be moved to the United States because he needed medical treatment available only in this country. So now Vance informed the President that the Shah was making a formal request to come to the United States for medical treatment. For the first time, Vance changed his position, stating that "as a matter of principle" it was now his view that the Shah should be permitted to enter the United States "for humanitarian reasons."

The President argued alone against allowing the Shah in. He questioned the medical judgment and once again made the argument about the interests of the United States.

I mentioned the political consequences: "Mr. President, if the Shah dies in Mexico, can you imagine the field day Kissinger will have with that? He'll say that first you caused the Shah's downfall and now you've killed him."

The President glared at me. "To hell with Henry Kissinger," he said. "I am President of this country!"

The controversy continued as Zbig and Vance—together this

time—stuck to the arguments of "humanitarian principle." It was
obvious that the President was becoming frustrated having to argue alone against all of his advisers and against "principle." Finally, he told Vance to "double-check" the Shah's medical
condition and needs and determine from the American Embassy
in Tehran what the reaction of the Iranian government would be
to the entry of the Shah for medical treatment—and to see if they
would guarantee the safety of our embassy.

Vance said he would cable immediately.

Carter had the last word: "What are you guys going to advise
me to do if they overrun our embassy and take our people
hostage?"

When the President returned to Camp David the afternoon of
October 22, after speaking at the dedication of the Kennedy Li-
brary, the State Department had received a response from Iran.
The senior American diplomat in Iran, Bruce Laingen, and Henry
Precht, a State Department official visiting Iran, had met with
Prime Minister Bazargan and Foreign Minister Ibrahim Yazdi.
They were strongly opposed to the Shah's being in the United
States but promised to protect the embassy just as they had in
February 1979.

The President instructed Vance to proceed with the arrangements to bring the Shah into the United States.

But all that was history. The job at hand was to resolve the
crisis (now in its third day) and get our people out of Tehran. We
still weren't sure how many were being held or if any had been
injured.

Khomeini's speech endorsing the takeover and Bazargan's resignation, Vance concluded, were ominous signs that made the
path to a quick solution less obvious.

"With Bazargan gone, who does that leave us to deal with?"
asked the President.

Vance, peering over his glasses, looked directly at him. "The
Ayatollah Khomeini."

"I'm afraid I had reached the same conclusion," Carter said
quietly.

Vance then put forth a suggestion made by Deputy Secretary of State Warren Christopher that the President send former Attorney General Ramsey Clark to Tehran. Clark had a history of outspoken opposition to the Shah's regime and had even met with Khomeini in Paris in 1979 and expressed support for his Revolution. He was one of a handful of people in the United States who knew the Ayatollah and might have credibility with the Iranians.

Ramsey Clark? I couldn't believe what I was hearing. Jody looked at me and rolled his eyes, and the President must have been thinking the same thing. He told Vance that he was receptive to the idea but concerned about Clark, whose years since he left the government had been spent on the fringes of different international "causes" and who more often than not seemed to blame most of the world's problems on the United States.

The President asked Vance the question that was on my mind: "Can Clark be trusted to go to Iran as my personal representative and accurately convey our nation's position? Or is there a chance that once he's there he'll say something sympathetic to Khomeini, compromise our position, and embarrass our country?"

Vance replied that, while he disagreed with many of Clark's views, he had worked with him before and knew he was an honorable man who could be expected to follow instructions as a Presidential envoy. He proposed that William Miller, a staff member on the Senate Intelligence Committee, who spoke Farsi and knew several of the Iranian leaders, be sent on the mission with Clark.

"I don't have any better ideas," the President said, and directed Vance to contact Clark. If Clark responded positively, Carter wanted to have written instructions prepared for his envoys and to meet with them before they left.

He admonished Vance, "Let's don't screw around with this Ramsey Clark thing. Let's move ahead with it. Every hour our people are being held, the chances increase that someone will get hurt or killed. I'll meet with Clark and Miller whenever you can get them here."

The President rose to leave for his regular weekly breakfast with the Congressional leadership, paused at the door, and said,

"By the way, Cy and Jody, I'm tired of seeing those bastards holding our people referred to as 'students.' Jody, you and Hodding [Hodding Carter, the State Department spokesman] get together and figure out what to call them. But they should be referred to as 'terrorists' or 'captors' or something that accurately describes what they are."

"Yes, sir," Jody replied. And as soon as President Carter had closed the door behind him, Jody quipped, "How about 'Islamic thugs'?"

At about four o'clock I checked the Oval Office, looking for the President, who had penciled a note on a memorandum: "See me on this." He wasn't there, so I knew he was in his study, where he often retreated. It is separated from the Oval Office by a short hallway. The Oval Office is handsome but awe-inspiring in both its size and its significance; by contrast, the small office is intimate and warm. The President had chosen warm colors and fabrics for the furniture and walls. On the wall facing his desk was an oil painting of Rosalynn Carter, with four-year-old Amy in her lap, painted by Thornton Utz while Jimmy Carter was still Governor of Georgia. Behind his desk hung the famous Childe Hassam impressionist painting "Flag Day." On the side wall were pencil sketches of old, weather-beaten Georgia farmhouses, a photograph of the President and Billy Carter at a softball game, grinning broadly, their arms hung loosely around each other's necks, and a touching black-and-white picture of "Miss Lillian" with Senator Hubert Humphrey, who wore a fur hat and smiled adoringly at the President's mother.

Behind his desk, and within arm's reach of his comfortable leather swivel chair, was the large globe that President Carter loved and referred to regularly. He once told me that in addition to the information that State Department briefing books supplied on nations and their leaders, the easiest and best way to understand a country, its history, and its vital interests, was to look at the globe—to observe the countries surrounding it, its proximity to richer and stronger nations, to international waters and ports. Before conferring with a foreign leader, Carter would often sit by his globe, poring over his briefing books and trying to imagine the political, economic, and military pressures experienced by the leader and his or her country. "I try·to put myself in their shoes," he once told me.

A large wooden bookcase stood by his desk and contained some of his most treasured possessions: the poems of Dylan Thomas, a number of biographies of his favorite Presidents (Jefferson, Lincoln, and Truman), and signed biographies of Brezhnev, Sadat, Begin, and other world leaders whom he had met during the course of his Presidency. Jimmy Carter spent some of the most rewarding and difficult moments of his term in this small office. When he wanted to put a visitor at ease or convey a particularly sensitive thought or request, he would excuse himself from the others in the Oval Office and walk the guest into his private study. Deng Xiaoping, Menachem Begin, Anwar Sadat, and the Shah of Iran had all spent time here with the President.

I seldom knocked before·sticking my head into the Oval Office, but always did so before entering his study. "Mr. President," I said quietly.

He answered in a voice that told me I should have left him alone. He had his glasses on and was writing on the light-green Presidential stationery that he reserved for personal communications of the highest order. "Maybe I should wait?"

"See me later if you don't mind—I'm writing a letter to Khomeini."

I was amused at the idea of the Southern Baptist writing to the Moslem fanatic. *What will he say to the man?* I thought. *Maybe he'll sign the letter "The Great Satan."*

At our 4:30 National Security meeting, President Carter said he wanted to be sure that Khomeini clearly understood the position of the United States. "I told him that the Americans being held were not spies, that it was inhumane for them to be held as hostages, and, for the sake of both nations, there should be a quick and honorable solution." He said he had been firm but not antagonistic or threatening, and he would have Clark hand-deliver the letter to the Ayatollah.

We reviewed the instructions Vance had prepared for Clark and Miller, who were already waiting in the outer office to see the President. Carter's military aide asked if they should be shown in. The President paused, shook his head no, and said he would prefer to see them in the Oval Office.

He wanted to impart to the envoys an idea of the sensitivity of their mission and also wanted to enable them to say when they reached Iran that they had come directly from a meeting with the President of the United States in the Oval Office. The President rose, asked Vance to join his conference with Clark and Miller, and our meeting broke up.

Jody walked back to my office with me, as he often did. It was a natural place to get together and rehash a meeting. We couldn't do it in Jody's office without being cornered by ABC correspondent Sam Donaldson or UPI reporter Helen Thomas. Jody and I watched the evening news in my office and ordered sandwiches from the White House mess. Jody stood in front of my set, perpetual cigarette in hand, flipping the knob from one channel to another. Just as a segment began, he would switch to another channel, so I could hardly keep track of what was happening.

Developments in Iran and speculation on our two NSC meetings dominated the news. There were clips of Secretaries Vance and Brown arriving and leaving the White House in their black limousines, accompanied by solemn aides clutching briefcases.

"At least it looks like the President is on top of the crisis," I said hopefully.

"They think we're doing more than we are," Jody said. "They don't know how lousy our options are. NSC meetings won't satisfy the American people for long."

Jody's hard-nosed judgment rang true. What was all this going to do to the President's image and his prospects for re-election?

When the White House limousine picked me up in front of the West Wing several hours later, I was ready to go home. It had been a long day. We were driving down Rock Creek Parkway and up Massachusetts Avenue when suddenly the traffic slowed to a crawl. Several hundred people were gathered in front of the Iranian Embassy. The D.C. police had roped off the sidewalk, ironically providing the Iranian building the very protection our embassy in Iran lacked.

I felt the anger of that crowd and saw it etched on every face.

Their rage, their very presence, seemed to be saying, *We've had enough! After Vietnam and OPEC price increases and gasoline lines, we've had enough. This is the last straw—Americans held hostage by a bunch of terrorists. We won't stand for it anymore!*

I was glad that the people cared, but bothered that they cared so much. *An ugly mood will develop in this country if the hostages aren't out soon,* I thought to myself.

I asked the driver to pull over and we sat watching for a while. Some people were singing, others chanted, "Let our people go!" People in passing cars honked their horns and shouted encouragement. Television crews had arrived and several correspondents spread through the crowd interviewing the protestors. After a few minutes, a bearded young Iranian came out of the embassy to talk with a police captain. The crowd began to boo and jeer. "Go home!" they shouted. "Let our people go!" I didn't want anyone in the press to see me hanging around the Iranian Embassy, so I slid down in the back seat and told the Sergeant to drive me home.

Jody was right, I thought. *The American people won't be satisfied for long with meetings at the White House.*

Ramsey Clark was an unlikely hero, but at least, after two days, something was being done.

November 7, 1979 (Wednesday)

We received word overnight that Clark and Miller had been denied permission to enter Tehran. They weren't "welcome" in Iran, a radio report said. And one of the captors at the compound reportedly asked, "Do you think the Spirit of God would meet with those two evil characters?" The President ordered the envoys to stand by in Turkey in case there was a change of attitude, but he was pessimistic. "I was feeling pretty good when they left, then I started thinking about it. If Khomeini wants to resolve this mess, it isn't likely that he'll use Americans to do it. He'll want to use the PLO or find some way to humiliate our country. We'll have to try a lot of different things."

Around noon, the legal counsel's office brought to my attention a memo concerning a parade permit that had been granted to a group of pro-Khomeini students who wanted to demonstrate in front of the White House.

Permits to parade and protest around the White House were routinely granted, and it was normal to see groups assembled in the park across Pennsylvania Avenue from the White House or on the Ellipse, behind the White House, protesting anything from abortion to U.S. policy in Africa.

The memory of angry Americans was still vivid in my mind from the previous night. If these Iranians protested in front of the White House, there would certainly be counterdemonstrations, and a damn good chance of fights and bloodshed. And if pictures of pro-Khomeini Iranians being beaten there were flashed to Tehran, the hostages' lives might be in immediate danger.

Vance had cautioned us earlier that day, "We don't know what's going on inside that compound or inside the minds of those people. We must be firm but cautious in dealing with this group of unknown and unpredictable Moslem fanatics," he had said.

It was possible that some of the captors were scheming to precipitate a crisis between the United States and Iran for the benefit of the Soviet Union. We couldn't afford to provoke the militants or give them an excuse to harm our people. I had to stop the demonstration.

I walked down the hall to the Oval Office. When I knew the President was alone, I didn't use the main entrance but slipped through a seldom-used door that opened directly into the Oval Office and was constantly guarded by a Secret Service agent. There was an electronic button under the carpet which, when stepped on, would unlock the door. I often went in this way to avoid the walk through the main lobby, where I would invariably have to stop and chat with people waiting to see the President.

President Carter was just finishing a call to Senator John Glenn, trying to persuade him to vote for the SALT II Treaty in the Foreign Relations Committee. The committee was going to give us a favorable vote, but we needed a solid majority to give the treaty some political momentum.

The President quickly read the memo on the parade permit, agreed with my assessment, and ordered it canceled. Back at my office, I called Lloyd Cutler, the President's legal counsel. Cutler was the quintessential Washington lawyer, with a bright, sharp, legal mind. Even more important, he knew people in the media and on Capitol Hill and could get things done quietly and efficiently. I outlined my concerns and told him of President Carter's decision to revoke the permit. He urged me to consider the arguments in favor of allowing the protest before doing so. In about forty-five minutes, I had a crowd in my office: the Mayor, the Police Chief, Attorney General Civiletti, and half a dozen aides. The Mayor of Washington, Marion Barry, expressed concern that a bad precedent might be set. The Police Chief, who had dealt with Iranian demonstrators before, feared their protest would become more violent if their permit to march in front of the White House were revoked; both the Attorney General and Cutler foresaw the possibility that the President might be dragged into Federal Court for violating the rights of the Iranians to assemble peacefully.

I stated plainly the President's concern and decision. "We are dealing with crazy people in Iran. If any harm comes to Iranian demonstrators, it will inevitably be shown on television and might cause the militants to kill the hostages. Obviously the Iranians don't understand our system of government." I continued: "If there were pictures of fistfights and bloodshed in front of the White House, they would conclude that whatever happened to the demonstrators was sponsored by the President and the government."

I argued the President's case for over an hour. Everyone else felt strongly that he had made his decision without the benefit of all the facts, and I was beginning to have some second thoughts myself. I thought, *Maybe I should have talked with Lloyd before running in to get the President to support my snap judgment.* The prospect of fighting the cancellation in court didn't worry me, but

I was bothered by the Police Chief's feeling that the demonstrators might cause more trouble if they were denied the right to march.

I suggested that we go see President Carter and explain their opposition to his decision.

It was 6:30 P.M. by now, and he was in the Residence having dinner with Senator and Mrs. Adlai Stevenson, trying to win support in Illinois to offset Chicago Mayor Jane Byrne's unexpected flipflop and endorsement of Ted Kennedy. The Residence was off-limits except in cases of genuine need or emergency. A President doesn't have much privacy, and we all regarded the Residence as Jimmy Carter's home. I called him anyway, apologized for the interruption, and told him that the Mayor, the Attorney General, the Police Chief, and Lloyd Cutler all disagreed with his decision to revoke the parade permit and wanted a chance to appeal it.

"As you know," the President told me, "I have had an awful day. The Clark mission has failed, and now I am trying to have a quiet dinner with the Stevensons, only to learn that a decision I made hours ago hasn't been carried out."

"OK," I said. "If you don't want to hear their appeal, I'll simply convey that your original decision stands."

He hesitated for a second, then told me to come upstairs alone.

I ran up the stairs. Carter glared at me as he excused himself and pulled me into a side room. I started to make the complicated legal arguments against revoking the permit, but he interrupted me. "I am not going to stand here and listen to this. I made my decision and I expect it to be carried out. I'm not going to risk a fight in front of the White House that gets shown in Iran and brings harm to the hostages," he went on. "I may have to sit here and bite my lip and show restraint and look impotent, but I am not going to have those bastards humiliating our country in front of the White House! And let me tell you something else, Ham, if I wasn't President, I'd be out on the streets myself and would probably take a swing at any Khomeini demonstrator I could get my hands on."

He turned and walked back to the dining room, and I left quickly. I was accustomed to being in the position of having to present an argument that I might not agree with, but as I presented it, the argument would seem to be my own. There was never enough time to explain that I was simply conveying someone else's point of view. But I understood his anger and frustration, and understood as well that one of the many things a staff member does for any President is to provide a private outlet for the expression of their feelings and frustrations.

I told the group waiting in my office that the President's decision was firm and final, but they weren't satisfied. The Attorney General and Lloyd Cutler scheduled a conference call with him after the Stevensons left. The call didn't last long: they got a dose of the same medicine I had received, and the permit was canceled that night.

The protests took place later that week, but not in front of the White House. Fortunately, there was no violence and no pictures flashed to Iran.

November 8, 1979 (Thursday)

President Carter was scheduled to leave for Canada for a state visit on Friday. It didn't feel right to me. Here we were in the middle of an international crisis, with the lives of numerous American diplomats at stake, and the President was leaving the country!

I lingered after our daily ten-o'clock staff meeting with the President to suggest that he postpone his trip. He barely considered my suggestion before saying no, explaining that no President since Lyndon Johnson had visited Canada, and his not going could be interpreted as taking our northern neighbor for granted. He could, he insisted, easily stay in touch with the White House from Ottawa, and his principal foreign policy advisers would be with him.

I didn't argue with him then, but returned to my office, settled into my green chair, and sat facing a small desk with my typewriter on it.

I had learned when Jimmy Carter was Governor that if I wanted to change his mind or challenge him on something that was important or complicated, it was best to do it in writing. If I went into his office to argue with him, armed with five reasons to do something, I would rarely get beyond point one before he was aggressively countering it. I seldom got to the second or third point.

But he couldn't argue with a piece of paper. I wrote a four-page memorandum. It was the symbolism of the trip that I felt was a mistake. The country was gripped by outrage and emotion, a lot of Americans were ready to go to war over the hostages, yet their President was leaving the country. American hostages in Iran and Jimmy Carter in Canada—it just didn't make sense.

I carried my memo into the Oval Office and placed it in his wooden "in" box, on top of his other papers, in the hope that he would see it soon enough to change his mind and cancel his trip.

The President was very particular about the handling of memos, most of which were confidential and some highly classified. He never gave me permission to put my memos on top of everything else in his "in" box; it was more a matter of my having the nerve to do it. Only a few of us—Jody Powell, Zbig Brzezinski, and Stu Eizenstat—"walked" our memos in when he was away from his office, circumventing the prescribed system for the circulation of memorandums going to the President. When I was anxious for him to pay immediate attention to something I deemed urgent, I would check and often find that one of the three had put his memo on top of mine. I would then dig mine out and put it back on top. I don't think Carter ever knew how often some of us shuffled papers in this way. And we never admitted it to one another.

If the President were going to seriously consider canceling his Canadian trip, he would check with Cy first about the consequences, so I needed to get to Vance first to make my case. I found him downstairs in the Situation Room, at one of the ongoing meetings about the hostages.

I walked through the long string of rooms filled with computer terminals, print-out machines spitting out cables, blaring television sets, and constantly ringing phones—it seemed more like the news room of a large daily paper or a television station than the place responsible for sending and receiving some of the most secret information in the world—until I got to the enclosed room in the center, the Situation Room. About fifteen by twenty feet, it was the only conference room in the White House with contemporary furniture. There was a wooden table surrounded by comfortable swivel chairs, and direct lights were recessed into the ceiling. The Situation Room was a lot less secretive and ominous than its name would suggest. The sign over the door was lit: MEETING IN PROGRESS.

When I stepped in, Secretary Vance was leading the group in a discussion of emergency measures to encourage, persuade, and, if necessary, compel any remaining American citizens in Iran to leave. I slipped him a note asking if he could drop by my office after the meeting.

I then went to see Mondale, whose office was next to mine. We often popped in on each other and had an easy and comfortable relationship. I started to tell him my reasons for opposing the Canadian trip, but before I had finished, Eleanor informed me that Vance was waiting for me in my office.

The Secretary frowned when he heard what I was advocating. He emphasized the same points the President had made—it would be difficult to call off the visit; to do so would embarrass the Canadian government. But, he said, it could be done if Carter felt strongly enough about it. Eleanor came in and told Vance that the President wanted to see him. I winced. *He's seen the memo,* I thought. I hoped he didn't know that Cy was in my office, because I didn't want him to find out that I was busy lobbying his advisers. I very seldom tried to sandbag the President; I was usually content just to present my arguments personally and then leave him alone.

In a half hour he called Jody and me in and told us he wasn't going to Ottawa. He didn't mention my memo.

I walked back to my office, satisfied that the President had done the right thing, and more than a little proud of myself for changing his mind.

Months later, when we were bogged down in what the press labeled our "Rose Garden strategy," unable to bring the hostages

home and committed not to campaign until the crisis was resolved, I kept remembering that incident. It was the first time we
had placed Iran above everything else in Carter's Presidency, and
I felt largely responsible for the public trap we later found ourselves in.

November 9, 1979 (Friday)

A somber mood prevailed at our foreign policy breakfast. When
the President bowed his head and asked a short blessing, he mentioned the hostages and everyone joined in the amen.

As usual, the meeting opened with Cy Vance's review of all
that had been done to date: cables to allies who had close relations with the Iranians, private meetings with ambassadors from
the Moslem countries, a meeting with Habib Chatty of the Islamic League (an international organization of Islamic religious
leaders), and contact with Moslem religious figures. The efforts
that week had been exhaustive and, I thought, impressive: we
seemed to have done everything humanly possible to get our people out. But they were still being held, and the rhetoric of both
the militants at the compound and Khomeini had become
harsher, with demands that the Shah be returned to Iran to stand
trial, that his assets be confiscated, and that the U.S. apologize for
past "crimes against the Iranian people."

For the first time it dawned on me that the hostage crisis might
not end so soon.

Zbig Brzezinski spoke up first following Vance's presentation.
"Mr. President, you can't allow this thing to settle into a state of
normalcy. If you do," he warned, "it could paralyze your Presidency. Yes, it *is* important that we get our people back. But," he
argued, "your greater responsibility is to protect the honor and
dignity of our country and its foreign policy interests. At some
point that greater responsibility could become more important
than the safety of our diplomats." He continued: "I hope we

never have to choose between the hostages and our nation's honor in the world, but Mr. President, you must be prepared for that occurrence. If they're still in captivity at Thanksgiving, what will that say about your Presidency and America's image in the world?"

Glancing first at Brzezinski and then turning to the President, Vance responded quickly. "The hostages have been held only five days," he said. "We're dealing with a volatile, chaotic situation in Iran, and negotiation is the only way to free them. The President and this nation will ultimately be judged by our restraint in the face of provocation, and on the safe return of our hostages," he argued. "We have to keep looking for ways to reach Khomeini and peacefully resolve this." He harked back to the Pueblo incident, which had plagued the Johnson Administration but which had finally been resolved honorably and without loss of life.

"But that went on for a year!" Brzezinski countered.

"And Johnson wasn't in the middle of a re-election campaign," I added.

As usual, Vance and Brzezinski, flanking the President, stated their arguments directly and without emotion. Carter gave his undivided attention first to the one and then to the other, listening carefully, weighing what both had to say. He considered himself fortunate to have the counsel of both the deliberate Vance and the feisty Brzezinski.

In 1972, when the Georgia Governor was quietly running for President, and seeking foreign policy experience and credentials, Jimmy Carter was invited to serve on the Trilateral Commission—a group of American, Japanese, and European leaders studying world problems. Later President Carter would recall, "Those Trilateral Commission meetings for me were like classes in foreign policy—reading papers produced on every conceivable subject, hearing experienced leaders debate international issues and problems, and meeting the big names like Cy Vance and Harold Brown and Zbig." (Zbigniew Brzezinski was the staff director of the commission.)

Governor Jimmy Carter admired the experienced Vance, who moved so easily and gracefully through the corridors of power.

And while Cy Vance became his acquaintance, Zbig Brzezinski became his friend. At first, Brzezinski was amused by the little-known Georgia Governor and his insatiable curiosity about foreign policy, and regularly sent him articles and books to read and later looked over his speeches on foreign policy. "Zbig became my teacher," Carter recalled. As the Carter candidacy progressed, demanding more thoughtful positions and public statements on foreign policy, it was only natural for Jimmy Carter to tell his staff, "Check this with Zbig."

In the meantime, Cy Vance had already signed up to support the Presidential candidacy of his old friend Sargent Shriver.

Vance was the odds-on favorite to be the Secretary of State under any Democrat elected President in 1976 (with the probable exception of Senator Scoop Jackson). President-elect Jimmy Carter resented the expectation that Vance would become *his* Secretary of State simply because Vance was the favorite of the foreign policy establishment. The week after his election, Carter told Fritz Mondale and me that he wanted to personally screen the candidates for that position and added, "I am going to keep an open mind."

A few days later, after making dozens of calls to knowledgeable persons, Jimmy Carter summoned Vance to Plains and asked him to be his Secretary of State. Later, the President-elect, Mondale, and I interviewed Brzezinski for the position of National Security Advisor. The banter between Carter and Brzezinski was easy, and after five minutes it was obvious to me that Carter had already made up his mind. Several days later, the appointment was announced.

In organizing his foreign policy team, Carter saw no inherent conflict between the men and the institutions they represented. Zbig would sit at his side, stimulating new ideas, creating long-range plans, and sifting through the mountains of foreign policy papers that regularly came to the White House for the President.

Vance would be the diplomat, meeting with ambassadors and foreign dignitaries; the manager, trying to control the sprawling State Department bureaucracy; and the implementer, responsible for making the policies work.

The President-elect was not worried about conflicts, and relished their different ideas and lively debate. The roles were clear to him: Zbig would be the thinker, Cy would be the doer, and Jimmy Carter would be the decider.

At another level, the two men reflected the different sides of the President's mind and personality. Zbig represented his boldness, the side of Jimmy Carter that had challenged the party establishment and won the Presidency; the part of him that disregarded the conventional wisdom and would bring Sadat and Begin to Camp David to hammer out a peace treaty and later rush off to the Middle East to salvage it when it was falling apart. Vance represented the more traditional and methodical side of Jimmy Carter; the side that would, once Begin and Sadat had been brought to Camp David, work eighteen or twenty hours a day, arguing over phrases and words, negotiating endlessly with the Israelis and the Egyptians, always searching for a way to overcome the problems. Like the President he served, Vance would arrive at work while it was still dark outside. Settling into his comfortable office on the seventh floor of the State Department, he would wade through cables and problems from all over the world, attend endless meetings where options and policies would be discussed, regularly travel to the Hill to testify before Congressional committees, and end most long days dropping by a reception at a foreign embassy.

By the end of the first year, the Panama Canal Treaties had been signed, the Administration was making quiet progress in its efforts to normalize relations with China, UN Ambassador Andy Young was making new friends for America in the Third World, and human rights had been made one of the hallmarks of American foreign policy.

There had been disappointments—an ambitious arms control proposal had been rejected out of hand by the Soviet Union, and the new Administration was just feeling its way in the troubled Middle East. But, all in all, the President was pleased with the way things were going in the foreign policy area. Looking back in January 1978, he said, "We've built a solid foundation for the first term."

Unfortunately, that wasn't the way it looked to the rest of the world. Governor Averell Harriman, the dean of America's foreign policy establishment, visited me to complain about news stories claiming that Vance and Brzezinski were engaged in a struggle for control of foreign policy. Leaning forward on his handsome walking stick, he told me in a gruff voice, "Young man, I don't care what the facts are. The perception is that there are two voices in foreign policy—and that is hurting the President! There can only be one spokesman in foreign policy—and that spokesman has to be the Secretary of State. The NSC Advisor should be a first-class clerk, but he cannot be a public spokesman. The National Security Advisor should be like a child at a formal dinner—seen but not heard."

I listened but respectfully disagreed, saying that the stories about Vance and Brzezinski were greatly exaggerated.

And they were. For when the President formally involved me in the foreign policy processes in January 1978, I was surprised to note how frequently the two men agreed on issues, the very important exception being U.S.-Soviet relations. When they did differ on Washington's policy toward Moscow, the President would side with Vance three out of four times.

However, that was not the perception outside the White House. And the notion that Dr. Zbigniew Brzezinski had the President's ear spread to the extent that many thought he had Carter's mind as well.

Cy Vance was solid as a rock and completely predictable. He went to the State Department with a clear idea of what he wanted to accomplish. While admiring some of Kissinger's achievements, Vance felt that there was a better way for the United States to do business. No diplomatic hocus-pocus, shuttles, or sleight-of-hand were needed to pursue America's interests. Just hard work and a steady course would get the job done.

Personally, Vance could not have been more different from his colorful predecessor. Henry Kissinger valued above all his image as a world leader, and nothing was more important to him than the time he spent polishing that image, nurturing the media with private interviews and late-night calls, and trading "inside" tidbits and goodies for a flattering column or favorable mention. One

White House staffer who had watched Kissinger operate said, "He fed the press like they were a flock of birds. They ate well and they ate regularly, and they sang and sang Henry's song."

Cyrus Vance operated differently. His contacts with the media were formal, structured, and infrequent. When he met the press, he was America's foreign policy accountant, methodically ticking off our positions, decisions, and options. Vance didn't have an ounce of the self-promoter in him. He wasn't concerned with his image: he was there to serve his President and his country.

And if Cy Vance didn't have an ounce of the self-promoter in him, then Zbig had several pounds.

Encouraged by the President, the proud Pole moved quietly into the vacuum that Vance left for explaining and defending the Administration's foreign policy. And more and more often, as the Administration progressed, I would bump into a columnist or reporter in the hallway or waiting in the West Wing to be shown into the corner office formerly occupied by Henry Kissinger.

Zbig relished his media contacts, scoffing at the columns and stories that were unfavorable, and often slipping positive articles and editorials about himself into the President's "in" box.

It was impossible for the media to resist the easy analogy between Kissinger and Brzezinski. It was foreign policy *déjà vu:* another professor (this time Columbia) with a thick accent (this time Polish) summoned to Washington to create a "global strategy" for a new Commander-in-Chief.

For me, the analogy didn't hold up. Henry Kissinger was a popular public figure and the darling of the media. Among the White House professionals who stayed on from Administration to Administration, "Henry" was a brilliant egomaniac who drove his staff mercilessly and was unconcerned about the personal problems of other people. Most of those under Kissinger admired his intelligence; some respected him; but very few liked him.

As a public figure, Zbig was perceived differently. Perhaps it was his clipped manner of speaking, his accent, or his angular profile that conveyed a brashness that bothered people. Zbig lacked Kissinger's self-deprecating sense of humor and his slow and relaxed way of speaking. Zbig's intelligence was intense and raw, and when added to his tough-guy image, it made many people uncomfortable. On the private side, however, he was as charming as Kissinger was abrasive. Zbig may have worked his staff hard, but they liked him and cared for him, and he developed an esprit de corps at the NSC that was lacking during the Kissinger years.

Although our offices were just a few steps apart—separated only by the Vice President's office—we did not get to know each other until the end of our first year in Washington. Brzezinski was preoccupied with "teaching" the new President, and I was burdened with the enormous chore of trying to organize the new Administration.

When I finally did get to know him, I found a playful, almost childlike quality about Zbig that contrasted sharply with his public image. Early on, I started calling him Woody Woodpecker because of the way his hair dipped down over his forehead then flipped back up—but I stopped when he countered by addressing me as Porky Pig. That's when I hit on the nickname "Dr. Strangelove"—and Zbig never seemed to object to that.

He was someone who went to great lengths to play a practical joke. One day in December, Eleanor rushed in with a "top secret cable" from the NSC. I was puzzled, and anxiously tore it open. It contained a letter that appeared to be written in Russian, along with a translation.

"It's from Dobrynin [the Soviet Ambassador to Washington]," I said, and read it aloud. "My Dear Hamilton: I would like to extend to you an invitation to visit our country over the coming American holidays. President Brezhnev has informed me that he would like to meet you and have you spend a couple of days. This would be, of course, purely unofficial in nature should you agree. Please contact me with your reply. Anatoly."

Eleanor looked worried. "It must be because of all those stories about you being the real power in the White House. What are you going to do? I don't see how you can refuse him, but this is a very, very delicate thing, Hamilton."

I didn't reply. I went over to my typewriter, pecked out my response, and read it aloud: "Dear Anatoly: I am greatly honored and flattered by the personal invitation to spend time with President Brezhnev. Unfortunately for President Brezhnev, I will be

in Cairo and Jerusalem the next several weeks on important diplomatic business which you can read about in the newspapers.
However, I do have two bright men here in the White House
who work for me—Carter and Brzezinski—whom I would be glad
to let off work and send as substitutes. They badly need this kind
of experience. Your friend, Hamilton."

Eleanor cackled. "Oh, it's a joke!"

"Send this to Dobrynin," I instructed. "Through the NSC, of
course."

Zbig and I occasionally played tennis on the White House court
(we referred to it as "the Supreme Court"). He was a good athlete
and played a hard, intense game—without subtlety. On every
shot, he would wind up and knock the hell out of the ball. If the
ball made it over the net and dropped inside the lines, it was
difficult to return, but his game was so erratic that rallies seldom
lasted more than several strokes. Either he smashed a winner, or,
more often, he hit into the net or out of bounds. One day I called
to him across the net, "Zbig, you play tennis like you conduct
foreign policy."

"You must mean that every shot is well-planned, crisply hit,
low and hard."

"Yes," I said, "and usually out."

Rather than choose between Vance's suggested restraint and
Brzezinski's call to protect our honor, the President turned the
discussion to the specific problem of reaching Khomeini. He said
that contacting Moslem religious figures was probably the best
way, but perhaps the envoys should be armed with theological
reasons against holding hostages. "If Khomeini is the religious
leader he purports to be," Carter said, "I don't see how he can
condone the holding of our people. There is no recognized religious faith on earth that condones kidnapping."

I slipped a note to Harold Brown: "Whose side is God on?"
Brown smiled, scribbled a reply, and pushed it back across the
table: "Ours, of course."

The President next asked for a military update. Secretary
Brown said that our forces in the Indian Ocean were ready to
move to the Persian Gulf, if necessary. It was important, he ex-

plained, to have a presence that was adequate but not large enough to provoke a Soviet reaction. On the President's order, the Joint Chiefs were preparing both punitive actions against Iran and emergency rescue plans in the event the militants started to execute their prisoners. But, Brown cautioned, Tehran wasn't Entebbe, where the Israelis had been able to fly in and snatch up their citizens from the airfield where they were being held. Our hostages, he explained, were locked up in a compound in the middle of a city of more than four million people, with the nearest airport nine miles away. The opinion of the Joint Chiefs was that a rescue would be extremely difficult but not impossible, and the Secretary recommended that they proceed with their planning.

Carter said that he wasn't inclined either toward the rescue action or punitive measures, but that both needed to be ready and in place for use as a "last resort." "The problem with all of the military options," he said, "is that we could use them and feel good for a few hours—until we found out they had killed our people. And once we start killing people in Iran, where will it end?" he asked quietly.

Vance mentioned that he had invited the families of hostages from the Washington area to the State Department for a briefing and asked if the President wanted to meet with them.

Jody urged him to see the families because they could play a critical role in shaping U.S. public opinion. If they demonstrated a quiet, calm attitude and a commitment to the peaceful resolution of the crisis, Powell reasoned, it would have a strong influence on the American people and would give the President more time. If they became frustrated and hostile, it might increase the public outcry for military action.

Carter agreed that since he was responsible for the hostages' safety and for the decision to let the Shah in, he must see them.

Both Vance and Jody suggested that a few of the visitors be taken to the Oval Office to meet the President. Jody pointed out that a small group would present less chance for an unpleasant confrontation. But Carter was worried that they might feel they were being exploited for publicity purposes if they were brought to the White House; he was adamant about going quietly to the State Department and meeting with all of the families there.

After our meeting, Vance, Jody, and I walked back down the hall toward my office. "Ham, do you have time to talk for a couple of minutes?" the Secretary asked. Vintage Cy Vance. One of the busiest and most important men in the world, and he wants to know if I have time for him. "Of course I do, Mr. Secretary."

Although I considered myself to be close to Cy, it was not normal for him just to drop by my office, so I knew he had something important on his mind. The three of us pulled up chairs around my conference table and I ordered a pot of coffee from the mess.

Vance slid down in his chair, propped his leg up on my table, and started talking about Carter's options, all the while twisting his dark-rimmed glasses in his hands, finally saying, "Don't forget—in the long run the President will be judged by whether or not we get those Americans back safely and alive."

That's it, I thought. *He's worried that Jody and I are so preoccupied with Carter's re-election that we might encourage him to do something foolish because of political pressures.*

I assured him that I agreed with the present strategy and the ultimate objective of returning the hostages, but we also had to think about the posture of both the President and the nation.

"Even if the hostages come home today," Jody argued, "the slate won't be clean."

"We can worry about that after they come out," Vance shot back. A phone call came from the State Department and he left quickly.

The door had hardly closed when Brzezinski strode in. Cy was an unaccustomed visitor, but Zbig dropped by frequently. Standing before Jody and me as if he were lecturing at Columbia, Zbig was more blunt than he had been at our NSC meeting. "This is the first big test of Carter's Presidency," he said. "It is a crisis, for sure, but it is also an opportunity, a chance for the President to show the world that he is capable of handling a crisis with international implications." He paused. "A chance to show American resolve!"

Cy's calm approach sounded good, but Zbig's tough approach felt good.

Later, when I saw the President in the Oval Office after his meeting with the families of the hostages, he looked troubled. I had some encouraging poll results from Pat Caddell, but it didn't seem the right time to talk politics, so I asked if there was anything I could do to help him. He shook his head and settled into his black leather chair behind the large ornate desk.

"You know, it was my duty to see the families," he said, "but I wasn't looking forward to it. I knew that some of them must blame me, but they were very generous and supportive. They don't expect miracles and want their loved ones home, but they want them to come home only on honorable terms." He paused. "You know, I've been worried all week about the hostages as a problem for the country and as a political problem for me. But it wasn't until I saw the grief and hope on the faces of their wives and mothers and fathers that I felt the personal responsibility for their lives. It's an awesome burden," he said quietly.

I slipped out, sensing that he wanted to be alone.

Back in my office, I thought about the President's emotional involvement with the hostages through their family members. Zbig had refused to meet with the families of the hostages on the grounds that, should the time come when the country's honor was pitted against the safety of the hostages, he would be free of emotional pressures. I respected this logic, but I disagreed with it.

November 16, 1979 (Friday)

It had been a hectic week.

On Sunday afternoon the President had convened a secret meeting of the National Security Council and told his advisers— including Secretary of Energy Charles Duncan and domestic adviser Stu Eizenstat—that he was considering a total cutoff of Iranian oil. Carter did not want to simply reduce our dependence on foreign oil; he wanted Iranians and Americans to know that our dependence on Iran's oil was not influencing our efforts to free the hostages.

Someone argued that cutting off Iranian oil would decrease the world supply and drive the cost of gasoline even higher. Memories of the previous summer were fresh in everyone's mind: angry Americans in long gasoline lines. But the President stood his ground, firmly saying that it would be an act of "self-discipline" for the American people to boycott Iran's oil and a clear signal to our European allies that we meant business and expected their help. Most important, it would signify that American lives were more valuable than oil. The next morning he announced the cutoff.

On Tuesday we had canceled Carter's campaign trip to Pennsylvania, to the dismay of supporters and campaign staff. When I mentioned this unhappiness, he said, with a trace of a grin, "You persuaded me not to go to Canada because of the hostages. Do you think I should go to Pittsburgh?" In the early hours of Wednesday he had been informed by Treasury Secretary Miller and Legal Counsel Lloyd Cutler that the Iranian government was withdrawing its money from American banks. Miller and Cutler had been on the lookout for such an action; the papers were already prepared, and the President signed them, freezing billions of dollars in Iranian assets.

On Thursday, the President had talked tough at the AFL-CIO convention, saying that Iran would be "held accountable" for any harm done our diplomats, and that the United States "would not yield to international terrorism and blackmail." Later, in the Oval Office, he spoke frankly about his speech. "You know, I've got to give expression to the anger of the American people. I guarantee that if I asked the people of Plains what I should do, every last one of them would say, 'Bomb Iran!' I've got to keep a lid on their emotions. If they can perceive me as firm and tough in voicing their rage, maybe we'll be able to control this thing."

Months later, the Monday-morning quarterbacks would question the President's handling of the crisis in the early stages, arguing that we complicated the hostage problem by focusing so much public attention on it. They argued that Carter should have put the problem on the back burner. But that was never possible. From the very first day, the hostage crisis dominated the news: nightly the networks showed interviews with the captors at the embassy in Iran or crowds of demonstrators in Tehran, flagellating themselves with chains and burning American flags, and pictures of spontaneous demonstrations in Houston and Los Angeles, with fistfights between Iranian students and angry Americans. We certainly did not downplay our own reaction to the crisis, but we never had the chance to "control" the news, as many critics contended, and put the hostages on the "back burner."

By Friday we seemed to have tried everything, but nothing had worked. However, at our breakfast meeting Vance told us that informal word from Iran was that "some" of the hostages might soon be released. *This is it*, I thought as Cy spoke. *This is the breakthrough*.

"I hope you're right, Cy. I'll believe it when I see it," the President replied. "It will be important, Cy, that if any of our people come home early, we not appear to be thanking Khomeini for letting some of them go. They don't deserve anything but condemnation. Also, we must be sure that we don't create the impression that a partial release reduces Iran's responsibility for every single American."

November 17, 1979 (Saturday)

Saturdays at the White House were leisurely, as the intensity of the week gave way to a slower pace. Many offices were empty, in others casually dressed staff members stood around chatting, reviewing their mail, or picking up their newspapers while their children ran through the hallways or pecked on typewriters. It hadn't always been that way. In the first year of the Carter Administration, Saturdays were like every other day: offices full, busy secretaries answering phones, a chorus of electric typewriters sounding a constant staccato throughout the building, and a steady stream of busy people entering and leaving meetings in the Roosevelt Room, the large room in the center of the West Wing used by the staff. There was so much to learn that first year in office that I was working against the clock—as though we had been elected for four months instead of four years and had to accomplish everything right away.

During those early months there was still a newness and excitement about our work. But the novelty wore off quickly, and the beautiful, white, historic building where we spent long hours became simply "the office." It was always there, as were the work and all the problems. And I soon found that I could spend twelve hours a day, seven days a week, at the White House, as many of us did during those early months, but still the headaches and paperwork and telephone calls piled up.

The President's job was much worse, and shortly after our first several months in office, he called a luncheon meeting with the senior staff to review our progress and problems. He told us that he was concerned about our work habits, and that all of us, himself included, were going to have to pace ourselves, to try to lead more balanced lives, spending more time with our families and away from our desks. "You're not any good to me or to the country if you're here around the clock, every day, emotionally and intellectually exhausted. I don't plan to sustain the pace of these first several months and don't want you to either."

Stu Eizenstat, the brilliant and intense domestic policy adviser who worked longer and harder than anyone but who was also extremely devoted to his family, smiled. "But you're the reason that my staff and I have to work so hard. Am I supposed to ignore your demands and requests?" he said with a twinkle in his eye.

"I give you permission to selectively ignore my requests," Jimmy Carter said with a sly grin.

Since that meeting, the pace had slowed a bit. Now, weekends usually presented a good opportunity for some quiet, thoughtful work, and I arrived at the White House this Saturday at about ten o'clock, to try to concentrate on some campaign problems. The campaign was right where I wanted it to be—slowly but surely we were gaining on Kennedy. If anything, we were ahead of schedule, and I was even a little scared by how quickly the race was changing—just one more indication of how fickle the electorate is. I had predicted from the outset that once the Democratic voters started contrasting Jimmy Carter, the man, with Ted Kennedy, the man, and made a serious decision about which of them they wanted sitting in the Oval Office, Carter would be in good shape. The President had said during the late summer of 1979, when Kennedy had a huge lead, "I am running against a myth of perfection now, but I'll do better when I am compared with another human being." He was right.

The early Democratic contests looked good. When we defeated Kennedy in the Florida straw vote in October, the Senator had said in a taunting way, "Wait till Iowa—that's the first *real* contest." But I was sure we would win Iowa, possibly by a decisive margin. I hoped that we then could turn around and ambush Kennedy in his own backyard in the New Hampshire primary. To beat a Kennedy in New England would really be something! But nothing could be left to chance; the stakes were too high and there was no way to measure the negative effect of the hostage crisis on the President.

And while I was confident of the early contests, I was anxious about our effort in Illinois, which would be the first battle in a big state. If we defeated Kennedy in Iowa and New Hampshire, Illinois would be critical: it could be the place where Kennedy bounced back after early defeats or where we buried his hopes for winning the nomination. I made a couple of calls to Illinois to check on our campaign there. Chicago Mayor Jane Byrne had promised to endorse the President in exchange for his attendance at her major annual fund-raising dinner for the Cook County Democratic Party. The President went to Chicago on October 15 and received her warm endorsement; weeks later Byrne endorsed Senator Kennedy. We were shocked when it happened, but Carter said, "Anybody who does business that way must have a hell of a lot of enemies. If we can get everyone in Chicago who doesn't like Jane Byrne to vote for me, we can win."

I was eager to finish Kennedy off, and although the Chicago machine was against us, as were the odds, Illinois seemed as good a place as any. Every extra week and month we were forced to campaign against Kennedy sapped our strength and made the chances of winning the general election more difficult.

We'd seen it happen in the 1976 Presidential campaign, Ronald Reagan's challenge to President Gerald Ford had permanently divided the Republican Party—which had a lot to do with our winning a very close general election. For in every state we ran against Kennedy, his television commercials would attack Jimmy Carter's record, exaggerating our mistakes and shortcomings. And, of course, we would have to retaliate. In every contested primary, the Democratic leaders and the voters would have to choose sides, and, regardless of who won the nomination, considerable damage would have been done along the way to the party's nominee. The only real winner of a protracted Carter-Kennedy struggle would be the Republican Party. We had to dispose of Kennedy—and quickly!

Bob Strauss dropped by my office in the morning, just before he left for the Middle East to continue his negotiations with Israel and Egypt on the Camp David accords. When he returned from his trip, he'd move to the campaign as chairman. I wasn't worried about the nuts and bolts; a tightly organized election effort had been the historical strength of every campaign that Jimmy Carter had run. What we needed was someone to raise money and be the spokesman for the President's re-election. The consummate Washington insider, Bob Strauss was ideal for that role. His pretense for stopping by was to talk about the campaign, but his real intention, I was sure, was to hear the latest on the hostages. In Washington, especially among the group that Strauss dealt with, information was power, to be gossiped about over cocktails in Georgetown or traded over lunch at the fashionable restaurant Sans Souci with a friendly newsman for favorable mention in a column. The result was that in Washington circles Bob Strauss's opinion was informed, authoritative, and ultimately very important. What made him unusual and attractive in a community of political and social climbers was that he made no attempt to disguise his own considerable ego and freely admitted to both playing the game and enjoying it.

One of Strauss's favorite tricks was to call me or the President's secretary to find out when the President had a gap in his schedule. He would then place a call to Carter at that exact time, hoping that the President would accept it. When he got through to the President, as he often did, Strauss would offer some political advice, report some news from the Hill, or, if the President's mood seemed good, even tell a joke. His call would last three or four minutes, but for the rest of the week Bob could go around town prefacing his comments on any number of things with, "Well, I was chatting with the President the other day, and I think . . ." He would talk authoritatively on any subject, and by implication his opinions and ideas seemed to come from the mouth of the President of the United States. It was always helpful for me to hear what Strauss was saying, because I knew that his "ideas" were more accurately an amalgam of the collective thoughts and opinions of the Washington political and media establishment.

"The President has to do something," he said. "We can't stay in this posture much longer." He paced back and forth before the large windows in my office. Bob Strauss was usually on the move, and his smooth tongue was always going. "We can't continue to cancel campaign trips or people will say that the President is hiding in the White House," he insisted. I asked him what we should do. "Hell, *I* don't know—and I can't advise you what to do when I don't know what's happening on the inside!"

I ignored his gibe about not being more fully involved in formulating policy and said, "Our hands are tied. If we take any kind of aggressive or punitive action, it would probably just get the hostages killed. There's no government to negotiate with other than Khomeini, and he doesn't want to negotiate. It's a tough damn problem."

He shook his head and said of the President, "Poor bastard—he used up all of his luck in getting here. We've had our share of victories and defeats, but we've not had a single piece of good luck in the past three years."

I was struck by how accurate that was. "The American people like the way Carter's handled this hostage thing so far," he continued. "He's been decisive and firm. But it won't last. At some point their patience will run out."

"And you'll be sitting over there," I razzed, "in charge of a losing campaign for an incumbent President."

"Hell, no, I won't!" he retorted, turning to face me and smiling broadly. "I can read the mood of the American people better than you can, and by the time that happens, I'll be back in Texas, making a million dollars, hanging around the country club with my rich Republican friends, cussing you and Carter."

"Give my regards to Begin and Sadat," I said as he put on his coat.

"I will," he replied, pausing at my door. "But they don't even know who you are!" I laughed. As usual, Bob Strauss had the last word.

I walked down to the Oval Office to check with the President before he and his family left for a much-needed rest at Camp David over Thanksgiving week.

Carter appeared to be cheerful. I had expected him to be disappointed that he couldn't spend the holiday in Plains, but he was obviously heartened by reports that some of the hostages were coming home. He stood behind his desk in the Oval Office, very carefully sifting through the large stack of memos in his "in" box, deciding which papers to take with him to Camp David. Declining my offer to help, he said that he was in good shape and was looking forward to the week away from the White House. As the President was packing his briefcase, Rosalynn walked in. His face lit up when he saw her, and they exchanged a few words in Spanish, as they often did in front of staff members. The President always said it was their way to brush up on their Spanish, but I always suspected that the dialogue was peppered with terms of affection.

Several of the White House staff had made plans to spend Thanksgiving at Camp David with their families, assuming the Carters would be in Plains. The President allowed us to use his retreat as much as we liked, but I had made a rule that no one could visit Camp David when he was there, because he would feel obligated to spend time with us instead of relaxing. However, he insisted that we not change our plans and all spend Thanksgiving together.

Out on the South Lawn, the press and some members of the White House staff with families and visitors had turned out to see the Carters off. Some applauded and others waved as the President, Rosalynn, and Amy climbed the steps to the helicopter, paused to wave, and took off. It seemed an upbeat moment.

Maybe by the time we get back from Camp David it'll all be over, I thought.

November 18, 1979 (Sunday)

We received a report that some of the hostages would definitely be released that day. But that good news was more than offset by another announcement from Khomeini that the remaining hostages would be tried in Islamic courts as "spies" unless the Shah were returned to Iran.

From Camp David, the President ordered our foreign policy team to meet and formulate a response to the Ayatollah's ultimatum. Bearing in mind the President's earlier admonition not to allow the release of some of our hostages to reduce Iran's responsibility to let them all go, we decided that the Vice President would make a public statement to the effect that "the last remaining hostage is as important as the first." Carter approved that strategy and the statement was made.

The Sunday *New York Times* carried a full-page ad, paid for by the Iranian government, which contained the text of the Ayatollah Khomeini's speech rejecting the plea made by Pope John Paul II to release the hostages and chastising the Catholic Church for its years of silence during the Shah's regime. *What a contradiction,* I thought. The Iranians were sophisticated enough to understand the role of the modern media and the importance of the *Times* as a newspaper with a large and influential readership, but they failed to realize that a paid advertisement criticizing the beloved Pope was not the way to influence the American people.

November 19, 1979 (Monday)

The President called me from Camp David to report on some telephone calls he had made at my request to key people in Illinois. Everyone he spoke with committed to our campaign effort, but despite his success, Carter sounded down.

"Isn't it great about the hostages coming home?" I said, trying to cheer him up. "Maybe this is the beginning of the end."

"I'm not so sure," he replied quietly. "Khomeini's statement worries me. He actually thinks that by releasing the black and female hostages there'll be some political uprising here against our government. I'm glad we're getting some of them home, but it bothers me that he misunderstands us so badly."

November 20, 1979 (Tuesday)

Eleanor walked into my office, looking worried. She handed me a wire story from Tehran. The headline read that Khomeini was calling for trials and was ridiculing military threats. Earlier statements had indicated that there might be spy trials, but this one left little room for doubt. I shuddered, visualizing the public trials and executions of our people as we sat helpless in the White House. I called Jody, who hurried over to my office. Zbig came in, armed with a full text of Khomeini's statement.

Particularly irritated by the taunting nature of Khomeini's speech, he read to us in a loud voice to emphasize the harsh rhetoric: "'Why should we be afraid . . . Carter is beating an empty drum. Carter does not have the guts to engage in a military action.'" We were interrupted by Vance, who called to say he had already talked with the President at Camp David and we were to meet about drafting a response to Khomeini's latest statement.

An ominous atmosphere hung over the Situation Room as our regular group—Mondale, Vance, Brzezinski, Brown, Turner, Powell, and I—assembled. We half-heartedly exchanged the usual superficial greetings as we gathered around the conference table. The Vice President sat at the head of the table and gestured to Vance to begin.

Cy said he had a better translation of the Khomeini speech, and while it did refer to "spy trials," it did not claim unequivocally that they would take place. "Khomeini is trying to bait us," he said. "His Revolution isn't working, and the hostage crisis takes the attention of the Iranian people off their other problems. We must understand that they would like us to do something rash, something that would galvanize public opinion against the United States. We have to bite our tongues for a while longer." As always, Cy's voice was calm and rational. He peered over his half-moon glasses, looking slowly around the room at each person to reinforce his point.

"They may be baiting us, Cy," Zbig shot back, "but they're also humiliating our country and our President." He went on, doodling on the notepad before him, his eyes fixed on his drawing. "Can you imagine how helpless we must look to the world right now?" he asked disgustedly.

"But what the hell can we do?" Jody demanded, pausing to take a long drag from his cigarette. "Words don't seem to help, and may even be counterproductive. We don't have a lot of cards to play, and most of them are facecards. If we play them now, God only knows where it leads us."

I jumped into what was becoming a lively discussion. "We've got the continuing problem of our people being stuck in Iran, but our focus should be on the immediate problem. What can we say or do to dissuade them from putting our people on trial?"

Jody replied that we had to answer Khomeini's statement immediately. We couldn't remain still; something had to be said. "You can't let a thing like that just sit out there. If we don't answer it—and answer it fast—it'll make us look unsure of ourselves."

Zbig agreed but said that an "empty statement" would be worse than none at all.

Cy picked up the Situation Room phone and called the President at Camp David to tell him that while there was some debate as to what exactly should be said, we all agreed a quick response was necessary.

"The Boss is coming back," Vance reported when he hung up. "He said that the American people need to hear from him."

"Well, that's just great!" Jody added sarcastically. "If he comes back, that just raises expectations—and the press will go absolutely wild."

I instinctively trusted Jody's judgment and wanted the President to hear him out. We both got on the phone and called him at Camp David. "Don't worry," Carter said. "I know what I'm doing."

In less than an hour, we watched from the Cabinet Room as the green Presidential helicopter, Marine One, swayed back and forth before gently setting down on the South Lawn. The President skipped confidently down the steps, his black briefcase in hand, and walked quickly toward the West Wing. He always walked erect, but today there seemed to be a special determination in the way he moved. He held his head high in an exaggerated, almost defiant way, as he marched toward the Cabinet Room. *He must have read what Khomeini said about him,* I thought. Jimmy Carter was a proud man, and the last thing in the world he would ever want would be to appear unsure of himself or afraid of Iran.

"Poor bastard," Jody said. "He's got a terrible job."

"Yeah, and we're all busting our asses to help him keep it for four more years," I replied.

The President was all business when he entered the Cabinet Room, nodding grimly to the group and asking that we all be seated. He turned to Cy and, as though to signal in advance his own resolve and his weariness with being "restrained," said, "Cy, go ahead with your report—but we are going to have some serious disagreement in a few minutes!"

Vance painted a picture that was certainly not encouraging, but it was not as pessimistic as we were all beginning to feel after seventeen long days and nights.

"Mr. President," he said, "we do have ten of the hostages back, and, while our people have been mistreated, we have no hard evidence that any are hurt or seriously injured. We can talk to the Iranians through both the UN channel and the PLO. I am very concerned about the threat of trials, but I don't want us to do anything rash or foolish that plays into the hands of Khomeini. Khomeini is trying to bait us," Vance continued, repeating for the President the views he had shared with us earlier. "His Revolution is not solving Iran's economic problems and it is losing momentum. He has seized on the hostage crisis to unite his people and turn their attention away from Iran's other problems. Mr. President, we should take seriously the threat of trials, but we shouldn't overreact," cautioned Vance, "Khomeini is taunting us."

"Cy," said the President quietly, "he may be taunting us, but it's about to work. Did you see what he said about our country and about me? We keep talking about the cultural differences and Khomeini's irrationality, but we can't respond to irrationality with irrationality." He paused. "We have to begin to spell out for Iran the serious consequences of harming a single one of our people or putting them on trial. I will not just sit here quietly as President and see our people tried!"

Zbig, clearly heartened by the President's tough words, jumped into the discussion. "Khomeini exploits weakness. His life is a study of stubbornness and resolve, ultimately winning out over less steadfast opponents. We have to show that there are costs . . . and we have to be ready to explore all of our options—including the military options."

"Well, I've had several days at Camp David to think about nothing but this thing," said the President, slipping his glasses on and glancing at a notepad filled with his own handwriting. "This is the way it looks to me," he said, referring to his notes. "Iran can continue to hold our people, or try our people, or kill our people. We can condemn Iran, break diplomatic relations. Among the military options, I can order punitive strikes against economic targets like their oil fields, or mine and blockade their harbors. Other things we can do that might affect the situation are to move the Shah from the United States, exhaust our legal options through the United Nations and the World Court, and encourage our allies to remove their embassy personnel from Tehran as a prelude to breaking relations. I'd like to talk about the overall situation, and start by discussing this latest threat to try our people."

"Mr. President," said Vance, "I think we should start by making a distinction between the threat of a trial, the commencement of an actual trial, and the possible result of such a trial. For example, there are Iranian specialists inside the State Department and some outside experts who think that trials could actually be a mechanism for freeing the hostages. My experts could foresee, for example, that the Iranians will try all our people, find them guilty of spying and then, in a gesture of Islamic forgiveness, have Khomeini pardon and expel them."

"Make no mistake though," CIA Director Stansfield Turner added, "Khomeini's talk of spies and trials is not just political rhetoric. Our Iran specialists at the Agency think he really believes that they are spies and that he would be fully justified in either trying or executing them."

"I agree with your analysis, Stan," said Vance.

"But where does that leave us?" asked Brzezinski.

The President was still concentrating on what Vance had said. "The problem, Cy, with your scenario is that it would be impossible for me just to sit quietly during a public trial of our people in hopes that it might be part of some scheme that might ultimately lead to the release of our hostages. Because if our diplomats were used as part of some enormous propaganda stunt, the damage to America's standing in the world would already be done."

"I agree completely," said Zbig. "You have to lay down a marker, Mr. President, saying what you will do if they try our people."

"But doesn't it need to be a somewhat ambiguous marker," Jody asked, "that allows them to think the very worst?"

"Not so ambiguous as to be misunderstood by Khomeini and those around him," retorted Zbig.

"Well, we can argue about these distinctions in the abstract, but let's look at what I need to say today about the trials," said the President.

Jody circulated copies of several statements he, Vance, and

Brzezinski had drafted. The language was firm in all three versions, with subtle but important distinctions as to what could and should be said about the use of force. After some discussion, the President was satisfied with the final draft. "Any other thoughts on the hostages?" he asked the group.

The Vice President hadn't said much. Some of Mondale's critics contended that he was not forceful or effective in internal debates with the President. Nothing was more untrue. In fact, perhaps the most admirable characteristic of Fritz Mondale as Vice President was that he fought hard for what he believed in on the inside, yet would accept the President's decisions and go out and defend them publicly. But very wisely, Mondale did not get involved in every dispute or waste himself on matters he didn't deem important. He saved himself for those occasions when he thought the President was making a mistake or wasn't getting good advice or didn't have all the facts. And using his relationship with Jimmy Carter, which had blossomed into a real friendship, and sometimes his keen sense of humor, he would usually have more success than the rest of us in arguing a second or even a third time matters which the President had already decided. When Fritz Mondale spoke, it was usually worth listening.

"Mr. President, I agree completely with the statement and what you've said about the trials," Mondale began. "It would be intolerable for us to just sit here if they tried our people. The American people wouldn't stand for it—and they shouldn't! I see the beginning of trials as a very ominous act that we would have to respond to in some way. But I'd like to get back to something you said earlier—the role of the Shah in this thing. I believe that Khomeini has the initiative. He has our people and a world forum for preaching his nonsense. I believe that the single most important thing we can do is to encourage the Shah to leave as soon as his health permits. He was the reason, ostensibly, for the embassy being seized, and I can't imagine the militants will release the hostages as long as the Shah is in the United States almost as if he were a ward of our government."

"I agree with what you are saying, Fritz," said Vance, "but we had better think that through. Some of my experts are worried about how the militants would react if the Shah left the States."

"Mine too," added Turner. "I worry that when and if he leaves, the Iranians just might feel that the United States has denied them their prize, and they could take it out on the hostages, killing them out of a sense of frustration."

"He finishes his treatments in New York next week—he could be ready to return to Mexico within a couple of weeks," Vance added.

Zbig shifted restlessly in his chair, then spoke, "Frankly, Mr. President, I think it is disgusting for us to be talking about getting the Shah out of the country. As you know, I always thought it was a mistake to make his coming to the U.S. an issue. But to allow him to come here on humanitarian grounds for medical treatment and then to hustle him out of the country to satisfy some terrorists is not right. I'm afraid that it will simply be read by Khomeini as another sign of weakness."

The President responded, irritated: "It's not a matter of principle or weakness, Zbig, to allow him to return to Mexico. He was in Mexico when he requested to come here for his treatment, and when it's completed, it's natural for him to return. I don't intend to rush him or jeopardize his health, and I don't want the government to be involved in his move. But when he's ready to return to Mexico, he should. Fritz is right, they're not likely to end this as long as the Shah is sitting in New York."

Carter instructed Vance to get him an updated report on the Shah's medical condition, including an estimate of when it would be safe for him to travel. The President walked out through the Rose Garden, boarded the chopper, and returned to Camp David.

I drove up to Camp David later that afternoon to join my mother, brother, sister, and their families for Thanksgiving, hoping to get my mind off Kennedy and Khomeini for a couple of days. I was not thankful for either of them. I wasn't surprised that the adults in my family wanted to talk about the hostages, but hadn't expected my nephews to know about the situation and to express their feelings so freely.

The two younger ones, Jordan and Lawton, subjected me to an endless stream of tasteless "Ayatollah" jokes. But my oldest nephew, Jay, age twelve, was more serious when he asked, "Why doesn't the President do something?"

"Like what?" I replied, amused by his question.

"Bomb Iran and wipe 'em out!" he shot back without hesitation. "A lot of my friends at school say that Jimmy Carter doesn't have the guts to do anything."

I didn't know what to say. My sister explained that Jay had a lot of "Republicans" in his class. That didn't make me feel much better—my nephew and Khomeini both doubted the President's resolve.

Thanksgiving Day 1979

I slept late, then sat by the fire and read the morning papers, which were filled with news about the hostages. When my mother got up, she and I sat drinking coffee and talking about them. From our cabin, we saw the President and First Lady in their warm-up clothes, returning from a morning jog around the Camp's perimeter trail.

They loved Camp David, but it had taken them a while to discover the Presidential retreat, tucked neatly away in the Maryland mountains. Gerald Ford had encouraged his successor to try Camp David out the first weekend in office, but the new President felt that he had been sent to Washington to do a job, not to relax away from the White House. But finally, in late February 1977, Rosalynn and Jimmy Carter went to Camp David. The newness of his Presidency had worn off by then, and, more important, he had come to need an occasional holiday from the endless meetings, paperwork, and problems of the White House. The Carters fell in love with Camp David that first weekend. When he returned to the White House, Jimmy Carter was like a little boy telling everyone who would listen about the wonders of Camp David. When the budget for the next fiscal year was being prepared and the President was looking for a way to sharply reduce federal spending, frills, perks, and limousines were special symbolic targets. But at one budget meeting he said to Bert Lance, then still Budget Director, "Don't tell me how much it costs to maintain Camp David. I don't ever want to know."

After that first visit, the President and his family began to spend almost every other weekend at Camp David. In fact, over the course of his Administration, his family spent the equivalent of nearly an entire year (including the two weeks of the Mideast Summit) there, using the retreat more than any other First Family. I was always a little worried that someone in the media might make the same calculation and criticize us for it.

The Presidential helicopter always landed precisely on the three red markers on the pad in the open field near the entrance to the camp. An identical auxiliary chopper stood nearby. The camp commander was on hand to welcome the Commander-in-Chief with a crisp salute. A flagpole near the helipad flew the Presidential flag, which was raised and lowered by the Marines in ceremony as he arrived or departed. The President's limousine, surrounded by Secret Service agents, would be waiting near the pad at the end of a narrow walkway. Unless the weather was bad, Carter would hand his briefcase to a waiting aide, take the First Lady's hand, and they would walk along the narrow road which wound through the beautiful, thick woods to the Presidential Cabin, Aspen, about a mile from the landing site. It made a strange procession—the Secret Service, the Presidential limousines, and the assortment of military and civilian aides riding or walking a dozen feet behind them, trying to give the couple a little sense of privacy.

The President and the First Lady would fall into a very natural routine. They would read together in Aspen or catch up on paperwork. At Camp David, the President tended to concentrate on big problems—major speeches or critical decisions that required a lot of study and reflection. Sometimes he didn't shave, and they enjoyed dressing casually, even when they attended the modest church service on Sunday morning in the recreation room converted temporarily into a chapel and presided over by a military chaplain or a minister from a nearby town. The Carters spent days outdoors, taking walks on the nature trails, bowling, jogging, and playing tennis, and during the warm spring and summer months, after they exercised, the couple often jumped into the pool outside their cabin, still in their sweaty clothes. They spent quiet evenings together in Aspen, often watching a movie with Amy after an early dinner.

It was impossible to get away from the problems of the Oval Office, but at Camp David the President could put them at a distance. Staff and Cabinet members who would call him at the White House wouldn't call him at his Maryland retreat. There was an aura about his being there that discouraged subordinates from bothering him with matters that might not, after all, demand Presidential attention. Cabinet and staff members went ahead and took action they probably should have taken anyway, and critical decisions were either delayed a day or so or brought to the attention of one of his aides.

The families of several staff members assembled in Laurel Cabin for Thanksgiving lunch, and the President, Rosalynn, and Amy joined us. While we were waiting to pass by the tables heaped with turkey, dressing, sweet potatoes, and cranberry sauce, the President asked for quiet and said a brief prayer, ending it by expressing thanks for our freedom and praying for the safe and quick release of the American hostages.

November 30, 1979 (Friday)

The Shah had made a steady recovery from surgery and was preparing to return to Mexico when a news report arrived from Mexico City: the Foreign Ministry wouldn't grant him a new entry visa.

"López Portillo is a liar!" Carter said furiously of the Mexican President. "They just double-crossed us," he complained, "and I doubt there's any other reason than just wanting to cause problems. Unless they think they are currying favor with the Third World by mistreating the Shah."

He turned to Vance. "Cy, I want you to really lay it on the line with our friends to help us by providing a home for the Shah."

Vance went right to work, and later that morning "flash" cables went out to friendly capitals all over the world; American ambassadors were instructed to ask their host governments: Would you be willing to accept the former Shah to assist the United States in its efforts to resolve the hostage crisis? After two days of this flurry of diplomatic effort, Vance reported that he had come up with several "shaky" offers but nothing firm. The only definite invitation was from Egypt.

The Shah was scheduled to leave New York Hospital on Sunday, December 2. The President asked Lloyd Cutler to fly quietly to New York to see the Shah and invite him to move to Lackland Air Force Base, Texas, where there were good medical facilities. Cutler assured the Shah that while he recuperated at Lackland, the President would continue his efforts to find a suitable permanent home for the royal family. The Shah and his entourage left for Lackland that Sunday.

December 11, 1979 (Tuesday)

It was a crisp, dry, winter day, the kind of cold that stimulates instead of numbing. The bare, black limbs of the leafless trees provided a stark contrast to the massive white buildings and monuments of the nation's capital. I was enjoying the morning drive along Rock Creek Parkway to the White House when the first call came. The military driver told me that "Deacon" was calling on the car radio, and I was to report to the Oval Office as soon as I reached the White House. Deacon was the code name given the President by the Secret Service for use on open communications.

I had worked for Jimmy Carter all of my adult life—over thirteen years—but I still couldn't help being a bit nervous whenever he called. I wondered what he wanted.

Only a few minutes passed before I heard the same radio operator calling again, asking the driver where we were and how long it would be before we got to the White House.

"The President is really anxious to see you, Mr. Jordan," the driver commented.

I agreed and sighed. "It can't be anything very good."

Jimmy Carter was not given to small talk, nor was he accustomed to heaping praise on those who worked for him, so when he was anxious to see someone, it meant that either there was a problem or he had a specific request. I skimmed through the morning *Washington Post* and *The New York Times*, looking for a clue as to what he might want. A Gallup poll showed us ahead of Kennedy for the first time in over a year, but the hostage story continued to dominate the front pages. I couldn't find any hint of what he might be calling about.

I stopped by my office only long enough to drop my briefcase, and walked quickly to the Oval Office. Eleanor, at my side, went over changes in my schedule for the day, her short legs working double-time to keep up with me.

Pushing open the heavy wooden door to the Oval Office, I said, "Good morning, Mr. President—I understand you wanted to see me."

He glanced up from the papers stacked neatly on the ornate wooden desk, looked at his watch with a slight grin, and said, "Good afternoon, Ham. It's almost nine forty-five."

It was common for the President to remind Jody and me that we were late. It was also a not-too-subtle reminder that our Boss was an early riser and had been at his desk for quite a while.

I smiled. "Well, it's important to the American people that at least one member of the Administration get a good night's sleep. If you slept eight hours a night, Mr. President, we'd probably have inflation down to five percent."

Carter grinned broadly and quickly turned serious. "Ham, we've got a real problem. I received a report from Cy this morning on potential homes for the Shah. We've gone to every possible country and we've completely struck out. Only Sadat is willing to take him, and after talking to Ghorbal [Egypt's Ambassador] and Mubarak [Egypt's Vice President] I'm convinced that would be trouble for Sadat. Mexico's refusal to allow the Shah to return there has only made it more difficult for other countries, who must be thinking, 'Well, if Mexico is scared to accept him, why should we?'"

I nodded.

"All the European countries where the Shah would like to go don't want him. Most of them are dependent on Iranian oil and have embassies in Tehran. I don't see any prospect for getting our people out as long as the Shah is in the U.S."

I wondered why he was telling me all of this.

"Do you think that you could get Torrijos to allow the Shah to go to Panama?"

I was surprised at his suggestion—surprised both at the idea of Panama as a possible home for the Shah and at the thought that I was being asked to make the request of General Omar Torrijos, the military strongman of Panama. It was true that I had become a close friend of Torrijos' during the ratification of the Panama Canal Treaties. In fact, a number of people in the White House had jokingly referred to me as "Secretary of State—for Panama."

"Mr. President," I said, "I don't know. I'd have to try to think about it from Panama's perspective."

"Ham, Panama had offered to take the Shah when he first left Iran. We've picked up some hints that they might still accept him, but we really don't know." He paused. "Panama isn't dependent on Iranian oil, and I doubt that they even have an embassy in Tehran."

"Of course the canal itself is terribly vulnerable to sabotage or commando attack, and a lot of ships around the world fly the Panamanian flag," I responded. "All that aside, Torrijos is a gutsy guy and might do it simply to help our country."

The President sat quietly, obviously waiting for me to work it out in my own mind.

"Torrijos would probably catch hell from the left in his own country and from some other Latin American and Third World countries for being a puppet of the U.S.," I said, thinking out loud.

"Yes," the President said, "but the bottom line is that if Torrijos wants to do it, he will—particularly if it helps us resolve the hostage crisis."

We talked on, trying to examine what the consequences of the Shah's going to Panama would be from Torrijos' perspective. Carter finally said that the only way we would know would be to ask. "And it's too damn important a thing to be done by telephone. It's easy to say no on the phone, and if Torrijos turned me down on the phone, we'd be in a hell of a fix—the Shah sitting at Lackland and nowhere to go. No, Ham, I think you should go see Torrijos and make the request in person," he concluded.

"I'm willing to give it a try," I said, attempting to disguise both my excitement and my nervousness.

Before I left the Oval Office, the President cautioned me to keep my trip absolutely quiet, reasoning that it would be bad for everyone involved if it were known that we tried to get Panama to accept the Shah and failed.

I took his admonition literally and told Eleanor only that I was going out of the country for the President and no one should know. I walked into my office, picked up the red "secure" phone on my desk that was immune to being tapped, and called Secretary of Defense Harold Brown to request a small military jet to carry me to Panama. I had never used a government plane for travel before. In fact, in keeping with guidelines imposed by the President when he took office, I had always traveled tourist class on commercial airlines when on government business. I told Harold that I needed a jet plane immediately to carry me "south" on urgent business.

After making arrangements for my flight, I called the U.S. Ambassador to Panama, Ambler Moss, and asked him to arrange for me to meet with Torrijos. Because we were on an "open" line that could easily be tapped, I didn't want to go into any details, so I only gave him my approximate time of arrival, told him I needed to see General Torrijos, and stressed the importance of keeping my trip absolutely confidential.

Just as I was finishing my call, Vice President Mondale walked in unannounced, as he often did. He began to talk about the campaign against Kennedy, but I interrupted him and told him that if he didn't mind, I was going to have to excuse myself because I was on my way to Panama.

"How many delegates do they have?" he asked.

The President confided totally in Mondale, so I knew I could be open with him and told him the purpose of my trip. He became very serious and talked about how surprised he had been by the patriotic, patient reaction of the American public to the hostage crisis. But Christmas, he said, would be the turning point. "If our people aren't out of there by Christmas," he said, "I'm afraid that an ugly mood will develop in this country, and we'll be in for a rough time."

I rushed home, packed a small bag, and headed for Andrews Air Force Base. What Mondale had said was very much on my mind. He was right about Christmas. The patience of the American people wouldn't last forever.

I better not mess things up, I thought as the small Air Force jet lifted off and headed toward Panama.

I began to worry about keeping my secret mission a secret. Suppose the press learned we were trying to move the Shah to Panama? If the militants in Tehran heard about it in advance, they could threaten to kill their prisoners if the Shah left the States. What would we do then? Perhaps there were Panamanians in Iran who might be seized. I took out a piece of White House stationery, wrote a note, and handed it to the pilot: *Colonel, I am on a secret and very delicate mission on behalf of the President. It is absolutely essential to the success of my mission that no one know about this trip or my presence on your plane. Thanks, Hamilton Jordan.* The pilot read it, signed it, and passed it around to the other members of the crew to read and sign. No one said a word.

I began to think about what to say to Torrijos. I wanted to construct an argument that would make it almost impossible for him to refuse me. I took out my legal pad and started writing. In one column I listed all of the reasons that Torrijos might accept the Shah:

1. *To help Carter.* Torrijos and the President developed a mutual respect during the treaty negotiations and ratification. Just as Carter would find it difficult to turn down any

reasonable request from Torrijos, Torrijos' inclination would surely be to accommodate Carter whenever possible.

2. *Panama's relationship with the United States is critical to its economy and political posture in Latin America*. If Panama played a role in freeing the hostages, it would create a more friendly climate in the States toward the tiny country.

3. *For Torrijos to be center stage*. Torrijos is bored with the day-to-day affairs of government. By allowing the Shah to come to Panama, he and his country would be at the hub of a great international drama. The General would love that!

4. *Panama's tradition of welcoming exiles*. Of all the Latin American countries, Panama has the richest tradition of hospitality for exiles and political dissidents. The General even invited Patty Hearst to Panama for her honeymoon, and she was his guest for several weeks. Allowing the Shah to come would be in keeping with that tradition.

Then I listed the reasons he might not:

1. *Harm to Panama's shipping*. Many countries fly the Panamanian flag on their ships. If Panama welcomed the Shah and aligned itself with the U.S. in this crisis, its shipping business could be hurt.

2. *Harm to the canal itself*. The Panama Canal is an amazing but very fragile engineering feat and extremely vulnerable to sabotage. Iran could send a hit squad to Panama and easily close it with a single stick of dynamite.

3. *Political problems for Torrijos*. The General is constantly performing a juggling act in his own country, trying to maintain an environment for economic growth and prosperity with the business community while at the same time communicating with the leftist, anti-American elements. If the Shah came to Panama, there could be riots, and Torrijos certainly would be accused by the left of being a U.S. "puppet."

4. *Harm to Panama's image in the Third World and Latin America*. It is important to Panama politically and economically not to be perceived as either a Communist state or a

U.S. "puppet." Torrijos is the only leader in the world who counts both Fidel Castro and the President of the United States as his "good friends."

5. *There might be Panamanians in Iran who could be seized or harmed.*

I didn't feel any better after finishing my list. There were damn good reasons for Torrijos not to accept the exile, but the General was such an independent and unpredictable man that it was impossible to second-guess him. Based on my knowledge of him and experience with him, I knew I'd rather depend on the "Panamanian dictator" than most of our nation's other "friends" and "allies" who proved their friendship only when it was in their own interest.

We had to stop at Homestead Air Force Base, Florida, to refuel. I wanted to get out of the plane, stretch my legs, and get a little fresh air, but was worried about keeping my trip secret, for there were military men scurrying around to service the plane, as well as an officer who had turned out to greet it. I put on my bulky topcoat, turned up the collar, and, when the officer faced the other way, quickly skipped down the steps and off the plane as inconspicuously as possible. I walked several hundred yards down the runway, feeling very much like a spy in a James Bond thriller. After refueling, we took off on the four-hour flight to Panama. I reclined in my seat but I couldn't sleep as the gravity of the mission sank in. What in the world would we do if he turned us down?

It was 9:45 P.M. when we landed in Panama and taxied to a dark corner of the airport. Before we had even come to a stop, several cars wheeled up. I walked down the ramp and was immediately shown into the car where Ambassador Moss waited for me. I had first met Moss during the Panama Canal Treaty negotiations. He was a young lawyer on the staff of Sol Linowitz, who, along with Ambassador Ellsworth Bunker, had negotiated the treaties with the Panamanians. Ambler spoke fluent Spanish and was considered very able. After the treaties were completed, he became a part of the group assigned to explain their meaning to the U.S. Senate during the fight for ratification. After ratification, the President felt it was important to have an Ambassador who understood how to implement the treaties and who could establish a close working relationship with the Panamanians. Ambler was the natural choice. I considered him a real friend, and we greeted each other warmly in the car. He had already phoned Torrijos, and the General agreed to see me right away.

I began to tell Ambler the purpose of my trip, but he interrupted me. "I bet you want the Shah to come to Panama."

"You're exactly right," I responded, astonished that he had already figured out the reason for my trip.

As we drove into the city, I reviewed with Moss the appeal I would make to Torrijos. He made a few suggestions but generally thought that my approach was correct. And, knowing Torrijos well, he was cautiously optimistic that Panama would allow the Shah to live there.

I heard later that Ambler told friends the night of my arrival in Panama was the only time he had ever seen me visibly nervous. And I *was* nervous. At a relatively young age, I had done a lot of things in my life and was accustomed to responsibility. I was Chief of Staff at the White House and exercised considerable authority on behalf of the President. In Jimmy Carter's Presidential campaign, I had made major strategic and tactical decisions as well as budget and personnel decisions without even consulting the Boss. But this was different. Lives depended on the whereabouts of the Shah, and at that moment, his whereabouts depended on me. If he left the States, it seemed likely that we could soon end the crisis. If he remained in the States, it could drag on for weeks or even months. And God only knew what would happen to the hostages and to Carter's re-election prospects.

Ambler Moss's description of me as "nervous" was a major understatement.

The house where I was to meet Omar Torrijos was one of eight or ten of his places scattered about the city and the countryside. He kept no regular schedule and moved abruptly, according to whim. Even his associates were not informed, except in a vague way, of his plans. I had suspected that this was primarily a safety precaution against attempts on his life or possible coups. But after

I got to know Torrijos well, I finally asked him the reason for this policy. He told me that a political leader had to have the popular support of his people; that he had to maintain a mystique and at the same time be able to relate to persons in all walks of life; that if he traveled to any part of his small country, the common people would say proudly, "Omar lives here." "And besides," he added, "you can't overthrow a leader if you can't find him."

We drove down a sidestreet in the heart of Panama City and parked in front of a modern, Spanish-style home. I recognized it as the home of Rory Gonzales, a businessman and close friend of Torrijos'. It was Torrijos' favorite place to stay, his "base" as he described it, and I had been there a number of times. The moon was out, and I could see the silhouettes of the Guardia Nacional scurrying around, whispering into their walkie-talkies as they cleared us through the metal gate.

A young officer in dark-green khakis escorted us into the house. General Torrijos, in white slacks and the traditional embroidered white Panamanian shirt, drink in hand, rose quickly from the sofa to greet us. With him was Sergeant Chu-chu Martínez, a slight, dark-skinned man who was the General's chief security guard, his occasional interpreter, and constant companion. Chu-chu spoke several languages, had written several books of poetry, and considered himself an amateur philosopher and a student of Marx.

"*Buenas noches*, Papa General," I said, calling out the nickname that I had given him during the difficult days of the treaty negotiations. Torrijos used to tease that I was but a child in the art of political thought and he was my teacher. From then on, I had affectionately called him "Papa General" and he had called me "*hijo.*"

Torrijos laughed heartily. "It is good to see you again, Mr. Jordan!" said Sergeant Chu-chu, giving me a firm *abrazo*.

Turning back to Torrijos and pointing to Chu-chu, I said, "I see that you still have that Communist hanging around."

Chu-chu grinned as he interpreted for Torrijos.

Torrijos smiled and spoke in rapid Spanish, gesturing first at Chu-chu and then at himself. "The General says yes he does, but I am *his* Communist!"

We all chuckled.

The General said something to Chu-chu, who left the room and returned moments later with several cold bottles of the local beer, Balboa. Ambler and I sat down. The room was open and pleasant, with a tile floor bordered with greenery in large pots, wooden chairs stuffed with colorful cushions, and a large window that looked out on a lighted blue pool.

"You look good, General," I said. Although Omar Torrijos was in his early fifties, he had the body of a much younger man, made lean and hard by years in the military and by the frequent daylong tromps that he still took through the dense jungles of Panama. He was under six feet tall, but his confident swagger and rugged physique suggested a much larger person. His hair was black with traces of gray and, despite his attempts to paste it back on his head, a wild lock usually dangled onto his brow. Torrijos was always running his hand through his hair, trying to press it back into place. His dark skin and hair were accentuated by pearl-white teeth and black, intense eyes that took in everything around him. Women usually found Omar Torrijos very attractive; he was, as one female journalist put it, a "Latin Bogart."

"I feel good, too," Torrijos responded. "Since the popular elections, I have turned over day-to-day control of the government to President Royo. I spend most of my time studying and thinking about foreign policy." He paused and added with a slight smile, "But I manage to keep my finger in the pie."

"It's a big finger," I retorted.

"But a very small pie," he shot back, obviously relishing the exchange, even through a translation.

I burst out laughing. Torrijos' quick wit reminded me of all the difficult but good times we had spent together working on the Canal Treaties.

But my stomach was still in a knot, and I couldn't hide my anxiety about my mission. Still, I couldn't just rush in and blurt out my request, so I tried to disguise my fears and waited for the proper moment.

We began to reminisce, swapping stories about our efforts to sell the treaty to both of our countries. I had a second beer and was beginning to relax a bit when Torrijos suddenly asked, "What brings you here in the middle of the night?"

"General, the President wanted me to come and see you," I said. "Would you mind if we talked alone?"

As soon as Chu-chu relayed my request, he nodded, and the three of us rose and walked out onto the enclosed porch, leaving Ambler, Torrijos' staff, and several security guards in the living room. We sat down in facing chairs, with Chu-chu close by, translating. Torrijos waved away the servants who were hovering, lit one of the large Cuban cigars his friend Fidel had sent him, and gestured for me to speak.

"The President believes that it will be impossible to resolve the hostage crisis as long as the Shah remains in the United States. To his credit, the Shah does not want his presence in the States to interfere, and he has said that he would leave. The problem is that we have been unable to find a country that would accept him. All the countries he knows and would like to go to— Switzerland, Austria, and Great Britain—withdrew their invitations after the hostages were seized. In the past two weeks, the President and Secretary Vance have canvassed the world community to find a place for him to go. The only country in the entire world that has offered to take him is Egypt, and the President opposes that because he fears it will only contribute to Sadat's other problems."

Torrijos shook his head and said softly, "The President is right."

I took a short breath, leaned forward, and looked him directly in the eyes. "So we have run out of options. We don't want to take advantage of our friendship by asking you to do something that ignores your own country's interests, but the President wanted me to ask if you would be willing to accept the Shah in Panama until the hostage crisis is resolved."

The General leaned back in the large wicker chair. He closed his eyes briefly and took a big puff on his long cigar. I could almost hear him thinking, but I couldn't read his mind. Maybe he was preparing his answer, just as I had prepared my question on the plane. The seconds that passed were like long minutes to me.

Torrijos sat up straight again. Nothing about him revealed his decision. He began to speak slowly, in a low voice. "Hamilton, the crisis is first and foremost the problem of the United States,

because those people are Americans and they represent your
country and your government. But it is also the problem and the
responsibility of the world community. As long as diplomats can
be held like those in Tehran, no diplomat is safe anywhere. You
can tell the President that we will accept the Shah in Panama. We
are a small but proud country. If we can make even a small contribution to peacefully resolving this crisis, we will be happy to do
so."

Months of debate in the councils of our government had preceded the decision to allow the Shah to come to the United
States. Omar Torrijos, sitting alone in a private house in Panama,
puffing on his cigar, had made his decision in seconds.

I wanted to shout with joy—at last the exile had somewhere to
go. That should speed up the release of the hostages. I was glad
not to have failed the President on what would certainly have
been my first and last venture in big-league diplomacy, and I was
overwhelmed with appreciation for this remarkable man. All of
the great and powerful nations in the world had turned the Shah
down, but tiny Panama had said yes. I was proud of our friendship with Torrijos and his country. It proved the basic point of the
Canal Treaties: that when a large and powerful country like the
United States treats a small nation like Panama with dignity and
respect, it pays off in the long run.

"General, thank you for your positive response. I hope that we
will be able to do something someday for Panama which adequately expresses our appreciation."

"Don't worry about that—just get the hostages out. But first, I
believe that we should tell your Ambassador in the next room. It
will probably be the only time I know something before he does,"
the General said with a smile. We walked into the other room.
Torrijos said a few words in Spanish to Moss, who responded in
that language.

"To Panama, to Papa General—and to the early release of our
hostages," I proposed, raising my Balboa high.

"To the wonderful Christmas present brought to me by my son
Hamilton and President Carter," Torrijos responded. We all
laughed and then began to talk about the arrangements for bringing the Shah to Panama.

I realized our discussion was a bit premature: the Shah now had a place to go, but there was no guarantee that he would agree to the move. Time and secrecy continued to be critical.

"Only half my job has been done," I explained. "We don't know if the Shah will accept your kind invitation. I'll have to go to Texas and extend your invitation to him. Quite frankly, he is a European in his thinking and is not at all familiar with Latin America, so I may have to answer a lot of questions about Panama."

"But you are an expert on Panama!" Torrijos said sarcastically.

"If I told him everything that I know about you, General," I said, "he wouldn't want to come here!"

Torrijos roared.

"Now I owe the President a telephone call," I said.

"Use the telephone in my bedroom, but be careful what you say on that line," Torrijos advised.

I wondered who he thought was bugging his phone: the Soviets, the United States—or both? In the bedroom several television sets and phones surrounded the king-sized bed blanketed with a bright-red spread. The walls were covered with Torrijos' pictures and memorabilia. Most prominently displayed were shots of him and Carter signing the Canal Treaties.

I reached the White House operator and asked for the President. She said he was in bed, and had left a wake-up call for 5:30. I told her to wake him. A few seconds later Jimmy Carter came on the phone.

"Mr. President, sorry to wake you. I'm with our friend down south, and he's willing to accept that gift," I said, using some of Torrijos' own code words to disguise my message.

"Thank God!" he said. "I'm glad and very relieved. I've been worried all day about what we could do if he said no."

"Well, I'm relieved too, Mr. President, but I suspect that it will take some selling to convince our other friend to come here, as he prefers other places and knows very little about this place. At any rate, I'd like to leave for Texas right away and try to persuade the other person to accept this invitation. I don't want to waste any time trying to tie this down. The longer we wait, the greater the chance it will be publicized."

The President agreed with my plans. "You leave as soon as possible. Keep me posted and call me if I can do anything to help move things along."

"Yes sir, I will. I do think it would be good if Lloyd could meet me in Texas tomorrow morning. It might help to have a little gray hair on our side of the table." Although I knew I could present my proposal to the Shah, I wasn't sure how he would react to a thirty-four-year-old he hardly knew. Lloyd Cutler was an experienced negotiator who knew the Shah and had dealt with him and his staff in New York prior to the move to Lackland.

"Good idea," the President said. "I'll call Lloyd now and ask him to get down there tomorrow. Now let me speak to the General."

I went to the door and motioned Torrijos to the phone. The confident leader I knew was visibly nervous when he was dealing with President Carter, and he picked up the phone hesitantly. It was a brief conversation, but I could tell as I watched the serious expression on Torrijos' face that the President was thanking him in Spanish for his help.

"*Gracias, buenas noches, Señor Presidente,*" the General said before hanging up.

I had complete faith in Torrijos, but I wanted his commitment to accept the Shah to be airtight before I left. I hoped that being thanked by President Carter would seal it.

As we walked back into the living room, Torrijos said, "Why don't you stay here tonight and get some sleep?"

"I'd like to, but I think it would be better for me to fly on to Lackland so I can see the Shah first thing in the morning. If I leave now, I can get there by six or seven. I'd like to nail this thing down."

We then spent about thirty minutes more talking about the Shah and the problems he would face if he came to Panama, particularly his security and medical needs. Torrijos had several ideas as to where he might live and mentioned a house in the mountains as well as one on a nearby island that was "suitable for a king." The General also suggested that if the Shah was interested in Panama but not convinced, we might bring a small team from his entourage down for what Torrijos called "a Chamber of Commerce tour."

"Above all else, Hamilton, please let the Shah know that he will be welcomed here and will be treated with dignity and respect."

We embraced and I left.

My car was just pulling away from the house when I heard the General shouting. I turned to see him running toward us with something in his hand. He thrust a brown sack through the window. I looked inside: a six-pack of cold Balboa. "*Gracias*, Papa General!" I yelled out the window as we sped off. I couldn't see him, but I heard him laughing in the dark.

December 12–13, 1979 (Wednesday–Thursday)

I boarded the plane for the long flight to Lackland Air Force Base. The base commander and Steve Oxman, an attorney and former assistant to Warren Christopher, who had been recruited to baby-sit with the Shah, met me and drove me directly to the Officers' Quarters. I told Oxman of the plan to transfer the Shah to Panama and he informed me that the Shah's wife and his assistant, Robert Armao, would be influential in his decision.

I hadn't slept in over twenty-four hours, so I went straight to bed, hoping to be refreshed when I saw the Shah at ten Thursday morning. But I couldn't sleep; all I could do was worry about how to persuade him to make the move. It was a relief to me to see Lloyd Cutler arrive from Washington in the morning; it was good to have the experienced, smooth counsel with me.

Armao was to accompany us to meet the Shah, and I asked Oxman to fill us in on him. "He was a Nelson Rockefeller advance man . . ." Oxman began. Before he could say any more, Armao joined us, and I was left to form my own impression. What I saw was a carefully groomed young man in an expensive suit and a sculpted hairdo. He presented the appearance of an elegant man of the world, but he was unable to conceal his nervous anticipation of being center stage in an international drama.

"Bob, the hostages will not be released as long as the Shah

remains in the States," I said bluntly. "The Shah has graciously agreed to go somewhere else if we can find a country that will accept him. Luckily for him, General Torrijos of Panama has offered to take him in."

"I'm skeptical," Armao said to me. "His Majesty has been badly treated and taken advantage of everywhere he has been since he left his homeland. You are welcome to make your pitch, but His Majesty knows very little about General Torrijos or his country."

He walked us to where the Shah was being lodged. Then, as though reminding a child to mind his manners, Armao whispered in my ear outside the door, "Be sure to refer to the Shah as Your Majesty when you address him."

"I understand," I assured him as we walked through the door.

The Shah and his Queen were living in a three-room apartment in the Lackland Officers' Quarters. It could easily have been a $75-a-day Holiday Inn "suite" in Peoria. The room where he received me conveyed a drab feeling, intensified by the awful blue and green curtains and carpet. The Shahanshah, King of Kings, Defender of the Faith and Descendant of Darius the Great, was seated on a vinyl couch.

He seemed to totter as he stood to shake hands with me and Lloyd Cutter.

"You know Mr. Jordan, Your Majesty," Armao said in a formal voice that could have been introducing me to the Shah's court.

"Of course," he said in a voice without feeling. "I remember Mr. Jordan from my visit to the White House in 1977."

I remembered the visit well. President Carter had seen an incredible number of heads of state during that first year and a half in the White House. I was worried both that he was spending too much time with foreign visitors and that he might be perceived as being overly attentive to foreign policy at the expense of domestic problems. I did a quick study which showed that Carter, during his first year in office, had met with over forty heads of state, many more than Kennedy, Johnson, or Nixon. The President, at a senior staff meeting, said he agreed with my analysis, resolved to do something about it, but continued to spend large amounts of time on foreign policy. Still, of all the people we had seen during that period—Sadat, Schmidt, Callaghan, Giscard, and scores of others—the Shah was easily the most impressive. At their first bilateral meeting in the Cabinet Room at the White House, the Shah had conducted a *tour d'horizon* of the world, describing with great accuracy the problems facing the West, the strategic importance of Iran, and the critical nature of the U.S.-Iran relationship. He spoke for almost an hour without notes. It was more than a presentation—it was a performance.

The President wanted to confront the Shah with reports of human rights violations in Iran and the lack of progress toward democratic reforms. But he did not want to embarrass the proud man in front of his entourage in the Cabinet Room, so he invited the Shah to join him in his private study. There Carter outlined his concerns about the violations of human rights in Iran and urged the Shah to accelerate efforts toward political reform. The President told me later that the Shah had been very "forthcoming" in his response, promising a renewed effort on human rights and democratization. By the time the Shah's visit was over, we felt reassured about the political situation in Iran and fortunate to have this strong leader as an ally.

But here we were, less than two years later, and the firm and decisive world leader looked emaciated and weak, his face pale and gaunt. *It must be his health,* I thought. But I also sensed that he had lost his spirit. He was wearing a blue Air Force robe with "USA" across the back—like a boxer's robe. I wondered if he knew . . .

"Your Majesty," I said, sitting down on the sofa opposite him, "it is good to see you again. I am glad you are looking so well, and I appreciate your receiving us on such short notice."

He stared hard at me silently, as if sizing me up. The one thing that hadn't changed in the two years since I had seen him were his piercing black eyes, like gleaming bits of the darkest onyx. I squirmed a bit, hoping that I didn't look as uncomfortable as I felt. I suspected those eyes had stared down many, many people over the years.

Finally the Shah spoke. "What brings you to Texas? Usually when I have contact with the U.S. government these days, it is at their request and because they want me to do something."

I was determined to be successful, and I knew that I had to

earn a little of his trust. He was welcome to score whatever points might make him happy.

"We are not here, Your Majesty, to make a request, but to describe for you the hostage situation as we see it and to review with you possible options for your travel to another country."

"Well, as I am sure you know, I would like to do everything possible to help your country resolve the hostage crisis. I don't want to be blamed by history for this terrible thing!"

"Quite frankly, Your Majesty, the problem in Iran is not likely to be resolved as long as you are in the United States."

"That may or may not be correct, Mr. Jordan. What you and the President must understand is that the people who are holding the hostages are crazy Communists who have been my enemies for years and will ultimately destroy Khomeini, just as they destroyed me. You are not dealing with rational people, Mr. Jordan, so ordinary standards of behavior do not apply. I am grateful for my thirty-seven-year friendship with the American people and I want to help resolve the hostage problem."

"I certainly can't quarrel with your assessment, Your Majesty, but we believe that whatever chance exists of peacefully resolving the crisis will be enhanced if the hard-liners and Communists are not able to charge that the Shah is in the United States preparing to return to Iran."

Smiling wryly, the Shah said, "That is certainly not true, is it, Mr. Jordan?"

"No, Your Majesty, it is not."

Turning serious, he then said, "I am prepared to travel soon to another country—but where can I go?"

"Your Majesty," Cutler said, "in the last twelve days, the President and Secretary of State have made requests of the countries you expressed an interest in and they've questioned additional countries where we might be influential. I regret to inform you that we have not been able to develop a lot of attractive choices."

"But what about Austria and Switzerland?"

"Neither is willing to receive you at this time."

"Are you sure?" the Shah asked, disbelieving.

"Yes, Your Majesty. Our ambassadors have seen the foreign ministers of both countries in the last forty-eight hours."

"I must admit that I am surprised and disappointed," he said in a low voice, loaded with grief. "It seems that no one wants me."

I jumped in. "That's not true, Your Majesty. I have just come from Panama, where I spoke with General Omar Torrijos. He is willing, indeed eager, to welcome you to his country," I said, trying to sound positive about his only possibility.

"That is very kind, Mr. Jordan, but I have to admit that I know very little about Latin America, or Panama, or this man Torrijos—and I would much prefer a European country."

"But, Your Majesty, there are no European countries available. In fact, I am afraid that Panama is the only country in the world that has expressed a desire to receive you—other than Egypt. And it is the view of the Administration that your going to Egypt now might be difficult for President Sadat."

"No, I don't want to burden my old friend Anwar with my problems."

"I hate to be so blunt, Your Majesty, but I am afraid that Panama is the only other country available at this point."

The mood of our conversation changed quickly, as the Shah said almost sympathetically, "Mr. Jordan, you are a young man only trying to do your job. Don't worry about disappointing me with your bluntness. After what my family and I have been through, nothing disappoints me anymore."

I didn't know how to respond. We sat for several minutes while the Shah looked down and seemed to be collecting himself and his emotions. Ending the silence, he said, "Very well—I must face reality. Tell me something about Panama and this man Torrijos."

Enormously relieved, I laid out everything I knew about Panama—its history, the recent treaty negotiations, even the Canal. Before I left Panama, Ambler Moss had handed me a copy of David McCullough's very fine book about the Canal to give to the Shah. I presented it to him.

"Very interesting. I thank you. But I have heard that Torrijos is a typical South American dictator," he said as he thumbed through the book.

I was shocked by his use of the word "dictator," which had been applied so many times to him, but the irony seemed to escape him. "Your Majesty," I responded, "with the possible exception of President Sadat, General Torrijos is the most fascinating person we have met since President Carter took office. He is a man without much formal education, but he is shrewd and wise. He led a group of young officers to power in the sixties. Although the military provided his political base, he has taken steps over the years to give control of his government to civilians. His country is small, but he is very active in foreign policy matters in Central and Latin America. He is a maverick and his actions are unpredictable. But from our dealings with him, we know him to be a man of his word."

I took a breath but didn't invite comment as I went on about Torrijos. "In the past several years, and particularly since the ratification of the Canal Treaties, he has moved to democratize his country rapidly and has handed over day-to-day control of the government to some capable technocrats and economists." As I spoke these words, I was tempted to blurt out to the Shah that this man whom he had referred to as a dictator had done the very things that might have saved his own regime.

"Mr. Jordan, I appreciate your observations and the General's invitation to Panama. But I have medical and security problems, and responsibilities to my family and staff. I would feel comfortable getting on a plane right now and flying to Austria or Switzerland, as I know these countries and their leaders, but it is not easy to wake up one morning and learn that my only choice is to go to a country I know nothing about."

"I understand, Your Majesty."

Turning to Armao, the Shah said, "Bob, how do we proceed?"

"Your Majesty," said Armao, "we have a number of things to consider. I would first want to meet with your doctors and be assured that adequate medical facilities exist in Panama for your continuing care and treatment."

The Shah nodded.

"Secondly," Armao went on, "I would want to have our own security people travel to Panama to determine if we can find a comfortable and secure place for the Royal Family to live and see what role the government of Panama will play in providing for your security. Finally, I would hope that Mr. Jordan and the Administration would give us some minimal assurances about re-entry to the States in the case of emergency."

"I am sure that our government will be able to provide reasonable assurances," I said. "But how long will it take to consult your doctors and security people and make a decision?" As soon as I said it, I knew I had made a mistake by appearing to be too anxious to move the Shah and not sufficiently concerned about his health and safety.

"It will take as long as it takes!" Armao snapped back. "Or is there a deadline—and are you telling His Majesty that he *has* to leave the United States?"

I glared at Armao, feeling foolish and trying to hide my irritation. "Of course not, Bob. If the Shah decides to go to Panama, we would simply like to make the move quietly and safely. Every hour that passes increases the chances that the media will find out about it. That's my main concern."

"Well, if it pleases Your Majesty, I'll check with your doctors this morning and give you a report," he said. "If they are positive about Panama, we can talk with our security people."

"That's fine," said the Shah. "I will talk to the Queen. She will have a lot of questions."

The Shah seemed in no hurry for me to go, and I felt comfortable enough with him to chat a bit.

"Your Majesty," I asked, "how do you evaluate what is happening in Iran?"

"Mr. Jordan, I wish that the President or someone had asked me that six months ago," he said curtly.

Not knowing how to respond, I simply waited, hoping he would continue talking.

After a moment, the Shah began a rambling analysis of what was going on in Iran. "My country is in chaos and is falling apart. Khomeini and his henchmen are ruining Iran. I cannot tell you how bad I felt to pick up the morning papers in the Bahamas and see that men who had worked for me for years and years trying to improve Iran had been executed. I am sure that will be a part of your nation's human rights report," he said with a pleased and wry expression. "But the educated middle class and technicians are leaving Iran, oil production is very low, and the economic outlook is bleak. With the Soviets now in Afghanistan, I fear that Iran is ripe for the plucking."

"Your Majesty," I asked, "what happened?"

"Mr. Jordan, I can't really explain it. I have had a lot of time to reflect on what I might have done differently and what your government might have done differently. I had trouble understanding what your President expected me to do. I would see your Ambassador [William] Sullivan one day and he would urge restraint or ask that I negotiate with the very people who were trying to destroy me! Sometimes on the same day, I would get a message from Dr. Brzezinski, advising that I crack down. As you know, Mr. Jordan, the President's public statements vacillated between support for the monarchy and doubt about my ability to lead my country." He paused, as if to regain his strength. "If I had to do it over again," he continued, "I would have been firmer. Iran is worth fighting for, and I should have led that fight! If I had, I would still be sitting on the Peacock Throne today and not having to sneak around the world like a criminal," he said in a quiet voice, filled with despair.

There was another awkward silence, except this time the Shah stared hard at me, as though he wanted me to share some of his burden and bitterness. I pitied him.

"I really cannot understand what happened," he continued. "One month, hundreds of thousands of people lined the streets to greet their Shah, and two months later, hundreds of thousands filled those same streets screaming for my death." Lowering his head, he said softly, "I really don't know what happened . . . I really don't."

He rambled on, saying finally and with great satisfaction, "This madman Khomeini has come to power by exploiting Islam. He in turn has been duped by the Communist elements in Iran, who know how to appease him. They will turn on Khomeini and destroy him! God willing, I will be around to see this happen. It won't be long," he said, obviously relishing the prospect.

I couldn't tell if he really believed it.

He said he wanted to freshen up before his twin sister, Princess Ashraf, arrived from New York.

"What a brave woman she is," he said admiringly. "I have lost my country, but she has lost her country and her son. I'm sure you know that her son was killed by some of Khomeini's assassins. But her sole concern now is for my health." He rose and said, as he offered a weak handshake, "Thank you, Mr. Jordan and Mr. Cutler, for your visit. I am sure that we will be talking again soon."

"Thank you, Your Majesty, for your time and understanding."

In the hall on the way out, we ran into Princess Ashraf. I paused, held out my hand, and said, "Nice to meet you, Your Highness." The Princess glared at me with jet-black eyes like her brother's. She didn't accept my hand, simply brushed by us as she entered the Shah's room.

December 13, 1979 (Thursday)

Bob Armao, Colonel Jahnbini (the Shah's security chief), and I flew to Panama to survey the places where the exiled monarch might live, while Lloyd Cutler remained at Lackland to talk with the Shah's doctors about medical facilities in Panama.

We all thought that Gabriel Lewis's vacation home on Contadora Island was the most suitable. "It's easier to protect him on the island," Jahnbini explained. "With Panama City only a few minutes away, hospitals are close," Armao observed. "And the Queen will like the warm weather and the water and the resort atmosphere. This is fine, Hamilton."

Torrijos sent for us. "It is an honor to meet you, Your Excellency," Armao said as he was introduced to Torrijos. I almost laughed out loud at his inappropriate formality.

"I understand that you have had a difficult time in other countries," Torrijos said, and Chu-chu translated. "Please tell the Shah that if he accepts my invitation, he will be treated as an honored guest. And if I hear that anyone tries to take advantage of the Shah, I will have that person thrown in jail."

Armao smiled. He liked what he was hearing. Before we left,

Torrijos wrote the Shah a warm letter inviting him to Panamá. We boarded the plane back to Lackland. "It's up to the Shah and his doctors now," Armao said.

December 14, 1979 (Friday)

Lloyd Cutler had worked out the Shah's medical needs by the time I returned from Panama. We met with the Shah's doctors and agreed, on behalf of our government, that the Shah would be allowed to return to the United States in case of a "medical emergency." This oral commitment was known later as the "Lackland agreement."

I then went to see the Shah, who had already been briefed by Armao. I presented Torrijos' letter to him, and he seemed touched by it, saying several times, "I actually have an invitation from this man."

We discussed his medical and security needs, and finally the Shah smiled and said, "You have convinced me. I will go to Panama."

We talked about travel arrangements and I volunteered a military plane to take him the next day. After saying goodbye to the Shah and checking one last time to see that all of the plans had been made for an early and quiet departure, I boarded the plane at Lackland and flew back to Washington. I was dead tired, but couldn't sleep on the long flight home.

I arrived about nine that night, feeling as if I had spent most of the last four days on an airplane. Eleanor was at her desk when I arrived. I hugged her and told her what I had been doing. The White House operator called to say that the President wanted me at the Residence, where he and the First Lady were hosting the annual Christmas party for the staff.

I was glad to find him and Rosalynn waiting for me in the small office off the State Dining Room. I was still anxious for the Shah to take off unnoticed and didn't want to have to explain to my colleagues where I had been.

The President extended both hands, greeting me warmly. I reported to him about my meeting with Torrijos and the Shah and said that whatever else we might think about him, the former King of Kings was a sad and tragic figure. The President promised to phone the Shah that night and wish him a good trip and to write to Torrijos the next day.

"Well, it was a hell of an interesting week," I said. "I just hope it helps get our people out of Iran."

"I am sure that it will," Carter replied. "There is no way to bring the hostages home as long as the Shah stays in the States."

He congratulated me on completing my mission and said I should go home and get a good night's sleep.

I told him that I intended to retire from diplomacy while I was ahead, but he quickly retorted that he was sending me to Tel Aviv the next day to see Menachim Begin about the West Bank.

The three of us laughed.

I was totally exhausted when I got home. I hadn't slept more than two or three hours a night for four days. I lay down on my bed with my clothes on and tried to stay awake through the eleven-o'clock news to see if there were any reports about the Shah's departure. I didn't make it.

December 15, 1979 (Saturday)

The phone rang. It seemed like the middle of the night, and I fumbled in the dark. The call was from the Situation Room.

"Mr. Jordan, we have an important development on the hostages."

I sat up straight, immediately wide awake, thinking, *Maybe this is it—maybe the hostages are on the way home*. "Yes?" I asked expectantly.

"There are news reports that the Shah of Iran left Texas over two hours ago for an unknown destination. There are additional reports that he might be going to Uruguay or to South Africa. We have confirmed his departure from Lackland, but do not know what his destination is," the voice told me.

I glanced at my clock. It was 8:30 A.M. I smiled. Our secret move was working—even the Situation Room hadn't caught on yet! I went back to sleep reassured. *Getting the Shah out of the country should speed up the release of the hostages,* I thought. And now I could turn my thoughts back to the campaign. *If only getting Kennedy out of the Presidential race could be this easy. . . .*

December 16, 1979–January 3, 1980

But nothing happened with the hostages the next day or even the next week. The Iranian government condemned the flight of the "criminal Shah" and threatened Panama with reprisals for accepting him. It was soon obvious that the Shah's departure alone would not free the captive Americans.

An even deeper gloom settled in at the White House as Christmas approached. The President canceled his plans to go to Georgia—the first time in twenty-seven years that the Carter family would not spend the holidays together—and ordered that the national Christmas-tree lights not be turned on until the hostages returned from Iran.

I went to south Georgia to be with my family. One night after a holiday party I received an "urgent" call from the Situation Room. *Maybe this is finally it,* I thought as I dialed. *Maybe Khomeini, in a gesture of Islamic mercy, is releasing our people.*

"Mr. Jordan," the duty officer said, "the President asked us to inform you that we have reason to believe that an invasion of Afghanistan by the Soviet Union is under way."

"What?" I said incredulously.

The Situation Room does not say "reason to believe" without damned solid evidence. I asked them to keep me posted.

I didn't sleep very well that night. First the hostages and now this! I got up early the next morning and listened to the news broadcasts. The Soviets had already invented a pretext: they had been invited by the Afghan government to help quell anti-Communist forces.

I put in a call to the President and asked simply if there was anything I could do. "No," he said, "unless you can get the Soviets out of Afghanistan." I thought for a second he was kidding, but his tone made it clear he was frustrated. I offered to go back to Washington immediately, but he said no, it would take several days for the Afghanistan conflict to be clarified.

"As if we didn't already have our hands full with the hostages," I said.

"This is more serious, Hamilton. Capturing those Americans was an inhumane act committed by a bunch of radicals and condoned by a crazy old man. But this is deliberate aggression that calls into question détente and the way we have been doing business with the Soviets for the past decade. It raises grave questions about Soviet intentions and destroys any chance of getting the SALT Treaty through the Senate. And that makes the prospects of nuclear war even greater."

I was chilled when I heard his analysis.

January 4, 1980 (Friday)

In a conference call over the holidays the President told Strauss, Rafshoon, Powell, Caddell, and me about his decision to cancel the scheduled debate with Ted Kennedy in Iowa. We tried to make the counterarguments, but he wouldn't listen. "Look, you guys—if I go out to Iowa to debate Ted Kennedy, I go out there as a President and return as just another political candidate. I'll undermine my leadership position in trying to deal with the Congress and with our NATO allies if I look like I'm just down in the trenches fighting for my political life. I'm sure that what I'm doing is right."

Carter had already agreed to withdraw SALT II from Senate consideration, and we were planning to impose economic sanctions and seek UN condemnation of the U.S.S.R., but we had to decide whether to levy a grain embargo as well; the Soviet Union was heavily dependent on U.S. grain for cattle feed, so an embargo could create a severe meat shortage and a serious domestic problem for the Kremlin.

To our allies, the real test of American resolve in the face of Soviet aggression was whether or not a President, in the middle of a tough re-election campaign, would embargo grain sales from the United States and possibly alienate our farmers. As Mondale put it: "Mr. President, we need to be strong and firm, but that doesn't mean you have to commit political suicide!"

Carter listened to the substantive arguments for the embargo and the political arguments against it all week, and at our foreign policy breakfast said, "How I am going to lead the West and persuade our allies to impose sanctions against the Russians if we aren't willing to make some sacrifices ourselves? What can I say to Margaret Thatcher or Helmut Schmidt if we fail to exercise the single option that hurts the Russians most?"

No one responded.

"God knows," he continued, "I have walked the fields of Iowa and know those farmers and realize that I promised them in the seventy-six campaign that I would never embargo grains except in the case of a national emergency! But this is an emergency and I'm going to have to impose the embargo, and we'll just have to make the best of it. Farmers are patriotic people."

The President made a television speech that night, calling the Soviet invasion "a deliberate effort of a powerful atheistic government to subjugate an independent Islamic people. . . . Aggression unopposed becomes a contagious disease. . . . The world simply cannot stand by and permit the Soviet Union to commit this act with impunity. Neither the United States nor any other nation . . . can continue to do business as usual with the Soviet Union."

I watched the speech in my office and waited for the inevitable reaction. Senator Bob Dole said, "Carter took a poke at the Soviet bear and knocked out the American farmer." Kennedy charged, "A weak foreign policy can't be redeemed by suddenly getting tough on farmers." Ronald Reagan, who had been calling for an Administration that would get tough with the Russians, said: "Pigs, cows, or chickens" had not invaded Afghanistan and "no one segment of the economy should be asked to bear the brunt of American countermeasures to deal with the Soviet invasion of Afghanistan."American Farm Bureau President Allan Grant said, "The President took aim at the Russians with a double-barreled shotgun, and hit the American farmer instead!"

All the Democratic and Republican candidates were crisscrossing Iowa (it was only a few days before the caucuses), blasting the President's decision. I talked to a nervous Tim Kraft. "Ten days ago we were headed for a solid win in Iowa," he reported. "Then the President drops out of the debate and sticks it to the farmers. All bets are off, Hamilton."

January 11, 1980 (Friday)

I had just arrived at Camp David and sat down in Laurel Lodge for a nice meal and a relaxed evening with friends when I got a telephone call. It was Sergeant Chu-chu, calling from Panama with a message from Papa General. It was direct: He wanted me to come to Panama the next day. It was an unusual request and would wreck my weekend. I tried to beg off, asking if the message couldn't be sent by courier or passed to me through our Ambassador, but Chu-chu said again and again, "I cannot talk on the phone. The General thinks it is important."

I told Chu-chu that I would call him back. I sat down and thought about Torrijos' request. He was not the kind to make unreasonable requests, and whether his business was important or not, I could hardly refuse him. I called Warren Christopher, the solid number-two man at the State Department, for his advice and later talked with the President, who said, "Maybe it's about the hostages. Even if it's not, you ought to go. We can't turn Torrijos down after all he's done for us."

I called Chu-chu and told him I would come. He told me that the General suggested we revise our plan. We would meet instead in Florida "for security reasons," and he would not come himself but would send "representatives" who could speak for him.

January 12, 1980 (Saturday)

I jogged around the perimeter trail at Camp David early in the morning, then drank a cup of coffee while I shaved and dressed.

I didn't want to leave, but we owed it to Torrijos to hear him out. It was obvious the President was taking this seriously when he offered to send his helicopter to pick me up and take me directly to Andrews.

Warren Christopher called to say that he was tied up with foreign visitors and would send Henry Precht in his place to brief me on our current efforts on behalf of the hostages in case I needed the information for my meeting with the Panamanians.

I had never met Precht. In those critical months preceding the Shah's downfall, Zbig had identified him as the person at the State Department who was "undermining" the President's policy and our relationship with the Shah. When I landed at Andrews, I saw an average-sized man dressed in a sweater and slacks get out of his government car and walk over to the plane. Brushing a lock of gray hair off his face, he approached me.

"Hello," he said, shaking my hand. "I'm Henry Precht."

"Hello, Henry. I've heard about you."

"I bet you have," he said, smiling. "I've been instructed to brief you on our present policy about the hostages and the sanctions we're pursuing at the United Nations."

We boarded the plane and Precht reviewed the Administration's official position on every aspect of the crisis. He seemed very intense and was taking my trip more seriously than I was. Later, I would understand: Precht had personally recruited and convinced some of the diplomats who were now hostages to go to Iran against their own wishes. After about twenty minutes, I felt comfortable enough with the subject to leave. "Well," I said with a grin, "off I go on my wild-goose chase!"

"I hope not—it's time for a breakthrough."

The small jet taxied to the end of the runway and shot up into the sky like a bullet. I was on my way to Homestead, Florida.

I arrived at 3:00 P.M. The minute I got off the plane at Homestead, I was hustled into a car with the base commander. All the windows in the car were blackened, so that while I could see out, no one could look in. I was whisked away to a small brick building containing conference rooms, offices, and elaborate communications capabilities. I had told the Defense Department that I needed access to secure communications so I could stay in touch with the President and Vance if necessary.

A final UN vote on sanctions against Iran was scheduled for that afternoon. At our foreign policy breakfast the day before, Cy Vance had argued that sanctions would just complicate the chances of negotiating the release. I had argued strenuously for the sanctions. Politically, it was important for the President to be seen taking every possible action against Iran.

The Panamanians were late. While I waited for them, the base commander and several officers fell all over me, trying to make small talk. Finally, to make things easier for all of us, I said I had to use the telephone. I spent the next couple of hours calling various campaign workers, mostly in Iowa. Although the grain boycott had shaken our support among farmers, they seemed to be coming around in support of the President. Finally they arrived, led by my old friend Gabriel Lewis. Lewis had been Panama's Ambassador to the United States during the fight for the ratification of the Panama Canal treaties. Carter had called Lewis his "secret weapon" in persuading senators to support the treaties and his "favorite ambassador."

I embraced Gabriel Lewis. "I bring you greetings from your 'Papa,'" he said.

"You and Papa General have ruined a beautiful weekend for me," I chided.

"I believe you'll find this worthwhile," Gabriel said. He introduced the slim young man with him as Marcel Saliman, and a dignified older man as Panama's Ambassador to the UN. We were led to an oversized conference room and began our meeting.

Saliman had curly black hair and was very attractive. He was known to be sympathetic to revolutionary movements around the world. Torrijos had a stable of people around him who reflected all shades of political thought; Saliman was his "leftist" and Gabriel was his businessman.

Saliman did not speak English and Gabriel served as interpreter. Saliman took out a thick file of notes and documents. I saw immediately that this was probably going to be long and complicated, so I began making notes on my legal pad. Saliman began with the comment that two "Frenchmen," one of whom was an Argentinian political exile living in Paris, had come to Panama on behalf of the Iranian government. I thought, *Here we go. The Panamanians are trying to get involved in the hostage negotiations.*

"I have just returned from Tehran," Saliman continued, "where I met with Foreign Minister Ghotbzadeh."

I almost fell off my chair. "You met with Ghotbzadeh?"

Gabriel didn't even have to translate. Saliman just shook his head up and down, enjoying my surprise.

"Why?"

"Don't be too impatient, my young friend. Let Marcel tell you the entire story," Gabriel said.

Saliman recounted that on Christmas Day, the two men had arrived with extradition papers for the Shah. He quickly added that they had no real hope of extraditing him, but wanted to use the process as the means to peacefully resolve the crisis.

"Why did they want to make contact with you?" I asked.

Marcel smiled briefly, spoke quickly in Spanish, and Gabriel translated: "So they could make contact with you."

"With me?"

"Yes, with you."

"Me! Why?"

"Because they knew you are close to the President and you are not in the State Department. Also, they knew that we know you."

"But why do they want to avoid the State Department?"

"Because they believe that the State Department is controlled by Kissinger and Rockefeller," replied Saliman.

There was no need to try to get into that. "Please continue," I said.

Saliman's account of his meetings with Ghotbzadeh convinced me that the Iranians wanted to use the charade of the extradition process as the basis for releasing the hostages. Ghotbzadeh had explained to him that the students who seized the embassy were radicals who feared that the Revolution was straying off course. Within one week, they had seen Brzezinski meeting with Bazargan and Yazdi at a funeral in Algeria and the Shah returning to the United States. They believed there was great danger that Iran was drifting slowly back to its traditional position of being dominated by the United States. The "students" who had led the attack on the embassy believed that Bazargan and Yazdi were "pro-Western" and were not following "the line of the Imam."

The so-called students had consulted with Ayatollah Koeini, a militant follower of Khomeini's, and planned an attack on the embassy as a way of purifying the Revolution and separating the followers of government doctrine from the followers of Khomeini. They had not informed Khomeini of their plan to overrun the embassy, and had expected to occupy it for only several days before the government would step in and force them to release the hostages. They were surprised, Ghotbzadeh told Saliman, when they became national heroes overnight and when television crews and newspeople from all over the world converged on the compound begging for interviews and statements. They were even more surprised the next day when Khomeini publicly congratulated them for capturing the "den of spies." That was when they began to take their own rhetorical demands seriously. Khomeini's endorsement and the resignations of Yazdi and Bazargan were proof that they were a powerful political force to be reckoned with.

Saliman had been going on for over an hour, and I was becoming restless. "Where do we go from here?" I asked.

"The first thing you must do is postpone the UN vote on sanctions against Iran," Gabriel responded quickly, then turned and related to Marcel in Spanish what he had told me. Saliman nodded in agreement.

"I'm not sure I agree—and even if I did, I don't know that the President or Secretary Vance would pay attention to me. We've got to have some kind of promise first," I said.

Gabriel responded, "Don't you see, Hamilton—Marcel has opened up a channel for negotiation. If you impose sanctions, you will undermine those people in Iran who want to resolve the crisis quickly, and you'll be playing into the hands of the militants, who want a total break with the West."

"What you say, Gabriel, makes sense, but it would be difficult to explain publicly why we're not retaliating."

"You are going to have to take some chances, my young friend."

I went into the other room to call the President on the secure phone. I told him that I thought the Panamanians had opened a channel to the Iranian leadership and that postponing the imposition of sanctions might allow us to pursue this lead more effectively. I was surprised when he quickly accepted my recommendation and worried afterward that I was in over my head.

I told Gabriel and Marcel that the President had reluctantly agreed to postpone the sanctions, and we talked about how to proceed. I said that we needed direct negotiations, and we agreed that Marcel and Gabriel might make a quick trip to Iran.

"There can't be any misunderstanding," I warned. "General Torrijos gave me his word that the Shah would not be extradited. If the Shah gets scared and asks to come back to the States, we'd have to accept him."

"Don't worry," Saliman assured me. "I don't even think the Iranians want him back."

"I don't understand."

"There would be a tremendous fight—they wouldn't know whether to torture him, shoot him, or hang him."

After reiterating our desire for direct negotiations with Iran and thanking the Panamanians for their help, we boarded our planes and headed our separate ways.

I was excited as I thumbed through the long documents in French and Arabic stamped with official seals. *Could these Frenchmen be a way to contact the Iranians and free the hostages?* I called the Situation Room from the plane and told the duty officer that I would arrive at Andrews at about ten or eleven and asked if Assistant Secretary of State for the Near East Hal Saunders could meet me. I had seen him tirelessly hammering out the Camp David peace treaties. Iran was Hal's responsibility, and he was the natural person for me to report to late on a Saturday night.

I tried to disguise my own excitement as I reviewed with Saunders what I had learned from Saliman.

"You actually think they went to Iran?" he asked.

"I do. I have no reason to think otherwise."

"Why didn't the Panamanians check with us earlier?"

"Torrijos probably wanted proof that this thing was real before dragging us into it."

Hal was particularly interested in Saliman's discussion with Ghotbzadeh. I took out my notes and spent about ten minutes describing Ghotbzadeh's analysis of the takeover and how the deadlock might be broken.

I didn't want to sound too optimistic or naive in my hope that the Panamanians could help us. "I don't know if it's for real or not, Hal," I said.

"Maybe not—but it's too important not to pursue every angle. How do you plan to proceed?"

"I'll write all this up in a memo to the President, with copies to Mondale, Vance, and Brzezinski. The Panamanians are ready and willing to continue discussions in Iran or do whatever we suggest. The ball is in our court."

"Are the Panamanians considering extraditing the Shah?" he asked.

"No, but they're willing to go through the charade."

Hal said that he had to go home to his children. I stayed at the Situation Room until three in the morning waiting for the documents to be translated while I typed up my report on the meeting. I stamped "top secret" all over the envelope and left instructions with the duty officer to have it delivered to the President first thing in the morning.

January 13, 1980 (Sunday)

I expected President Carter to call me early, but he didn't. I hung around my apartment all morning, waiting for the call that didn't come until early in the afternoon.

"Ham, I've read your memo and talked with Cy. We'll get together tomorrow and talk about it."

I couldn't tell from the way he sounded if he took it seriously. "What do you think?"

"Well, I intend to pursue it. We can't afford not to."

When he hung up, I realized that perhaps I had overreacted. Nothing was likely to come from my trip.

January 14, 1980 (Monday)

Mondays were always the worst day of the week at the White House. By then two days of telephone calls and problems had piled up, and something always happened over the weekend.

I had to speak to the Time-Life executives in the middle of the day, and we had one of our regular weekly campaign meetings with the President in the afternoon. I had to talk to Mondale, Strauss, and Kraft and prepare an agenda for the campaign session. Also, I was to review the first group of television advertisements that Jerry Rafshoon had ready.

But I couldn't seem to put my heart into the campaign. All I could think about was the remote chance that my Panamanian friends might have the key to reaching the Iranians. Hal Saunders reported that the documents had been found to be authentic copies of an extradition request. Hal said he was anxious to pursue the "Panamanian connection" and had said the same thing to Secretary Vance.

"You think we've got something here, Hal?" I asked.

"I'm not saying that, but it's more promising than the other leads we've been following."

After our regular 10:00 A.M. meeting, I hung back to talk with the President.

"I want the Panamanians to help us contact the Iranians," he said. "But I don't want them to get carried away with this extradition thing."

"Torrijos wouldn't do that to us," I protested.

"I don't think he would either. But if the Shah got the notion he was going to be extradited and wanted to leave Panama, we would be in one hell of a fix. Cy's reviewed the papers, and, while he wants to pursue it, he's worried that the Panamanians might really extradite the Shah."

I was beginning to get the feeling that Carter was even less enthusiastic about the Panamanian connection than he had been yesterday. "Well, what's our next move?" I asked cautiously.

"You should simply let the Iranians know through the Panamanians that we are ready and willing to talk and want to find an honorable way out. The Panamanians will have done their part if they can just make contact for us. We need to negotiate directly—that's our goal."

I talked to Saunders, Ambassador Ambler-Moss, and Gabriel Lewis during the course of the day and told them all the same thing: we were ready to continue the discussions that Saliman had begun with Ghotbzadeh and wanted direct contact with Iran. Lewis and Moss said that they were meeting with Torrijos, who wanted to send Saliman back to Tehran in pursuit of direct contact between the U.S. and Iran. I asked them to stop off in Washington to be briefed. I trusted the Panamanians but wanted to be absolutely sure that we understood one another. It was too damn important to leave anything to chance.

January 16, 1980 (Wednesday)

Hal Saunders, Henry Precht, Stan Turner, Gary Sick, Charles Kirbo—the President's best friend and lawyer—and I met in the Situation Room with Gabriel Lewis and Rory Gonzales from 7:30 to about 10:00. Saliman was sick and didn't come. We outlined our position on the hostages and conveyed our strong desire to begin negotiations. I tried to subtly address Cy Vance's fear that the Panamanians might try to negotiate for us.

"How do you see Panama's role in this?" I asked.

"Omar's instructions were plain," Gabriel Lewis replied. "He said he hoped Panama could help open the door, but that the Americans would have to walk through it. Our job will be done when you are negotiating with the Iranians."

Everyone was satisfied with our discussion, and I arranged for an Air Force plane to fly them to New York to catch the Concorde to Paris, where they would meet the two French lawyers—and continue on to Iran. For the rest of the day, I anxiously awaited Gabriel's call, but I heard nothing until the middle of the next day.

January 17, 1980 (Thursday)

I was having lunch with Israeli Ambassador Ephraim Evron in the White House mess when the phone was brought to our table and the White House operator told me I had a call from Paris. I made excuses to Eppie and ran upstairs to take the call in the privacy of my office.

Gabriel's message was plain: he and Rory Gonzales had met with the lawyers and shared Saliman's evaluation that their intentions were honorable. "It makes no sense for us to go to Tehran now," he said. "What you should do is hop on a plane and come to Paris and meet these two men."

I resisted. "That wasn't the plan, Gabriel. You and Rory were going to go to Tehran, try to arrange for direct negotiations with the Iranians, and present our position."

Rory got on the phone. "Listen, Hamilton—you can sit on your ass in the White House and wait for something to happen, but it isn't going to. That's the problem with your country—you're not willing to take any chances. We can spend several days going to Iran, but our recommendation is still going to be the same: sit down and talk with these two guys. They understand what's going on in Iran, and they know the leaders. We've stumbled on a way to reach the Iranians. Don't play hard to get."

I was taken aback at Rory's straight talk, but it made sense.

"Give me a couple of hours. I'll have to check it out with the Boss."

I returned to my lunch with Ambassador Evron and tried to appear interested in the Middle East and how matters in Iran and Afghanistan would affect Israel.

Charles Kirbo was still around, and I told him about Gabriel's call. He said I should go. I called Vance and said I was going to talk to the President about it. I hesitated to get in over my head and suggested to Vance that if I did go, Hal Saunders should accompany me.

"That would be a good idea." I could almost hear the relief in Vance's voice.

Kirbo and I went to see the President at 3:45. I tried not to sound overanxious and mentioned the idea of taking Saunders along. I must have understated my case, because Kirbo, who usually just sits and listens, jumped into the conversation. "I think Ham ought to go on over there. We have nothing to lose, and I wouldn't be surprised to see it develop into something."

"I agree," Carter said. "And taking Hal will make Cy feel better. Go ahead."

"I doubt if anything will come of this," I added as Kirbo and I left the Oval Office. I didn't believe it but wanted to appear to be properly skeptical.

I reported my meeting with the President to Vance, who had Hal Saunders call me to make our plans. I then called Gabriel and suggested that we meet with the Frenchmen in London on "neutral ground." Hal arranged for us to meet at the residence of the number-two man at the American Embassy in London.

"The Panamanians have dragged me into this hostage thing," I told Eleanor. "It's absolutely essential that no one know about it."

"I figured as much."

"I'm going to London tomorrow. Hal will call you with the plans."

We spent some time rearranging my schedule in order to arouse the least suspicion. I would leave midday Friday, but would be sure to show my face around the White House in hopes that my absence would not be noticed.

January 18, 1980 (Friday)

Afghanistan dominated the discussion at the weekly foreign policy breakfast.

President Carter was stern. "There is a tendency on the frazzled edges of our government to drift away from the tough decisions we made. I am not going to abide that. We cannot wince now or seem unsure of ourselves. If we do, we'll get very little help from our allies."

Vance brought up our decision to withdraw from the Moscow Olympics, which the President would reveal Sunday during his appearance on "Meet the Press."

"It's the toughest question of all for me," Carter said. "I don't want the onus for the failure of the Olympics to fall exclusively on the United States. . . . It must be seen as a legitimate worldwide political reaction to what the Russians are doing in Afghanistan. After the grain embargo, the farmers raised hell." He smiled slyly. "But after I announce our Olympics boycott, we'll have to face the wrath of an even more powerful force—Howard Cosell, telling the sports fans that Jimmy Carter killed the Olympics."

He told the group that I would be going to Europe to meet with two French lawyers who had approached the Panamanians. No one said anything except Vance, who merely mentioned that Hal Saunders was going along and that the basic objective of our trip was not to negotiate but to make contact with the Iranian government. I felt that no one took it very seriously or expected anything to come of it.

Zbig flashed a smile at me. I wasn't sure if he was envying my secret mission or laughing about it.

I wrote a note to Lloyd Cutler asking him if there was any message I could carry to the British about the Olympics as a cover for the trip in case I was discovered. If the press found me in London, it would surely raise questions. What was the President's political adviser doing overseas in the midst of the campaign?

Lloyd wrote back that I could ask if the U.K. would back us if we tried to move the Olympic games away from Moscow.

Because the plane took off from Dulles around the middle of the day, I left the foreign policy breakfast, dropped by the senior staff meeting for a few minutes, and went to my office to look over paperwork and telephone calls and see to last-minute details.

"Here are your tickets and passport . . . Mr. Thompson." Eleanor was smiling slyly.

"What?"

"You are traveling incognito, courtesy of the State Department and Hal Saunders—excuse me . . . Mr. Sinclair," she said with a wink.

I assured Eleanor that I would check in with her regularly and set off on the forty-five-minute drive to Dulles Airport. The State Department had arranged with British Airways for us to board the Concorde inconspicuously. They waited until the plane was loaded and escorted us to it right before takeoff. We ducked in and took the two seats that had been saved for us near the front. A few minutes after takeoff, we were 60,000 feet above the Atlantic, moving at twice the speed of sound.

During a long meal we discussed the Panamanians and our strategy for dealing with the mysterious lawyers. We had only one interruption, when we both glanced up to see a well-dressed gentleman standing over us with his hand extended. "Good to see you!"

I gulped, sure that my cover was blown—but he was speaking to Hal. They exchanged brief pleasantries and Hal managed not to introduce me.

We had been in the air barely three hours when the captain announced that we had begun our descent into the London area. We were met by the deputy chief of mission, Edward Streator, and driven to his home.

I went to my room and called Gabriel and Rory at the Dorchester Hotel to tell them where we were. We agreed to start negotiations at 10:00 the next morning at the DCM's fashionable town house. I stayed awake most of the night, tossing and turning as I thought time and again about our encounter the next morning with the two who might help bring the hostages home.

January 19, 1980 (Saturday)

I was so nervous about meeting the intermediaries that I could hardly eat breakfast. The embassy interpreter arrived at the DCM's home and I swore him to secrecy. Then Gabriel Lewis and Rory Gonzales came in with a man they introduced as Hector Villalon. I shook his hand, then turned to Gabriel and Rory and kidded, "I thought I was through with you two after the Canal Treaties, but you seem to be involved in all of our problems."

"Once we get the hostages out, General Torrijos is sending us to Moscow to see Brezhnev," Gabriel shot back.

We laughed, moved into the drawing room, and sat down in a

semicircle around Villalon. After an awkward silence I said, "Mr. Villalon, we appreciate very much that you have come to London to meet us. We have a single objective: a peaceful, honorable, and quick resolution of the problem, and are here to understand the situation in Iran and to learn from you how this might be accomplished."

I paused while my comments were translated into French for Villalon, who neither spoke nor understood English. Throughout our conversation Hal scribbled notes in a little black book which fitted neatly in his hand.

I hadn't quite imagined what to expect the French lawyer to look like. He turned out to be a middle-aged, Latin-looking man, immaculately dressed in a light-brown suit and expensive leather shoes. He had a small black mustache and a prominent, hawklike nose and bushy eyebrows. His jet-black hair was combed straight back.

Although Hector Villalon was a native Argentinian and successful international businessman, he and Bourguet came to be known as the "French lawyers" because they both lived in Paris and worked inseparably during the negotiations.

"Mr. Jordan," the interpreter replied, feeding back Villalon's comments, "we thank you for traveling all the way from the United States to meet with us. First, I would like to apologize for the absence of my colleague, Monsieur Bourguet, who is arriving in London this morning from meetings in Iran with government officials there. He will join us as soon as he arrives."

I nodded. *Maybe Bourguet will be carrying a proposal that'll wrap this thing up in the next few days*, I thought hopefully.

"Mr. Jordan, you said you wanted to resolve the hostage matter peacefully. That is our objective as well. But you also said something even more important—that you want to understand Iran. Only by understanding the Revolution can we hope to reach a solution."

"We are anxious to learn, Mr. Villalon."

"I will try to be your teacher then," he said with a little smile.

He began with a lengthy explanation of the Ayatollah Khomeini, Khomeini's concept of the Islamic Republic, and his notion of ruling by broad consensus. He talked about the internal strug-

gle in Iran for the "soul" of the Revolution, and Khomeini's inclination not to get personally involved, but to stay in Qom, aloof
from political disputes. He told us that, despite Western reports
that the hostage seizure had been planned by the Islamic government, he could report authoritatively that both Khomeini and the
leaders of the government knew nothing in advance of the embassy takeover.

I slipped Hal a note. "Does this guy know what he is talking
about?"

"I think he does," he wrote back.

Villalon continued: "You see, a number of Western-educated
people around Khomeini believe that holding the hostages is
hurting Iran economically and damaging Iran's image with other
nations. On the other hand, most of the mullahs around Khomeini do not care about the opinion of other nations. They view
the seizure as a justifiable reaction to years of rule by the Shah
and manipulation by the United States. These two groups are
struggling for power. Elections are scheduled for the end of this
month, and the hostage matter has become an important political
issue in that campaign. Both groups are trying to gain electoral
advantage without going beyond the Imam's line."

Just one more irony, I thought. *Elections in both countries and
the hostages are issues in both campaigns. At least Khomeini
doesn't have anybody running against him.* "What is 'the Imam's
line'?" I asked

Villalon smiled. "The Imam's line is the thinking and logic of
the Ayatollah Khomeini. In the West, we would describe it as
trying to anticipate the wishes of one's superior. In every action
and decision, politicians on both sides will claim that their approach to the problem is in keeping with the Imam's line or that
they are doing something the way the Imam would do it."

I was taking copious notes on my legal pad. What I was learning was too important to be forgotten. I had to convey these no-
tions to the President.

We went on for two hours. Finally Villalon glanced at his watch
and said that he had to leave to meet Bourguet at the airport.
This gave us a welcome break, an opportunity to assess everything he had told us.

"So, Hamilton—was it worth the trip over to hear this?" Gabriel asked.

"You know it was!" I replied. "What do you think, Hal?"

"Everything he told us squares with what I've heard. He obviously knows the players and their relationships. Whether his analysis is correct, who can tell? But he is for real."

Villalon soon returned with a stick figure of a man with a thick, dark beard, a mass of shoulder-length hair, and heavy black-rimmed glasses. After a couple of hours with the urbane Villalon, I had expected his French companion to be equally dapper and polished. "This," Villalon said, "is Monsieur Bourguet."

Through the interpreter, Bourguet told me that he had just returned from Tehran, where the problems were "very difficult." He expanded on Villalon's summation of the political climate, describing in detail both the Imam's ultimate power and his deference to any consensus of the Revolutionary Council. Villalon interrupted occasionally, and the two men seemed comfortable in their disagreements and respectful of each other's point of view. Essentially, they said the same thing. They were sympathetic to the Iranian cause but also flatly opposed to the holding of hostages.

"You have to understand, Mr. Jordan," Bourguet said, "the Iranians feel there is reason for this action. They are the sons and brothers of people who have been tortured by Savak or murdered by the Shah. The Shah is a very evil man. You must understand the grievances of the Iranians."

I began to lose patience. "What can we do to resolve the crisis?"

He did not wait for the interpreter, but spoke slowly in English. "You must return the Shah to Iran!"

I was surprised by his plainly stated demand. "It is absolutely impossible!"

"Why can he not be returned and placed on trial? Is America not a country of law? This evil man must return and face his crimes!"

I didn't respond for a minute. "I appreciate very much your willingness to meet with us, but there is little sense in our debating whether the Shah is a good or evil man. Frankly, I don't know the answer to that myself. What I can tell you, Mr. Bourguet, is that the President will never allow the Shah to be extradited. We will permit Iran's grievance against the Shah and our country to be taken to the United Nations after our people are freed."

After a while, Bourguet began to let his guard down. He ceased posturing and making points and seemed to be searching, just as we were, for some way out of the box we were in. He acknowledged our different ideas and obligations but recognized that a continuing dialogue was the only way to resolve the mounting conflict between Iran and the United States. I urged them to continue their role as "middle men" and to prove their credentials.

"As well-intentioned as you are," I said, "we have no proof that you speak for Iran."

When the meeting broke up, Bourguet asked if he could use the phone. I hardly paid attention as he picked it up, dialed, and started speaking—in French, of course. I was startled when the translator alerted me that he was talking to Iranian Foreign Minister Sadegh Ghotbzadeh. Bourguet explained afterward that he was trying to persuade Ghotbzadeh to speak to me on the phone, but Ghotbzadeh had refused, saying that the Ayatollah Khomeini had "forbidden" anyone to talk to the Americans.

I didn't know if his intention was to impress me. But he certainly did.

January 20, 1980 (Sunday)

It was now necessary for me to go through the little charade that would insure my cover story for being in London, so the DCM and I drove to the home of an official in the British Foreign Office. I delivered a rambling, poorly prepared speech on the Olympics, ended the meeting, thanked the gentleman and his wife for their time, and dashed for the plane. The visit took twenty minutes at the most, and the puzzled British official must have wondered what it was all about. I probably confirmed his notion that Jimmy Carter's foreign policy was being handled by amateurs.

I felt relaxed and optimistic on the Concorde. "I'd call our trip a success," I said to Hal.

He was more cautious. "We did open up contacts which could lead to something. Did you see the way Bourguet just picked up the phone, dialed Tehran, and had Ghotbzadeh on the line in less than a minute? That's when I was sure it was all real. However, we never really addressed what any of us could do about the basic problem."

"I'm going home with one strong feeling: we can stick to our position of not agreeing to do anything until the hostages are released, but they'll never be released unless we take some chances."

"True," said Hal, "but this is an election year. Can the President afford to take chances? Whatever we do will be a gamble."

"If we don't get those people out quickly and safely, I don't see how he can be re-elected."

Saunders had sent Carter and Vance a cable from London summarizing our meeting. When I arrived in Washington, I phoned the President at Camp David. It was clear to me that he had begun to take the "Panama connection" seriously. I told him that I would give him a written report the next day.

January 21, 1980 (Monday)

I slept late the next morning, knowing that Carter wouldn't be back from Camp David until that afternoon. I had left word with the operator that I didn't want any calls unless they were urgent, and was startled by the phone when it rang. It was Vice President Mondale, calling about the Iowa caucuses tonight. I told him that Tim Kraft, who had run our first Iowa campaign, was the best source. Tim was confident that we would win again and "win big." I passed that assessment on to a nervous Mondale, who reflected the mood at the White House.

But my worries about Iran overshadowed political concerns. When I got to the office, I checked first with Hal Saunders and continued talking to him and Henry Precht throughout the day. Precht had told me about a professor at the University of Pittsburgh who was an expert on Iran. I asked him to put me in touch with the man so I could verify what I had heard in London.

The basic question raised by Hal after our trip was, Where do we go from here? We'd had a nice meeting with the two lawyers, who seemed so genuine and obviously had contacts with the Iranian leadership—but how to translate that into a plan to free the hostages?

The next step, as Hal pointed out, was to translate our "French connection" and fresh knowledge into a plan of action. I told Hal that I couldn't work on it today, as everyone at the White House was preoccupied with the Iowa caucuses, but I would put my thoughts in writing and was going to argue for changing our posture, dropping our insistence that the hostages had to be freed before we would agree to do anything. We would have to take some risks. I asked Hal how Vance would respond, and he said the Secretary would probably support this position as long as the basic principles of the Administration were not violated.

People were in and out of my office all afternoon, and the calls were pouring in. We started a pool on the results of the Iowa caucuses. I bet that we would beat Kennedy 55 to 30. Everyone thought I was too optimistic.

I went to the home of Cynthia and Tim Smith to watch the returns. Tim was a close friend and the legal counsel for the reelection campaign. When I got there about 7:30, the major networks were already predicting a big Carter victory in Iowa. It was over before it started, but it didn't feel at all like the 1976 victories.

"Kennedy will get out," I predicted confidently. Twenty people stood at the television set cheering when Jody appeared on the screen, and hissed when Kennedy's representatives came on.

Minutes after the victory was projected, Carter called me. We congratulated each other, but I said, "Frankly, neither one of us had much to do with it. The credit goes to those Iowa people who stuck with us."

"I know," he said. "Who should I call and thank in Iowa?" I gave him a list of ten or twelve people.

"It's a great night, isn't it?" I said.

"Ham, it would be a great night if the hostages were out and the Soviets weren't in Afghanistan."

"I know what you mean, Mr. President."

I had a couple of beers and went back to my apartment, glad that the Iowa caucuses were behind us, thinking again about Villalon, Bourguet, and the hostages.

January 22, 1980 (Tuesday)

The mood at the 8:30 staff meeting was upbeat. We had defeated Kennedy in Iowa by a two-to-one margin. Kennedy had made a statement that he was in the race to stay, but I tended to discount it. I was sure that he and his people were shocked by their lopsided defeat and hadn't had time to assess his posture before having to face the television cameras and their supporters in that state. I repeated my prediction that Kennedy would get out of the race, but told everyone that we had to expect the worst and get to work on the next contest, Maine, which was in his backyard and only nineteen days away.

I couldn't focus on it, though. My thoughts kept returning to Tehran. The Panamanians had "opened the door," as Gabriel had put it, but how to walk through it? I was particularly uncomfortable that I had so little knowledge of Iran. I called Dr. Richard Cottam, the Iranian specialist at the University of Pittsburgh who had been recommended to me, and asked if I could meet with him. He agreed to donate whatever time I needed. Then I called Stan Turner and asked for any information the CIA could assemble on Hector Villalon and Christian Bourguet. I had to be sure about these fellows and not proceed simply on my instincts.

I canceled all my appointments, locked the door to my office, and sat down at my typewriter. I wrote to President Carter that I had been persuaded by the lawyers that we would have to modify our position before we had any hope of getting the hostages out. I said I thought there was a way to minimize the risk to our country's honor and his image while at the same time creating the mood in Iran that would lead to the release of our people. We would have to negotiate in advance reciprocal steps, and a precise scenario that would be agreed to by both countries.

I took the five-page memo into the Oval Office, handed it to the President, and in spite of his extremely heavy schedule, he read and returned it within the hour. In the corner he had written: "Good ideas. Discuss with Fritz, Cy, and Zbig."

I then delivered the memo to Mondale's office and sat there while he read it. "I agree," he said. "We've got to try something different. What we've been doing hasn't worked."

I was afraid that the whole scheme would sound far-fetched and amateurish to Zbig, so I was a little relieved to find him busy with West German Foreign Minister Hans-Dietrich Genscher and the President of the European Community, Roy Jenkins, discussing sanctions against the Soviet Union and Iran. His secretary, Trudy, assured me that he would read my memo at his first opportunity.

I was reviewing the draft of the President's State of the Union address, paying particular emphasis to what he said about Iran, when Zbig popped in. He wasn't opposed to the ideas I had expressed in my memo, but said, "I'm a bit skeptical, Ham, about these Frenchmen. I don't think the Iranian government will challenge the militants, and there is such chaos in Iran that ultimately only Khomeini has the power to order the release. Can these Frenchmen get to Khomeini?"

I told him that I didn't know. Changing the subject to the election, Zbig asked me what I thought Kennedy was going to do. I said again that he would probably drop out. Zbig suggested some things the President might do that would smooth his path in that direction.

"We ought to swap jobs, Dr. Strangelove," I replied. "You should be running the campaign and I should be conducting foreign policy."

"Could I use nuclear weapons in the Presidential campaign?" he asked, poking fun at his image as a reckless warmonger.

Kennedy's defeat in Iowa was the big story on the evening news, but there was no indication he was quitting. I called Bob Strauss. "It looks to me like he needs a nudge," I said, suggesting that we begin an active effort to have party leaders and members of Congress call for Kennedy's withdrawal.

I went home feeling pretty good. Not only had the press played up Kennedy's defeat, but the Boss had responded positively to my ideas on Iran and there weren't even any objections from his foreign policy team. Bourguet and Villalon were in Tehran by now. What were the Iranians saying to the two lawyers?

January 23, 1980 (Wednesday)

Just as I was getting up, the duty officer at the Operations Center of the State Department called. "Deputy Secretary Christopher wanted you to have this information," he said. "According to a news story from Panama, the former Shah of Iran is under arrest in Panama and awaiting extradition procedures."

Oh no, I thought. *The Panamanians are playing games with Iran.*

I rushed to the office. Warren Christopher had called twice. He told me that the story had upset Vance, who didn't really trust Torrijos. "Ham, we will have to respond to the story."

"The Panamanians think they are taking risks that we can't afford to take," I said. "Torrijos would never really consider extraditing the Shah, but he's probably playing this game in hopes of helping us get the hostages out. They're going to screw everything up without even trying. This is going to scare the hell out of the Shah, and if he decides to leave Panama and come back to the States, we'll be in a hell of a mess!"

"And it puts the President in a terrible posture," Christopher added, "looking as if we've handed the Shah over to someone who is going to send him back to Iran."

I promised Chris that I would phone Gabriel, President Royo, and even Torrijos, if necessary, and get back to him.

I immediately called Gabriel in Panama to find out what was going on.

He spoke calmly in his raspy voice. "Take it easy, my young friend—the Shah has not been arrested. He is still sitting at my house on Contadora Island. Nothing has changed. Under Panamanian law, when a request for extradition is made, the government is obliged to detain that person and proceed with a hearing. Since the Shah is being protected by Panamanian guards, we can easily claim that he has been 'detained.'"

"Gabriel, we are not talking about just anybody—this is the Shah of Iran!"

"The *former* Shah of Iran," Gabriel corrected me with a chuckle.

"Well, I'm not sure what's going on, but it is going to mess up our plans. If the Shah believes he's going to be extradited and asks to return to the States, we couldn't refuse him," I said, trying not to lose my temper. "Gabriel, you must tell the General and President Royo that they are playing with fire!"

"You Americans are funny people," Gabriel came back. "You are always pushing us to democratize and criticizing us for violations of human rights, and now you are asking us to disregard our own laws. When you asked us to accept the Shah, we said that we would and promised not to extradite him, but we did not say that we would ignore our own legal processes. We have a legal obligation to proceed with the extradition process, even though nothing will come of it."

"I'm only asking that you understand the position we are in with the Shah. If the public perceives that the U.S. government has somehow or other acquiesced to his being extradited to Iran—"

Gabriel cut me off with assurances that he would check with Torrijos and Royo and call me back.

In the meantime, Ambler Moss called. He shared my concerns and worried about what to tell the Shah, but agreed with Gabriel that we couldn't ask the Panamanians to publicly ignore their own law. He planned to meet with Royo and work toward getting the Panamanians to clarify the news stories that the deposed monarch would be extradited and also figure out some way to calm him down. We agreed to talk later.

I phoned Warren Christopher, told him that Gabriel and Ambler were working on the problem, and asked him to reassure Vance that the Panamanians weren't even considering extradition.

The President told me to arrange a meeting with Mondale, Vance, and Brzezinski to discuss my memo on Iran. We gathered in the Oval Office. "I assume that you have all had a chance to read Ham's memo," President Carter began. Everyone nodded and he continued. "For over two months we have stood firm and not agreed to any of Iran's demands until the hostages were released, and nothing has happened. We have tried unsuccessfully since November to reach Khomeini through every possible channel, and all of a sudden these two characters appear out of nowhere who can pick up the phone and talk directly with Ghotbzadeh. Ham has met them and is more inclined to trust them than I am, but at this point I don't see that we have any alternative to proceeding along the lines suggested in Ham's memo."

"Mr. President, I agree," Vance said simply.

Carter turned to Mondale, who said, "Mr. President, I don't see where we have any choice but to take some chances. We need to minimize our risks and not give anything away."

Zbig echoed the Vice President's sentiments and offered no objection to my memo or the President's decision.

Carter admonished me to stay close to Hal Saunders and the State Department in all that I did, and the meeting was over. We had been in the Oval Office less than ten minutes.

I wandered back to my office to reflect on what had just happened.

I had just argued for and won a significant change in the government's policy on the hostages. My presentation had been largely based on my faith in two people I had met only once in London. And yet, in just a few minutes, the President and the Secretary of State had gone along with my recommendation. *My God*, I thought. *Suppose this thing is wrong or doesn't work or compromises the President in some way?* I became more and more anxious. I was operating out of my league. Maybe I had pushed it too far, too fast.

I glanced at the President's daily schedule, which was taped on my desk. He still had a few minutes before his next appointment.

After thirteen years of working for a man whose time is vital and who rations it carefully, I had learned to read Jimmy Carter's moods. When he had his glasses on and was doing paperwork, and didn't look up when you entered, it was a signal that he was preoccupied and a bad time to try to get his full attention for your problem or need. When you stuck your head into the door and he looked up, it meant that he was prepared to deal with you and whatever problem you might be bringing him.

I opened the large white wooden door to the Oval Office. He looked up, smiled, and said, "Come on in, Ham!"

I could see that he was working on his State of the Union speech. "Can I have a couple of minutes with you?"

"Of course," he said, taking off his glasses and coming around to sit in one of the chairs arranged in the semicircle in front of his desk.

"Mr. President," I said, "I've been thinking about this Iranian thing. I hope we're doing the right thing. Cy seemed a bit reluctant, and maybe I pushed too hard. I'm betting a lot on these guys' being able to help—"

The President interrupted me. "Ham, don't worry. What choice do we have? Those bastards have held our people for two months now," he said sharply. "Nothing we have tried diplomatically has worked. The UN can't do anything, our allies have tried and struck out, everything imaginable has been attempted. We've got to take some risks. Don't worry. You just pursue this thing aggressively and we'll see where it leads. Nothing is more important!"

"Yes, sir."

I stood to leave and he went around his desk and slumped into his chair. "But, Ham . . ." he said plaintively.

"Yes?"

"Don't completely forget about the campaign," he said with a wistful smile.

However, at times I almost did forget, as I found myself increasingly immersed in the business of the hostages. I began to hear gossip around the White House that I wasn't paying enough attention to getting Carter re-elected. Campaign workers were complaining that I was late for meetings or even absent and was inattentive to their requests and problems.

 somehow the hostages and the election were woven together in my mind. When I wasn't thinking about Kennedy, I was thinking about Khomeini, and when I wasn't thinking about Khomeini, I was thinking about Kennedy.

I made plans to go to Pittsburgh late in the day and see Professor Cottam. The Defense Department assigned me a small military jet.

Hal Saunders was next. I called to tell him that I had the go-ahead on my memo from the President and the foreign policy group. Hal was testifying on the Hill but said he could be through in time for lunch and would bring Henry Precht.

We had sandwiches at the oval mahogany table in my office. I listened carefully to Hal's analysis: we had to proceed along reciprocal steps that were agreed to in advance and that tested the intentions of both governments. Hal listed the questions and the problems: Were Bourguet and Villalon empowered to negotiate on behalf of the leadership in Iran? If so, could they represent Iran's point of view while also recognizing U.S. interests? If we did negotiate something with them, could they sell it to the Iranian leadership and could that leadership implement an agreement? Iranians were great hagglers, but would they be able to negotiate in a Western sense?

Hal talked about the complexity of the frozen assets, the exchange of hostages for money, the demands for apologies from the United States, and the Shah's extradition. In his cool, level-headed manner he warned, "Ham, I don't want to appear pessimistic, but we should recognize the problems on the front end of negotiating this thing."

"Maybe we should focus all our efforts on contacting the Iranians directly rather than negotiating through a third party," I suggested.

"I'm not sure we have that choice. Who knows? Direct negotiation might be more difficult than dealing with Bourguet and Villalon. But I don't think the direct approach is in the cards right now."

We kept talking, trying to examine every possibility and to be aware of the many pitfalls. Bourguet and Villalon came up time after time. However we wanted to proceed, they were the key.

"Hell, let's get back together with them," I said finally. I was eager to get moving, feeling the pressures more acutely than either Saunders or Precht. They were worried about the hostages—I was worried about the hostages and the campaign. We agreed to contact Bourguet and Villalon through the Panamanians and try to persuade them to come to the States immediately. I thought the weekend would be best, as there would be fewer distractions, and my absence from White House and campaign meetings would be less obvious.

I left for Pittsburgh to meet Dr. Cottam. I didn't tell the President or Saunders and Precht that I was going: it was, after all, a not-so-subtle indication that I wanted to get a different perspective on Iran than the State Department and the CIA had been giving me.

The National Guard provided me with a room at the airport, and it was there I met Professor Cottam, one of the few persons in America who understood Khomeini's Iran. Ghotbzadeh had been his student, Yazdi was a friend, and he had interviewed Khomeini while he was in France.

"Funny thing," Cottam said. "I spent a lot of time trying to offer Washington my advice on Iran, but no one listened. Now I have the President's top man coming to me asking for my opinion. President Carter inherited a flawed policy and continued it," he observed unabashedly. "You may not think you continued it, but you did."

Everything he told me about Khomeini—his deep religious faith, his total disdain for the West, and how he goes into a trance to make a decision—was compatible with what I heard from Saliman, Bourguet, and Villalon. The only way out was to let Khomeini believe he had humiliated the United States, Cottam reasoned.

"That's impossible," I said.

"I know."

All I understood about Iran after my meeting with Cottam was that we didn't understand that country and its people. How in the world do you negotiate under those circumstances?

I made it back to the White House in time to hear the State of the Union Address. "If the American hostages are harmed," Carter said, "a severe price will be paid." And the Soviets "must pay a concrete price for aggression."

Congress received the speech enthusiastically. I suspected his audience was responding to the President's tough rhetoric—and perhaps to the fact that we had cleaned Kennedy's clock in Iowa two nights ago. Politicians respect a lot of things, but nothing so much as success.

January 24, 1980 (Thursday)

The morning news reported that Khomeini had been taken to a cardiac unit in a Tehran hospital. I found myself worried about the health of that evil old man. If he died, there would be a struggle for power which would complicate the task of freeing our people. At least, with Khomeini alive, we knew whom we had to deal with.

Hal called to report that Bourguet and Villalon would catch the Concorde and arrive midday on the 25th. I was elated and considered it a good sign that we had arranged a meeting so easily.

The Prime Minister of Italy was in town for a state visit. The top item on the President's agenda was to encourage the Italians to support us on the embargo against Iran and also on the boycott of the Moscow Olympics. I didn't want to bother Carter with the details of our work, and simply left a note in his box that Bourguet and Villalon were coming. He scribbled "good" on the note.

The situation in Panama was settling down a bit. President Royo made the promised statement explaining that the Shah was in the "care" of the Panamanian government, not "under detention," and that, although Panama had no extradition treaty with Iran, his government would process Iran's request. However, Royo linked serious consideration of the extradition request to the release of the hostages. Like most foreign policy agreements, his statement was not exactly what we wanted, but it helped a lot. I felt better after I read a cable from Ambler saying that Royo would visit the Shah and reassure him that the Panamanians had no intention of extraditing him.

January 25, 1980 (Friday)

There was more political good news. *The Washington Post* carried the headline, FUND DEPLETED, KENNEDY JUGGLES CAMPAIGN PLANS. Kennedy had canceled his appearances for the weekend and promised a "major policy address." It looked as though my prediction was coming true: he was dropping out.

When the subject of the hostages came up at our foreign policy breakfast, I was surprised when Vance turned to me for a report. I mentioned that Bourguet and Villalon were coming in the afternoon and that we would meet with the objective of either establishing direct contact with the Iranians or negotiating with them along the new lines that the President had approved. To reassure the group, I emphasized Hal Saunders's involvement.

I interpreted Vance's gesture as a vote of confidence. If he took my actions seriously, everyone else would too. Throughout our discussion of Iran and our negotiating posture, I kept waiting for Vance or Zbig or even the President to ask to meet the Frenchmen or sit in on some portion of our discussion, but the request never came.

I left the meeting knowing that, for better or worse, the secret negotiations were my baby. I was excited and scared.

The CIA report on Villalon and Bourguet was waiting for me in my office. The information on Bourguet was scant and squared with my impressions: he was described as a political activist, a left-wing French lawyer who represented the new Iranian government in a number of lawsuits. The report on Villalon was longer and disturbing: he was called an international wheeler-dealer, and the sources from Buenos Aires and Paris painted the picture of a man who was at least an opportunist and possibly even a scoundrel. There was a news report from Paris that Villalon had been jailed for kidnapping a Fiat executive. *Just who in the hell are we dealing with?* I thought. I considered for a minute whether or not to show the report to the President or Cy or even to Hal. *No*, I decided. *We can't pick our intermediaries at a time like this. I'd better keep this to myself. It would certainly cool the President and Vance on our negotiations.*

The only person I shared the report with was Eleanor. She was shocked. Then, laughing, she said, "Well, you're probably the first person to entertain a kidnapper in the White House!"

"I picked a fine pair to deal with," I groaned. "Bourguet *looks* awful and Villalon *sounds* awful. My main goal is going to be to keep Vance and the President from seeing Bourguet or reading this report about Villalon."

The two lawyers were met by State Department officials and taken to the Hay-Adams Hotel, where they checked in and rested before our working lunch at 12:30 in my office.

Hal had asked Stephanie van Reigersberg, a State Department translator, to be at our meeting. Stephanie was fluent in both French and Spanish and frequently interpreted for the President when he met with other heads of state. I had first worked with her during the Panama Canal Treaties and knew that she was capable and tough. I would never forget the day I saw her stand down Zbig. President Carter was on the phone in the Oval Office with Torrijos, with Zbig on an extension, during the critical stage of the treaty negotiations. Stephanie held a phone in one hand, listening and translating nonstop, and with the other hand she was writing furiously. When the conversation ended, Zbig ordered a transcript of the conversation immediately. Stephanie replied, "Don't you want me to sweep and clean up before I leave, Dr. Brzezinski?"

Stephanie was one of the best in the business. She had the ability to step quickly from language to language and from culture to culture as well. She always seemed to enjoy her work and the challenge of expressing not only literal meanings but also the many subtle but important nuances of oral exchanges. We said hello warmly and I briefed her on what we hoped to accomplish with Bourguet and Villalon. I knew I didn't need to remind her of the great sensitivity of our work. She was accustomed to dealing with matters of national security and could be trusted completely.

When our guests arrived, we greeted one another formally. I could tell that for the moment they were more interested in the White House than in talking to me. As they glanced around my spacious corner office, I gave them a bit of the history of the place. I pointed out the window to the old Executive Office Building and told them that when young Franklin Roosevelt was Assistant Secretary of the Navy, both the State and War Departments were housed in that building, which now contains the Budget Office. I also told them a little about my own office, listing some of its former occupants and showing them gimmicks, such as the box over my desk that tracked the President's movements, which H. R. Haldeman had installed. I joked that I hoped my fate would be better than his.

Villalon asked what I meant, and I told him that Haldeman had been sent to prison. The minute I said it I thought about Villalon, the alleged kidnapper, right there in my office. My joke about jail was particularly inappropriate. I quickly tried to cover my embarrassment by promising to take them on a grand tour of the White House after our discussion. They seemed pleased at that prospect, and we settled in to work.

Bourguet opened the large, tattered leather bag that he used for a briefcase, took out a cassette tape, and with a big smile handed it to me. "Hector and I brought you a present from Iran."

"Thank you," I said. "But what is it?" There was Arabic writing on the case.

"It's a tape of a meeting of the Revolutionary Council," Bourguet explained.

I couldn't hide my surprise. "You're kidding."

"No. And it was a rather special meeting," added Villalon, "the meeting in which Secretary General Waldheim addressed the Council."

That's it, I thought. *It's the proof I need to convince everyone—myself included—that Bourguet and Villalon are authentic and are trusted by the Iranian officials. There's no other way they could have gotten such a tape.*

"In London," Bourguet said, "you asked us to produce our credentials. That is why we brought this tape."

"This will help a lot," I said calmly. An understatement—I was overjoyed. I carefully locked the cassette in my file cabinet.

"But there is another reason," he continued. "This tape should show you and the President that Waldheim's trip to Tehran was not a success. He failed to convey the American position to the Revolutionary Council. A great misunderstanding still exists."

That didn't worry me. I was more concerned with the future than the past, and at least the tape gave me hard evidence of their legitimacy. "Well, I'll listen to it carefully and see that the President does as well."

Taking turns speaking, delayed further by the translation into English, the two men gave a very detailed report on their most recent trip to Tehran. Bourguet would be describing a meeting or discussion when Villalon would interrupt to elaborate or make a special point, usually stressing that it was *"très important."*

In the middle of our meeting, Eleanor walked in with a copy of a cable from the Situation Room: initial returns from Iran showed that the former Foreign Minister and French-trained economist Bani-Sadr had taken a strong lead in the election for Iran's first president. I told Bourguet and Villalon the news and they were visibly disappointed.

"Habibi is the best person for President," Bourguet said, "and Ghotbzadeh would have been good."

"This is bad, then, for the hostage situation?" I asked anxiously.

"Not necessarily," Bourguet explained. "Bani-Sadr has called publicly for the release of the hostages because it is hurting the Revolution. The bad thing is that he may not be strong enough and lacks the political skills and experience to govern effectively."

"Bani-Sadr and Ghotbzadeh are competitors," added Villalon. "If Bani-Sadr wins, it will be important for him to keep Ghotbzadeh on as his Foreign Minister."

"But Sadegh Ghotbzadeh will be terribly disappointed in defeat," continued Bourguet. "Sadegh is a proud man, and when both men were political exiles in Paris, Bani-Sadr was his subordinate—not even a very important subordinate. When we get back to Tehran, we'll have to spend a lot of time bolstering Sadegh's spirits."

Putting aside the election results for the time being, they told me that our frank discussion in London and our willingness to listen had made it easier to explain the U.S. position to Iran. Villalon said, "When we arrived in Tehran we had a four-hour meeting with the Foreign Minister before he spoke to the Revolutionary Council."

I listened to him speak and my heartbeat quickened as I heard Stephanie's translation. *It's happening*, I thought. *It's real—we are beginning a dialogue with the Iranians . . .*

Ghotbzadeh had returned from a lengthy meeting of the Revolutionary Council to report: First, the Foreign Minister was to assume responsibility for the negotiations. Villalon explained that while this might seem like a vote of confidence in Ghotbzadeh, it also provided a way for his enemies on the Council to make him the scapegoat. If the negotiations failed, they would make it Ghotbzadeh's failure. And if negotiations succeeded, his enemies would charge he had struck a bad deal for Iran. Second, that the Foreign Minister was to personally report all major developments to the Ayatollah Khomeini and keep him informed. Third, since the campaign for President of Iran was under way, the Foreign Minister was instructed to keep all of the other presidential candidates informed about the negotiations.

Hearing that Ghotbzadeh had been "instructed" by the Council to do these things made me feel better and lessened my apprehension that he was a free agent, operating independently of the Council and Khomeini.

Bourguet and Villalon then launched into a detailed description of the personalities in the Council and the power struggles that were going on. I interrupted to order lunch, which was served while their analysis continued. Stephanie never had a chance to eat. A couple of times Hal Saunders and I exchanged impatient glances, but I remembered the high premium they had placed on our "listening and learning" about the Iranian Revolution. I bided my time, feeling that in the long run it was worth hearing them out—and a better way to gain a little more of their confidence.

After more than an hour, Hal could stand it no longer. "Understanding this is very helpful and important for us—but where do we go from here? What's the next step?"

They moved quickly to the heart of their proposal. "Based on our discussions with the Minister," Bourguet explained, "we envision that the Iranians will call upon the United Nations to form a commission to investigate Iran's grievances. The United States should oppose the formation of that commission since it is important that it look as though it has been formed over the opposition of the United States and that Iran has won a political victory over the United States in the United Nations."

"But that's not credible," I argued. "It would be easy to block the creation of such a commission in the United Nations if we really opposed it."

With a smile, Bourguet said, "Let me finish explaining the idea, then you and Mr. Saunders can destroy it!"

His joke helped everyone to relax.

"This commission would go to Iran to inquire into Iranian grievances and the condition of the American hostages. After a week, the commission will issue a report to the UN and to the Ayatollah Khomeini, stating that the hostages are being held under conditions that are not acceptable by Islamic standards. The Ayatollah, in an act of Islamic forgiveness, will order the hostages released on an important religious holiday. Then the commission will return to New York and issue a public report on Iran's grievances."

Bourguet made it sound very straightforward and simple.

"What about the frozen assets and our other bilateral problems?" Hal asked.

"The chairman of the commission would negotiate the other existing differences. Obviously, it would be better to try to set up a process for addressing the other problems than to try to solve them before the hostages could be released."

"I agree," said Hal. "But the frozen assets are very difficult and complex!"

"I know," Bourguet replied. "I am Iran's lawyer."

I was really feeling encouraged. The proposal that Bourguet and Villalon had brought with them was certainly a start. More important, it was an indication that the Iranians wanted to negotiate. There was none of the rhetorical nonsense about returning the Shah or having Carter apologize for past U.S. policies. I wanted these men to know that our reaction was basically positive, so I said, "It's a constructive proposal and a good place to start."

"I agree," added Hal.

"How do we proceed?" I asked.

Since we had worked for four solid hours and they were still on Paris time, we decided to break and start out fresh the next day.

I took my guests on a tour of the West Wing. I showed them the offices where Mondale and Brzezinski worked, and, since the Carters had left for Camp David in the middle of the afternoon, I was able to walk them into the Oval Office. They chatted in rapid, excited French.

I whispered to Stephanie, "What are they saying?"

"Bourguet asked Villalon if he ever expected to be standing in the Oval Office. Villalon said, 'Never in my life!' Villalon is commenting about the art and furnishings and Bourguet mentioned how much smaller the Oval Office is than he had imagined."

I pointed out John Kennedy's desk, Harry Truman's THE BUCK STOPS HERE sign, and gifts from foreign governments. I gave them a glimpse of the President's private study and escorted them through the building, to the Cabinet Room and the Roosevelt Room, and, after first checking to be sure that the press corps had left when the President did, I stopped by Jody's office and introduced them to him. Then I walked them out to their car.

In London, the two men had seemed like our adversaries, but after this second session, they were more like comrades, working with us toward a common goal. I felt warmly toward both of them.

I raced back to my office, locked the door, took out the cassette, and, handling it delicately as if it were a rare jewel, placed it in the tape player. I heard voices speaking a foreign language, a man interpreting in broken English, and then the recognizable voice of Kurt Waldheim. I could just imagine the scene—the tall, slim international diplomat, standing before a group of turbaned Iranians trying to explain who he was, what the United Nations was, and why he was in Tehran.

I listened to the cassette for about an hour, and, not trusting anyone else to deal with so sensitive a matter, I asked Eleanor to transcribe the English parts for me.

"I'm not sure why," I told her, "but I trust those two guys."

"But what about Villalon's reputation?"

"What about *my* reputation? I don't care, if he helps us get the hostages out!"

(My intuition was right. I found out later that Villalon had been framed, and he was exonerated.)

January 26, 1980 (Saturday)

Hal Saunders, Henry Precht, and Stephanie came to my office an hour before the two intermediaries were due, and we went over the job ahead. Hal said we should push hard to get our ideas on paper.

I told them I had listened to the tape and that it was indeed a recording of Waldheim's meeting with the Revolutionary Council. I told Hal that I had a transcript of it for him to take to Vance.

"Cy said he didn't want a transcript."

"Why?"

"He doesn't think it's fair to Waldheim to pass around his remarks when he didn't have any idea he was being taped. If the story ever comes out, Cy would rather be able to truthfully say that he had never heard the tape," Hal explained. "You know he's a very honorable man."

I thought for a moment. I knew Vance was honorable, but perhaps this time, too honorable. "Well, at least convey to him there's no doubt about the tape's authenticity."

When Bourguet and Villalon arrived, I played the first card.

"We might," I said, "consider dropping our insistence that the hostages be released before we would agree to an airing of grievances before the UN—if," I said, then repeated, "*if* that was the first step leading to the release."

The two intermediaries politely disagreed with each other in the discussion that followed. It was a good sign, I thought, that they were relaxed enough to speak honestly and frankly.

We went step-by-step through the process, analyzing each suggestion and idea from both the U.S. and the Iranian perspective. Bourguet and Villalon tended to lapse into interesting, lengthy, and sometimes convoluted explanations of why something would or would not work in Iran. I found it frustrating that it took so long to deal with a specific point and whispered my concern to Hal, who had suffered through so many meetings and negotiations. He smiled back with a "be patient" look.

The creation of a United Nations commission to hear the grievances of the Iranians and to visit the hostages was a critical element of our plan. "The creation of the commission will have to appear to be a victory for the Iranians," Bourguet reasoned.

"There must be some balance to this," I objected mildly. "We are making a major concession if we agree to establish the commission before the hostages are released."

"I understand. But this same commission must win credibility with the Iranians from the outset if it is ultimately going to call for and gain the release of the hostages. Don't forget the political pressures in Iran!"

"Don't forget the political pressures here," I replied, smiling. "President Carter will have to be able to publicly explain and defend our actions to the American people. Khomeini doesn't have to run for re-election."

"Yes, he does," Villalon shot back. "But there's only one voter."

We ended up conferring for over twelve hours. There were several hour-long digressions on minute points before Bourguet, Villalon, Saunders, Precht, or I came up with a suitable way to solve a problem with a sentence or phrase. Hal kept track of all our ideas and suggestions in his tiny book. I was sure he would have to buy a new one after this session. And by the time we had finally hammered out what we called "the scenario," it was a five-page document that stated precisely what each country would say in response to each step, day by day, hour by hour.

I was surprised to learn that Bourguet and Villalon planned to fly to Panama on the 27th to see Torrijos and Royo. Bourguet said that while he never expected the Panamanians to even consider extraditing the Shah, it was important to the "political climate in Iran" for Ghotbzadeh and others to be able to claim that legal action against the "criminal Shah" was proceeding in Panama. Bourguet chuckled and told how Ghotbzadeh had handled the Shah's departure from the United States. "Some people in Iran were ready to use it against Ghotbzadeh, saying that the Shah had escaped their grasp. Ghotbzadeh went on television to say that the Shah's 'escape to Panama' proved he was a criminal, having to move around the world like a thief in the night. Sadegh's explanation was quickly accepted and used by the political leaders to explain why the Shah went to Panama."

I told them they were playing a dangerous game with the Panamanians. "My greatest concern is the Shah's state of mind. I know that you are going through a charade, and you know it—but the Shah doesn't. We have already had a number of indications that he's getting nervous about being extradited. We'll be in a hell of a mess if he decides to leave."

"I understand," said Bourguet, "but I am Iran's lawyer in this matter, and we have to continue the legal process."

I wasn't so sure he did understand.

We parted friends, all pleased with our work, agreeing to meet again in a few days when Bourguet and Villalon came back from Panama through Washington, en route to Paris and Tehran.

I took the scenario home and read it over again and again. It seemed to be a practical and workable plan. I tried to envision how the public would receive it. We would catch hell from some of our political opponents as the plan unfolded, but ultimately our actions would be judged by whether or not we got the hostages out safely and without compromising our nation's honor.

And we would have very little political flexibility if Kennedy didn't drop out. *Damn Ted Kennedy*, I thought. *Damn, damn, damn Ted Kennedy!*

January 27, 1980 (Sunday)

For a change, reading the bulky Sunday papers was mostly enjoyable. There were a couple of campaign stories which were hard on Kennedy, saying that he faced a real test in Maine and New Hampshire, and that if he couldn't beat Jimmy Carter in New England, where could he beat him and why was he running? There was also a story that Kennedy had met with Waldheim to discuss the hostage crisis. I thought it made Kennedy look superficial. Still, there was no indication he would withdraw or accept defeat. Instead, he had planned a "major address" at Georgetown University on Monday. Obviously, they were trying to orchestrate a new beginning for his campaign, but his campaign could be turned around only in New Hampshire and Maine, not in Georgetown, I thought.

The final election results in Iran showed Bani-Sadr the overwhelming victor, winning almost 75 percent of the vote. He had made a statement saying that the American hostages were a "minor issue" that could be solved easily. It sounded like he was softening up the Iranian people for a quick resolution. Perhaps Bourguet and Villalon were too close to Ghotbzadeh to be objective about Bani-Sadr.

I was anxious to see the President Monday and review our scenario with him, and I also wanted to show it to Jody so that he could list his major points of concern for me. Implementing the plan would be like walking through a minefield, of course, and this presumed that Bourguet and Villalon would be able to sell our proposals to the Iranians. Hal was pretty skeptical. "Don't worry," he told me. "Our two friends will come back from Tehran with a lot of ifs and buts."

But we couldn't accept many changes—we had gone about as far as we could. Maybe not. I sat down and reread the scenario.

January 28, 1980 (Monday)

In the morning I went straight to the President with a transcript of the Waldheim tape. Carter said he had already talked with Cy and decided that we should get a small group together to review the scenario.

Hal and I defended it and told what we had learned about Iran to the President, Mondale, Vance, and Brzezinski. I felt odd "explaining Iran" to the foreign policy group, so I prefaced most of my remarks by saying, "Villalon thinks" or "Bourguet says."

Hal and I were able to answer their questions satisfactorily, and although the President suggested a few minor modifications, the basic proposal was left intact. I was relieved because I didn't want to present the intermediaries with a revised scenario that had been ripped apart by our own bureaucracy. Also, it would damage our credibility with them in the future if the ideas and concepts that Hal and I had okayed were reversed by the President and Vance.

I was looking forward to seeing Bourguet and Villalon and telling them we had official approval from the President.

Jody and I watched the evening news on Kennedy's Georgetown speech. It was a strong call for the Democratic Party to return to traditional liberalism: "The time has come to speak the truth again . . . ," he told the student audience, admitting that on many issues he was "sailing against the wind."

"Bullshit," Jody said disgustedly. He jumped up from his chair, paced for a few seconds, and sat back down. "He's against our grain embargo, against the boycott of the Olympics, and against draft registration. 'Sailing against the wind'? The only time Ted Kennedy sails against the wind is when he can't figure out which way it's blowing."

I was disappointed that the Senator had decided to continue his candidacy, and I reflected on my earlier predictions that the race wouldn't last long. We kept knocking him down and he kept getting up, obviously not knowing he was beaten.

January 29, 1980 (Tuesday)

Bourguet and Villalon returned from Panama and arrived at my office a little before Hal, Henry, and Stephie. We welcomed each other warmly but stood in awkward silence—I didn't know a single word of French.

"I have studied English for years, but speak the language not good," Bourguet said haltingly, but clearly.

"You speak very well," I said.

I motioned for Hector and Christian to sit down. Just then Eleanor walked in with a wire story: the Americans who had been hiding in the Canadian Embassy in Tehran had escaped safely. Their story had been one of the best-kept secrets in the American government. We had learned several days after the embassy take-over that a few of our people had made it out of the compound and were hiding in the Canadian Embassy, and we'd worked hard to keep it out of the press. Some enterprising reporters figured out that there were more Americans "missing" than were counted as hostages. The President and Vance had directly contacted editors and publishers of major newspapers and magazines to ask them not to print any stories about missing Americans. We had been working quietly with the Canadians from the outset to develop a plan to free them. The CIA kept the President up-to-date on escape plans. Admiral Turner had described two possibilities: either sneak them through the Tehran airport or allow them individually to cross the Iranian border at some obscure point. "Maybe, Mr. President," he said, "we should give each one his choice."

"I disagree, Stan. There is no telling about the mental and emotional state of those people. Some speak Farsi, some don't. Some can stand up under pressure better than others. My feeling is that you and the Canadians should make a decision as to which escape plan has the best chance of success and then simply tell them what they are to do. I think it would place an enormous burden on them if they had to choose their own escape route. I wouldn't know what to do."

"That makes sense to me, Mr. President, and my belief is that bringing them out together through the airport is our best chance."

"Let's do it, then!"

Now they were free, and I was faced with informing Bourguet and Villalon. What a coincidence. I hoped it wouldn't mess things up.

"Christian," I said, making a special effort to speak slowly and clearly, "I have something to tell you. Six Americans who were hiding in the Canadian Embassy since the takeover have just escaped from Iran." I explained everything.

Bourguet looked shocked and mumbled something in French that I was sure was either obscenities or a prayer.

"We had no choice," I explained. "They were there, they would be discovered . . ."

"I understand," Bourguet said quietly, "that you had to get your citizens out—but what will the Iranians think and what will they do?" Bourguet stopped and said something in French to Villalon, who threw his arms up and exclaimed, "Ooooh, la la!"

They spoke some more in French, then Bourguet turned to me. "Hector says their reaction is predictable. The Iranians will say that once again they have been tricked by the CIA and the Americans. We have been telling them the Americans could be trusted—and now this happens!"

"We had no choice, Christian. If we had left those people in Tehran they would have become hostages."

"I know, I know, I know . . . but it makes things very difficult . . . very, very difficult."

The two men continued to confer in French.

"What can we do to soften their reaction?" I asked.

"Hector says I must call Ghotzbadeh immediately. I must give him reasons for this that will make less danger to the hostages. But what can I say?" Bourguet wondered out loud.

My mind raced. "I know: the Canadians are right in the middle of an election. Tell Ghotbzadeh that it was simply a re-election ploy by Prime Minister Joe Clark. Say it was Clark's attempt to win favor with the Americans and his own people. Blame it all on the Canadians!"

"Good! The Iranians always look for conspiracies," Bourguet responded. He sat quietly for a moment, then spoke again to Hector. "Where is a telephone I can use?" Bourguet asked.

"You can use this one here. I'll step outside."

"No, there is no need for that. It isn't tapped, is it?"

"No," I said with a smile, wondering if he believed me.

With that he lifted the receiver, dialed a number, asked in French for Ghotbzadeh, then said, "*Bonjour*, Sadegh."

My God, I thought. *He just picks up the phone and calls Ghotbzadeh directly from my office*. They talked for about ten minutes, and since Hector and I had no way to communicate with each other, we both just sat there, watching Bourguet.

Hal, Stephanie, and Precht arrived while Bourguet was on the phone. Precht asked me, "Who's Bourguet talking to?"

"Nobody important—just Ghotbzadeh," I said, enjoying his surprise. "He's telling him about the escape from the Canadian Embassy."

"I'm relieved they're out, but I've been worrying about how it will affect the hostages, not to mention our negotiations," Saunders said.

"I told Bourguet to blame it all on the Canadians."

"They just might buy that," Precht said.

When Bourguet hung up, I asked anxiously, "What did he say?"

He responded in rapid French, Stephanie began translating, and our dialogue moved quickly. "He was very, very concerned about the escape. He said that he will do his best to control public opinion, but he wasn't sure what will happen at the American Embassy. He will try to turn all the Iranian anger and frustration toward the Canadians."

"We were lucky they were here when the story broke," I said to Saunders and Precht.

"Sadegh is anxious for Hector and me to complete our work here and get back to Tehran. He says there is a religious holiday coming up that could provide the excuse for the release. He even thinks it could happen by February seventh!"

We worked late into the night, debating and perfecting the scenario. When we were finished, we had a very precise document that we all believed would work.

Bourguet and Villalon left Washington the next day for Tehran to present it to the Iranian leadership.

They told us they would be in Tehran by Thursday, and we started waiting for their call Friday.

February 4, 1980 (Mcnday)

The two intermediaries had been in Tehran since last Thursday, and we still hadn't heard from them. I left numbers where I could be reached every minute over the weekend and called both Saunders and Precht a dozen times, asking if they had heard anything. It bothered me. They had said they would call Friday or Saturday, and we still hadn't been contacted. Had my trust in the two men been misplaced?

By Monday, President Carter was becoming a little antsy himself. What had gone wrong? Television and news accounts indicated that the Ayatollah Khomeini and others had agreed in principle to the idea of an international commission that would travel to Iran and hear the grievances against the Shah and the United States. I knew that Bourguet and Villalon must have delivered the plan. This was Iran claiming "victory" for the creation of the commission—just as we had designed it.

It all looked and sounded good, but we didn't know how to proceed until we heard from the lawyers on what was happening in Iran.

They still hadn't called us, and I was beginning to despair.

February 5, 1980 (Tuesday)

Philip Alston, one of the President's oldest and dearest friends, who was serving as Ambassador to Australia, dropped by as he always did when he was in the States. While we talked about how the Administration was perceived in that part of the world, Eleanor popped in with reminders that Tim Kraft was waiting to see me.

Alston was about to leave when Eleanor came in again. This time the note she handed me said there was a call from Paris. She thought it was Villalon's office but couldn't be sure.

My heart was pounding as I grabbed the phone. It was Villalon's secretary, speaking broken English. I could barely understand what she was saying. I asked her if she spoke Spanish; she said yes, and I thought of Kraft, in my outer office, who had been in the Peace Corps in Guatemala. I rushed Kraft in, told him what he was about to hear was very confidential. He picked up the phone and began speaking. While he was talking to her, I called Hal at the State Department on my other phone and said, "The call has come through." He told me he would round up Henry and Stephanie and come right over.

Tim had been on the phone with Villalon's secretary for about thirty minutes, taking careful notes, when Stephanie arrived, took the phone, and made the poor secretary repeat the entire message. Both Kraft and Alston excused themselves at this point, realizing what they had overheard was more important than either Australia or the campaign.

At last the conversation ended. Stephanie stood before my desk and read her notes. Hector had spoken Spanish to his secretary in Paris to make things more difficult for the Iranians if they were tapping his phones. "'Mr. Villalon is calling in regard to the business contract that he has been working on.' We laughed at Hector's attempt to disguise his message. Stephanie continued. "'He says that he was "quite optimistic" that the contract will be approved and would be implemented, and it is going to be taken to the hospital [a reference to Khomeini, who was still hospitalized]. The President of the company [Bani-Sadr] will soon make a statement in reference to the contract, but Mr. Villalon is quite anxious first to make contact with the representative of the Swiss watch company.'"

I chuckled. Villalon was referring to the Swiss Ambassador, who was handling all U.S. communications with the Iranian government.

"'Finally,'" Stephanie read, "'Mr. Villalon says that he will be back in Paris Friday, and although he has not slept for several days, he is feeling happy and optimistic about the contract.'"

"Is that all?" Hal asked.

"Yes, that's it."

"Well, that doesn't tell us much," I said. "We've got to have more from Bourguet and Villalon than that. It sounds good, but what are we supposed to do—proceed on the basis that the scenario is intact, or what?"

We decided that Stephanie should try to reach Hector at his hotel in Tehran. A little after three that afternoon, Hal, Henry, and Stephanie returned to my office to attempt the call to Hector.

Stephanie sat at my desk and dialed the hotel. Speaking in Spanish, she said it was Madrid calling for Señor Hector Villalon. She said hello, and, covering the phone with her hand, told us that she had awakened him. "He sounds irritated," she whispered, "and says that it was a big mistake for me to call him." She listened for twenty minutes, writing furiously and occasionally sharing some little funny or interesting tidbit.

"He repeated in essence what his secretary told us," Stephanie said after hanging up. "But he sounded really upset with me. I thought it was because I woke him, but when we finished the conversation, he said very plainly, 'Don't ever call me about the contract. I will call you or the Swiss watchmaker.'"

"I hope we didn't screw up by calling him," I said.

"They've got to keep us better informed if they want this thing to work," said Saunders.

We were all disappointed and frustrated. We had people in Iran working for release of the hostages and were still unable to find out what was happening.

February 6, 1980 (Wednesday)

Hal Saunders called around noon to tell me that the Swiss Ambassador was delivering a "message" from the "French lawyers." I wandered around the office, trying to make the time pass more quickly. After a couple of hours, I finally called Hal, who said the translators weren't finished, but promised to let me know as soon as they were.

Finally, around 6:30, he rang me on my secure phone and read me the text of the message from Bourguet and Villalon. They claimed that they would have the support of Bani-Sadr, Ghotbzadeh, and the Revolutionary Council for the scenario. They had some "minor" changes. "They may be minor to them," Hal interjected, "but I bet they're not minor to us!" Much of their message gave reasons and explanations for things Khomeini and Bani-Sadr had said or done but didn't address the specifics of the scenario. Hal and I agreed that to perfect it we should probably have another meeting.

February 7, 1980 (Thursday)

Hal reported during the evening that he had received a message from Bourguet and Villalon saying that they wanted to see us right away—but not in Paris. The French press was about to expose their role in the secret negotiations.

He suggested that we go to Switzerland, but I hesitated to bring yet another group of bureaucrats into this. "You know," I said, "if we arranged a meeting for someone in the States, dozens of people would know about it and there would be a lot of memos floating around."

Hal smiled. "The Swiss Foreign Ministry isn't like the State Department. It's very small."

"And very discreet?" I shot back.

Saunders laughed. "They would probably execute anyone responsible for a leak."

"Switzerland sounds like a great place for us to meet."

February 8, 1980 (Friday)

By morning, Hal had worked it out for us to leave in a few hours. Meanwhile, Henry Precht reported on a "press problem" that Bourguet and Villalon had mentioned. Reporters from *The Washington Post* and *Newsweek* were calling my office asking about my meetings with "the French lawyers" and seemed on the verge of writing major stories about our negotiations.

My worst fears were about to be realized. Our negotiations would be exposed, the channel we had opened to Iran would be destroyed, and the President would then have to explain why his political hack from Georgia was engaged in secret, high-level negotiations. I rushed down to the Oval Office and suggested that the President call Katharine Graham, chairman of the board of The Washington Post Company, which owns *Newsweek*. Carter reflected on it for a few seconds, then said, "Check with Jody and have Cy call her right away. If he strikes out, I'll try."

The President's logic seemed sound. Contrary to what the public believes, contact between Presidents and news executives is rare. Even when the appeal was, as in this case, not to publish because of national interest, it was difficult to request that a story be killed. Jody, agreeing, called Vance, who said he would telephone her immediately. I was a nervous wreck for the next hour until he called to say that she was sympathetic to the problem and would take care of it.

I breathed a sigh of relief and reported Cy's conversation to Jody and President Carter.

The four of us—Stephanie, Henry, Hal, and I—took a military plane to Boston, where we boarded a Swissair flight to Zurich. I was sorry to learn we were not all seated together. Hal said the only reason he could get the State Department to approve even two first-class tickets was that I was along. "I assumed you always fly first class."

"Never! Carter would kill me if he knew I was flying first class now."

"Then don't ever let him see the price of that Concorde ticket," Hal said, laughing.

"He already has. It's coming out of my paycheck!"

I usually have trouble sleeping on planes, and I sat up the entire time, rehashing the scenario and trying to identify the problem spots.

I was back in the spy movie after we landed in Zurich. Two Swiss diplomats met us at the airport gate, rushed us through customs and into a private room, where we had coffee and reviewed our plans. They drove us to Bern, where we checked into the Bellevue Hotel under our assumed names.

It was midafternoon and Bourguet and Villalon were not due in until evening. We stayed in our rooms to avoid being discovered. At about six o'clock, our Swiss escorts took us for a walk through the streets of Bern.

At about eight, Bourguet and Villalon arrived, tired and hungry after a long trip from Tehran. We hugged one another with affection. My initial caution and skepticism had been transformed in just a few weeks into friendship and trust.

Over a light supper in my suite, we worked until midnight. I was pleased to discover that the changes the two intermediaries brought from Tehran were very minor even in our terms.

While Saunders and Precht were in another room drafting a cable to Carter and Vance, and Stephanie was taking a break in her room, Bourguet and Villalon pulled me aside. Speaking slowly so there would be no misunderstanding, Bourguet said, "We think it is time for you to meet with the Iranians."

I was stunned. Our initial objective had been to negotiate directly with the Iranians, but things were going so well through Bourguet and Villalon that it no longer seemed necessary to make direct contact. However, I could hardly refuse the opportunity. And the prospect was exciting.

"I have to check with the President, but I feel confident that he will want me to meet them. But what would be the purpose of the meeting? We've got the scenario worked out."

"This meeting would be"—Bourguet paused, searching for the right word—"an investment in the future. It may make the release of the hostages faster. More important, it would begin a dialogue between the United States and Iran which could be the foundation for future relations."

"Who would I meet with?"

"I will tell you, but there is one condition: you must promise never to reveal the name of the contact and you must keep it from ever appearing in the press."

Making such a commitment troubled me. "I can keep it quiet, but I can't promise anything on behalf of our government. We read things in the newspapers every day that are classified but have been somehow given out by government officials—things that harm our country. If I meet this person I promise only that I will try to prevent any leaks. Of course, you have my personal promise that I will never reveal the name of the contact."

"That is all that we can ask." He told me the name of the Iranian contact and said that we would talk soon about the details of the meeting.

I never knew how much of the impetus for the meeting came from Iran and how much came from the lawyers. The two men had dedicated themselves to helping Iran establish better relations with the United States in order to offset Iran's dangerous proximity to the Soviet Union. Perhaps Bourguet and Villalon told the Iranians that I insisted on direct contact just as they were pushing me now saying the Iranians wanted to meet.

February 11, 1980 (Monday)

We all flew to Paris in the morning in a U.S. Air Force plane. We dropped the French intermediaries at a special gate, then proceeded to another gate to catch the Concorde. We arrived in New

York midmorning, and Hal and I went over the revisions with Vance before a luncheon meeting with Waldheim at his residence on the East River.

The Secretary General greeted us at the door and introduced his chef de cabinet, Rafi Ahmed. Over lunch, Vance began the delicate process of outlining our plan and enlisting Waldheim's cooperation in a scheme that had been created without him.

Waldheim was very sincere about wanting to help, but wanted to be sure that both parties were equally committed to the precise plan that Vance outlined. "Cy," he asked, "can you assure me that Iran agrees to this—even the Ayatollah Khomeini?"

"As best we can tell, yes, Kurt. Ham, do you want to elaborate?"

I told the Secretary General about Bourguet and Villalon, though I was not anxious to have him check them out and develop any doubts of his own. I described their friendship with the Iranian exiles in Paris, and how they traveled freely to Iran and could meet with all the leaders, including the Revolutionary Council. I couldn't help thinking about that tape we had of Waldheim. "Mr. Secretary General, nobody knows for sure—not even our French intermediaries—what the Ayatollah Khomeini knows. As you are well aware, he is not the kind of man to pay attention to the details of a plan. We do think that he has been informed that the Revolutionary Council has unanimously endorsed a procedure that allows for the world to hear Iran's grievances and leads ultimately to the release of the hostages."

"I see," said Waldheim, seeming not to be fully satisfied with my answer. "What are the names of these French lawyers?"

"Christian Bourguet and Hector Villalon."

"I don't think I know them. Do you, Rafi?" he asked, turning to his aide, who shook his head. "All the same, the plan looks workable and reasonable, and I and the UN stand ready to do whatever we can."

We went on to discuss the makeup of the commission. Waldheim knew all of the proposed members and approved of our selections. He would contact them all, ask them to serve, and brief them thoroughly before their trip to Iran.

Saunders, Vance, and I took a small, twin-engined Air Force plane to Washington. The Secretary was in a good mood and seemed relaxed. I asked him how he really felt about our plan.

"Ham, we have been disappointed so many times that I have trouble being optimistic. But you and Hal have gotten more on paper than I ever thought you would." Pausing, he said with a smile, "I have a feeling that this just might be it. We'll know soon enough, since the scenario calls for Kurt to phone Ghotbzadeh tonight to announce the formation of the UN commission."

Back in Washington late in the afternoon, we briefed the President. He was pleased with the progress but was concerned about the public statements that both the U.S. and Iran would have to make when it was all over—in accordance with the scenario. I shared his concern, but assured him that we could find language that would satisfy both the American people and our obligations under the scenario.

I was exhausted and ready to go home, but there had been three calls from Gabriel Lewis and two from Ambler Moss. *Something must be going on in Panama*, I thought. Ambler told me that the friction between the Shah's entourage and the Panamanians had reached a new high. Allegations were flying: Armao said the Panamanians were overcharging the Shah. There was fresh talk of extradition, and general ill will between Armao and his hosts. I knew that none of it was true, as did Ambler, but the problem was that the Shah was beginning to believe it and Armao and others were talking openly about making public their complaints about Panama and their demands to return to the States.

I went home very tired but very optimistic. The call from Panama had been the only unpleasant note in a long and productive day.

February 12, 1980 (Tuesday)

The papers carried reports of an interview Bani-Sadr had given to a French journalist, Eric Rouleau, who revealed that the Revolutionary Council had approved a plan which required the United States to make a "self-criticism" of its past crimes against Iran. I knew that it was important to Bani-Sadr to create the right political atmosphere in Iran, but at the same time, we had our own political problems. We couldn't allow the Iranians to publicly claim just anything that suited them. The President suggested that Jody, Saunders, Hodding Carter, and I get together every morning so that we could speak with "one voice" on the hostage crisis as the scenario unfolded.

February 13, 1980 (Wednesday)

President Carter's first formal press conference in weeks was scheduled for 8:00 P.M. We had to convey the idea that the Administration was doing something behind the scenes, without in any way compromising our plan. Today's papers had Bani-Sadr saying that the Ayatollah had approved a "secret plan" for the release of the hostages. After several months of nothing but harsh rhetoric coming out of Tehran, the American press had worked itself into a frenzy trying to find out what was going on. We needed to dampen expectations of an immediate release—if the scenario were followed to the letter, the hostages would not be freed for nearly two weeks.

As Jody put it to the President, "A lot is going to happen in the next couple of weeks that will be difficult for the public to understand and impossible for us to explain. I think the principal objective of your news conference, Mr. President, should be to buy some time and patience. We want Americans to know that we're involved, but we don't want to have to say so. We need them to understand that there's a method to our madness."

"That's easy for you to say, Jody, but hard for me to do. I've got to stand up there in front of those friends of yours [the White House press corps] and try to answer their questions. What do you suggest?"

"Maybe you could read your prepared statement to the American people and then wink at 'em."

Jody, Hal, and I got to work on the President's remarks. Charles Kirbo was in town and sat in with us as we struggled with the draft of the opening statement. I left my office only once all morning, to call Stan Turner. I had been thinking a lot about my meeting with the Iranian contact and was worried to death that we would be found out, probably destroying any chance of implementing the scenario. I had to be sure that this didn't happen. "Stan, I would like to have someone from the Agency who works in disguises meet me this afternoon. Is that possible?"

"Of course, Ham. Should he come with equipment—and where do you want to meet?"

I tried to think of an inconspicuous place. "Tell him to come to the South Gate. I'll have him cleared and taken to the White House barbershop—it's closed on Wednesdays. I'll come down when the guards announce him."

The opening statement for the press conference was finished by midafternoon. Hal took a copy to the State Department for Cy to review; he called back with some minor changes, which we incorporated. By four o'clock, we had completed the draft statement, and Jody, Kirbo, and I spent forty-five minutes with the President in the Oval Office going over it.

When I came out, Eleanor pulled me aside and with a puzzled look said, "There's a man from the CIA waiting for you in the *barbershop*." I smiled at her, enjoying the rare moment: I was doing something Eleanor knew absolutely nothing about.

"Mr. Jordan?" A soft voice reached me from the back of the darkened barbershop.

"Yes?"

"The light switch is on the wall to your immediate left."

I groped around, then flicked on the light, and a very ordinary-looking man, carrying a briefcase, came into focus. He introduced himself and went right to work.

"What is your objective, Mr. Jordan?"

"I want to be able, if necessary, to quickly put on a disguise that I could use to get in and out of a building unnoticed."

He asked me where I would be using the disguise and how long people would see me in it. Then he asked me to walk around the room. "I need to see how you carry yourself. Your walk is noticeable," he commented, "and you carry yourself very confidently. I think I want to make you more obscure by adding years to your look. But you'll need to move a little more slowly and shrug a bit—and try wearing some type of topcoat if the weather permits."

He opened his briefcase. In a couple of minutes I was looking into a mirror at a man with graying black hair and gold-rimmed, tinted glasses. "This looks great," I said with a snicker. I looked like a sleazy Latin businessman.

"Well, I'm not through." He placed a strip of gray and black hair on the counter, then smeared some liquid from a small bottle on it.

"What's that?"

"Your mustache, Señor Jordan," he replied gravely as he meticulously pressed it above my mouth and combed the ends around my mouth. He brushed the wig over my hairline and said, "What do you think, Mr. Jordan?"

"I think it's great—but I know it's me under there. What do *you* think?"

"I think your mother wouldn't recognize you. If I do say so myself, it is very, very good! Let me take a couple of pictures."

He pulled out a Polaroid camera, snapped several shots, and gave one to me. He was right. My mother wouldn't recognize me.

The CIA man took a few minutes to review the instructions for putting the disguise on, then he packed it all in a small green case and gave it to me. He turned off the light in the barbershop, and, in a low voice said, "I am leaving now. Count to sixty before you go out."

I felt like a make-believe 007, standing in the dark in the deserted White House barbershop with my disguise in my little green kit, counting. When I got back to my office, I hid the Polaroid shot in my safe, determined that no one would ever see it.

I had agreed to meet with several workers from the campaign to review final plans for the New Hampshire primary. They didn't really need me, but I knew some people were beginning to resent the fact that I hadn't been spending much time on the campaign. I struggled to act interested, but was glad when it ended so I could go down to the Oval Office with Jody, Zbig, and the others to have a session with the President before his press conference.

Afterward, we went back to my office, ordered dinner from the mess, and watched President Carter's performance on television. He made his statement, cautioned against excessive optimism, and refused to be dragged into further discussion of the hostage matter. We all thought it went well.

February 14, 1980 (Thursday)

And the morning reviews confirmed our feelings.

Strauss called ecstatic. "The Boss did very, very well last night! But I tell you what—this city is a beehive of rumors and stories about the hostages. He talked about not expecting anything on the hostages in a hurry, but I'm not sure that it's possible to control the public's expectations anymore. This thing's got to end soon!"

"How soon, Bob?"

"The Monday before the New Hampshire primary would do just fine," he said. I didn't answer, but smiled and thought to myself that it wouldn't be too long after then that they would be on their way home.

I shared Strauss's assessment that the President had appeared firm and tough and had scored a few political points on Kennedy.

He had effectively refuted the charge that he was afraid to campaign, and took Kennedy to task for trying to claim in a speech at Harvard that the UN commission was the Senator's idea and that Carter had possibly prolonged the hostages' captivity by not acting on Kennedy's suggestion earlier. "What causes me the deepest concern," Carter had said, "is that his statements have not been accurate, they have not been responsible, and they have not helped our country."

Jody was worried that the President's comments were too strong. "Even when it's true, it sounds bad for any President to claim that criticism of him is damaging to the country's interests. It smacks of arrogance."

Nonetheless, the mood around the White House was upbeat. The press conference, the good news on the hostages, and political reaction had bought us a little more time.

Late that afternoon, Stan Turner called. "Ham, my special effects got over to see you yesterday, I understand," he said cautiously.

"Yes, and he was very helpful."

"I assume that this relates to your special assignment on Iran?"

"Yes, it does. Is there any problem?"

"No. I just wanted to check and be sure. Our special effects folks over here have been burned before, and I just wanted to be able to say that this was for official government use."

"Stan, I'm afraid I don't understand." I was tempted to say, "I'm not going to a costume party, Stan."

"Well, let me put it this way, Ham. The last time that a CIA employee was called over to the White House with a disguise, it was for Howard Hunt."

"Oh, I understand. Tell them the difference is this is not for a break-in, it's for a break-out."

Turner laughed and hung up.

February 15, 1980 (Friday)

At the foreign policy breakfast, Cy reported that Waldheim was putting the commission together and had four acceptances and only one refusal. We discussed candidates for the fifth position and, once again, we went over the scenario. "I am going to have real difficulties with that final step," the President said, "finding words that will be acceptable to the American people and that will allow the Iranians to claim victory."

"We've got three languages to play with: English, French, and Farsi," I pointed out. We can take an English word, find a French synonym that is weaker or even vague, and find a Farsi word that is even more so. We'll stick with our English word and let them give it their best possible Farsi interpretation."

The President was not reassured. "You can play with words all you want, but I am going to have to be able to stand up in front of the American people and defend whatever statement I make." He then asked Cy to have Warren Christopher work with Saunders and me on drafting the statement.

Rather than talk about my meeting with the "Iranian contact" in front of the whole group, the President asked Cy, Hal, and me to meet with him at three o'clock before I left. I asked Hal to draw up some "talking points." I wanted to have specific objectives for my secret meeting and written instructions approved by both the President and Secretary; if anything happened, the President and I would be better protected if there were a written record, stating clearly his instructions to me.

Hal prepared my instructions. My task was to push hard on the scenario and try to pin the Iranians down on some of the troublesome questions, particularly the timing of the release and the logistics of removing the hostages from Tehran. I was to talk about the future of U.S. relations with Iran, and how to counterbalance Soviet interests in the area. The President and Cy studied Hal's draft and made a few small changes.

Eleanor sent me a message that Henry Precht was on the phone. I excused myself and took the call. Bourguet and Villalon had called to say that the "Iranian contact" wanted only me and the interpreter to come.

"But what about Hal?" I asked Henry.

"They say specifically that Hal should not come. They are emphatic about it."

"Why?"

"The Iranian does not want to be in the same city with anyone who has been a part of the—and I quote—'Rockefeller-Kissinger cabal.'"

I was afraid the President and Vance wouldn't want me to go alone, but when I returned with the message, they all laughed.

"Hal, you have finally been discovered," the President said. Then he added in a somber tone, "I don't like the Iranians telling us who to bring."

"I don't either, Mr. President, but I think Ham should go ahead alone. To cancel the meeting would be a big mistake," Vance said.

I was flattered by Cy's confidence, but I was a little more apprehensive now about my trip.

Once again I made a point of being very visible around the White House the rest of the day so that my absence Saturday and Sunday would be less obvious.

Note to Reader:

There was much speculation in the press about my meetings with "Iranians" in Europe and the Middle East, and several articles claimed I had traveled clandestinely into Iran. In accordance with my promise to Bourguet and Villalon, I never confirmed either the site of any meetings or the persons in attendance. The most frequent allegations were that I met with Ghotbzadeh, although others speculated that I had conferred with Bani-Sadr or the Ayatollah Beheshti or Ahmad Khomeini, the Imam's son.

Every account I have read about these alleged contacts is flawed in one way or another, and no one in a position to know authoritatively would have confirmed any one of them. I am the only source for what really happened, and I will not break the promise I made to my friends Hector Villalon and Christian Bourguet.

Zbigniew Brzezinski, Cyrus Vance, and Jimmy Carter
walking on the South Lawn of the White House *(November 8, 1979)*.

Pat Caddell, Hamilton Jordan,
Jerry Rafshoon, and Jody Powell at Camp David.

The President toasting the Shah in Iran (*New Year's Eve 1977*).

Foreign policy breakfast in the Cabinet Room:
to the President's left, Brzezinski, Walter Mondale, Hedley Donovan, and Lloyd Cutler;
to his right, Vance, Harold Brown, Warren Christopher, Jordan. and Powell (*November 9, 1979*).

The President talking with Vance (above) at the foreign policy breakfast, before meeting with families of the hostages (below) at the State Department *(November 9, 1979)*.

General Omar Torrijos at his "home" on the Pacific Ocean.

Carter and Brzezinski discussing the hostages (*November 20, 1979*).

Marine One, landed on the South Lawn, bringing the President (above) back from Camp David to discuss Khomeini's threat with his advisers (below): Jordan, Brown, Vance, Brzezinski, Mondale, and Admiral Stansfield Turner *(November 20, 1979)*.

Señor Hamilton Jordan
in disguise.

Hector Villalon.

Christian Bourguet.

Arriving at Camp David: General David Jones, Turner, Brown, Vance, Mondale, Brzezinski, and Jordan, with Secret Service agents following *(November 23, 1979)*.

Carter and Brzezinski conferring at Laurel, Camp David *(November 23, 1979)*.

Jordan and the gerbils fighting the Kennedy forces at the
1980 Democratic National Convention.

Senator Ted Kennedy leaving the podium
the last night of the Convention (*August 14, 1980*).

Election evening in Hamilton Jordan's White House office: (above) Pat Caddell, Jordan, Carter adviser Bob Lipshutz, Jody Powell, Frank Moore, Phil Wise, Jerry Rafshoon, and Bob Strauss; (below) Powell, Moore, Wise, Tim Kraft, Strauss, Jordan, and Rafshoon (*November 4, 1980*).

Waiting for news of the hostages. Jordan, Carter, Cutler, and Mondale in the Oval Office on the eve of Ronald Reagan's Inauguration *(January 19, 1981)*.

Dozing in the Oval Office *(January 20, 1981)*.

Carter dressing before the Inauguration while awaiting news of the hostages with Cutler, Jordan, and Charles Kirbo *(January 20, 1981)*.

Last hours in the Oval Office: Carter, Brzezinski, Edmund Muskie, Cutler, and Gary Sick *(January 20, 1981)*.

I took the Concorde to Europe where I was secretly met and driven to a private residence.

February 16, 1980 (Saturday)

We spent the morning at the home of an American official, preparing for my meeting with the contact. Bourguet and Villalon took turns telling me what they knew about his life and interests. Time and again they stressed that I should assume a learning posture and show a willingness to hear what he had to say. "Don't forget that you and he have different objectives," Bourguet reasoned while Stephanie translated. "You are anxious to end the hostage crisis. He is anxious to explain the Revolution to you. He sees you as the way to reach the President."

Hector added that it was *"très important"* that I listen more than talk.

After two hours of this preparation, I excused myself and went upstairs to the bathroom. On the way back, I noticed my little green bag and had a devilish thought. I spent about five minutes in front of the mirror, dabbing the sticky glue on the little mustache and pressing it on my lip, combing the wig over my own dark hair, and adjusting the glasses and my brown topcoat.

I walked back toward the sitting area, where Stephanie, Hector, and Bourguet were chatting in French. No one paid attention until I was halfway down the stairs. Suddenly Hector jumped up and shouted in French, "There's an intruder here!" (Stephanie translated it for me later.) Christian and Stephanie looked up, both startled. Before they got too carried away, I said, "It's only me—Señor Jordan."

Stephanie roared, then translated. Bourguet shook with laughter and Hector smiled broadly. I took off my disguise, and we sat around the house the rest of the afternoon and night, then walked out the rear door and down the alley, where a small car waited to carry us through backstreets to the site of our meeting.

February 17, 1980 (Sunday)

Shortly after midnight, Stephanie and I entered the apartment. I put my disguise kit on a table by the door and sat down on the sofa. Stephanie knew I was uptight and tried to relax me with small talk, but she quit after a few minutes.

It was almost two hours before we heard the sound of footsteps in the corridor, then words in a foreign language and the door being opened. *That's him,* I thought. *That's our contact.* I swallowed hard and stood up.

A man stepped into the room. He walked up to us, smiled, and held out his hand confidently. "Monsieur Jordan," he said.

"I trust you had a safe trip here," I said.

"Yes, thank you. And, more important, I don't think it received any public notice."

"I came on the Concorde to Europe and then traveled here secretly," I told him. "It took twice as long to do this part as it did to fly across the ocean."

"I have heard about the Concorde but have never flown on it."

"We must both be sure to do it while we can charge it to our governments. It's very expensive!"

He laughed heartily.

The host, speaking French while Stephanie interpreted, escorted us into a small dining area, where the beautiful mahogany table was set with fine china, crystal goblets, and ornate silver. The candlelight made it seem more a setting for lovers than for two men whose countries were sliding toward armed conflict.

We sat down across from each other. The Iranian looked as nervous as I felt. "This is a very lovely setting, and I am very hungry!" he said.

A manservant came in with a bottle of red wine, filled my glass, and started to pour into the Iranian's glass, but he quickly covered it with his hand. I wondered if he didn't care for wine or if he had refused because of his Islamic faith.

I intended to listen, as Bourguet and Villalon had suggested, but I wanted to extend a gesture of friendship. "I appreciate the great risk you have taken in coming here and meeting with me," I said.

"It is a risk that I take freely in the cause of peace. Don't worry about me, but also I must trust you never to reveal my identity."

"You have my word. But what would happen?"

He laughed heartily. "Well, my friend, first I would lose my job and then I would lose my neck!"

I tried to smile at his joke and thought about how little I had at stake by comparison. "Why are you taking such a chance to meet with me?" I asked. "We seem to have agreed on a plan for ending the crisis."

He nodded. "The immediate conflict will soon be over. I wanted to talk about the future. We must not let the misunderstanding that exists today between our people be repeated time and again. Contrary to what you may think, I do not hate your country!"

I nodded for him to continue.

"The reason that I wanted to meet with you, Mr. Jordan, is to try to penetrate the wall of people surrounding your President who have kept the truth from him about the criminal Shah, Iran, and our Revolution."

Here we go again, I thought. *The same old anti-American Islamic crap.*

I didn't want to begin our meeting with an argument, and remembered Bourguet's admonition about listening, so I simply replied, "Which people are you talking about?"

"Kissinger, the Rockefellers, and all the other Jews in the State Department who have kept the truth from the President!" he said sternly.

I sat quietly, letting him have the floor for a while. *Maybe,* I thought, *he'll get all of this rhetoric and bitterness out of his system and then we can talk about the hostages.*

He seemed pleased to have me as his audience. As I sat listening, I wondered if his presentation had been practiced.

He launched into a long monologue on the Ayatollah and the

Revolution. With great reverence in his voice, he recited the sufferings of Khomeini. He told of the death of Khomeini's father at the hands of a wealthy landlord when the Imam was just a child; of his steadfast opposition to the Shah, which led to his exile from Iran in 1963; of the killing of his son by "your CIA"; and finally of his trip to Paris and triumphant return to Tehran. The main course—filet mignon—had been served, but the contact was so totally immersed in his worshipful story of the Imam that he had not even touched his food.

As I listened to his impassioned speech, I began to realize that it was not just rhetoric or polemics but a sincere attempt to make me comprehend what a wonderful man the Ayatollah Khomeini was.

"Tell me," I said, "how do you perceive President Carter in terms of Iran and the Revolution?"

"I don't think he is a bad man, but I think he has made decisions about the Shah and Iran based on very poor advice. In short, your President has been duped by the State Department!" He paused, smiled, and then added, "And I realize now that he is anxious for the hostages to be released so that he can be re-elected!"

Now it was time for me to speak. "Of course he wants to be re-elected and wants the hostages out. Any President would. If you put aside your grievances against the Shah and the United States, how does Iran benefit from holding our citizens and isolating itself from the West, particularly with the Soviets in Afghanistan ready to exploit the chaos in your country?" I replied angrily.

"But, Mr. Jordan—we *cannot* put aside the case of the Shah! That man is so evil, he has tortured and murdered so many of our people, he has stolen so much of our money! The Shah and Kissinger and Rockefeller made our country an instrument of U.S. foreign policy. The Shah is the reason for the hostages! You must understand that!"

I wasn't going to back down. I stared hard at him and he returned my glare.

He broke the tense moment with a slight smile, then said, "I see your newspapers and replays of your television news, and all I have heard about the last three months is hostages, hostages, hostages. Your press does not tell the story of the Shah's crimes or the events leading to their seizure. It is very frustrating for us. I disagree with what those students have done. It isolates and hurts our country and our Revolution. But holding fifty-three Americans is a slight injustice compared to the killing and torturing of thousands and thousands of Iranians by the criminal Shah!"

"The policy of our country for the past thirty years is not the fault or responsibility of this Administration," I responded, "nor is it the responsibility of the captured men and women."

"Mr. Jordan, it is hard for my people to separate the guilty from the innocent. Your country and your Presidents have made it possible for the Shah to rule. As far as the Ayatollah Khomeini is concerned, you all have blood on your hands."

Clearly, it was futile to argue about the past. I decided to be blunt. "How do we resolve this crisis peacefully, honorably, and quickly?"

The contact paused and smiled slyly. "It is easy to resolve the crisis."

"How?" I shot back.

"All you have to do is kill the Shah," he said in a quiet voice.

I was shocked. "You're kidding."

He stopped smiling. "I am very serious, Mr. Jordan. The Shah is in Panama now. I am not talking about anything dramatic. Perhaps the CIA can give him an injection or do something to make it look like a natural death. I'm only asking you to do to the Shah what the CIA did to thousands of innocent Iranians over the past thirty years!"

"That's impossible!" I told him. "It's totally out of the question!"

He smiled again. "You asked me how to quickly resolve the crisis. I want to remove this thorn from our side just as badly as you do, Mr. Jordan," the man said, "but for very different reasons. Your purpose is to have the President re-elected, and my purpose is to refocus the attention of the Iranian people on our Revolution and to keep the United States and the Soviets from subverting it. You think we hate the United States. The truth is we hate both the United States and the Soviet Union. Both countries have used and exploited Iran! Our hatred of the United States is simply more recent."

He was obviously enjoying hearing his own voice, so I decided to wait for the right opening to bring up the matter of the hostages again.

"You know, Mr. Jordan, I will admit that the United States is a better country than the Soviet Union, but the Russians do a better job than you do of selling their philosophy. One of the great ironies of the Revolution is that the new Iran—after the hostage matter is behind us—will be a better ally of yours against the Soviet Union than the Shah ever was. Under the Imam, the Iranian people will fight to the last man to defend the country against aggressors of all types! All I want is for Iran to remain free of foreign interference. You know, it doesn't make any difference if I am hit by a Soviet bullet or an American bullet. Either way I am dead."

I did my best to hide my frustration and tried again to turn the conversation back to the hostages. "But how do we resolve these differences between our leaders so that Iran can remain independent of both superpowers? We can't have normal relations as long as you are holding our diplomats."

"Correct." He then spoke frankly about the secret negotiations and the scenario. "If President Carter will only be patient, not say things that are inflammatory, and stop talking about sanctions and pressure on Iran, your citizens will be released soon."

"What is soon?" I asked. "Weeks or months?"

"Weeks," he replied. "The plan is a good one. It is fair, and it has the support of our leaders and the Revolutionary Council."

"I say this not in a threatening way—but you should know that the patience of the President and the American people is running out. What assurance can you give me that the plan will be followed by your government?"

He bristled when I said this, and lapsed into a very formal response. "Mr. Jordan, you may tell the President of the United States that my government will abide by every detail of the scenario drawn up by you and the French lawyers."

"What about the Ayatollah Khomeini? Has the scenario been approved by him?"

He paused, perhaps collecting his thoughts, then spoke. "We argued the details of the scenario in the Council. Although some of the clergy tried to use the plan for their own political purposes, the vote of the Council was unanimous. We then went to Qom, asked for an audience with the Imam, and told him that we had shamed the United States sufficiently and taught it a lesson, and now we needed to resolve this problem so we could be strong and not vulnerable to the Soviet Union."

"And what was his response?"

He smiled. "The Imam often does not respond. He listened to our explanation and nodded when we told him that the elected leadership and the Revolutionary Council had approved this approach. If he had objected to our proposal, he would have said so. We talked about other matters, prayed together, and we left."

We had spent three hours together, talking mostly about the future. I had tried to pin him down on the scenario—how much had I accomplished?

I gave the contact the numbers of the private line at my apartment and the phone that rang directly on my desk. "If you ever need to talk with me or want to say anything to me directly, feel free to call. No one answers either of those phones but me."

He seemed to appreciate the gesture. We rose, shook hands, and said farewell.

I waited at the apartment for a long hour in case anyone had been following him, and was in the car before I remembered the green kit sitting on the table by the entrance. I ran in and got it, then returned to the house where I was staying.

The adrenaline was still flowing. The time difference meant that the President probably hadn't gone to bed yet, and I decided to call him. Because I was on an open line, I kept my conversation vague. "Mr. Carter, I just wanted you to know that the meeting took place and was satisfactory from our perspective."

"Any startling news?"

"No, but I think everything is on track."

"Any breakthroughs?"

I realized that he was hoping that my meeting might accelerate the release of the hostages.

"Sorry, none that I know of. But I do think it reinforced what was already under way."

"I understand."

"I'm heading home in a few hours and will give you a full report then."

Back in Washington, I drove straight to the White House to give the President the twelve-page report I had written on a legal pad on the plane.

"The bad news," I said, "is that the contact didn't want to talk too much about the hostage situation. The good news is that he was so confident that they would be released soon that he wanted to use our time to talk about relations between the U.S. and Iran after they're free. I would say, Mr. President, that he will return to Iran with a greater stake in the release of the hostages."

Carter nodded and said that he was looking forward to reading my report and my impressions of the contact. I sensed he was a little disappointed that the secret meeting hadn't produced more tangible results, but he didn't say anything.

February 18, 1980 (Monday)

Officially, it was Washington's birthday, so the pace at the White House was leisurely. I had to recap my report throughout the day for Jody, then Lloyd Cutler, and then Brzezinski. It became increasingly obvious to me that everyone had been expecting a breakthrough. I started to wonder myself if our strategy had been correct or if I should have pushed harder to talk about the hostages.

But I kept remembering that Bourguet and Villalon had stressed the importance of letting the Iranians know we were willing to listen to their grievances instead of just expressing our own. I'd done my best, and felt good about it. I'd just have to quit worrying and second-guessing myself.

Vance and Saunders were in New York. They first met with Waldheim and Andres Aguilar, of Venezuela, chairman of the UN Commission; then with Mohammed Bedjaoui, of Algeria, a commission member whose government had close ties with the Khomeini government. Hal called to report that their meetings had gone well.

I also talked with Henry Precht, who was in Paris and had been in touch with Bourguet and Villalon. They reported that the contact gave them a very positive report, which reassured me.

I had a couple of conversations with Chris Brown, who had engineered our '76 victory in the New Hampshire primary and was trying for a repeat. Chris was hard-nosed, and cautious in his predictions. When I could squeeze an optimistic report out of him, I knew we were in good shape. "Don't tell anybody, but we're going to win this damn primary, and it might even be big," he told me. I started to relax. Iowa, Maine, and now New Hampshire—how could Kennedy continue?

Jody called in the middle of the day to ask if I had seen *Newsweek*. "There's a story revealing that you've been negotiating with Bourguet and Villalon."

"But that's impossible!" I protested. "Mrs. Graham assured Vance they wouldn't do that."

"Maybe that word didn't get to *Newsweek*. Don't be too upset. I can use personal leverage with the White House press. I just wanted you to know about it. Since you can't deny it, you should just avoid any calls or contact with the press and refer them to me."

I got a copy of *Newsweek*. The lead story was "A Break in the Hostage Deadlock." "It's going to compromise Bourguet and Villalon and make the President look silly," I said to Eleanor.

For my greatest fear all along had been that my role in the negotiations would become known, compromising Bourguet and Villalon with the Iranians and destroying the channel we had worked so hard to open.

But I also knew that it would be politically disastrous if it were discovered that I—of all people—was in charge of negotiating the release. For after three years in the White House, I had become an object of ridicule and controversy. I didn't like it, but knew it was true.

I could just imagine the reaction of the American people to the news that I was negotiating for the President: the political cartoonists and columnists, saying, "Jimmy Carter has his first big crisis on his hands, and whom does he turn to? . . . Hamilton Jordan. Unbelievable!"

I thought about the long road to the White House, those hard years when I would drive the ex-Governor of Georgia in my beat-up green VW to the Atlanta airport to catch a plane to Iowa or New Hampshire. In those early days, we often couldn't afford two tickets, and Jimmy Carter would fly tourist class and be met by volunteers who would drive him around and put him up in their homes. People didn't laugh at us openly, but many of my friends and even some of my family had snickered behind our backs—a peanut farmer from Georgia as President? Preposterous.

The only thing that kept me going through those years was the dream of Jimmy Carter being President. Working in the White House was not a goal of mine, but when I was offered the opportunity to go with the President-elect to Washington, I was caught up in the excitement of the moment and said yes to that once-in-a-lifetime offer. I never wanted to be a public figure, and never dreamed that I might become a controversial figure and a political liability.

Because Jimmy Carter was not a product of Congress and was not well known to the Washington establishment, there was an inordinate curiosity about him. It is not easy to get to know a man after he has become President. As a result of their years in Congress, Presidents Ford, Nixon, Johnson, and Kennedy were well known to the press and the political establishment. Jimmy Carter was both a surprise and an enigma.

Many people sought to answer .the question, Who is Jimmy Carter? by trying to understand the persons around him, for it was easier to reach and try to read the President's staff than the new Chief Executive himself.

Jimmy Carter's success was at the same time celebrated and resented by the Democratic political establishment. It was bad enough that they didn't know him and had no stake in his candidacy, but to make matters worse, Carter had defeated their various darlings in the battles around the country. There was a subtle but strong feeling when we arrived in Washington that "Well, OK, you Georgians—you won the big prize through gimmicks, good fortune, and by running against Washington. But now we are going to show you who's boss in this town!"

As a result of Carter's unexpected success in the primaries, Jody Powell and I were the only two persons with high public profiles. Jody was always at Carter's side and became a familiar and popular figure to the members of the press who traveled with Carter and covered the campaign. If anything, his influence on candidate Carter was discounted because he was inaccurately perceived as playing the traditional and limited role of mouthpiece. Because I was the campaign manager and was given exaggerated credit for the strategy that carried Carter to the White House, there was great curiosity about me and my future role in the White House. I had never traveled with candidate Carter, and only rarely had granted interviews, so I was naturally a mystery to the national press.

After the general election, I worked closely with the President-elect and with Vice President-elect Mondale in the selection of the Cabinet, and ended up in the office in the White House that had been occupied by the Chiefs of Staff of recent Presidents. But the media would not accept our protests that I was not the new H.R. Haldeman.

I realized I was in trouble when I read an article in *The Washington Post* by Sally Quinn describing me as "the second most important person in Washington." "Jody," I said, "I have been set up for a great big fall."

I was not a public person nor could I think of myself as one. But the mistake I made was failing to appreciate that anyone working at the White House, particularly someone who had the relationship I enjoyed with the President, was a public person whether he liked it or not. And that position carries with it certain responsibilities.

Despite my later image as a playboy, I spent most of my first year at the White House working twelve and fifteen hours a day. Because of my work, I never went out socially, nor did I try to become a part of the Washington party scene. That was interpreted by many as a sign of contempt, and one of the constant complaints you heard about the "Georgia mafia" was that it was difficult to get them—"particularly Jordan," to attend any of their gatherings.

One of the few social events I attended that year was a dinner party given by Barbara Walters in honor of the ambassadors to Egypt and Israel. I was seated between the ambassadors' wives, at a table that included humorist Art Buchwald and Henry Kissinger.

Several weeks after the dinner, an article in the Style Section of *The Washington Post* criticized the social practices of the Carter White House. The liveliest tidbit described me, saying I had gazed at the Egyptian woman's ample front, pulled at her elasticized bodice, and said out loud, "I've always wanted to see the pyramids."

I couldn't believe my eyes when I read the article. Several friends called to kid me about it, but I didn't find it very funny. I denied the outrageous allegations, and after Mrs. Ghorbal herself denied the story and said she was "upset by its even being written," and Henry Kissinger said he could recall "nothing improper" about my conduct and didn't believe the reported incident had occurred, I was sure that my innocence wouldn't be questioned. The Israeli, Mrs. Dinitz, said that she was "shocked" by the story and that I had been a "model of decorum," and Art Buchwald denied seeing or hearing anything at our table that night that resembled the story reported. But the *Post* stuck to its story, which made the front page all over the country and was treated as a serious item on the evening news.

Then there was the rumor—based on an anonymous source—which appeared in a gossip column, alleging that, at a Georgetown bar, I had spat an Amaretto-and-cream drink over the head of one person and down the dress of a young woman. I had been at that bar that night with Tim Kraft and others eating a hamburger and having a couple of drinks. Jody called me at Camp

David, where I was relaxing with my brother and his family. "We've got to draw the line on this stuff, Ham. I want to fight this."

And he did, sending White House lawyers to question witnesses and take affidavits and to poke holes in the accusations. It was one of the few mistakes I thought Jody made while he was press secretary, this overreaction on my behalf, a thirty-three-page document refuting the allegations—and that only drew more attention to them. The President was supportive. "You ought to get out of government and go in the circus if you can do that," he kidded. The bar where the incident allegedly took place started selling Amaretto and cream with a new name: Jordan's Lotion.

These "funny" tales about me gave rise to a stream of "Hamilton Jordan stories" that ranged from the very trivial to the very serious. One of the more famous ones was about my refusing to give Speaker Tip O'Neill inaugural tickets (something that never happened); another was about my coming to work in blue jeans (I hadn't owned or worn a pair in twenty years). I knew that people had stopped taking me seriously when Jody was asked at one of his official White House briefings if I wore underwear or not. Jody told the female reporter that she would be the last to know one way or the other. Everyone else on the White House staff thought that was hilarious, but I didn't.

In less than a year, I had become a caricature, embodying all of the bad things—real or imagined—that the Washington establishment didn't like about Jimmy Carter and his Administration: I was seen as an arrogant, impolite rube.

Then the rumors and gossip gave way to more serious charges.

In the middle of the Camp David negotiations with Begin and Sadat, Jack Anderson wrote a story stating that Charles Kirbo and I had received $10 million from fugitive financier Robert Vesco as part of a scheme to fix his case with the Justice Department. After months of FBI investigations and weeks of front-page stories, Kirbo and I proved conclusively to a grand jury that Anderson's story was absolutely untrue.

In August 1979, shortly after I had been named Chief of Staff, I was charged with using cocaine at Studio 54 by two men indicted on charges of federal tax fraud who were plea bargaining with the

Justice Department for lighter sentences in exchange for information against me. I decided to treat the allegation seriously when I
learned that one of the attorneys for my accusers was Roy Cohn,
the close friend and former aide of Senator Joseph McCarthy. A
special prosecutor had been appointed by the Attorney General
to investigate the allegation, and months later I was still fighting
that charge.

After the cocaine charge, I went even further into my hole,
stopped granting any press interviews, and became even more of
a hermit. I went to extremes to stay out of the public eye, not
going to Presidential press conferences or to events where I
might be caught by the camera. Maybe people would just forget
about me.

When Jerry Rafshoon was filming a campaign commercial about
life inside the White House, I told him to avoid shots of me.
"You're being too sensitive," he objected. But when the commercials were completed, I was nowhere to be seen in them. For
Rafshoon recognized—just as I did—that my presence would only
remind the American people of me.

One of my worst moments in the White House occurred when
I went into the Oval Office one day soon after the Studio 54
charge to see the President, who was just finishing a telephone
call to Lew Wasserman, the Democratic fund raiser and movie
mogul, in Los Angeles. "How did Lew say we are doing in California?" I had asked.

"Not so good. He says that all people are talking about out
there is the story about your using cocaine."

I blushed, muttered that I was sorry, and started to leave, for-
getting the reason for my visit. The President stopped me and
said, smiling, "Don't let it get you down, Ham. Look what they're
saying about me!"

I changed the subject, finished my business, and left the office.

Now I was terribly concerned about keeping my own involvement in the hostage crisis out of the papers. And on more than
one occasion when it looked like my negotiations with Bourguet
and Villalon might bring our people home, I allowed myself the
selfish thought that if I helped to free them, it would erase my
bad image and possibly even help the President.

When Cy and Hal returned from New York, the three of us went to the Residence where Jimmy Carter, his family, and some senior staff members were watching *Coal Miner's Daughter*. The President left the movie and met with us for about half an hour. He seemed relaxed and happy, and I couldn't tell whether he was confident for the first time about the hostages or just enjoying the movie.

February 19, 1980 (Tuesday)

I was awakened before dawn by the Situation Room. A French news agency had reported that I had met with Iran's Foreign Minister Ghotbzadeh in Paris on Monday. Ghotbzadeh had denied it. Later in the morning, at his press briefing, Jody denied the story about Ghotbzadeh, confirmed that I had "traveled abroad" on behalf of the negotiations, and refused to say any more. I was deluged with press inquiries, which I referred back to Jody's office. By the end of the day, Jody described himself as being "pleasantly surprised" at how little follow-up there had been on my role. "But," he said, "it was probably overshadowed by the story out of Tehran that Bani-Sadr had cabled Waldheim to welcome the UN Commission and hinted strongly that Khomeini would publicly endorse their trip to Iran."

The actors were waiting offstage, ready to play the roles assigned to them by Bourguet, Villalon, and myself in our carefully constructed political scenario. Now if they would only remember their lines . . .

I skipped a regular meeting with the President so that I could begin work on the tricky wording for his statement regarding the final stages of the plan. The campaign was increasingly becoming a nuisance for me.

February 20, 1980 (Wednesday)

The wake-up calls seemed to be coming earlier and earlier. Today the White House operator rang me up at 3:35 A.M. to add me to a conference call already under way with the President, Warren Christopher, and Hal Saunders.

"Mr. President, the news from Tehran this morning is not good," Christopher began. "Iran's official government news agency has released a statement from Khomeini supporting the 'students' at the compound and calling for the return of the Shah as a condition for the release of the hostages."

"No, that's certainly not very good news, Chris. And it calls the whole scenario into question. Ham, what do you think?"

"Mr. President, it doesn't sound good, but we mustn't over-react. I think we should try to get in touch with Bourguet and Villalon and get their reading on this. Khomeini's rhetoric is often ad hoc and contradictory. He might even be softening up the militants prior to ordering them to release the hostages."

"That's an optimistic analysis, Ham," Carter said quickly. "Khomeini's statement can really screw things up."

Hal and I reached Precht in Paris and he tracked down Bourguet, who tried to reach Ghotbzadeh on his tour of European capitals trying to prevent the imposition of permanent sanctions against Iran. Bourguet had no explanation for Khomeini's statement and called it "very disturbing"; he said, however, that the announcement of the UN Commission had not made the formation of the commission look enough like a victory for Iran. Also, Bani-Sadr didn't have his copy of the scenario when he sent his telex to Waldheim, so he hadn't used the precise language it called for. "But don't worry about that," Bourguet assured Henry. "Ghotbzadeh said he would straighten that out."

Later that morning we received the disturbing news that the commission's trip to Iran had been delayed by the Iranians for three days. I was very depressed. The combination of Khomeini's statement and the commission's delay shook my confidence in the scenario.

February 21, 1980 (Thursday)

It was 5:30 A.M. when Henry Precht called from Paris. He had just heard from Bourguet, who had talked to Ghotbzadeh. The reason the commission was delayed in going to Iran was "technical," Ghotbzadeh had explained, and we shouldn't worry. "Bourguet said the delay wasn't a big concern. The Iranians just weren't ready for them," Precht reported.

"What do you mean, 'not ready'?"

"Not ready with hotel accommodations and office space. Also, Christian suspects they've done a poor job of assembling their 'evidence' against the Shah. Bourguet said that Ghotbzadeh was anxious for him to come to Tehran, and suspects it's because they need help in compiling those charges."

Precht told me that Villalon was en route to Geneva to make contact with the chairman of the commission.

"Henry, it hasn't been easy explaining all these stops and starts and statements coming out of Iran that seem to violate the scenario. You should tell that to Christian. Everybody here is still on board, but there are some doubts now," I said.

"I understand—hell, I have some doubts too."

February 22, 1980 (Friday)

At the Friday meeting, Warren Christopher reported that Vance's trip to Europe was generally upbeat. He said prospects were good that our European allies would join us in boycotting the Olympics. "They've each got their own domestic politics to consider, but sooner or later I think they'll all join us," he told us.

We went on to talk about SALT II. The President said he knew that ratification of the treaty was not feasible anytime in the near future, but he hoped we could keep the treaty alive until after the election. "I would hate to think," he said, "that we'd have to start from scratch with the Soviets a year from now."

Finally, Carter asked me to report on Iran. I summarized the events of the last few weeks, the mixed signals from Tehran, and the reasons the Iranians were not ready to receive the commission. "But there's no doubt," I said, "that the UN team will be able to travel tomorrow, and Bourguet reports that everything's on track."

As discussion of the commission's work ensued, I found myself having to rationalize and defend some of the statements made by the Iranians that week. I didn't like the posture that I was put in, but assumed that it went along with negotiating with the Iranians and believing that they would live up to the scenario. Both the President and Christopher were unquestionably concerned that what Khomeini had been saying tended to suggest that he was not following our script.

I also had to inform the group that the Shah was getting quite nervous, sitting on his private island and hearing what was going on. I suggested that we send a special emissary to reassure him, as we were about to enter a critical period when statements from him would be counterproductive. "Also," I reasoned, "he needs to be prepared for the commission and what it might say about him and us."

Christopher suggested that William Bowdler, a State Department expert in Latin America, would be a good person to send. The President agreed and asked that I draft talking points for him and Christopher to review.

A short time later, while I was in my office working on the message to be delivered to the Shah by Bowdler, Precht called from Paris. He had just spoken with an optimistic Bourguet, who was in Tehran meeting with the Iranian leaders. Bourguet reported that, while there were "problems" between the government and the "students" at the compound, "the Revolutionary Council remains committed to the scenario."

I went to the Oval Office to share the good news with the President and returned to finish the message for the Shah. I typed, "While this commission might receive information and accusations that are unpleasant and untrue about President Carter, the

United States, the Shah and his family, we hope that Your Majesty can understand that their work will very likely lead to the release of our hostages." I offered reassurance from our government that the United States would not tolerate his extradition under any circumstances and that we had received similar assurances from General Torrijos that we believed were made in good faith. I ended with the suggestion that Ambassador Bowdler obtain a renewed commitment from Torrijos on the extradition question prior to visiting the Shah. *Maybe that will reassure the King,* I thought.

February 23, 1980 (Saturday)

I was reading the morning *Post* when the phone rang at my apartment. It was the signal operator from Camp David. Customarily, the operator said that the President was calling, waited on the line until Carter picked up, and then announced him. But this time he didn't get the chance. "Ham—what the hell is going on?"

I jumped up, startled by the anger in his voice. "Mr. President, I'm afraid I don't know what you're talking about."

"Well, I just got a call from Cy Vance, who said that Khomeini had made a statement this morning saying that the hostages would be dealt with when the Iranian Parliament assembles!"

"Oh, my God, no," I groaned, shocked to hear this news and unable to explain it. "That's terrible. I don't know what to say. I'll try to reach Bourguet and Villalon and give you a call back."

"Please do—and let them know that they are playing with fire. The commission is probably already on the way to Tehran now, believing that we have an agreement on a plan leading to the release of the hostages. And now this—it makes us all look foolish!"

"I understand, Mr. President."

"In fact, Ham, it looks as if we have everybody in the world roped into our scenario—our government, the UN, French law-

yers, Argentinians, Panamanians, the Revolutionary Council—
and it's starting to look as if the only person not involved is the
Ayatollah Khomeini!"

I told the operator to get me Hal Saunders and Henry Precht
immediately.

Maybe the President is right, I reflected as I waited for my calls
to go through. *Maybe Khomeini doesn't know anything at all
about what we're doing, and his minions are playing games with
us in hopes that when the time comes, he'll order the hostages
released.*

The phone rang. Hal said, "I bet I know why you're calling: the
Khomeini speech?"

"Yep. What do you think—and where does this leave us?"

"My first thought is that I wonder if Khomeini even knows
there's a scenario."

"You're reading my mind," I replied.

"Second—if he does, why would he say this? I wanted to have
someone here study his speech before we talked. Tentatively,
some of the people in the Department who are familiar with Khomeini's rhetoric and manner of speaking doubt that he made such
a speech and say it could have been written by someone else and
released to the news service as coming from the Imam. But
whether he made it or not, the effect is the same: the news media, the American people, the Iranian people, the commission,
and the militants at the compound now believe that the Parliament will deal with the hostage question."

"We're in a hell of a fix," I said. "Can you or Henry try to track
down Bourguet and Villalon and get a reading from them? And let
them know that there's a limit to American patience. Tell them,
Hal, that our credibility on the scenario with both the President
and Vance is very much in question, thanks to the Khomeini
statement today. I'm not kidding about Carter—he's upset."

"And you're not kidding about Vance—he's not going to like or
understand this one bit."

I talked with Hal and the President a dozen times during the
course of the day. Bourguet, Villalon, and the Iran experts had a
number of different theories about the Ayatollah's statement. Several thought it was the work of his son, Ahmed Khomeini, who
was working to establish himself as a power in Iran and might

have released it to thwart Bani-Sadr and curry favor with the hard-line militants at the compound. But I couldn't avoid the nagging doubt that Khomeini had never heard of the elaborate scheme that Bourguet, Villalon, and I had drafted with such painstaking care.

Bourguet's message was: "Tell Hamilton that one thing is sure: Khomeini can change his mind tomorrow and give the order for the hostages to be let go and it will be done. Don't be pessimistic yet. Let us see what the commission's work produces."

I passed this recommendation on to President Carter. He accepted it because we really had no choice, but I could tell that he didn't like it at all. Once again the head of the most powerful nation on earth was being asked to sit silently and patiently and wait.

February 24, 1980 (Sunday)

I spent most of the day at the White House on the phone with Saunders and Precht.

Bourguet and Villalon said that the members of the UN Commission had met satisfactorily with Ghotbzadeh and Bani-Sadr and planned their work for the week, including the steps to be taken for considering the evidence against the Shah and their visit to the compound to see the hostages. The chairman of the commission, Ambassador Aguilar, asked Bani-Sadr if Khomeini's public statement that the Majlis, the Iranian Parliament, was the ultimate authority for resolving the hostage question would jeopardize the work and schedule of the commission. Bani-Sadr replied, "No, we have a secret plan and we are going to execute it."

The commission staff reported to Saunders that the first day in Tehran had been "very constructive."

"We're on a damn roller coaster, Hal," I said at the end of the day. "Yesterday we were down, today we are up."

"Yes, but we can't stand many more days like yesterday--or I know a couple of American passengers named Carter and Vance who'll want to get off the ride!"

I went home as exhilarated as I had been depressed twenty-four hours earlier.

February 25, 1980 (Monday)

The morning was crazy, filled with mixed reports out of Iran. There was a long cable from Lang, the Swiss Ambassador to Iran, who communicated with Iran for the U.S. government. The cable attempted to analyze Khomeini's Saturday statement. There were last-minute calls to and from New Hampshire, where a critical primary would take place tomorrow.

In the middle of it all, we stopped to greet the United States hockey team, which had been invited to the White House for lunch with the President to celebrate its stunning win over the Russians and its gold-medal victory over the Finns. Jerry Rafshoon and I were relishing the favorable publicity the President would gain from this on the evening news.

Wagging her finger at Rafshoon in mock anger and laughing, Eleanor said, "It's the most shameless thing I have ever seen—the President is boycotting the Summer Olympics and welcoming the heroes of the Winter Olympics at the White House!"

"No," Rafshoon told her, "the most shameless thing we have ever done was to get Governor Jimmy Carter on 'What's My Line' when he was quietly running for President."

"And they couldn't guess who he was," I recalled.

"They didn't even know who he was when the emcee told them," Rafshoon said with a chuckle. "Now, Ellie, if we can just dream up a few more shameless things, Jimmy Carter will be re-elected."

February 26, 1980 (Tuesday)

Waldheim reported that the commission's co-chairs were feeling "optimistic," and that the Ayatollah Beheshti, leader of the clerics and the Islamic Republican Party, had told Western newsmen that the Majlis would not be organized and ready to deal with the "hostage question" for six to eight weeks.

Also, Bob Armao called me and Lloyd Cutler to report that relations between the Panamanians and the Shah's staff were "very, very bad."

February 27, 1980 (Wednesday)

From the glum look on Jimmy Carter's face early in the morning, you would never have guessed we'd just won a primary.

"Congratulations on New Hampshire," I said, hoping to brighten him up.

He painfully forced a smile. "There's not much joy in winning this year," he said in a low voice, "with everything else going wrong. Ham, I'm getting discouraged on the commission visit. We're sitting here helpless, being buffeted back and forth by events, being kicked around in the press, just watching and waiting. God knows, I realize that Bourguet and Villalon are doing the best they can, but we need to take the initiative."

"I share your frustration, Mr. President, and I'd like to do something—but what would you suggest?"

"Ham, I want you to get in touch with Bourguet and Villalon and make it plain to them that my patience is growing very thin. Tell them that Khomeini's statement over the weekend rocked Washington and created real doubt in my mind. Tell them that if something doesn't happen soon, we'll reveal the contents of the scenario."

"What do you mean by 'reveal'?" I asked.

"Publish 'em in the damn newspaper! If our hostages aren't going to get out, at least the American people and the world will know that we have been negotiating in good faith and the fault lies with Iran."

"I'm not sure that threat means much to them, but I've often heard that negotiating with Iranians is like haggling in the bazaar: they'll wait until the very last minute, when the deal is just about to fall apart, before closing it. Maybe some pressure from here will help."

"Well, frankly, Ham, I'm not asking for you to analyze what I'm suggesting and decide whether or not to do it—I just want you to follow my orders!"

"Yes, sir," I said quietly. I wasn't sure that what he was suggesting was right, but I knew that he had made up his mind and my job was to implement his decision.

I called Henry and Hal to my office right away. They had yet another long cable from Ambassador Lang. As was so often the case with reports from Iran, there were so many rumors, theories, and conspiracies floating around that you could find support for any assumption about events there. I was now sure that we were coming to a showdown between the factions in Iran that were using the hostages for their own political purposes, and the commission that was there to implement the scenario and free the hostages.

Saunders, Precht, and I drafted a message for Villalon incorporating the elements that the President had suggested, but leaving out the threat of publishing the scenario. We decided to do that in a written message that Bourguet and Villalon could show the Iranians. We got Stephanie on a conference call at the State Department and gave her the message to be read to Villalon. I recognized Hector's voice when he picked up the phone in his room. It sounded like he was half asleep. He and Stephanie exchanged greetings, then she began to read our message in Spanish. I listened for a while, then put the phone down and worked with Hal and Henry to draft a message through Lang for Bourguet and Villalon reinforcing the points we had made in the call plus the very direct threat to hand the scenario over to the press and demonstrate the bad faith of the Iranian leadership to the world.

"Hector was really angry that I called him at the hotel," Stephanie reported. "He said that it was a matter of life and death that I never, never call him there again. He was quite provoked. Then," she said chuckling, "he talked for over an hour."

He told her that Ghotbzadeh had met that morning with the commission, which was pushing him to stick to the terms of our plan. Hector said that perhaps we had created a Frankenstein's monster in the commission, as it was showing very little flexibility. Very confidentially, Villalon reported that the Revolutionary Council had approved the commission's visit to the compound in the next twenty-four hours and that Bani-Sadr had named Ghotbzadeh to orchestrate the details of that visit. As a show of good faith, Ghotbzadeh had arranged for the commission to visit the three hostages—Bruce Laingen, Victor Tomseth, and Mike Holland—at the Foreign Ministry, and that had already happened.

"And if they don't have enough problems," Stephanie continued, "relations between the commission and Ghotbzadeh have gotten so bad that both sides want Bourguet and Villalon to serve as middlemen."

I smiled. Hector and Christian always seemed to end up in the middle of everything.

I asked Stephanie to get me the "memcon"—memorandum of conversation—as soon as possible.

"How big a rush are you in?" she asked.

"Not much. But if you don't have it over here in the next hour, the President will probably just go ahead and bomb Tehran!"

The President and Vice President were having their weekly lunch, which was the "Vice President's time." They always lunched alone, and I never bothered them, but because of the urgency of the President's request that morning and the news that Villalon had conveyed, I took a chance and interrupted them. I told them what Villalon had said. Carter smiled and said to Mondale, "When things look bad to us here, Ham's friends say that everything is going well. When things look good, they say it looks bad!"

I knew he was teasing. He was clearly satisfied with what we had done to implement his orders.

February 29, 1980 (Friday)

All during the foreign policy breakfast I kept trying to find out the news from Iran.

Stephanie managed to talk with Hector again, this time at the Swiss Ambassador's residence in Tehran. "He's really upset," she told me. "He said that he and Bourguet are in great danger, that there have been threats against their lives, that the government has assigned them bodyguards, and that we should never again phone him at the hotel."

"Wow," I said. "That doesn't sound too good. They're under a lot of pressure. Maybe we shouldn't have called."

"That's not all," Stephanie continued. "Hector said to tell you that they were offended by the message delivered to them through the Swiss about revealing the contents of the scenario. He said that he and Bourguet are considering resigning from their assignment, that they are doing their best and don't appreciate being in the unusual position of being threatened by both sides, that they're trying to help. Hamilton, he really sounded serious and was almost rude to me."

I wanted to quickly repair any hurt feelings. We couldn't afford to have our intermediaries miffed just as we were going down the home stretch. "Stephie, try to call Hector back and tell him that they shouldn't take offense at our cable. We were simply stating what we would have to do if everything falls apart. But mainly tell them how much all of us here, the President included, appreciate and admire their courage and contribution. The last thing we intended was for them to take it as a threat."

We spent the next hours waiting for some word from Tehran.

At three o'clock, I went up to Lloyd Cutler's office to meet with Bob Armao, who had come to complain about conditions in Panama and to express the Shah's desire to move elsewhere. His presentation was peppered with "His Majesty this" and "His Majesty that."

I cut him off. "Bob, we are in the middle of some very delicate negotiations that could lead to the release of the hostages. The Shah's leaving now would be very damaging to what we are trying to do."

I promised that I would look into the situation, and would if necessary fly there to see Torrijos and the Shah. I was sure that Armao was exaggerating the Shah's grievances, but I thought it was important for the President to understand the Shah's state of mind. "Mr. President," I told him in the Oval Office, "he is scared to death. He doesn't trust the Panamanians and really believes they're going to either extradite or kidnap him."

"Ham, he's got my word and Torrijos' word that he won't be extradited. I don't know what else we can do," Carter said, exasperated.

"Well, according to Armao, his greatest fear is that some of the Panamanian guards will be bribed to kidnap him. He thinks that he'll be bundled up in the middle of the night and flown back to Iran."

The President paused for a second, then replied, "Ham, you can tell the Shah that, as President of the United States, I promise if the Panamanians try to fly him back to Iran, I will personally order the plane to be shot down."

I was first startled, then saw a grin creep across his face, and we both burst out laughing.

I considered the Shah's fear of kidnappers to be ludicrous, but on at least one occasion Bob Armao and Ambassador Ambler Moss had reason to assume otherwise.

According to one Panamanian official, Moss received a call one night at his home. It was from a panicked Bob Armao. "He's gone, he's gone!" Armao shouted into the phone.

"Who's gone?"

"The Shah—the Shah is gone! The Panamanians have taken him away!"

Moss was horrified. His first thought was, *I can't believe that*

Torrijos would allow this. But if he isn't on Contadora, where is he?

He asked Armao to please calm down and explain what had happened. Armao said that the Shah and the Shahbanou were scheduled to fly to Panama City the next day to look at a house they were considering buying, but two Panamanian security guards had come to their home with a change in plans: the Shah was to go to the mainland alone, spend the night in Panama City, and look at real estate in the morning. The Shah had reluctantly consented.

Then Moss panicked. He knew that Torrijos was extremely protective of the Shah—but had someone bribed a guard or even an officer? Moss began making inquiry calls, and even debated calling the State Department. But what could they do? After checking his regular contacts, Moss called "a very high official."

"Relax, my friend," the man said.

"What do you mean 'relax'? It'll be my ass if anything happens to the Shah. *Where the hell is he?*"

"I'm sitting here with my wife," the official whispered.

"I don't understand."

"Well, isn't the Shah entitled to a good time like an ordinary man?"

"What are you talking about?"

"A night on the town," the voice replied. "Omar has arranged for the Shah to have a night on the town."

Moss breathed a huge sigh of relief, and once again begged the Panamanians to be careful with their "friend."

(The Shah recalled that evening very differently in his book, *Answer to History*. He wrote, "I flew to Panama City for a secret meeting with the American Ambassador, who said he had a message from President Carter. My adviser, Robert Armao, planned to come . . . but Panamanian officials refused to let him attend.")

March 1–2, 1980 (Saturday–Sunday)

The UN Commission had been in Tehran for a solid week now, and still there was no guarantee that they were going to be allowed to see the hostages and implement the scenario. Messages from Bourguet, Villalon, and Swiss Ambassador Lang were all the same: "We are coming to a critical time. Please be patient." Khomeini left the Tehran hospital where he had been for some time, but he stayed in Tehran instead of returning to his home in Qom.

"Maybe he's staying there to be accessible to the Revolutionary Council and the militants to implement the release," I said to Hal Saunders in a telephone call.

"Ham, that's a very optimistic interpretation," he replied.

March 3, 1980 (Monday)

The day started out slowly. Snow was paralyzing traffic and staffers arrived late at the White House telling tales of trying to negotiate icy roads with drivers unused to bad weather conditions.

The President returned from Camp David at midday. I went down to see him, and found him outside in the Rose Garden, which was covered with several inches of clean white snow. He was helping his three-year-old grandson and namesake, James Carter, build a snowman. He adored the little boy, and they chatted nonstop while taking turns packing handfuls of snow on their creation. When the President saw me, he waved and walked inside, where he stood rubbing his hands before the blazing fire in the Oval Office. "This is one of those days when I'd much rather play with James than be President."

That afternoon Precht reported that Ghotbzadeh was pushing hard for the commission to see the hostages under the decision taken by the Revolutionary Council, but that the militants at the compound were stalling. "They claim, Ham, that President Carter had said the reason for the commission's visit was to gain the release of the hostages, and that they won't allow the visit until that is clarified," Precht explained. Both Bourguet and Villalon seemed to think that the visit would take place in another twenty-four hours.

I didn't really have the stomach to give the President one more explanation of why the visit hadn't taken place and ask him one more time to be patient. So I typed a brief memo, and left it in his "in" box. He wrote a note in the corner—in larger handwriting than usual—and sent it back to me: "Ham, they are crazy. J."

March 4–10, 1980 (Tuesday–Monday)

We were on a roller coaster again Tuesday and Wednesday: one hour we would get positive news stories, and the next they would be contradicted by discouraging cables from Bourguet and Villalon via the Swiss; then, several hours later, upbeat messages would come from Bourguet and Villalon, and in the meantime the news reports would be negative.

The commission was becoming frustrated and embarrassed by its inability to carry out its mission as prescribed by the Secretary General. The five members, all prominent diplomats in their own right, were sensitive about their own honor and that of the United Nations. Hector and Christian complained that they were spending half their time baby-sitting the commission and the other half pushing Bani-Sadr and plotting to complete the visit to the compound and the transfer of the hostages.

I received a call before dawn Thursday morning. "Mr. Jordan, I have a statement that I think you'd be interested in," the Situation Room duty officer said. He read: "A leader of the 'students' at the American Embassy released a statement today in Tehran which said that they, and I quote, 'are prepared for the Council to take the hostages, the American spies, and do with them what they wish.' They went on to say that this was their own decision and was not an order from the Imam."

"Thank God," I said to the duty officer. "It's finally happening." I rushed to the White House.

Eleanor didn't allow herself to get excited too often. Someone, she reasoned, had to maintain a level head and some degree of sanity. But when I reached the office, she was beaming. "Congratulations, Hamilton, it sounds like this is it!"

"I think it finally is, Ellie. I think it finally is."

I ran down to the Oval Office to tell the President, and my enthusiasm was chilled by his response. "Really?" he said, looking up from his paperwork. "I'll believe it when it happens." And he turned back to his work.

Precht called at 9:30. Bourguet and Villalon had advised us to respond to the announcement in a "nonjoyous way" and said that the defeat of the "students" was a great victory for the government and Ghotbzadeh. "They said the transfer would take place Sunday, Hamilton."

"Why in the hell are they waiting so long?" I said. "Anything can happen over there in a few days. They ought to move while they have the momentum."

"That's what I told Christian, but he said there were a lot of problems. For example, there are mines at the compound that have to be cleared, places have to be found for the hostages to stay, and they have to work out a safe way to take them from the compound to wherever they're staying."

After talking to Henry, I was still optimistic but realized that the transfer was iffy.

I spent Friday, Saturday, and Sunday on the phone, trying to find out what was happening in Tehran. It was obvious that the UN Commission was sitting on the sidelines while the struggle for control of the hostages was being played out. Ghotbzadeh and Bani-Sadr were trying to implement the scenario, and the clerics, led by the Ayatollah Beheshti, were trying to thwart the release.

By Saturday, Bourguet and Villalon reported that the plans for the transfer of the hostages to the Iranian government were proceeding, that Ghotbzadeh was actually meeting with representatives of the "students" from the compound and the military commanders who were to fly into the compound and take the hostages out to the Foreign Ministry. There, fifty beds had been set up and the windows had been covered to protect the hostages from rocks thrown by demonstrators or even possible sniper fire. When I heard these practical details, I allowed myself to be excited again: "Eleanor, it sounds like it's actually happening!"

At the suggestion of Bourguet and Villalon, we had the President cut a tape, which would be played to the hostages once they were released. But by late Saturday afternoon, the reports were gloomy. "Ham," Henry Precht said to me over the phone, "I hate to tell you this, but I'm afraid everything's turned sour again." The "students" had refused to turn the hostages over to Ghotbzadeh, whom they accused of lying to them about having Khomeini's support for his plan. Also, a statement put out by Khomeini's son, Ahmed Khomeini, had cast doubts as to whether his father really favored the transfer. Ghotbzadeh had tried and failed to convene a special meeting of the Revolutionary Council to deal with the "students"; the scheduled transfer had been put off once again.

On Sunday, Ghotbzadeh met with the Council but failed to persuade them to confront the "students" and issue an ultimatum. The Council agreed only to meet with Khomeini on Monday morning to seek guidance. Khomeini then said he would order the "dear students" to allow the commission to see the hostages if the commission chairman would first make a public statement of its findings of the Shah's crimes. Ghotbzadeh tried to persuade the commission to agree to the substantial deviation in the scenario, but before they had time to even consider it seriously, Khomeini's "plan" was broadcast on Tehran radio and television, and the commission members, feeling they had been compromised, began to make plans to leave Iran.

Ghotbzadeh, Bani-Sadr, Villalon, and Bourguet made a last-ditch effort to keep the commission in Tehran. Saunders, Precht, Jody, and I sat in my office, talking back and forth, directly now, with Bourguet and Villalon, who were in one room of the Hilton

Hotel in Tehran while the UN representatives were in the next room, where Ghotbzadeh was trying to persuade them to stay. The President's position was plain: he wanted them to remain and work on the scenario if they were willing to, but not if the scenario were to be changed. "We can be flexible on the details of the scenario, but not the principles," he told me.

At about 7:00 P.M. Monday, the President walked into my office, "What's happening now?" he asked.

"Mr. President, I'm afraid the commission is going home."

"I don't think the Iranians had any intention of following the scenario," he said sharply, adding, as he turned to walk out, "and I'm not sure if our people will ever come back." (It would be alleged afterward that President Carter had talked with Bani-Sadr on the phone and had pleaded with the commission members to ignore their mandate and stay in Iran. Neither is true.)

The failure of the commission prompted Bourguet and Villalon to suggest that we get together right away in Bern.

March 13, 1980 (Thursday)

I arrived midmorning in Bern and found Bourguet, Villalon, Precht, Saunders, and Stephanie hard at work in the same room at the Bellevue Palace we'd been in weeks before, as though they had never left.

They were all smiles and jokes when I walked in. "Here comes the problem," Hector said, as Stephanie translated.

I was surprised by everyone's good humor. I soon learned why. Bourguet explained that although the commission visit had not succeeded, its failure and the confrontation between the government and the "students" had embarrassed Bani-Sadr and the Revolutionary Council. "They met after the UN Commission left," Villalon reported, "and addressed the question: Who is in charge of this country?—the 'students' or us? They are going to try to answer that question affirmatively."

"Hamilton," Bourguet said, "we bring you a message from Bani-Sadr. He told us to tell you that the government will take control of the hostages within fifteen days. That is a promise from him to you!"

As I heard it, I got excited once again. I had been disappointed so many times before. What was a promise from Bani-Sadr really worth? Maybe not much, but it was the first time during the entire crisis that they had taken the initiative in pledging a date for action.

"I hope it's true, but we need to nail his promise down so Bani-Sadr will feel pressure to deliver. I think I'll write him a letter."

While the others worked in the sitting room area, updating the scenario—as the basic elements were still valid—I sat in the bedroom and wrote out on Bellevue Palace stationery a three-page letter to the President of Iran.

March 13, 1980

Dear President Bani-Sadr:

I was pleased to receive your message of March 10th that the fifty-three American hostages would be transferred to the custody of the Iranian government within fifteen days. I have conveyed that message to President Carter, and he considered it an encouraging development.

[I then described the growing impatience of the American people, and how, despite pressures to the contrary, the President had shown restraint.]

However, the atmosphere of restraint created and sustained by President Carter is diminishing every day and cannot last forever. A growing number of political figures in our country are calling for extreme measures against Iran, but still the President has refused to use anything other than peaceful means for resolving this crisis between our nations.

[I then talked about the objective we had of trying to build a new relationship with Iran after the crisis.]

But, quite frankly, the possibility of having a relationship in the future will not be possible unless all the hostages are returned safely to our country at an early date.

Sincerely,
Hamilton Jordan

Bourguet and Villalon thought the letter was the right tone—firm in saying the hostages must come home but not antagonistic; and restating and taking for granted Bani-Sadr's pledge that the captives would be released within fifteen days.

We stayed up all night completing the work on the revised scenario, which I would take home with me the next day with the letter to Bani-Sadr, which I wanted Carter and Cy to see before it was sent.

March 16, 1980 (Sunday)

I had been from Washington to London to Bern to Paris to Washington in seventy-two hours, and I hadn't had any sleep at all during the twenty-four hours I had been in Bern, so I slept late and well Sunday morning. The failure of the UN Commission had made me feel frustrated with the Iranians, but the optimism of Bourguet and Villalon was contagious. When I arrived at the office at midday, I was sure we could get the scenario back on track. I was surprised that Eleanor was at the office on Sunday. She handed me my messages: there were calls from Gabriel Lewis; Dr. Garcia, Torrijos' friend and personal physician; Warren Christopher; and Ambassador Ambler Moss.

"Oh, my God," I said. "Something must be happening with the Shah—and it can't be good!"

I soon had the story. The Shah's recovery and weight gain had reversed quickly and dramatically. His Panamanian doctors, monitoring his condition through regular blood tests, had concluded that his spleen had to be removed right away. Dr. Adan Rios, the Panamanian oncologist whom Dr. Kean had charged with the Shah's care during his stay in Panama, had been trained in blood cancers at the M. D. Anderson Clinic in Houston. He contacted oncologist Dr. Jeane Hester there, outlined the Shah's medical condition, and they concluded that a splenectomy should be performed immediately.

When Dr. Kean learned that other American doctors had been consulted without his approval, he flew to Panama immediately out of concern for the Shah's health and anxiety that control over the Shah's treatment was slipping from his grasp. He invited Dr. Michael DeBakey, the world-famous heart surgeon, to meet him in Panama and perform the surgery.

DeBakey arrived in Panama unannounced. The doctors there, unaware that he was coming, resented the implication that no local surgeon was deemed qualified to perform the surgery. Their national and professional pride was injured, and, feeling that they had been treated shabbily by the Shah and his American doctors, they issued a public statement that demeaned Dr. DeBakey, calling him an "itinerant physician."

Their acrimony was further complicated by a hot debate over which hospital would be used: Gorgas, a U.S. military hospital, which was technically on American soil, or Paitilla, a small Panamanian hospital with a solid medical reputation. Predictably, the Panamanians insisted on Paitilla and the Shah's American doctors demanded to operate at Gorgas.

Ambler explained that the Panamanian doctors were still angry with Kean but had already regretted their public insult to De-Bakey. Moss tried to appease both Panama's leading surgeon, Gaspar Garcia de Peredes, and DeBakey by striking a compromise that would allow DeBakey to operate at Paitilla, under satisfactory conditions, and allow the Panamanian doctors to save face.

Later, Ambler called to report that the Panamanian doctors had now invited DeBakey to join their operating team, assuring that DeBakey would be the lead physician, although they planned to leave that word deliberately vague. DeBakey accepted the invitation, but because of the conflict, plus a respiratory infection that was plaguing the Shah, they agreed to a two-week postponement of the surgery.

"Ambler earned his pay today," Eleanor said after reading his cable.

"Yeah, but I wonder what the Shah must think—he's probably scared to death."

March 17, 1980 (Monday)

Stories about the Shah's medical controversy began appearing on the television and in the papers, so I went in early to brief the President. I also told him that I thought we could get the scenario back on track.

"I don't see why you are so optimistic. Those bastards failed to live up to their commitment when the commission was there, so I'm not hopeful they will now."

The President sounded more than frustrated—he was beginning to sound angry. I made up my mind to keep working on him to give the plan a chance.

I talked with Saunders and Precht about the next step. Villalon was scheduled to go to Iran and would take my letter to Bani-Sadr.

Later that morning DeBakey phoned me from Panama. "Mr. Jordan, I have been in unusual medical situations before," he said. "I have operated all over the world and behind the Iron Curtain, but I have never encountered anything like what I saw over the weekend in Panama."

He went over the whole sequence of events. "I know that you have been involved with the Panamanians and the Shah, and I just wanted you and the President to know that I face a very, very difficult situation here."

"I understand, Dr. DeBakey, and I deeply appreciate your calling and keeping us informed. I don't have all the facts, but I think a basic mistake was made when the Panamanians were not informed of your coming and were not asked to participate in the Shah's operation. They feel like they were good enough to take care of the Shah up to now but are being ignored when surgery is needed. It's a matter of both national and professional pride."

DeBakey laughed. "I understand that very, very well from my meetings and discussions with the doctors. Mr. Jordan, I realize that I may have to come back here to Panama to perform the operation, so I have gone to great lengths to make amends with them."

"Can't the operation be safely performed in Panama at Paitilla hospital?" I asked.

"Of course—I can operate in a tent if I have to—but you must understand that my sole obligation is to the Shah's health. I have to tell you that I have qualms about operating in Panama after the experience of the past few days. I can't be in the middle of surgery and make a decision on a procedure or medication that may be questioned or challenged," he explained.

"I understand, Dr. DeBakey. I can't say a lot about it on this phone, but let me also tell you unequivocally that it is important that the Shah have the operation in Panama at the Panamanian hospital. If the Shah left Panama, it could jeopardize our negotiations and could mean the death of the hostages."

"That is your responsibility and the responsibility of the President, Mr. Jordan—just as the Shah's health is my responsibility."

March 18, 1980 (Tuesday)

Arnie Raphel, Cy Vance's executive assistant who had served in Iran, called to say that Ambler had met with the Shah and Bob Armao, and that my offer to go to Panama to meet with the Shah might have bought us a couple of days, but that while the Shah seemed resigned to the surgery, he was convinced that it could not be done safely in Panama. "They have promised to keep quiet, Hamilton, but from Ambler's report, I believe that you had best get on down there."

What a crazy day! It was the day of the Illinois primary, the first test of Kennedy strength in a large industrial state. And it was the day my lawyers were scheduled to spend the afternoon with me reviewing questions prior to my appearance before the special prosecutor on the Studio 54 cocaine charges. Actually, we had been meeting almost every week now for more than eight months, going over and over every aspect of my case, playacting the scene in the courtroom, each of them asking me questions that the special prosecutor might pose. This afternoon we were interrupted constantly by calls from Panama and from the campaign.

I went home early that night to watch the results and made calls to Illinois thanking our supporters. We won 163 of the 179 Illinois delegates. It was the sweetest victory of the campaign, for not only had we defeated the Senator but we had also embarrassed Mayor Jane Byrne in her own city. I talked to a jubilant Strauss, who was in Chicago. "Kennedy ought to get out," he said.

"I think so too, and this ought to do it. But I've quit predicting he'll get out because I'm not sure he ever will."

I relayed to Strauss a bit of wisdom that Charles Kirbo had shared with me on his last visit to Washington. "You know, Ham," he had said, "it takes a lot of guts to stick your neck out and run for any public office, particularly President. But the only thing that's tougher than announcing for office is withdrawing from a race, 'cause when you drop out you are saying that you are quitting and that you're beaten. That's hard for a Kennedy to say."

March 19, 1980 (Wednesday)

When I arrived at the White House I had a message that Zbig needed to see me right away. An intelligence report had arrived: the Shah was planning to leave Panama for Egypt.

"What can we do?" I asked, appalled.

"Hamilton, Panama and the Shah are your specialty. I'm in charge of current leaders and big countries—you're in charge of former leaders and small countries."

I started making plans to go to Panama.

Elsewhere in the White House the mood was upbeat. The decisive Illinois victory was large and real and couldn't be ignored by either the media or the political community. We worked once again to orchestrate statements from party leaders calling for Kennedy to get out of the race before he permanently divided the party. We were already looking to the New York primary. Our polls looked good, but Joel McCleary, our bright and effective New York organizer, was nervous that the UN vote was still reverberating through the Jewish community. In early March, our UN Ambassador, misunderstanding the President's instructions, cast his vote in favor of a resolution condemning Israel. An embarrassed President Carter stated two days later that the vote was a mistake, but the political damage was already done.

"Are we going to win?" I asked Joel.

"I'd be satisfied with a one-vote victory. Everyone says we're going to win big, but it doesn't feel good."

I tried to discount his uneasiness.

I arranged for a plane to Panama. If the Shah was hell-bent on going to Egypt because he was afraid the operation couldn't be performed safely in Panama, I believed that the best way to convince him to remain there was to win over his doctors. I called DeBakey and asked if I could come quietly to Houston to visit for a few minutes on the way to Panama. He said he'd be glad to see me.

I had worked at a hospital while I was in college and had flirted briefly with the idea of going into medicine. I admired doctors, but also knew how easily they could intimidate laymen. The Shah had been allowed into the States because a doctor believed he was dying and needed emergency medical treatment "available only in the United States." We had not adequately questioned that judgment, and as a result our people were captives in Tehran. I was about to step into the middle of another controversy in which a medical decision was going to have enormous political implications. I needed some good, balanced advice.

I walked over to see Dr. William Lukash, the President's physician, a soft-spoken man who exuded confidence. I asked him to find someone who could accompany me to see DeBakey and possibly go on to Panama. He called me later to say that Dr. Norman Rich, a professor and chairman of the Department of Surgery at the Military Medical School, had volunteered to go.

I told the President about my plan. I started to say that I hated to be away with so much happening, but he interrupted. "We've got to try to keep the Shah in Panama. It will be bad for Sadat in the Arab world to have the Shah there now, not to mention the reaction of the militants against the hostages if he moves again."

The President asked Zbig to call Egyptian Ambassador Ashraf Ghorbal, who confirmed that Sadat had invited the Shah and that the Shah had accepted.

"It sounds like an open-and-shut case," Brzezinski reported.

"I'm afraid so," Carter said, "but Ham ought to get on down there and give it a try."

I spent another hectic afternoon with my lawyers, preparing for my meeting with the special prosecutor. Our time was again cut short by calls from Panama and from the campaign—this time about the New York primary. "If we beat Kennedy there," Rafshoon said, "that will be the nail in his coffin."

Late in the afternoon we had a campaign meeting in the Residence with the President and First Lady. There was a lot of laughing and joking about the pasting Kennedy had taken in Illinois, but Carter directed his attention instead toward the next battle—New York. Bob Strauss and Tim Kraft told about last-minute plans, and Rafshoon and Caddell reviewed the polls and media arrangements. The President liked and trusted Joel McCleary and asked me what I had heard from him.

"He's nervous, Mr. President, particularly about the Jewish community," I said. "But Joel is always nervous."

March 20, 1980 (Thursday)

Arnie Raphel and Norman Rich were waiting for me at Andrews Air Force Base when I arrived, and we took off immediately for Houston. Raphel and I began briefing Dr. Rich, a quiet and unassuming man who seemed knowledgeable and confident about facing DeBakey and the foreign doctors. He was sensitive to the fact that American doctors often underestimated medical practices in other countries.

I said, "I'm going to try to appeal to DeBakey's sense of patriotism and ask him to help us persuade the Shah to remain in Panama for the operation."

Rich warned me to be subtle, as DeBakey's first obligation was to his patient; but Rich felt that the spleen could be safely removed in Panama and that DeBakey and the Panamanian doctors could jointly perform the surgery.

By the time we reached Houston, I was sure we had the right man.

We went straight to DeBakey's office. He seemed surprised that we had a doctor with us. He looked spry and much younger than his seventy-two years. And his gracious manner belied the "Black Mike DeBakey" reputation he had among his colleagues, who feared both his ego and his drive for perfection in the practice of medicine.

He showed us into a handsome conference room which was dominated by a large wooden table. Dr. DeBakey and I sat at opposite ends of the table, and Rich and Raphel took seats on either side. DeBakey offered us coffee and began chatting about his work.

"But you didn't come this long way to talk about the clinic, Mr. Jordan. Tell me what I can do to help you."

"Dr. DeBakey," I started, "we understand that the Shah is considering leaving Panama, primarily because he isn't convinced that the operation can be safely performed there."

"Can you blame him, Mr. Jordan, after what he has been through? It is very tragic for a sick man to see his doctors fighting over his care. Let's say it doesn't inspire confidence."

DeBakey was obviously still burning over what had happened in Panama.

"No, I can't blame him, Dr. DeBakey—but the Shah of Iran is not your average patient. We're dealing with crazy people! His leaving Panama could bring harm to the hostages . . . they could even be killed. We would like your advice as to what can be done in Panama to make both you and the Shah comfortable about having the operation done there."

"I'm not sure if there is an answer to your question, Mr. Jordan. I can operate anywhere, but my obligation to my patient—the Shah or anyone else—is to secure the best possible circumstances for surgery and recovery. I've made peace with the Panamanian doctors—in fact we really parted friends—but I can't forget their earlier behavior. Now I'm left with the question, despite any promises, of what could happen during surgery or postoperative care. Am I in charge or not? Will my orders be followed? Mr. Jordan, I don't mind taking responsibility for my patients, but I won't take responsibility without authority." He was beginning to sound like the Black Mike of medical legend.

He paused and described the Shah's condition to Dr. Rich. "It is not difficult or unusual surgery, but it is not without risk. Again, Mr. Jordan, I'll operate where I have to, but I cannot be pleased about the prospect of doing it in Panama. And even if you could satisfy me, Mr. Jordan, I'm not sure if anyone can persuade the Shah to have it done there."

My heart sank. It looked as though we were in a trap. "But, Dr. DeBakey—think about the hostages," I pleaded.

He stared hard at me and then said in a gentle voice, "Mr. Jordan, that is your problem and the President's problem. The Shah's health is my problem. I don't want to appear insensitive to the consequences of the operation, but our basic obligations in this instance lead us in different directions."

Raphel and Rich joined in, but DeBakey did not yield. We were going to have to change the Shah's mind.

We got back on the Air Force jet, which headed for New Orleans to refuel. On the way, one of the pilots reported that the radar wasn't functioning. He said we could probably make it to Panama without radar as the weather looked pretty good, but that it would be safer to swap planes.

"Are you kidding?" I said. "Don't take any chances for our sake. I'm not crazy about flying anyway—I was in two air mishaps in Vietnam."

A substitute plane was going to have to come all the way from Washington; we waited for several hours at a small private terminal at the end of the field in New Orleans. We boarded again and were just above the city when the new plane turned and headed back to the airfield.

The pilot, obviously embarrassed, came back and explained: a malfunction. It couldn't be repaired quickly so they were radioing for yet another plane.

Again we cooled our heels at the airport. To make use of the time, Arnie and I sat down and drafted a cable for the President and Vance outlining what we had learned from DeBakey. At the end of the cable we said that our objective in going to Panama was to convince the Shah to have the surgery there. If we failed, we analyzed that, given Sadat's political situation in Egypt and the Middle East, the Shah would be allowed to return to the United States in keeping with the terms of the "Lackland Agreement," which provided that he could return in case of a "medical emergency."

But I was determined that we wouldn't fail.

We had been in the small terminal in New Orleans for five hours, and two more hours passed before the next plane arrived from Washington.

I did some thinking about the Shah and his time in Panama.

When the Shah had stepped off the plane in Panama on December 15, 1979, he did not look well to the Panamanians waiting to greet him. He was pale and drawn; his suit hung on him. Accompanying the Shah and his wife were a few Iranian and American aides, the Shah's Great Dane, and his wife's French poodle.

Omar Torrijos, who had great disdain for pomp and was offended by the myth of the Pahlavi dynasty, remarked later, "Twenty-five hundred years of the Pahlavi dynasty reduced to twelve people, a pile of luggage and two dogs."

The Shah forced a smile and shook hands with those who received him, waved weakly to a waiting press contingent, and climbed aboard the U.S. helicopter for the brief flight to the quiet island of Contadora. Once in the helicopter, a grim look returned to his face, and his wife rubbed the back of his neck.

After landing on Contadora, the group had driven in a golf cart to the home of Gabriel Lewis. Lewis, making constant apologies for the condition of the house, showed the Shah and his wife their new home, a dark, wooden house, surrounded by thick green trees and shrubs, perched high on a ridge overlooking the azure waters of the Pacific. The Shah did not say much but seemed to be satisfied. The Shahbanou was visibly pleased.

The group walked the quarter mile to the hotel for lunch. Word of the Shah's presence had swept through the hotel, and small groups of tourists gathered to gawk at him and his party. The Panamanian guards, noticeably nervous, kept even the children away.

They sat down in the hotel restaurant and began to make small talk. The conversation was light and easy. The Shah was obviously not feeling well, but he picked at his food and made an effort to be pleasant. It fell to Ambassador Moss to carry the conversation, and he tried to tell the Shah something about Panama.

The only time the Shah seemed genuinely interested in the conversation was when Ambassador Moss was explaining the progressive changes made in Panama as a result of Torrijos' emphasis on education. As a result of a concentrated effort, Moss reported, Panama had the highest literacy rate in Latin America.

The Shah told of his hope to educate his people by satellite, beaming lessons to every village in Iran which could be picked up on television sets supplied by the government. Teachers would not be necessary, the Shah explained, in most schools. In that way, he could conquer the widespread problem of illiteracy in Iran in one generation.

But sadly, he said, because of "that crazy man Khomeini, my dreams for educating my people will have to wait for the next Shah."

Moss didn't know much about Iran or its culture, but he questioned the wisdom of trying to educate by satellite. Did the Shah really think that he could replace the mullahs, the teachers, and the leaders of the villages, with satellite schooling? The Shah's ideas of modernization didn't seem to take into account the culture of his own people. No wonder he was overthrown, Moss had thought at the time.

For a while it seemed that the Shah might find in his new home the peace of mind that had escaped him elsewhere. The weather was warm, the island was beautiful, and the Panamanians were friendly. In the second week of their stay, the Shah told one of his Panamanian hosts that Contadora was his "Paradise Island."

The Shah regained some of the weight that he had lost after his operation, his healthy coloring returned, and he was even well enough to stroll around the island with his wife. He reported to his doctors that for the first time in months he was sleeping comfortably.

General Torrijos had made arrangements for a cook and valet to help the Queen in managing the house and for a secretary to assist the Shah in handling the hundreds of letters he received weekly. He took great pride in the sympathetic mail he received, and, when introducing his secretary to visitors, he would explain, "She is in charge of my fan mail."

The Queen went out of her way to be pleasant, brushed up on her Spanish and chatted easily with her new servants. But the Shah was as detached and aloof from the Panamanians as she was comfortable with them. His Panamanian valet, Cristóbal Valencia, recalled, "He was the King, and we were the servants—and we both played our proper roles."

The Shah and the Shahbanou fell into a routine which they followed the first two months on Contadora. They would sleep late in the morning and take a light breakfast of fresh fruit and coffee on the terrace overlooking the water. Torrijos had made special arrangements to fly American newspapers from the mainland to Contadora early each morning so that the Shah could read *The Miami Herald* or a day-old issue of *The New York Times*.

The Queen loved the outdoors and the sun, and she quickly immersed herself in life on the island. The Shah would spend his mornings reading books and news magazines and would occasionally write a letter or review his mail while his wife swam or water skied or dove for shells in the ocean.

To the delight of the Panamanian frogmen, positioned guarding the Shah against a possible commando attack from the sea, the Shahbanou often swam topless. Her dips in the ocean were major events for the security guards.

The King and Queen would have a light lunch alone, and in the afternoon the Shah could be seen walking the golf course with his huge black Great Dane or wandering over to the tennis court to watch his wife play. He would applaud her exceptional shots, and on at least one instance, cautioned the tennis instructor not to stand so close to the Queen when coaching her.

As had been their custom in Tehran, there was always tea in the late afternoon. During his reign, the Shah would use tea time to meet with a visiting American businessman or to flatter some Western journalist with an interview. But in Panama, their guests for tea were different. Sometimes Gabriel Lewis would drop by to chat or Ralph Tursi, the manager of the resort hotel on the island, would come by to ask if everything was to their liking. Tony May, the Queen's tennis instructor, was one of her favorites and often stopped in to see her. To their guests, the Shah would be polite but quiet, sitting on the terrace, staring out at the expanse of water.

Instead of being times of relaxation and enjoyment, the cool Panamanian evenings were filled with intense activity for the Royal Couple. After an early dinner, the Shah would study the television news broadcasts and then spend hours fiddling with his large shortwave radio, trying to get the latest news on Iran from the BBC. Occasionally he would pick up Iran and shout excitedly to his wife to come and hear the news "from home."

Because it was her only contact with the outside world and their own past, the Shahbanou spent four or five hours on the phone each night, talking to Mrs. Sadat or Jordan's President Hussein or to friends in America and Europe. Because of the time difference, her early evening calls would be to the States, and later she would talk with her friends in Europe and the Middle East, chatting easily in English, French, and Farsi. Occasionally she would convince her husband to abandon his radio long enough to speak briefly with the friend on the other end. On most nights when he retired or the servants were dismissed to go home, the Queen was still on the telephone.

The only time the Shah seemed to have any zest for life was when his children visited.

Their daughters, at school in the States, had wanted to move to

Panama to be with their parents, but the couple thought it more important that they continue their educations. The Crown Prince, who had been groomed all of his life to be Shah, had a strong sense of his own duty and never raised the possibility of moving to Panama.

When the children came, the Shah would immerse himself in his family, and they would spend long hours playing games, talking, and laughing. He would test his children on questions of world history, countries and their capitals and the names of rivers, switching from English to French to their native Farsi.

The couple kept up the pretense of the Shah's eventual return to Iran when their children were there. Whether he actually thought he would resume his throne was difficult to tell. There was no doubt, however, that the Shah firmly believed that his son would someday sit on the Peacock Throne—just as he had and his father before him. The Shah and his son talked constantly about events in Iran, with frequent references to "when we return."

One evening after dinner, the entire family sat on the porch and talked late into the night, enjoying the cool breeze. For hours, the Panamanians heard them laughing and speaking Farsi. Repeatedly, the Crown Prince would stand up, wave his arms wildly, raise his head to the sky, and shout loudly. His antics made his parents and sisters laugh to the point of tears. After several such outbursts, the valet asked the Queen what was so funny. "He is imitating that crazy man Khomeini," she replied, laughing.

But much of their conversation was about their homeland. The first several months after leaving Tehran were difficult for the Shah and Shahbanou. All the news was troubling. For hour after hour, he would sit by the radio, learning of the deaths of his old friends and colleagues: members of his Cabinet were denied trials and ruthlessly executed by Revolutionary courts; the officers of his armies, who had served under his father and himself, were dragged from their beds and murdered in cold blood. It was a terrible time for the Shah and his wife, and there were many nights when they went to bed in shock from the radio reports.

During their first few months in exile, the Queen had tried to discourage the Shah from listening to the radio reports, fearing it was more than he could bear. "It is my duty," he had said simply to his wife.

But the news now was of a different sort. There were stories about the chaos in Iran, the shortage of food and consumer goods, the news that Iran's precious oil production was reduced to only a trickle. In short, it was a nation and a people being torn apart by the constant struggle for control between the secular people and the clerics. The Shah took a perverse pleasure in recounting in detail the news broadcasts that described this situation. His very worst predictions about the "Iranian Revolution" were coming true, and he reveled in it.

By the middle of February, his diseased spleen, friction between his staff and the Panamanians, and news stories about his "extradition" had ended the Shah's tranquil life on his "Paradise Island."

Almost overnight, the enlarged spleen acted up, his general health deteriorated, and, in the words of Omar Torrijos, he looked like "a living dead man."

The relationship between the Shah's American staff and the Panamanians became as hot as the tropical sun. His American aides arrived in Panama with unhappy memories of their stays in the Bahamas and Mexico. Bob Armao had told me, "Every time we turned around in Mexico, López Portillo was bugging me to bring in some friend to see the Shah, trying to convince him to invest in a business deal." It came as no surprise to me that the Shah, believed by many to be a billionaire, would be the target of schemers and con artists, ambitious servants and entrepreneurs.

Armao and his assistant, Mark Morse, brought their suspicions and prejudices with them to Panama, and it wasn't long before the Shah's entourage was accusing the Panamanians of robbing His Majesty. They never appreciated either the Panamanian hospitality or the problems their presence caused their hosts. Because of the serious allegation that the Panamanian government had "ripped the Shah off," we were obligated to interview a number of persons and to examine voluminous financial records. From our research, there is no evidence that the Panamanian government charged the Shah's party for anything more than meals and lodging for the sizable contingent of persons assigned to protecting the exiled monarch. There were over two hundred security guards and frogmen on Contadora Island alone, working three shifts, guarding the royal family, their home, the island, and its approaches. Extra personnel were added to airport security to screen possible assassins.

In addition, because of Torrijos' decision to admit the Shah, there were demonstrations and even some rioting in Panama City. The Shah's presence also hurt the Panamanian tourist economy. The Contadora Island resort with its casino—both owned by the government—were popular vacation spots in Central America. The Shah's entourage arrived at the height of the tourist season, and the news of his being there and the fear of possible violence resulted in a sharp drop in reservations—occupancy at the island hotel went from close to 90 percent in December, when the Shah arrived, to less than 40 percent in January. The hotel's losses were estimated to be close to a million dollars.

The Shah's staff never documented the charges. A few scoundrels may have tried to take advantage of the Shah, but I am certain that their efforts were neither known nor condoned by the Panamanian government.

Torrijos was offended when Armao's complaints about overcharging reached him. He later told me, "That sissy [Armao] and his friend [Morse] get paid a commission by the Shah every time they accuse someone of overcharging them."

In addition to worrying about his spleen and his pocketbook, the Shah began to have concerns about his safety. The Iranians had announced publicly that he was "under arrest" in Panama and would soon be returned to Tehran for trial. Despite a personal visit from President Royo, who explained the Panamanian law to the royal visitor and assured him that they had no intention of extraditing him, rumors and news stories persisted through February. And the Shah, convinced by Armao that he was being exploited financially, began to speculate that he might be sacrificed at some point by Torrijos and Carter to liberate the hostages.

So I was headed into a hostile atmosphere to convince a sick, frightened man that he should stay. As we boarded another plane,

I wondered if I was going to be able to pull it off.

We took off and were at thirty thousand feet over the Gulf of Mexico, an hour into the trip, when we heard a loud explosion. The plane headed into a dive, the cabin filled with smoke, and the floor became so hot that I could feel it through my shoes.

The pilot didn't have to come back to see me this time. When the plane leveled off, I bolted to the cockpit and asked what was wrong. "Probably nothing serious," I was told. But I didn't believe them, as we were now skimming low over the water and both pilot and copilot looked worried. As they searched frantically for the problem, I thought, *Maybe this is it. I won't have to worry about the Shah or the hostages, Kennedy or the special prosecutor. We'll just vanish in the Gulf. They'll probably never even find us.*

The pilot and copilot were working feverishly. I knew I was a distraction in the cockpit so I returned to my seat, soaking with sweat from the terrible heat and the prospect of dropping into the water. I felt miserably helpless. Arnie and I talked nervously. I woke Dr. Rich and told him what was happening; he calmly said there was nothing he could do, and went back to sleep. I was both amused and disgusted by his logic and composure.

We headed back toward New Orleans, and I breathed easier when I spotted the faraway lights of the city. I had never felt better walking on solid ground than when we hopped down the steps at the New Orleans airport. We were in a routine: another plane was ordered and showed up in a couple of hours. It was now about 2:30 A.M. We'd left Washington fourteen hours before and, with the exception of the flight to Houston and an hour's stopover there, had spent the entire time waiting for planes and returning them. Tired, frustrated, and shell-shocked, we boarded our fourth airplane. I was almost too tired to worry. We had a couple of drinks and joked about our bad luck.

"I can just see it," said Arnie, "the newspaper headline: HAMILTON JORDAN DIES IN PLANE CRASH TRYING TO SAVE HOSTAGES. And over on page thirty-four, 'an unnamed State Department official and a military doctor were killed as well.'"

"Hell no, Arnie," I replied. "The headline would read, JORDAN CRASHES, SWIMS 200 MILES TO SAFETY and a small subtitle, TWO OTHERS DROWN."

After unwinding a bit, Norm Rich and Arnie went to sleep and I got back to thinking and worrying. *Dammit,* I thought to myself, *we almost got killed on this flight—the least the Shah can do is to consider the effect of his operation on our hostages. But maybe he doesn't care . . . maybe the tragic figure I talked with at Lackland is as cold and uncaring and even as cruel as his critics say.*

We landed at the Panama airport at 7:15 A.M. Poor Ambler, who had been getting up and going back to bed all night with each report of our new arrival time, was there to greet us. He took us right to his residence in La Cresta, the American Ambassador's home, a sprawling white house on a luscious green lawn atop a hill overlooking Panama City. Every time I visited the beautiful old house, with its high ceilings, fans, and tropical greenery, I felt I was in a Graham Greene novel.

March 21, 1980 (Friday)

After a couple of hours of uneasy sleep, I was awakened by Ambler. Things were happening, he said, and I'd better get to work.

"I've already talked to Torrijos," Ambler said, "and he's on the way to see you."

"Here?" I said, knowing that it was very unusual for the General to come to the American ambassador's residence.

"Yes, he knows that something is up with the Shah. And your being here just reinforces his suspicion. He may have heard about the Shah's plans. Torrijos doesn't miss much of what goes on around here."

We reviewed our strategy: the basic goal was to keep the Shah in Panama for the operation. "But to do that," I contended, "we must first have the cooperation of the Panamanian doctors. And then we have to persuade the Shah to stay."

"What if he insists on leaving?" asked Ambler. "I think he's dead set on it."

"We can't let that happen. We've got to figure out a way to keep him here."

Torrijos arrived shortly with Chu-chu and Dr. Carlos Garcia, his personal physician and the dominant force in Panama's medical establishment. Dr. Rich and Garcia began to talk, and Torrijos motioned me to join him in the library. He and I and Chu-chu settled into the cushion-stuffed wicker chairs.

"We've got problems, Papa General," I said. "We have information that the Shah has decided to leave Panama and go to Egypt."

Torrijos looked surprised as he listened to Chu-chu's translation. "Are you sure of this?" he asked.

"Yes, I believe it's true. We have confirmed it with the Egyptians."

"That would be bad for everyone—for the hostages, for the Shah, and even for Panama," mused Torrijos as he stuck a Cuban cigar with his name on the band into his mouth and turned to Chu-chu, who had a match waiting. "What can we do to change his mind?"

"We'll have to start with the doctors. I stopped off in Houston to see Dr. DeBakey on the way to Panama. He will operate here if he has to, but he'll not take an active role in persuading the Shah to stay. If the Panamanian doctors would invite DeBakey to perform the surgery, he might just consider it. Then the Shah would feel better about remaining."

I could tell that Torrijos was thinking as Chu-chu relayed my message.

"Doctors are strange animals with big skills and big egos," said Torrijos.

"I considered being a doctor," I replied.

"Your ego alone qualifies you," he shot back, enjoying his joke. "I can handle the Panamanian doctors, but I am not sure that the doctors alone can solve this problem."

We sat silent for a few seconds, then Torrijos said, "I'll do whatever you want me to—just tell me. We can let the Shah go or keep him here—and I'll make him stay here even if he doesn't

want to. I have observed this King—he cares about no one but
himself. He does not have the right to jeopardize the lives of fifty-
three others. All I care about is helping the President solve the
problem of the hostages."

I was surprised at the General's harsh words about the Shah
and his offer to force him to stay in Panama for surgery. *It would
be an extreme measure,* I thought, *but we are in a hell of a mess.
On the other hand, it would look terrible for the Shah to be detained in Panama against his will—and Torrijos isn't kidding.* I
wanted to acknowledge the generous offer but discourage him at
the same time.

"Let's try to keep him here first, then worry later about what to
do if he insists on leaving."

"I agree," said Torrijos. "Men of action usually succeed. Men of
inaction wait for something good to happen and it never does.
What is your plan?"

"I called Lloyd Cutler this morning. He's on his way, and we're
planning to see the Shah later this afternoon. That meeting could
very well be our first and last chance to change his mind."

Torrijos nodded, rolling the Cuban cigar around in his mouth.
After a long pause, he began to speak in a rapid, excited voice.
"We'll have to work to soften the mind of the Shah before you see
him. Don't worry about the doctors—I'll take care of them. Before the day is out, Dr. DeBakey will get a telephone call officially inviting him to return. Then I will call the Shah and try to
put him on the defensive by telling him that my feelings are hurt,
that I have been his host and have tried to be his friend for three
months, only to learn now through rumors that he is unhappy and
leaving Panama. I'll ask him why he is unhappy and sound a little
irritated. If he is really scared about being extradited, then I still
have some leverage on him."

While Chu-chu was relaying Torrijos' message, the General
rose and paced back and forth. I could tell that he was ready to go
to work. He stopped abruptly, half waved, and walked out of the
room into the foyer and out the front door, his entourage of security people and Panamanian doctors scurrying to keep up with
him.

"Armao has called again, asking when you are going to come see the Shah," Ambler reported.

"That's strange. I wonder why they're so eager to see me?" I replied uneasily.

"Maybe they just want to get your meeting out of the way so they can prepare to leave," Ambler mused.

"I've got a sick feeling that they might be anxious to see me so they can put in their request to return to the United States," I replied. "I made a real mistake at Lackland when we moved the Shah. I thought the hostages would soon be released and was so anxious to get him out of the country that we made it easy for him to return to the States. Under the agreement, he merely has to claim that he needs to return for medical treatment."

"The same way this whole mess started," added Arnie.

"Well, let's get on down to the embassy so we'll have access to the secure phone to Washington and the telex," Moss suggested. "It'll be a better place to work, and I'll have the driver bring Lloyd directly there when he arrives."

We went to the top floor of the embassy and camped out in Ambler's office, where we spent the balance of the morning outlining our plan of attack.

"I almost didn't make it," Lloyd announced as he walked into Ambler's office and shook hands around. "We lost an engine when my plane landed."

"We can top that," I told him, and gave him a rundown on our misadventures.

"We'll have to tell Harold [Brown] about that when we get back," Cutler said.

"I'll never again oppose increases in the defense budget," I assured them, and we all laughed.

I told him about our meeting with DeBakey, about Ambler's belief that the Shah had already made up his mind to go to Egypt, and about Torrijos' offer to hold the Shah in Panama against his will.

Lloyd was amused—and offended—by Torrijos' threat. "That's just talk, isn't it? He wouldn't really do that—would he?"

"Don't ever underestimate the General," Ambler said. "If we

gave him the nod or even winked, he'd do it all right."

"But that would put the President in a terrible position," Lloyd said.

"I agree—but isn't it funny to think about Torrijos telling the Shah that he can't leave?"

We agreed that because of the fluid situation we should check in with the President, and Lloyd and I called him on the secure phone. Much as Carter wanted the Shah to stay where he was, if this turned out to be impossible, he was adamant that the Shah not go to Egypt. "I will not do that to Anwar," Carter said. "He's got enough problems without having us dump the Shah in his lap. If he insists on leaving Panama, our position should be that we want him to come back to the States."

I was chilled. "But, Mr. President, that would endanger the lives of the hostages, it could—"

"Dammit, Ham—I got a cable first thing this morning saying that you and Arnie recommended that we not allow the Shah to go to Egypt, that if he left Panama it should be for the States. Make up your mind!"

I considered telling him that that cable was written in the middle of the night between our second and third planes, but decided against it. "I've changed my mind, Mr. President. Our first priority should be to try to persuade him to stay here, at all costs. A poor second option is to encourage the Shah to go to Egypt. Only as a last resort should he be allowed into the States."

"Well, I disagree," Carter retorted. He was clearly irritated with me and my flipflops. "I do not want the Shah going to Egypt. It is not fair to Sadat!"

"Well, let's work on keeping him here," said Cutler. "Is there anything we can do with the doctors?" he asked me.

"I'm sure Torrijos will work out the problems with the Panamanians. Our problem is DeBakey. The President could call DeBakey and make a patriotic pitch for him to take an active role in persuading the Shah to have the operation performed in Panama for the sake of the hostages and world peace," I suggested.

"I'm not about to do that," Carter responded quickly. "I'm not going to call DeBakey and ask him to abandon what he obviously thinks is a matter of principle."

The President was so inflexible about keeping the Shah out of

Egypt and so annoyed with me that I decided to let him cool off a bit. "Mr. President, let us kick it around here for a while and call you back later when we have some concrete ideas."

He got in the last punch. "I fully expect you to have changed your mind by the time you call back, Ham."

Lloyd and I discussed the President's adamant stand. Ambler's secretary poked her head in the door—Hal Saunders was calling from Washington. "He must have seen our cable about the Shah coming to the States," Arnie said under his breath.

"That damn cable was a mistake—I don't know what I was thinking," I said.

Although Hal was my senior in age and experience, he was an Assistant Secretary of State, while I was the President's Chief of Staff, so he always deferred to me. But today there was an edge in his voice. "Ham, I got this cable that you and Arnie sent to the President and Secretary Vance. I can't believe that the two of you actually recommended allowing the Shah to return to the States. They'll kill the hostages if he comes here!" His frustration and anger were barely disguised.

I didn't even try to explain it. "You're right, Hal. Arnie and I are busting our asses now trying to keep the Shah here. I agree that it would be a disaster for him to go back to the States."

"The Secretary tells me that the President is dead set against letting him to go Egypt," Saunders continued. "Can't you just keep him in Panama?"

"We're trying, but it doesn't look good right now."

"If he absolutely has to leave, it would be better for him to go to Egypt than to come here."

"What will it do to Sadat?" I asked, trying to make the President's argument.

"Ham, Sadat is the best judge of what he can tolerate in Egypt and the Arab world. He couldn't be more isolated than he is now. I'm not sure that having the Shah will make a big difference. Think about our interests. If the Shah returns to the States, I think the least they will do will be to try our people and probably kill them. We'll have to respond strongly, and all of a sudden we'll find ourselves in a war in the Persian Gulf! That will be bad for our country *and* for Sadat."

Hal never exaggerated, and hearing him talk about war scared me. *Maybe Torrijos' offer to hold the Shah in Panama will have to be exercised after all,* I thought. *It's our only ace in the hole, although not a very attractive one.*

"Hal, I agree with you. We just screwed up with that cable. You work on the Secretary and we'll work on the President and try to turn him around."

"The best thing would be to keep the Shah there."

"Hal, I don't think that's possible now. He's a selfish bastard who is only concerned with his own life. Lloyd is here with me and we're trying."

Ambler told me that Armao had called again to ask when I was coming out to Contadora Island to meet with the Shah.

I started thinking about going out to see the Shah. The press knew I was in Panama and that something was up. Maybe I shouldn't go.

"Gentlemen, I've been thinking. All the signs are that the Shah has already made up his mind to leave Panama. I think I should stay away from him. I'd go see him if I thought it made a difference, but if I went to Contadora and the press got a picture of me with him, it could jeopardize my negotiations with the Iranians. It could look like I'm part of his effort to avoid extradition."

Raphel and Cutler agreed.

Before they went to see the Shah, I needed to touch base with Torrijos to see what progress he had made with the Panamanian doctors. I climbed into Ambler's car and drove to the General's "base."

I almost dropped my teeth when I saw Christian Bourguet sitting on the couch beside Torrijos. It seemed so strange to see him in this setting.

There was no one present who spoke French, so we spoke English slowly and carefully to each other. Shaking hands, I said, "My friend, what the hell are you doing here?"

"I am here to file the extradition papers," Bourguet said, enjoying my surprise. "The deadline is next Monday. What the hell are *you* doing here?"

"Christian, the Shah wants to leave Panama."

The smile vanished from his face. "Leave Panama. That is very bad news, Hamilton. Very bad news. Where will he go?"

"Either to Egypt or to the States."

Bourguet sat up quickly as if someone had pinched him. "To the States? Not to the States! You cannot allow it," he pleaded. "They will kill the hostages!"

I explained the medical situation and our obligation to allow the Shah back in the event of a "medical emergency."

Torrijos, who had been unusually quiet, just smoking his cigar and listening, jumped up, and, pointing his finger to his chest, began speaking in excited Spanish. "I can keep the Shah here if I want . . . whether Hamilton likes it or not, I can keep him here for the operation," Chu-chu translated, "but I will not do it unless the hostages are transferred from the militants to the government. Tell *that* to your friends in Iran . . . tell them that they have twenty-four hours to move the hostages or the Shah will leave!"

Torrijos was using the Shah's threat to leave to push the Iranians on the hostages. I decided to sit quietly, not wanting to encourage the General's scheme or oppose it.

Bourguet and Torrijos discussed the plan, then Bourguet ended the conversation abruptly, saying, "I must go to the hotel and call Sadegh [Ghotbzadeh]."

After Bourguet left, Torrijos winked at me and, wagging his finger in my face, said, "Remember, my son, in military battle and political battle, always attack . . . even when you are low on ammunition."

Torrijos escorted me into the living room, where several men were standing around. With a sweeping gesture, he said through his translator, "Dr. Jordan, I would like for you to meet the Panamanian medical oligarchy."

We shook hands. "There are three doctors here," Torrijos continued, "but twenty-five different opinions."

They all laughed, then Torrijos turned serious. "These are brilliant men. They may not always be wise men [a reference, I thought, to the way they had treated Dr. DeBakey], but they are fine doctors, trained as specialists in the finest medical schools. They went to the same classes as your American doctors. They studied from the same textbooks and took the same tests."

Torrijos stood up and imitated a doctor leaning over the operating table, sawing off a limb. "They learned side-by-side with the American doctors how to carve up the body," he continued, center stage. Everyone laughed delightedly at his antics.

The General stopped abruptly. "We welcomed the Shah here. Our doctors treated him as they were trained to do in the States. The Shah gets ill and an American doctor arrives unannounced to perform the operation without our knowledge. Is it surprising the way our doctors reacted? They are doctors, but first they are Panamanians."

But DeBakey was welcome, he said, to come to Panama and be "the general of the doctors." The Panamanian doctors nodded their assent as Torrijos spoke.

We went back to the embassy for instructions from the President and Vance on the secure phone before Lloyd and Arnie went to Contadora to see the Shah. Carter was still firm in opposing the Shah's travel to Egypt. "I want you to see that he stays in Panama for the operation. God knows, I don't want him coming to the States. Remember, Ham, I don't want him going to Egypt. But if he insists, we'll have to accept him."

Cy got on the phone and suggested that if the Shah wanted to come to the States, we should insist that he abdicate. *Good old lawyer Cy,* I thought. *Never dishonorable but often sly.* But the proud monarch would find it difficult to step down.

"You'll be walking a tightrope," I said to the departing Cutler and Raphel. "The more you discourage him from going to Egypt, the more likely he is to say, 'OK, I'll come to the States.'"

They left around 9:00 P.M. for Contadora Island. In an hour and a half, they returned to Ambler's office. "You can relax, Ham," Lloyd said. "I think he's going to Egypt."

"What happened?" I asked nervously.

Raphel told the story. "We got there and found the Shah, the Shahbanou, and Armao waiting for us. The Shah seemed pleased to see Lloyd. Lloyd told Their Royal Highnesses quite pointedly that he wanted to speak with them alone. It ticked Armao off, but he left."

"Good for you, counselor," I said to Lloyd, pleased that someone had taken the opportunity to put the cocky Armao down.

"They were both quiet and seemed depressed," Raphel continued, "but they listened carefully while Lloyd discussed the Shah's choices: staying in Panama, traveling to Egypt, or returning to the States. The Shah made it clear from the outset that he was anxious to leave Panama and inclined to go to Egypt. 'I realize I am a dying man, so my concern is for my family and my country,' he said. Then he stared at Lloyd. 'But I want to die with honor, not on the operating table . . . because of a mistake or a bribe.'"

What I didn't know then—and I suspect the Shah didn't either—was that there was some foundation for his fears about not leaving Panama alive. I learned later that a Panamanian physician who operated regularly at Paitilla Hospital was approached by someone who offered him a million dollars if he would see to it that the Shah's surgery was "not successful." The doctor rejected the bribe out of hand. The Shah may have been justified in his worries, but I was equally justified in my faith that the Panamanian doctors were above being bribed.

Arnie went on with his account. "The Shah repeatedly referred to Sadat's generosity to him—not a very subtle reminder that he felt we'd treated him unfairly. They listened carefully to what Lloyd said about returning to the U.S., including the bit about abdication."

Raphel digressed. "I learned enough Farsi when I was stationed in Iran to know what the Shahbanou was saying after Lloyd mentioned abdication. 'Don't you dare abdicate!' she fussed. 'Think of our son and our people! Abdication would be a disgrace!' The Shah just sat there like a henpecked husband," Arnie said. "He told Lloyd he'd think about the choices, but indicated that they were heavily inclined to accept 'Anwar's kind invitation.' He promised to give Lloyd the final answer in the morning.

"Just as we were getting ready to leave," Raphel added, "the phone rang. Lloyd glanced at his watch and asked who was calling so late. The Shah hung up and reported it was one of his Panamanian doctors, drunk, calling to complain that he had not paid the $1800 bill for his most recent 'housecall.' The Shah smiled. Then he said, 'You wonder why I want to leave this place?'"

I felt a little better as we drove back to Ambler's residence. The Shah was undoubtedly going to leave Panama, but he preferred going to Egypt, where he felt he was welcome, over returning to the States without a real invitation. But if President Carter tried to keep him from going to Egypt by encouraging him to come to America, the Shah would accept that invitation in a second.

So, when I went to bed that night in Panama, I wasn't thinking about the Shah, sitting on an island several miles from me, but about Carter, thousands of miles away and hell-bent on keeping the Shah from going to Egypt.

March 22, 1980 (Saturday)

I got up early and began my campaign against the Shah's coming to the States. First, I called Mondale and then was able to catch Vance away from the President at Camp David. They both thought the Shah should not come to America.

Then Lloyd and I called the President. "Mr. President," Lloyd reported, "the Shah is going to leave Panama. It's just a question of where he goes. As it stands now, we'll meet with him later this morning, and I'm sure he'll tell us he's going to Egypt."

Carter pressed Lloyd, who reasoned that if we "urged" the Shah to come to the States, he would quickly accept. I took a deep breath and said my piece. "Mr. President, you keep talking about what's best for Sadat. Isn't it a bit presumptuous for us to say we understand his situation better than he does? How do we know what he can or cannot tolerate? Hal Saunders says that Sadat is already isolated in the Arab world and that this will be just one more thing, but won't make a lot of difference. If the Shah comes to the States, and they kill our hostages, and we have to take military action against Iran, and have a war in the Persian

Gulf, will *that* be good for Sadat?"

The phone was silent for a few seconds. I waited for the explosion. "All right," he said, "I'll call Anwar and see what he thinks."

In less than ten minutes, a cheerful Carter was calling us back. "OK, Ham, you guys get your way . . . you must have coached Sadat. I called him and told him that I was concerned about the Shah's going to Egypt. He said, 'Jimm-ee, don't you worry about Egypt. You worry about your hostages.'"

The President agreed that when Cutler saw the Shah later in the morning, he could encourage him to go to Egypt. Raphel and Cutler went out to Contadora. They returned in less than an hour. "He's leaving tomorrow morning, Ham."

"Thank God, Lloyd. Good job!"

I relaxed at Ambler's the rest of the day, determined to stay until the Shah had taken off. We heard several times from Bourguet, who claimed that Torrijos' offer to keep the Shah in Panama had put some fire in the Revolutionary Council, which was meeting continuously. I listened politely to Christian, but just wasn't going to buy it this time.

March 23, 1980 (Sunday)

I slept well for the first time in several days, comforted at least that the Shah was not coming to the States. I got up and had breakfast with Ambler and his wife.

Lloyd had taken the small plane and returned to Washington, but I was not going to leave until the Shah took off, just in case of last-minute hitches.

We waited and waited, getting periodic reports from both the Panamanians and Ambler's people that the Shah and the Queen had such a mountain of luggage to pack and move from Contadora that takeoff was repeatedly delayed. It was a sultry day. I jumped into the backyard pool at Ambler's house and floated around on a raft for a couple of hours, trying to relax, but the phone rang constantly. If it wasn't the latest report on the Shah's progress packing, it was a journalist calling for a comment from me. I consistently declined, letting Ambler make excuses. There were several calls from Bourguet saying that he had been on the phone with Ghotbzadeh, who was seriously trying to transfer the hostages to the control of the Iranian government in accordance with Torrijos' promise to "hold the Shah" if the hostages were released. I simply repeated what had to be our position: that the Shah was free to leave when he wanted to, and that I couldn't be any part of Torrijos' ploy. I told Bourguet, "But make no mistake—he's on his way. He's packing his bags."

At 1:40 P.M., Ambler received a phone call from the airport. "The Shah of Iran left Panama today at one-forty-two," Ambler announced.

"Let's go home," I said to Arnie and Norm. "But I need to swing by and thank Torrijos for all he's done. Panama has lost both ways. Torrijos made a lot of people here mad by letting the Shah in and now Panama is going to catch hell when all these stories come out about what happened here. Armao and company are really going to dump on Torrijos and us. Ambler, you're on good terms with the press. As soon as we leave, you ought to get them in and give them our side of the story while the Shah is en route to Egypt." Ambler agreed. We began to pack.

Just as we were leaving, the phone rang again. Ambler picked it up and handed it to me. "It's Christian."

"What is happening?" Bourguet asked.

"It's over, Christian—the Shah has left," I said.

"No, no," he said.

"He took off fifteen minutes ago."

"Hamilton, it is very, very bad. I just talked with the Minister. The Revolutionary Council is in session now and they are going to take the hostages away from the militants."

I had heard this so many times before that I didn't allow myself to be·either excited or optimistic. "Well, I'm afraid it's too late, Christian. I could stop the Shah's plane when he reaches the Azores in several hours, but only if there's hard evidence that the hostages have been removed from the compound."

"Please stay in touch," he said urgently.

The minute I hung up, the wheels in my head started turning. Maybe I had dismissed Bourguet's scheme too casually. Maybe the reality of the Shah's flight from Panama would shock the Iranians into action. I told Ambler what Bourguet was trying to do and asked him to convey any messages from Bourguet to our plane.

"You know, each of your trips is crazier than the one before," Ambler said.

"We're lucky to have you here, Ambler. Thanks for everything," I said, meaning it.

We stopped by Torrijos' house. I ran in alone to say goodbye. He was in a surprisingly good mood.

"Well, the drama did not end as I hoped, Papa," I said.

"No, but I am glad he has gone. A strange man, the Shah— timid, insecure, and very weak."

"You do know how much we appreciate your having taken him in."

"Panama is not big enough for a king," Torrijos said. "It is barely big enough for a general."

Our meeting ended, as usual, with a laugh and an embrace. (It was the last time I ever saw him; he died in a plane crash on the way to one of his several "homes" in the summer of 1981.)

Norm, Arnie, and I boarded the large plane that Lloyd had flown down in.

We had barely taken off when I received a call from Ambler: Bourguet had called and said the hostages would be moved in the next hour if the Shah were prevented from fleeing to Egypt. I knew that Bourguet believed it, but I didn't allow myself to. I had been disappointed too many times before.

"Tell Christian I will need proof that the government has taken the hostages away from the militants before I can do anything. It'll take the Shah four or five hours to reach the Azores. But, Ambler, stress to him that I will need hard, absolute proof!"

I told Arnie and Norm what had happened, and found myself

talking excitedly about how we could hold the Shah on an island off Portugal, where his plane would be refueling at a U.S. military base.

"But what then?" asked Arnie.

"I could have the President call him and really put it to him that the resolution of this world crisis depends on his not going to Egypt, and appeal to his pride—tell him he'd be a world hero. We could ask him to either return to Panama or agree to have DeBakey and his team fly to the Azores to perform the operation. Or maybe Cy could fly to the Azores and try to persuade him. What do you think?"

"The only problem with your plan," Norm responded, "is that the Shah right this minute is a very sick man. His blood reports look bad, and he's had a fever for the past several days. It might be hard to make him sit still long enough for Vance to get there. He's dying and he's desperate."

"With Iranians," Arnie said, "there is always a lot of bluffing and the deal is struck at the very last minute. It would be typical of them to wait until the Shah is escaping to Egypt to take action."

"My God, what an ending," I said.

I walked to the front of the plane and asked the communications officer to get Secretary of Defense Harold Brown on the phone. When the call came through, I reminded myself to be careful, as our conversation could be intercepted. "Harold, as you know, our friend is en route to Egypt. I would like you to hold his plane in the Azores when they land there for refueling. It is very important and could resolve our problem." He assented without asking on whose authority I was speaking; I was sure he thought the President knew what I was doing.

Arnie, Norm, and I continued to talk—and wait and wait. I phoned Ambler a couple of times and also spoke with Bourguet as we traveled.

"It's about to happen, Hamilton—the Revolutionary Council is meeting this very minute. Ghotbzadeh just left the meeting to take my call and asked how much time he had to make the transfer public. It is about to happen!" Christian said excitedly.

"Don't forget, I'll need proof," I said.

We worked ourselves up into a state of sustained suspense. I talked myself into thinking it was going to happen. More calls came in and went out to Bourguet and Ambler. Still, nothing firm from Iran.

The five-hour flight passed quickly, and soon we were in Washington, where waiting limousines raced us to the White House. Brown called my office to say the Shah's plane had landed in the Azores, was being refueled, but couldn't leave until the base commander had permission from Brown. We got on the phone to both Ambler and Bourguet.

Christian's mood had changed. "I am sorry, my friend," Bourguet said haltingly. Everything in Iran had fallen through, and the scheme for holding the Shah in the Azores wouldn't work. I called Brown and gave clearance for the Shah's plane to leave the Azores. The delay was so short that neither the Shah nor anyone in his entourage was aware that anything had transpired.

The President was livid when he found out that I had stopped the Shah's plane, scolding that I had grossly overstepped my authority.

March 24, 1980 (Monday)

The morning news showed the Shah of Iran arriving in Egypt and being welcomed by Sadat in a manner reserved for heads of state. There they were, hugging each other and walking arm in arm to the helicopter that would take the Shah directly to the hospital in Cairo.

"Let them shout until the end of the world," Sadat said defiantly. "We have received the Shah in the true spirit of Islam, not the Islam they preach."

Henry Precht called to say that he had talked with Bourguet in Panama, who replayed for him the conversations he had had with Iran. Again, Bourguet was advising Ghotbzadeh to explain the Shah's latest departure as "justice chasing a criminal." Henry reported that Bourguet was "frustrated and very depressed."

I suggested that Bourguet come through Washington on the way back to Europe. *Maybe now's a good time for him to meet the President and get a direct sense of Carter's mounting frustration,* I thought.

Later that day, Torrijos issued a statement that he had made a "mistake" trying to deal with the government of Iran, that there was no government of Iran and he should have been dealing with the "students" all along, as *they* were the real power in Iran.

The President called me in the early afternoon and, obviously not wanting to be very precise, told me to "check with Harold Brown" about something "sensitive" that had been discussed at Camp David while I was in Panama.

I arrived at a nervous White House. The crucial New York primary was the next day. The polls were encouraging, but Caddell and Rafshoon, who were on the scene, and Joel McCleary, our campaign manager, were extremely wary. Although we had reversed our UN vote on the resolution condemning Israel and had been explaining our position, the flap hadn't cooled off, and the mood in New York's large Jewish community was very hostile.

I called Brown on my secure phone. The President wanted me briefed on a sensitive matter, he said. When could I do it? He seemed anxious so I said I had some time that afternoon. He said he would send General Pustay over.

General John Pustay, the top staff person to General David Jones, Chairman of the Joint Chiefs, arrived at my office with two cardboard tubes under his arm. "My instructions are to give you an update on the rescue mission," he said as he spread maps and charts on my conference table.

"Rescue mission?" I said, surprised. "I haven't heard anything about it for quite a while." I locked my door, picked up the phone, and told Eleanor to hold all calls, even from Strauss, Rafshoon, and Caddell.

A precise and articulate man, General Pustay began a presentation that I suspected had been carefully rehearsed. He told me that at the time of the seizure of the hostages, the initial estimates for a successful rescue mission were quite low. However, a team had been training and it was thought now the mission had a reasonable chance for success and could be seriously considered by the President.

As I listened to General Pustay's presentation, I began to be convinced that maybe it would work. After months of waiting and hoping, negotiating and failing, here was a way to go in and snatch our people up and have the whole damn thing over! Not to mention what it would do for the President and the nation. It would prove to the columnists and our political opponents that Carter was not an indecisive Chief Executive who was afraid to act. It would bolster a world community that was increasingly skeptical about American power. A daring mission would right the great wrong done to our country and our citizens.

"It all sounds so easy, General—but how confident are you that it will work?" I asked anxiously. "Are you highly confident?"

"No, sir. I would say at this point that we have confidence in this plan. To say that we are highly confident would be to ignore some of the risks and obstacles."

As Pustay was rolling up his maps and sliding them into the cardboard tubes, I asked him what was the official posture of the Joint Chiefs. "Are they recommending this mission?"

"That's not our job," Pustay said, carefully choosing his words. "The President asked us to come up with a plan for a rescue—and we have. It obviously will be his decision if he decides to attempt it."

"Of course," I replied, trying to hide my smile and thinking to myself, *It will be a great coup for the Pentagon if the mission succeeds—and Carter's ass if it fails.* But I couldn't even contemplate failure. After Pustay left, I returned a few calls to New York, but couldn't get my mind off the helicopters lifting off from the embassy grounds with the hostages. I wanted desperately for this Godforsaken crisis to be over and done with.

March 25, 1980 (Tuesday)

I was looking forward to seeing Bourguet—at least he would take my mind off the New York primary. Eleanor was in New York appearing before the special prosecutor for the second time on my case. Things never seemed to work very well around my office when she was away.

Bourguet arrived in time for lunch, and Stephanie, Hal, Henry, and Lloyd Cutler joined us. Bourguet looked haggard, clearly discouraged by the events in Panama. The rhetoric from Iran was not good. Some clerics were calling for the trial of the hostages in response to the Shah's "escape" to Egypt, and thousands of angry Iranians had gathered in front of the embassy.

We tried to cheer Christian up. After all, he and Villalon were all we had. Without them we had no reliable way to communicate with the Iranians; they had become indispensable to a negotiated settlement.

Mondale dropped by, and while he chatted with Bourguet, I went to the Oval Office to brief the President for his meeting with Bourguet. "Be sure to pat him on the back a little," I said. "He's really down right now. I'm hoping this meeting with you will give him a fresh incentive to get the scenario back on track when he returns to Tehran."

The President glared at me. "The scenario?" he said, almost mockingly. "It's beginning to seem like a deal that we made with ourselves. Everybody's on board except the one person who can free the hostages—Khomeini!"

I began to wonder if a meeting between a frustrated Bourguet and an irritated President was a good idea after all. I went back to collect Bourguet and Stephanie and escorted them over to the Map Room, a small, formal room on the ground floor of the Residence, where the President occasionally held private meetings. He was waiting for us, arms outstretched. "Welcome to our hero!" said the smiling President. "It is an honor to finally meet you, Christian."

A half-step behind, Stephanie was furiously translating in Christian's ear, although his immediate smile indicated that he had understood Carter's greeting.

"It is an honor to meet you, Mr. President," he said in French. "And I am not a hero yet because heroes are successful—and we have not been successful."

The President sat down on a small, ornate sofa, gestured to Christian to sit down in an easy chair directly across from him, and Stephanie and I took chairs off to the side.

"But you have tried and tried and tried, Christian. I'm sorry for what happened in Panama and hope it doesn't complicate the situation. We tried to persuade the Shah to stay in Panama, but he insisted on leaving. I am very interested in hearing your views and asking your advice on where we should go from here."

"Mr. President, it is an honor to be asked for advice by you. You must remember that I am someone whose finger was put into this pie by chance. But I cannot take it out now. The departure of the Shah from Panama was a turning point in the feelings of the Iranians."

"A turning point upward or downward?"

"First it was downward. The Iranians believed the United States had aided the Shah in escaping arrest in Panama. However, maybe it can be a positive turn because we are trying to present it as a victory for the Iranian government in that it demonstrates that the Shah did commit crimes and is having to flee from justice to avoid paying for them."

Bourguet then lapsed into a long analysis of the political climate in Iran. As he spoke, I realized that he was trying to convey to the President in a few minutes what he had emphasized to me during countless meetings and hundreds of hours of conversation: that fairly or unfairly, the Revolution and now the seizure of our hostages was a reaction of the Iranian people to the excesses of the Shah and to unwavering American support for his rule.

"Mr. President, we are witnessing a struggle for power. And unfortunately the hostages are caught in the middle of a domestic political struggle. This creates a state of affairs that is so delicate that any action from the outside can swing the balance within Iran. There is a constant battle between the different political elements to see who can be the harshest toward the United States. That is why sanctions and other punitive measures would be counterproductive. The actions you can take against Iran would play into the hands of the group of people who do not want to let the hostages go. It is very frustrating."

The President had slumped down on the sofa, his chin in his hand, listening. When Bourguet said it was frustrating, Carter suddenly sat up and leaned forward. "Frustrating? Look at the spot *I'm* in! I am the President of a great country. Fifty-three people look to me for support week after week and month after month while we watch this comic opera in Tehran. Neither Bani-Sadr nor Khomeini has the courage to take the hostages away from the terrorists. I would like to continue to be patient, but it is very difficult for us to do so. What is your advice, Christian?"

Bourguet went over what had been done so far. "Some progress has been made and we have almost succeeded several times."

"I don't see that there has been progress at all!" Carter snapped. "We're in exactly the same position as we were four months ago. The hostages are suffering every day. We are a strong nation and we do not have to prove it, but our patience is beginning to look like a demonstration of cowardice of which we cannot be proud and which I will not allow to become a way of life. Something has to change. I have no faith. I trust your judgment—but you must understand my feelings."

"Mr. President, you suggest that you cannot be proud of what you have done. On the contrary, it has not been easy to be patient and bear up under these circumstances. A country has to be strong to be able to do that. If anyone should be ashamed, it is certainly Iran and not you."

Carter did not respond.

"One last thing, you speak of the fifty-three people who have been detained. That is your concern and rightly the concern of the American people. But you must understand that your human-itarian arguments will never touch the Iranians—especially the Imam and the others in power. Why? Because these are the very same people who for years were imprisoned by the Shah, tortured, and have seen many of their friends and family members killed. Not fifty-three, but thousands. Many of them have lost their sense of proportion and values. The fact that the American hostages are allowed to read and are fed and allowed to bathe indicates to them that they are being treated quite properly and better than they were ever treated by the Shah. I do not accept that, but their reasoning is based on their own experience."

"I find that sickening!" Carter replied. "These fifty-three people have killed no one, while Khomeini has been responsible for the execution of six or eight hundred people. To punish fifty-three innocent human beings violates all the teachings of Christianity and the Moslem faith that I know of."

"But, Mr. President, you do not realize the extent to which the Iranians hold *all* American officials and diplomats responsible for the Shah's actions because the Shah has survived only because of the support of the United States."

I fidgeted uncomfortably in my chair as I heard Christian then begin a long review of U.S.-Iranian relations from the perspective of the people now in power in Iran. It implied that Carter was responsible for the actions of his predecessors. I could tell that he did not like what he was hearing and rejected the insinuation that he bore any responsibility for the Shah's excesses. On the contrary, he had urged the Shah to improve human rights in Iran.

"Christian," he interrupted, "I will have to go now. All we want is our hostages back, and, after a decent interval, relations with Iran based on mutual interests and respect. We do not want anything else—just those two things. Iran wants to embarrass me and the United States. It has done that. It wants to punish innocent human beings to pay us back for the Shah. They want to make their case against us and the Shah public—and we have agreed to that. What else do they want? Who can speak for them? Bani-Sadr? If I knew what they wanted, maybe I could be more forthcoming, but my lack of action seems to be approving of their punishment of our people and perpetuating the status quo. Americans are not a patient or humble people. They are a proud people." Then with a smile, he added, "Though perhaps not as much as the French."

We all laughed, and the light moment broke the tension.

"Mr. President," I said, "Christian is planning to return to Iran immediately. Do you have any message for him to take?"

The President took out a notepad and quickly wrote what he wanted:

a. The United States wants the captors released unharmed—quickly.

b. When desired, the U.S. wants normal relations with Iran under the existing government, recognizing the results of the Revolution.

c. The United States wants for Iran to air grievances through the UN International Court of Justice or media.

J.C.

"Give this to Mr. Khomeini or Bani-Sadr—or use it as you wish."

"Mr. President, it is my hope that our efforts will be successful."

As we walked back to my office, Christian said, "I must call the Minister and Hector and give them a full report on my meeting with the President. Also, I must make plans to leave immediately for Tehran."

I smiled. If the meeting had accomplished nothing else, Bourguet was invigorated and ready to get back to work on freeing the hostages.

Bourguet handed me Carter's note to read while he was on the phone. The President must have been irritated—the usually precise Carter had written "captors" instead of "captives."

By now, news from the New York primary had started to dribble in. I was shocked to hear that Kennedy was going to win big there. "It's the UN vote in the Jewish community," Caddell told me. "We're getting wiped out. It's almost as if the voters know that Carter's got the nomination sewed up but want to send him a message. It's a protest vote." A few minutes later, Pat called back to report the same thing was happening in the Connecticut primary.

For weeks and months, Kennedy's campaign lingered on the hope that sooner or later Carter's balloon would burst—when the combination of hostages and inflation became too much. *Maybe*, I thought, *it's finally happening*. Kennedy would have to win 1429 of the 2363 delegates left to be selected, or 60.5 percent—it was mathematically a near impossibility that he could overcome our lead in delegates, but if he started beating us regularly, a mood could develop in the Democratic Party to take the nomination away from us.

March 26, 1980 (Wednesday)

To top off a rotten week, which included shocking defeats in New York and Connecticut, I had to appear before the special prosecutor.

When the FBI called me for questioning late one night in August 1979, I asked, "What about?" I was not particularly alarmed; I had been interviewed by the FBI probably a dozen times in connection with one charge or another made against me or others in the Administration.

"I can't tell you on the phone, Mr. Jordan. Maybe we should do it first thing tomorrow."

"Hell, I won't be able to sleep for worrying. Have your men come on over now if they'd like."

Two agents showed up at my apartment at about 11:30 P.M. They began with, "Anything you say here can be used against you in a court of law. . . ." I started squirming and said to myself, *For God's sake, Hamilton, don't act like you're guilty of whatever it is they've come to ask about.*

Did I remember, they asked, being in New York with Jody Powell on a certain night in the spring of 1978, and did I remember going with Jody to a fashionable New York club called Studio 54?

"I don't remember the specific time or date, but I did go there once for about thirty minutes. I sure don't remember Jody's being with me."

They went on a bit and then showed me several pictures, none of which I could identify.

Finally, the real question popped out: "Did you, while at Studio 54, use the drug cocaine?"

"Absolutely not," I replied, somewhat relieved to know what a ridiculous charge it had turned out to be. "Who said I did?"

"These men, Schrager and Rubell," one agent replied.

"And who are they?"

"Owners of Studio 54—under indictment for federal tax evasion."

It all clicked. "I see. These jokers are trying to plea bargain with the Justice Department by claiming they have information about me."

"Mr. Jordan, I can't say anything about that. You understand."

"Of course I do."

They cautioned against talking with Jody (who happened to be cruising down the Mississippi with the President just then). "Until he has been questioned, it would be in no one's interest for it to appear that there was collusion."

I felt better when they left. Everybody in the press corps knew that Jody and I didn't use drugs. Nobody would believe this stupid charge. We'd get rid of the whole thing tomorrow.

Shortly after I arrived at the office the next morning, Jody called from St. Louis to say that he and the President were on the way back. I told him that we shouldn't be talking unless he had already been interviewed by the FBI. He said that they had gotten him up in the middle of the night on the riverboat and that the Attorney General had briefed the President.

"OK, we both know it's not true—but what will the press make of it?" I asked anxiously.

"Ham, it's hard to tell. But they can hardly ignore a story that centers around you, me, and drugs."

I was depressed. Right in the middle of the campaign and five weeks after I had taken on additional responsibilities as Chief of Staff, I was going to cause the President a serious problem.

I wrote him a memo which said simply that I had not used cocaine and had never used drugs, but feared greatly that my being under investigation while sitting down the hall from the President of the United States would be intolerable for him politically. Consequently, I wanted to resign.

I was waiting in the Oval Office when he and Jody arrived. Jody argued that we had to take the offensive. The charge was untrue and most of the members of the press would believe us. Carter agreed, but said he was going to have to refrain from talking too much with us about it as he was ultimately the chief law enforcement officer in the nation and the Attorney General's superior. I handed him my memo and left.

About twenty minutes later, he called me to his office. He came around to the front of his desk and put his arm around me. "Ham, your leaving won't solve anything. We lose both ways if you resign. I'll be deprived of your help, and a lot of people will think you are admitting guilt. You've got to stay and fight."

"Mr. President, I think you've underestimated this thing. Jody thinks it'll be big news."

"Ham, I'll reserve the right to change my mind, but I'm sure that what's best for you and for me is to fight it."

I walked to the door, feeling even worse to have the President bearing this latest burden with me. "But, Mr. President, my offer to resign is permanent. I don't want this to drag out like Bert Lance's."

He smiled but said nothing.

We did take the offensive. Jody and I met with *The New York Times* and vigorously denied the story. Still, it was big news and my heart sank as the networks and the newspapers were filled with a new round of "Hamilton Jordan" stories, cartoons, and editorials.

Lloyd Cutler was an immense help. "Hamilton, I know it's not true and you know it's not true, but you have to treat it seriously. You must avoid making the mistake many public people make of trying to fight it alone. Also, it will be improper for you to solicit the advice of government lawyers. Your top priority should be to retain good legal counsel."

By Friday afternoon, Lloyd had Steve Pollak, a lawyer formerly with the Justice Department, in my office. Henry Ruth, the former Watergate prosecutor, joined him the following Monday. It was the first of many, many meetings that I was to have with them in the ten months to come. Hardly a day passed without a telephone conversation with one of them or a week without a meeting in my office to review some portion of the investigations. Eleanor had to go through my records and account for my time for most of the past three years, as additional "anonymous" allegations against me surfaced all over the country and were investigated by the FBI and special prosecutor.

But that had been months ago. Ruth, Pollak, and I had become close friends, but they always took the investigation seriously, made me take it seriously, and never allowed it to get me down.

Now maybe it was all coming to an end with this trip to New York to see the special prosecutor.

I hung back after the intelligence briefing to talk about a few campaign matters with the President.

"Give me a report tomorrow on the next batch of primaries. Also an update on our delegate count," Jimmy Carter said.

"Mr. President, I've got to be in New York most of the day tomorrow, so it will probably be Friday before I can get that together."

"What are you going to New York for?"

I bit my lip and tried to sound matter of fact. "I've got to go see the special prosecutor on the Studio 54 nonsense."

"Oh, I see." He paused, then reminded me about his own ordeal with "special investigations," specifically the charge that the Carter Warehouse funds had been used improperly in his Presidential campaign. The charge was, of course, never substantiated and when special counsel Paul Curran completed his investigation, he stated that "Every nickel and every peanut has been tracked into and out of the warehouse, and no funds were unlawfully diverted."

The President talked about his meeting with Curran and his staff. "It was unbelievable. There I was, President of the United States, sitting in the White House, being questioned for hours by people who were paid by the Federal government. And when I asked who had made the allegation against me, all they could say was that there were news stories that raised questions."

"When our own Justice Department gets through investigating all of us," he said with a smile, "I'm going to have a blue-ribbon panel of lawyers take a good look at these laws covering people in government. It's not fair to be chasing people on frivolous charges when there are big-time drug dealers and gangsters to be prosecuted."

But that was a second-term project.

March 27, 1980 (Thursday)

With my lawyers, I took the shuttle to New York to see the special prosecutor. I tried to relax on the way up but found it difficult. We talked about Arthur Christy, the special prosecutor appointed by the federal court to investigate the Studio 54 charges. I wondered what kind of man would take an assignment like that: to drop a lucrative private practice to prosecute a misdemeanor against a public official. It seemed plain to me: a publicity seeker, an ambitious lawyer trying to get his name in the newspaper.

However, Christy surprised me. Not that he did me any favors, but I was impressed with his businesslike manner. He questioned me intensely, leaving the room occasionally to confer with one of the several lawyers and investigators on his staff. He was polite but kept a proper distance.

I appreciated his sensitivity to the publicity surrounding my case. He had made it possible for me to come and go to his office quietly and without any news leaks; he seemed as interested in keeping my visit out of the papers as I was. When we headed back to Washington, I felt better. At least I knew that an honorable man was investigating me and that he seemed determined only to find the truth. I hoped that he would.

March 28, 1980 (Friday)

Earlier in the week, the President had sent Bani-Sadr and Khomeini a tough message, stating that there would be "serious consequences" if the hostages were not transferred by April 1, as promised. I told the foreign policy breakfast that the Swiss were reporting that the Revolutionary Council was pulling itself together for one more attempt to free the hostages.

Carter was skeptical. "I'll believe it when I see it. Bani-Sadr promised you, Ham, that the transfer would take place in fifteen days. His deadline is April first!"

Pat Caddell called with good news for a change: "Wisconsin is going to be just like Illinois."

"Are you sure, Pat?" I asked, thinking of New York. If we lost two big ones in a row, we could really be in trouble.

He laughed. "I'm sure, and you'll see! Wisconsin isn't a Kennedy type of state. It's a state of traditional Democrats. They may not love the President, but they greatly prefer him to Ted Kennedy."

March 29, 1980 (Saturday)

Jody called me in a panic in the morning. "Have you heard about this story out of Iran?"

"What?"

"It says that the Boss sent Khomeini a letter apologizing for past U.S. behavior toward Iran and admitting our mistakes."

"That's absolutely absurd, Jody. The only letter we've sent the Iranians is a tough one."

"It may be absurd, Ham, but it's a major story. The text of the letter from the President has been released, and it sounds bad. You'd better get on down to the office."

When I arrived, Jody's office was swarming with the White House press corps. I didn't even try to get in, but walked back to my office, called, and asked him to come over.

"I've talked to the Boss, who of course denies that we sent such a letter. Here's the Reuters story from Tehran," Jody said.

"My God," I said. "Some of this is taken from the letter I sent Bani-Sadr. But there's nothing in that letter to worry about. It was approved by Carter and Vance. This other stuff is just phony! We've never sent any such letter. Somebody concocted the whole damn thing!"

"Our ass is in a crack now," Jody replied disgustedly. "I've denied it, but the press thinks this is part of some larger scheme leading to the release of the hostages."

"They don't believe your denial?" I asked, incredulous. Jody had, said many, many times that the bond between him and the White House press corps was based on their belief that he would never lie to them.

"Some think I'm lying and justify it because human lives are at stake; others think that something is happening and I've been cut out of it to protect my integrity. God knows, Ham, if that's true, I need to know about it," he said, lighting a cigarette from the stub in his mouth.

"Nothing is happening. Someone gave Khomeini a phony letter and he's released it, probably thinking it's evidence that he's humbled Carter and the West. I don't know what to do but deny it."

"Dammit, Ham, I have, and that's what I'm telling you—not a lot of people believe me!"

"Let's go see the Boss."

"Jody," the President said, "when you deny something and say that I deny it and then the press runs the story anyway and says it might be true, they're calling *me* a liar."

"Mr. President, I know. But look at it from where they sit. A letter is released by Khomeini. He says it's from you. The Swiss confirm that they have recently delivered messages from the United States to Iran. They end up very skeptical."

Carter took out his irritation with the press on Jody. "Well, you've denied that I sent such a letter and I've denied it. I don't know anything else to do. We're in a poor posture to deal with anything if they don't believe us on something this important. I have to get ready for a newspaper interview," he said, dismissing us.

Calls from Saunders and Precht awaited me at my office. Villalon had called from Tehran and begged that we not deny the letter Khomeini had released. Hal told him to forget it—the letter was bogus and we couldn't remain silent. I told Saunders to get a message to Bourguet and Villalon asking them what the hell was going on and telling them that our negotiating posture had been seriously compromised.

March 30–31, 1980 (Sunday–Monday)

The skeptical stories about the phony letter continued Sunday, and I knew that we had a real problem when two members of the White House staff pulled me aside and said, "Is that letter real or not?"

Carter was furious. "I say one thing, Khomeini says another— and who does the American press believe? Khomeini!"

But we had to do something, so an exasperated Chief Executive invited a small group of media people to the Residence Sunday night, told them unequivocally that he had not sent Khomeini the letter, and briefed them confidentially on what was happening behind the scenes.

Caddell called Monday morning with the good news that our lead in the Wisconsin primary was holding and that "the Boss is going to win big tomorrow."

I was relieved. We'd lost New York and Connecticut last Tuesday, and if we lost Wisconsin this Tuesday, it would look like the President's grip on the nomination was slipping. We couldn't stand back-to-back defeats.

We then received a long cable from Bourguet and Villalon, confirmed later by a phone call: BANI-SADR IS LIVING UP TO THE PROMISE MADE TO HAMILTON ON MARCH 15 THAT THE HOSTAGES WOULD BE REMOVED FROM THE COMPOUND IN FIFTEEN DAYS. HE HAS MET WITH THE LEADERS OF THE STUDENTS AND WORKED OUT THE DETAILS OF THE TRANSFER.

I was more than a little proud as I walked quickly to the Oval Office to share the good news with the President. Cy had already called him, and he seemed encouraged.

Later we learned the plan. President Bani-Sadr had obtained the approval of the Revolutionary Council for the transfer of the hostages and would announce it at noon Tuesday in a major speech in Tehran. We were expected to respond to the speech.

April 1, 1980 (Tuesday)

The President, Vance, Saunders, Jody, Brzezinski, Warren Christopher, Brzezinski's deputy David Aaron, Gary Sick, and I gathered in front of a blazing fire in the Oval Office at 5:00 A.M. to await the message from Iran. "Maybe this will finally be it," I said.

The President looked at me. "I've heard *that* before."

We sat around making small talk as we drank coffee and waited.

After about thirty minutes, Hal Saunders received a telephone call from the Swiss Embassy in Washington. "It's happened," he reported as he hung up and read from his notes. "Bani-Sadr publicly said a few minutes ago that his government would take control of, quote, 'the hostages from the students if the American authorities make an official announcement that they will not spread propaganda or say anything provocative about the hostages until the formation of the Parliament,' unquote. He calls on us to recognize the Parliament's right to deal with the hostage question."

The debate began. Had Bani-Sadr said enough? Did it indicate a real intention to resolve the crisis and should we now put off the imposition of sanctions?

I argued that it did. "I don't like the part about the Parliament, but if we can just get the hostages out of the compound, I believe that the government will find it difficult to hold our people very long."

"This is the strongest public statement yet from Bani-Sadr," said the President. "He's been so gutless before that I don't believe he'd have said this without the knowledge and approval of Khomeini."

"I don't think we have any choice but to treat it as serious and genuine," said Vance. "And that means holding off on the sanctions."

The next question debated was what the President would say as an official public response to Bani-Sadr's speech. "We should move fast," I pressed, "so that whatever momentum Bani-Sadr has with the Revolutionary Council and the militants at the compound won't be lost."

"It sounds to me that Bani-Sadr is trying to resolve the thing," said the President, "but we can't accept the notion that the Majlis has the 'right' to resolve the crisis. That implies that the hostages have done something wrong."

"Mr. President, I concur," said Vance, "because to recognize the 'right' of the Majlis to deal with the hostages would seem to condone whatever they decide to do. For example, they could choose to put our people on trial or sentence them and claim that we had agreed to it."

As usual, Warren Christopher came up with the right words. "Why don't we say that we recognize the 'competence' of the Majlis to deal with the crisis? We would be saying that they have the ability to resolve the problem but not acknowledging their right to punish or try our people."

Everyone agreed. The President would make a statement calling Bani-Sadr's speech a "positive development" and stating that we would delay once more the imposition of sanctions.

"When do you want to do it?" asked Jody.

Carter went over to his desk, looked at his calendar. "I have to prepare for a tough meeting with the Energy Committee at eight-thirty. Let's go on and do it and get it out of the way. That way my response will get back to Bani-Sadr immediately."

"OK," Jody said. "You want to do it in the press room or bring them in here?"

"You can bring them in here," Carter said.

At 7:20 A.M., the President stood behind his desk, surrounded by moving cameras and the White House press corps, and announced that he considered President Bani-Sadr's speech a "positive step" and as a result he was delaying the imposition of sanctions.

We spent the rest of the day talking with Bourguet and Villalon in Tehran and sending messages to the Iranians to reinforce the President's statement. But by the end of the day it had become obvious that the opponents of the transfer were succeeding in stirring up trouble against Bani-Sadr and the prospect of the transfer.

At least there was good news from Wisconsin: we defeated Kennedy handily.

April 3, 1980 (Thursday)

I slipped in the side door to the Oval Office to give the President the latest cables and reports. "Mr. President, the stuff coming out of Tehran this morning doesn't look good." He just looked at me without expression as I handed him the main wire story. I continued. "The Revolutionary Council met for hours and made a statement saying that, although it approved the transfer, the conditions they set forth have not been met by us. Bani-Sadr said that he is washing his hands of the entire matter and the fate of the hostages rests with the Ayatollah."

Shaking his head, Carter said, "Bani-Sadr is gutless. He had a chance to move the hostages and didn't do it. The Council approved the transfer, the militants agreed to it, and then nothing happens!" He tossed the wire story into his "out" box.

He stood, walked over to the window that looked out on the Rose Garden, and spoke quietly, as if thinking out loud. "I don't know what we do now. I really don't. Rosalynn and I talked last night about how wonderful it would be to spend Easter at Camp David, knowing that the hostages were out of the compound and maybe soon on the way home."

"Mr. President, Bourguet and Villalon haven't given up, they think that—"

"Ham," he interrupted me, "the only people in the world who think we're going to get our people back soon are you and your French friends. The people in Iran may want to solve this thing, but they don't have the courage to do it. And we look foolish. I go out and announce the plan, and forty-eight hours later it's falling apart. I'm not sure what to do now, but the options left aren't very attractive."

"Mr. President, I'm sorry."

"There's nothing to be sorry about. It's nobody's fault. You've done the best you could. But it just hasn't worked and I don't think it's going to work."

I told him that I had planned to spend the weekend with my mother in Georgia, but that perhaps I should stay in Washington and be available to him.

"Go on home, Ham, and be with your family. I'm afraid there's not going to be much happening here on the hostages. Stay in touch by phone, and if I need you back, I'll call you."

April 5, 1980 (Saturday)

I flew home and spent most of the weekend on the phone to Washington. By Saturday, even Bourguet and Villalon seemed to have given up. Bani-Sadr had had the green light for the transfer, but he never followed through.

What in the world do we do now? I thought to myself a hundred times over the Easter holidays. *There seems no chance to negotiate their release.* I kept coming back to the idea of the rescue mission.

April 7, 1980 (Monday)

A National Security Council meeting was called for 9:00 A.M. Khomeini had made a public statement through his son stating clearly that the hostage question would be handled by the Parliament when it convened. Our experts thought that would be months away.

The President flew back to Washington from Camp David, looking grim when he arrived. He was resolved to break diplomatic relations, expel Iranian diplomats, impose economic sanctions on everything but food and medicine, and insist that our allies support our actions. "It seems that every time I call Helmut [Schmidt] or Margaret [Thatcher] or Giscard [d'Estaing], I'm asking them to do something politically difficult. It's gotten so that they hate to get a telephone call from me anymore."

We were backed into a corner, I knew, and were being forced to protect the honor of our country and cover the President's political flanks, although it looked as if none of it would speed up the release of the hostages. But I kept quiet because everyone knew it.

Jody was usually at his best at such difficult times, but he was frustrated and worried when he stopped by my office after the meeting. "It's bad enough that everything fell apart last week, but on top of that, we've ended up with a credibility problem. Have you seen the news magazines?"

"No."

"They're filled with stories about how the President announced the 'good news' about the hostages in the early morning hours of the Wisconsin primary. Nobody would have said anything about it if everything had worked out, but now the press thinks we've been playing politics with the hostages. You know—Carter announces the good news the morning of a big primary, wins the primary, and then a couple of days later we find out that it all amounted to nothing."

Jody took a long drag on his cigarette and continued. "I could just kick myself for letting the Boss make that announcement himself. I should have realized the risk and done it myself. Or even if we had waited until nine o'clock to do it instead of seven-thirty . . ."

"Jody, we were so sure it was happening. After months of waiting, there was finally some genuine good news on the hostages. It seemed only right for the President to announce it. He's had to deliver all the bad news and eat crow so many times. Anyway, he had to respond to Bani-Sadr's speech."

"Look," Jody said, irritated, "you don't have to convince me, Ham—I'm just telling you that we are about to have an enormous credibility problem. The combination of not campaigning and that early-morning announcement has made skeptics out of even our friends in the press."

"That's ridiculous. We couldn't choose when Bani-Sadr gave that speech. I think you're overreacting."

As it turned out, he wasn't. First the press and then our political opponents began to charge that Jimmy Carter was manipulating the hostages for his own political benefit.

The President made his announcement on sanctions and other steps against Iran in the afternoon. I knew our hard-line approach wouldn't bring the hostages home any sooner, but I hoped that maybe it would buy us a little more time and patience from the public and possibly scare our allies into taking some strong actions.

"What do you think, Bob?" I asked Strauss, who was at my office before our weekly campaign meeting.

"Too little, too late, Hamilton. Goddammit, the President has to get out of the White House and lead this country! The American people want to see and feel their President. They'll understand his predicament better if he's out there explaining it."

"We're in a hell of a mess. How can he get out now just when the damn hostage thing is starting to look hopeless? If Carter starts running around campaigning, it'll look terrible."

Carter heard Strauss out at our regular campaign meeting but said now wasn't the time to change his posture. "We are all going to have to hold steady." And, looking directly at Strauss, he said, "Bob, you have to take the lead in making that case to the media."

April 10, 1980 (Thursday)

Harold Brown called on my secure phone. "The President must be thinking more and more seriously about the rescue mission—he and Zbig have been asking me a lot of specific questions."

"We're in a box, Harold. We've broken relations with Iran and imposed sanctions, but we still have no leverage on Khomeini. We've got to do something."

"That's right," Brown said. "Neither the naval blockade or mining the harbors will bring the hostages home."

"Except in boxes."

"And if they begin killing our people, then we'll have to take punitive measures—and God only knows where that will lead," Brown reasoned.

"The rescue mission is the best of a lousy set of options."

April 11, 1980 (Friday)

At the foreign policy breakfast the President talked about the problems of both mining and blockading the Iranian ports but didn't mention the rescue mission. I assumed that his interest in it had waned.

I was scheduled to be the "attraction" at two Carter-Mondale fund-raisers in Atlanta and was on the way to the airport when the driver said, "Deacon would like you to return to the White House."

When I got back, Phil Wise told me that I was to attend a "luncheon meeting" with the foreign policy group. I was surprised to find that CIA Director Stan Turner and General David Jones were in attendance, and that neither Lloyd Cutler nor Hedley Donovan, an advisor to the President who regularly attended the foreign policy breakfasts, was there. Warren Christopher was sitting in for Cy, who was in Florida on a long overdue vacation.

The President got right to the point. "Gentlemen, I want you to know that I am seriously considering an attempt to rescue the hostages."

I could feel my heart speed up: *He's going to do it! He's had enough!*

"As you know," Carter continued, "the first week the hostages were seized, I ordered the Joint Chiefs to develop a rescue plan that could be used in dire circumstances. A team of expert paramilitary people now report that they have confidence in their ability to rescue our people. Before I make up my mind, I want to know your reactions."

The President might say—or even believe—he hadn't made up his mind, but I knew he had.

"Harold," he said, "I'd like for you and Dave Jones to outline the plan, the risks, the problems—and the prospects for success."

General Jones spread a big map out over the table, and, using a pointer, showed the different stages of the mission. Harold Brown occasionally interrupted to elaborate.

"What do you think?" I whispered to Christopher, on my left.

"I'm not sure. Does Cy know about this?"

"The contingency rescue plan? Of course."

"No, no—does he realize how far along the President is in his thinking about this?"

"I don't know," I replied. "I assume they've talked about it." We went around the room to hear everyone's opinion. Mondale said he was inclined to attempt the rescue. Zbig made a forceful statement in favor of the mission and spoke glowingly about the members of the Delta team and their impressive training and backgrounds. Stan Turner was positive but cautioned, "The conditions inside and around the compound are good now, but they could change any day."

Jody and I briefly echoed Harold's sentiment that it was our best option. Chris said he hadn't discussed the mission with Cy and didn't feel he could accurately represent his feelings.

The overwhelming logic of Harold's point carried the day: the other military options and sanctions wouldn't bring the hostages home, but the highly specialized Delta team probably could.

The President said he would "explore the rescue option" very tentatively, that he still had a lot of questions. "I'm going to think and pray about it over the weekend. I hope you'll do the same, and we'll get back together the first of the week."

I flew on to Atlanta, excited by the prospect of a bold and successful resolution of the crisis.

April 12, 1980 (Saturday)

I spent the morning in an Atlanta hotel room, pacing and thinking about the rescue mission, beginning to regret that my support for it had sounded lukewarm. On a legal pad, I wrote an eight-page memorandum to Carter analyzing the situation in Iran. I concluded that it would be a long, long time before the hostages came home. "Once you are satisfied with the soundness of the rescue plan, I believe you should proceed with the mission," I wrote.

When I finished, I called the White House and ordered a military courier with top-secret clearance to pick up the memo and hand-carry it to the President. Several hours later, twó bulky young men knocked on my door, showed me their identification, and I handed them my message—sealed in a Sheraton Hotel envelope. I felt better after putting myself squarely on the side of the mission—advisers are no good if they don't advise.

April 15, 1980 (Tuesday)

I arrived back in Washington in the morning just in time for another off-the-record foreign policy luncheon.

The President and Vance, both stony-faced, entered the Cabinet Room together five minutes late.

The President began: "Cy has some concerns about the rescue mission, and I suggested that he share them with you. Cy?"

Vance leaned forward in his chair, his glasses perched on the tip of his nose so he could glance at the notes on his legal pad. "The hostage problem has been with us for a long time," he began. "It has been terribly frustrating for all of us at the State Department who know and identify with our people in Tehran. Most of all"—he paused, turning to Carter—"it has been frustrating for the President. We have all been repeatedly disappointed, as we seemed to be on the verge of a breakthrough only to see it all fall apart. This is a particularly difficult time, but my strong feeling is that we should not be discouraged; we must continue to look for ways to negotiate. I am strongly opposed to a rescue mission," he said firmly, looking at everyone around the table.

"Let me elaborate," Vance continued. "First, although I have not heard all the details, I have serious doubts that the mission will work. We would have to get into Iran undetected, move into Tehran, scale the compound wall, and remove all the Americans. I cannot imagine that all this could be accomplished without harming some of the hostages or rescuers. Consider the best outcome and suppose everything goes according to plan and everyone gets out alive. Several hundred Americans live in Tehran. Suppose the militants seize them next? What will we do? We'll be back where we are now."

He paused again and looked around. The President was staring hard at him.

"Finally, Mr. President," Cy went on, "we have to worry about the consequences of either a successful or unsuccessful rescue mission. What will the Soviet Union do in response? What will the neighboring Arab nations think if we go in and take Americans out but kill a lot of Iranians in the process? We call it a rescue mission, but it will be interpreted as a military action by others. For all of these reasons, I feel strongly that now is not the time to consider this option."

"Are there any reactions to Cy's comments?" the President asked.

There was an awkward silence as Vance scanned the room, looking from Zbig, to Mondale, to Harold Brown, to Jody, and finally to me, his eyes begging for support. I fidgeted, feeling sorry for Cy, who sat there all alone.

The President spoke first, "Let me respond, Cy. The Joint Chiefs didn't think it could be done back in November when the embassy was overrun. After four months of planning, they have confidence that it can succeed. As for Americans in Tehran, we have told them repeatedly that it was not safe to be there. Most of them, as I understand it, are teachers, or business people, or Americans married to Iranians. We are responsible for our diplomats—but we are *not* responsible for private citizens in Iran who have refused time and again to follow our advice to leave!"

"But they are Americans, Mr. President!" Vance protested.

"I understand and am not unconcerned about their welfare. But my obligation is to those hostages, who represent me, you, and our country!" Carter said firmly. "I disagree with your assessment of the reaction to a rescue mission. If it works, our friends all over the world will breathe a sigh of relief that it's over and that they won't have to impose further sanctions. The Moslem countries may make a few public statements for the sake of Islamic unity, but you know as well as I do that they despise and fear Khomeini and will be snickering at him behind his back. Cy, my greatest fear all along is that this crisis could lead us into direct confrontation with the Soviets. The chances of that are much greater if we exercise any of the other military options—a punitive air strike, mining the harbors, or a blockade—than if we go in, rescue our people, and get out. The thing will be over. I haven't made a final decision, but at this point, I am inclined to go ahead."

After the President spoke, there was another painful silence. Cy lowered his eyes to his pad. The President looked around the room and finally asked, "Are there any other comments?"

There were none, and Carter started to question General Jones. Everyone joined in except Cy.

April 16, 1980 (Wednesday)

Harold Brown sensed that Carter wasn't completely comfortable with the details of the mission and suggested a secret meeting of the foreign policy group with the leaders of the rescue team. Wednesday night the entire foreign policy group, preceded by President Carter, filed into the Situation Room.

You unlock the Situation Room door by dialing a special code on a box mounted on the wall by the door. With its men and women working at computer terminals and copying machines, the complex in which the Situation Room is contained gives the impression of an operations center of a modern bank. "The Room" itself is about fifteen by twenty feet, paneled in light wood, and has no windows. It is dominated by a wooden conference table surrounded by comfortable but very ordinary office chairs. A second group of chairs rings the wall, where, during the frequent meetings held on matters of foreign policy and national security, aides sit behind their principals and furiously scribble notes.

As we entered, the men all jumped to their feet, saluted, and said, "Good evening, Mr. President!"

I wondered if that welcome had been planned.

"Good evening, gentlemen," the President said. He put down his briefcase and began shaking hands.

"Mr. President, I apologize for our civilian clothes, but I didn't want to arouse any suspicion," said Chairman of the Joint Chiefs David Jones.

"Good, Dave. We have to be sensitive to things like that."

Harold Brown introduced Delta Force leader Colonel Charlie Beckwith, a tall, beefy man with a gray crewcut. As he greeted me, he enveloped my hand firmly. "Colonel," I said, "you sound like you're from the South."

"Sir, it is even better than that—I am from Georgia!" he said proudly. ·

"Where in Georgia are you from, Colonel?" the President asked.

"Schley County, sir."

"That's right next to Sumter County! You're my neighbor. Who are your folks?"

The President and Beckwith chatted for a moment about mutual friends and acquaintances. Harold Brown slipped me a note: "You've got to hand it to the Pentagon for finding a good ole boy to head up the mission." I scribbled an answer: "They might as well have chosen someone from Plains—maybe Billy? The Pentagon has never been known for its subtlety." Harold chuckled as he read my reply.

I learned later that Charlie Beckwith's selection was neither as recent nor as casual as Secretary Brown had led me to believe.

In 1977 the Army chose Colonel Charles Beckwith to form an elite paramilitary unit that could be utilized against hijackings, political assassinations and terrorist activities around the world. The fifty-one-year-old professional soldier still looked very much like the guard he had been at the University of Georgia. His large frame was topped with a mat of steel-gray hair and accented by blue eyes that squinted hard when he wanted to make a point with his raspy voice.

Charlie Beckwith was a soldier and a superpatriot. "People that complain about America and don't like this country ought to leave it," he once told an interviewer. Beckwith had fought in Korea and in Vietnam, making his reputation as a Special Forces officer who trained units for dangerous missions. Decorated repeatedly for valor and wounded seriously on one occasion, Beckwith was called "Chargin' Charlie"—he knew only one direction to move: forward, toward the enemy. "He's a man who won't take 'no' for an answer," one officer recalled. "That's not to say he was foolhardy or reckless, but if there was any way to do something based on guts and smarts, Charlie Beckwith was your man."

Someone suggested to an Army buddy of his that if they made a movie about Beckwith, John Wayne would have been a natural to play him. "No," the friend said, "John Wayne's not tough enough."

The President opened the meeting. "Gentlemen, I don't have to tell anyone why we are here tonight. We have been negotiating in good faith with Iranians who want to resolve the crisis but don't seem to have the will or guts to do it. If I had to predict, I would guess that it will be many months, or possibly years, before Khomeini orders the militants at the compound to release our people. That is intolerable for the hostages, for their families, and for our country's dignity and interests." Turning to General Jones, he said, "Dave, I am seriously considering going ahead with the mission but will make a final decision only after this meeting and after I've had several days to think about it. I would like you all to assume that none of us knows anything about it and provide us with a step-by-step rundown. The show is yours, Dave."

Jones gave the President the background of Lieutenant General Phillip C. Gast, Director of Operations, Joint Chiefs of Staff, and Major General James Vaught, the commander of the overall rescue mission, and then went on to describe their personal and professional qualifications.

"The Joint Chiefs' unanimous recommendation," he continued, "was for Charlie Beckwith to lead the rescue team."

All eyes were on Beckwith, who lowered his head and squirmed uncomfortably.

Jones then introduced Vaught, who began to recount each step of the mission. Carter put on his glasses and began to take notes on a small pad. Occasionally he stopped Vaught to ask a hypothetical question. Vaught was intense and impressive, rattling off statistics and possibilities to cover any circumstance.

"What is the most difficult part of the mission, General?" the President asked at one point.

"Getting in undetected," Vaught answered without hesitation. "That's why operational security is so important, Mr. President. The Iranian military is in a state of disrepair, but they have enough of our sophisticated equipment, provided it's operational and properly manned, to detect our entry. We're betting that they won't be prepared."

"What other critical elements, General, concern you most?"

"The helicopters, sir. They're not made for long-distance, heavy-duty flying at low altitudes with full loads. That's why we've added two extra choppers to give us a wide margin of safety. Our experts believe that we could lose a helicopter."

Carter nodded, apparently pleased with the answer.

Vaught said, "I will now turn it over to Colonel Beckwith, who will lead the team into Iran."

"Mr. President," said Beckwith, "I'd like to tell you first that the team assembled for this mission is made up of the finest group of military men ever to train and work together. They are all experts, and they are tough, good soldiers who have volunteered for the mission and believe in it. They'll be greatly disappointed if they don't have the chance to try to rescue their fellow Americans."

His presentation was clear, simple, and straightforward. He did not go into the particulars about the formation of the team, which he told me later. "There were some fellas in the Pentagon who wanted me to just round up a bunch of good ole boys, run around playing grabass for a few weeks, and claim we had an antiterrorist unit, ready for action," Beckwith said. "I refused to do that and said that it would take two years to put the right kind of team together. I tried to approach it like a fella named Bear Bryant would have," he told me. "You know, he's a fair-to-middling football coach, and one of his secrets is that his men function as a team. And that's what I wanted for Delta, a bunch of red-blooded American soldiers who lived together, ate together, worked together, screwed together, and if necessary died together. You can put together a half-assed team in six weeks, but I wasn't going to lead a half-assed team."

"Chargin' Charlie" got his way, and by fall 1979, he had trained a commando unit, stationed at Fort Bragg, North Carolina, that would have made Bear Bryant proud. Late in October the Pentagon gave the Delta Force its first major "validation exercise," a simulated, secret antiterrorist action, witnessed by experts from France, Great Britain, and West Germany.

"We worked our asses off, flying all over the country and going without sleep for four days and nights," Beckwith said. "Me and the boys did pretty damned good on it because when it was over, we were adjudicated to be a 'national asset' by the brass." The exercise ended at Fort Stewart, Georgia, and "I went to bed about four o'clock the night we finished, dead tired and real proud of my boys."

He didn't sleep for long that night. "Before dawn, they got me up and told me that our embassy in Iran had gone down. The minute I got that call, several of us rented cars and drove back to Bragg 'cause I knew this could mean we'd be called in. Soon as I got there, I got a call that the JCS [Joint Chiefs of Staff] wanted me to come to Washington.

"At the Pentagon," Beckwith said, "I met with some goddamn anxious generals. 'OK, Colonel,' they said to me, 'you've been playing around down there at Bragg for a couple of years, can you get our hostages out?' Well, shit, it was obvious to me that they were just trying to answer the mail. Word was out at the Pentagon that Brzezinski had already been there asking questions."

They pressed Beckwith for three hours to come up with a solution. Finally, he said, "'OK, I can put together very quickly an emergency assault plan for the embassy in Tehran.' Boy, that made 'em smile. Then General Jones, a man I have a lot of respect for, asked me, 'What is the probability of success and what are the risks?' I didn't bat an eye or hesitate a second. 'Sir,' I said, 'the probability of success is zero and the risks are high.'

"That wasn't what the brass wanted to hear. They told me that that was 'unacceptable,' and I told them that a rescue was impossible until they could give me the answers to some questions," Beckwith continued. "How many hostages are there? Give me a list of anybody who has been in that compound in the last six months. Do you have the architectural plans for the embassy? Who understands the way Iranians think and act, particularly the kind of revolutionaries inside the compound? And those are the easy questions. I've got a thousand more before I can make a recommendation to you gentlemen about a rescue."

It was General Jones who "answered the mail," telling the President several days after the embassy seizure that a rescue mission in the present circumstances was "nearly impossible." But Jones also obtained permission to begin planning a rescue option for use in the event that the hostages were put on trial or executed one by one. "We'd have to try to rescue them then, regardless of the odds," Carter had said grimly.

Charlie Beckwith went back to Bragg and started to put together a plan. Air Force Major General Gast, who had served in Iran, was assigned to the project with specific responsibility for planning the movements into and out of Iran. Army Major General Vaught was named overall commander. Although Vaught was ultimately in charge, he, Gast, and Beckwith worked as co-leaders for the planning and implementation of the mission. With information from the American intelligence network, they constructed a model of the American embassy in Iran and then began to figure out how to enter and operate inside. "It was like a gigantic jigsaw puzzle," Beckwith recalled, "with a thousand tiny pieces, and each time we got an answer to a piece of the puzzle, we plugged that in and adjusted our thinking and planning accordingly."

People throughout the military who had worked in Iran and might know something about the grounds of the compound, the streets in that area of the city, the traffic patterns—anything— were called in and interviewed. "Some knew things, others didn't," Beckwith said. "What we did with a guy after reading him in was General Vaught's problem. It was pretty damn obvious what we were doing, so after he became saturated, you'd have to icebox him—hold him where he can't get out in public. So, we were holding a lot of people, and folks were getting kind of concerned about it." (I hadn't known there were American hostages at Fort Bragg as well as in Tehran.)

He explained the interviewing. "For example, one person might tell us that there was a tennis court built recently in this part of the compound. Well, that may not seem so important, but if you come over the wall in the middle of the night carrying a hundred pounds of equipment and land on the tennis court, you might break your ankle. Was there a fence around the court? Which way did the court face? 'Cause, if you come over the compound wall at a certain point and run toward the embassy building, would you have a clear shot at the building or would you trip on the net and bust your ass and miss your assignment? So exactly where that tennis court is is an important goddamn bit of information."

In addition to the physical setup, they studied the personnel. "We got profiles on each of the hostages and studied them carefully. We knew every face and name and knew how they would look with beards."

The Delta Force began practicing the mission, flying out of Fort Bragg in the middle of the night to the Western desert where they would unload, board helicopters, and later "take down the embassy," a group of buildings with façades built to replicate the compound in Iran. They had eight full-dress rehearsals in all.

By the middle of December, the team had trained hard and was ready for a break. "General Jones wanted to stand everybody down for Christmas," Beckwith told me, "but I said bullshit to that idea. 'Cause, I know what people do when they go home and get in bed with momma: they whisper. I told them, 'I don't want Delta to have time off for Christmas. I got a family, too, but I want Delta isolated until after we get back from Iran.' General Jones said we'd just have to risk it and let the men off."

Beckwith explained to me why they were saying that the most difficult part of the mission was getting into Iran undetected. That was the part they couldn't rehearse, couldn't control.

"Shit, people laugh when I say that getting in and out of the embassy would be a piece of cake. It would be. But the toughest part was getting into Iran undetected. They had some pretty sophisticated radar equipment. That's why the helicopters were so damn important, because we could fly under their radar at tree-top level. One thing I learned in Nam is that if you need one helicopter, you ask for two more, 'cause they get sick real quick. And you gotta remember they were flying in low at night over a long damn distance. Choppers aren't made for that, so me and Vaught and Gast all agreed in December that we wouldn't leave Desert One for Tehran unless we had six birds. I figured we'd lose one on the way to Iran, one going into the compound, and maybe another one at the soccer stadium across from the embassy where we were going to take the hostages before lifting off. That would've given me three, worst case. We could have gotten out with three and made it to the desert for the flight out."

As to the question of getting into the compound and safely removing hostages held by armed terrorists, "Chargin' Charlie" explained: "Me and the boys have made a career of busting down doors and saving folks. I was prepared for the worst in Tehran: a highly trained badnik sitting by each hostage with a gun to his head. But I knew what we were going to find was Joe Shit, the raghead, sitting there picking his nose with a rifle he had never cleaned and maybe never fired. When I bust down the door and go in, what is that man with the rifle going to do? Aim it at the hostage or aim it at me? You bet your ass he's going to aim it at me because I'm going to bleed him with mine."

Delta had perfected the art of "busting down doors." Every day, they practiced breaking into darkened rooms, where dummies, dressed as "Iranians" or "Americans," sat in alternate chairs. Wearing infra-red glasses that allowed them to see in the dark, they would first drill a tiny hole in the door and slip in a detection device to try to "hear" into the room. Then they would put a small charge in the door that would cleanly blow the door off without hurting anyone, jump into the room, and fire a round into all the "Iranian" dummies. I asked Beckwith if they ever hit the "American" dummies. "Sir, Delta played in the Rosebowl, not the shitbowl. Any man that ever hit an 'American' dummy was not a Bear Bryant–type player." For each practice session the "hostages" and "captors" were set in different configurations. Beckwith and the other officers regularly sat in the darkened rooms in place of the "American" dummies, as the sharpshooters "busted down the door" and sprayed live ammunition all around them.

In mid-April, General David Jones had flown down to Fort Bragg to question the Delta Force leaders. On the way to the Delta camp, he said to Beckwith, who had picked him up, "Let's talk." They pulled off the road. "Charlie, tell me what you really think about the mission. Be straight with me."

"Sir, we're going to do it! We want to do it, and we're ready. Besides, sir, America needs a win. We need one real, real bad."

After talking with Vaught and Gast, Jones said that he wanted the three of them to come to Washington the next day, with a presentation for the Joint Chiefs. They had a presentation, they assured him, and the next afternoon they appeared before Jones and the Joint Chiefs.

After the presentation for the Joint Chiefs, they were told they were going to the White House that night. Now "Chargin' Charlie" knew that the rescue mission had gone from being a "last resort" to being a "live option."

Beckwith described in detail the plan to enter Iran at night in transport planes, which would rendezvous in the desert with the helicopters. The team would be flown to an overnight resting place in the mountains and then be driven by CIA-recruited Iranians in old Iranian trucks to a warehouse near Tehran. The next night, in the same trucks, the team would enter the city.

"And then, Mr. President," Beckwith said, "we go over that wall and get our people out."

"What is your objective in that compound, Colonel?" Carter asked.

"That's simple. To find and safely extract every American hostage and to bring back alive every one of those beautiful men that I have trained."

"What will your attitude be toward the Iranians?"

"To be successful, our mission must be kept simple. We will not allow ourselves to be distracted by other military targets or opportunities other than those absolutely essential to freeing the hostages."

"What does that mean, Colonel?"

"It means that there will be no unnecessary blood shed, sir. We will be concerned only with those who are physically in the compound holding our people hostage."

"I think it is important to keep your mission simple. It will be easy and tempting for your men to become engaged in gunfire with others and to try to settle some scores for our nation. That will interfere with your objective of getting our people out safely. In the eyes of the world, it is important that the scope of this mission be seen as simply removing our people. If innocent people are killed, the Iranians will make a great public spectacle of it and will say that we murdered women and children. For both reasons, you are to keep your operation simple," the President said emphatically.

"Yes, sir, Mr. President. I agree," Beckwith said.

"I have to admit," Beckwith told me later, "before that meeting in the Situation Room, I wasn't a big Carter fan, but the man impressed me. He wasn't gonna allow the mission to be run by a goddamn committee. It was going to be the President to Brown to Jones to us. And the President was going to stay out of it once we got under way. It was a slick command-and-control setup. The President pulled me aside at the end of that meeting and said, 'Colonel, I want to ask you to do two things for me. And one of them is very difficult. Before you leave, I want you to line up everybody that's going to Tehran, all the Delta guys, and I want you to tell them that if this operation is not a success, that it's not their fault, it's not your fault, it's my fault . . . the buck stops here. I'd also like to ask you, if there's an American that gets killed inside the embassy grounds, if it's a hostage or one of your guys, if you possibly can, without costing the life of someone else, try to bring his body back. I know what I'm asking is a tall order.'

"I told him, 'Mr. President, you know my track record. I ain't gonna leave anybody if I can help it.'"

For over three hours, Carter and others questioned the mission leaders. Vance hardly spoke. Finally the President said, "Well, gentlemen, I am impressed with your planning for this mission. I wasn't able to ask a question that you hadn't anticipated or hadn't thought through. I will make my decision in the next few days. If we go, you know that you'll have my full support."

"Mr. President," Beckwith said, "may I say something?"

"Of course, Colonel."

"On behalf of my men, sir, I hope that you will let us go. Unless you can get the Red Cross to go get the hostages, we want to do it and think we can."

The President smiled. "That will be a factor in my decision, Colonel. That I think you believe you can do it is very important to me. Also, Colonel, the fact that you are from Schley County, Georgia, is not a disadvantage."

I pulled Vance aside as we walked out of the Situation Room. "Do you feel any better about this after hearing their plans?"

"Yes, Ham, I feel a little better. But generals will rarely tell you they can't do something. This is a complex damn operation, and I haven't forgotten the old saying from my Pentagon days that in the military anything that can go wrong will go wrong. I'm just opposed to the idea of a military operation as long as there is any chance of negotiating the release."

As I left the White House that night, I reflected on how disgusted I was with Cy. His unrelenting opposition to the mission was putting President Carter in an uncomfortable position.

Earlier in the day, Zbig had said "Cy is the ultimate example of a good man who has been traumatized by his Vietnam experience."

He was right, I thought. *Cy was going to feel like a damn fool when the helicopters landed on the South Lawn and our hostages climbed out.*

April 17, 1980 (Thursday)

President Carter imposed further sanctions at his press conference. "If this additional set of sanctions and the concerted action of our allies is not successful," he affirmed, "then our next step will be some sort of military action. . . ."

Zbig worried that the public speculation about armed intervention could prompt Iran into a military alert. "We need to conduct a disinformation campaign that will relax the Iranians," he said.

"Maybe I could throw the Iranians off guard if I met with my contact and assured him that in spite of all this military talk, we want to keep negotiating," I said.

Another meeting with the contact made sense. We needed his current assessment of the hostage release date. If we received an encouraging report (which I did not expect), it might justify scuttling the rescue mission to give the negotiations one last chance. If we got a pessimistic report, then we would probably go ahead.

President Carter accepted my suggestion. I called Bourguet and Villalon in Paris. They arranged for me to see the contact immediately. I planned to make the first part of my trip on the Concorde, but discovered that former President Nixon was booked on the same flight. He would undoubtedly have press people traveling with him.

I scurried to make other plans, ordered a big military plane that could make the transatlantic hop, and called Stephanie, who dropped her other work to go with me. When I met her at midnight for our departure, she told me she had scrawled a message to her husband on the blackboard in her kitchen: GONE OVERSEAS WITH HAMILTON.

"I'm sure he'll sleep well," I said.

April 18, 1980 (Friday)

It was eerie to be the only two passengers on a plane that normally carries over a hundred people. Stephanie slept, but I couldn't. I stared at the empty rows of seats and thought about Beckwith and the Delta team, and what I would say to the contact.

That afternoon we arrived in Europe, were met by a waiting car, and driven to the home of an American diplomat, where we anxiously watched the clock until 3:30 A.M., the designated meeting time. The contact greeted me warmly when he arrived, but something seemed different as he slumped down in a large chair. The confident enthusiasm he had shown at our first meeting was gone.

"A lot has happened since we first met," I said, trying to open the conversation.

"Actual preparations were made for the Foreign Ministry to receive the freed hostages," the contact said. "Helicopters were waiting to take them from the compound to the Foreign Ministry. We came so close. But close is not enough." He paused. "It was a big mistake for the United States to break diplomatic relations with Iran. You have left Iran open to the Russians. Soon my country will be filled with KGB agents."

I tried to stay calm. "You are worried about the Russians—but your government will provide them the protection you never gave our diplomats. Look," I said, "what else could we do? This mess has continued for five months. We are sick and tired of—"

He held up his hand to silence me. "I understand your frustration. I understand that President Carter is running for re-election. But once countries break relations, re-establishing them is very difficult."

We talked on, and finally I got to the purpose of my mission. "When do you think the hostages will come home? And please don't give me a diplomatic response—tell me what you really think."

He lapsed into a political lecture on the failure of Iran's new regime to solve the nation's problems. "The hostages are not important anymore. If you traveled to Tehran, you would find no one concerned about them. They have become simply a political issue: a candidate who takes a soft position on the hostages can't hope to be elected."

"But how long will this go on?" I demanded, repeating the question that he had carefully avoided answering.

He looked straight at me. "My friend, I'm afraid that it will be a long time before your people come home."

"How long?" I insisted.

"Months and months," he said quietly. I was relieved. At least now the rescue mission could go forward. If he had said the hostages would be freed in the near future, as he had affirmed so many times before, I would have reported that to the President and maybe we would continue to negotiate. Now we had no choice but to send in the Delta Force.

"I'm sorry," the contact continued, "but there is no other way. I just hope your President doesn't do anything rash, like attack Iran or mine our harbors."

"Don't worry," I replied quickly, "he won't. President Carter is not a militaristic man." As I heard my words, I sounded convincing. I didn't like lying to him.

We bade each other farewell and pledged to get together in the next few weeks for a review. On the long flight home, I wrote out a verbatim report to the President and Secretary Vance. Back at the Residence, Carter read through the pages and called Harold Brown on his secure phone. The operator reached Brown within seconds. "Harold, my last remaining doubt about the mission has been removed. Tell Colonel Beckwith to proceed."

I was sobered as I heard him giving the order, and I thought about the Iranian contact. He was the reason for the continuing negotiations. Little did he know that he was also one of the reasons now for direct military action.

April 22, 1980 (Tuesday)

With the breaking of diplomatic relations, public speculation about the use of force had mushroomed, and the White House staff was becoming more and more concerned that the President might do something rash. We were, in the words of Presidential speechwriter Rick Hertzberg, "sliding down the slippery slope toward war."

Because I was so preoccupied with the hostage negotiations, I had been going to fewer and fewer staff meetings. But I agreed to attend the senior staff meeting to hear their concerns and offer reassurances. I told them we had been negotiating in good faith, had done everything possible to free the hostages, but that the present stalemate could not continue forever. "We've got to worry about the Americans in Iran," I said, "but we also have to think about our nation's honor."

Louie Martin, the President's Special Assistant and highly respected liaison with the black community, blurted out, "Hamilton, don't talk to me about honor! I sat in this room all through Vietnam and heard President Johnson and his Generals and McNamara talk about our honor. All we got to show for that honor was a lot of boys killed and the whole world mad at us."

Someone asked me point-blank if the President had decided to mine the harbors or impose a naval blockade on Iran.

"I can assure you that he has not," I replied firmly.

"How about a rescue mission?" someone else asked.

I swallowed hard. At that moment, Charlie Beckwith and his team were somewhere in the Middle East, preparing to leave for Desert One, Iran.

"The Joint Chiefs have told us from the outset that a rescue mission is impossible," I said quickly and, I hoped, naturally.

I had told a gigantic lie. But there was no other choice. I couldn't tell them the truth, and knew that when news of the successful rescue reached them, they would understand.

April 23, 1980 (Wednesday)

Pollak, Ruth, and I took the shuttle to New York, where a staff member from the prosecutor's office met and drove us into the city. On the way to the courthouse, one of the special prosecutor's staff members pointed out a building and said, "That's where your buddies Steve Rubell and Ian Schrager are serving their sentence for tax evasion."

I asked what he meant, and he told me the building was the jail.

"What's it like in there?" I asked.

"Oh," he replied quickly, "it's a nice minimum-security facility, with a game room and television sets. As prisons go, one of the best."

"Funny," I said, "I've always believed in prison reform, but I was hoping you would tell me that it was a rat-infested building and that those two bastards were eating only bread and water and being tortured every night."

The driver laughed, but I wasn't kidding.

The three of us sat in a dingy room outside the courtroom, waiting, waiting, waiting for Christy to take me to face the jury.

I felt as dirty and grimy as the room, and had to remind myself time and again that I hadn't done anything wrong. Finally I was led into the courtroom, where I raised my right hand, took the oath, and sat down on the stand. I had thought about my demeanor, putting myself into all those courtroom movie scenes of the accused establishing rapport with the jury by looking at them. I tried to appear relaxed and innocent, and glanced a couple of times at the men and women sitting in the double row of chairs to my left. But I felt uncomfortable and self-conscious and couldn't concentrate on the questions.

I couldn't help but wonder what they thought of me. I recalled all the bad press I'd received over the past couple of years: Jordan, who looks down ladies' dresses and spits drinks and wears blue jeans to work at the White House—it wasn't hard to imagine that such a fellow would use drugs. And there I was for them to judge me.

In response to the questions, I told the story of my trip to New York to speak at a dinner of Democratic leaders at "21," how a bunch of us had gone to a cocktail party at the home of a friend, and how one of the women with us was eager to show us Studio 54, the current New York "in" place. I told Christy that after my first year in Washington, after being accused of various outrageous actions, I practically became a hermit. But because it wasn't Washington, I had agreed to go along. I knew the minute I walked into Studio 54 that I had made a mistake. I drank a couple of beers with the group, stayed thirty or forty-five minutes, and returned to the cocktail party.

"Did you use the drug cocaine that night at Studio 54?" the prosecutor asked.

"I did not," I said firmly.

He asked me how I felt about drugs. I looked him straight in the eye as I said, "Mr. Christy, I believe that people, especially people who serve the public, don't have the right to pick and choose which laws they will obey. I don't use drugs."

Then we flew back to Washington. I was relieved to have it over, but also irritated. My day had been wasted. I hadn't done a thing to further the release of the hostages or help Jimmy Carter's re-election. And, halfway around the world somewhere, Charlie Beckwith and his team were getting ready to fly to Iran.

April 24, 1980 (Thursday)

I could hardly hide my excitement as the day passed. Every time I looked at my watch, I would try to think what Beckwith and the Delta team would be doing at that moment.

Remembering the warnings from the military, the President was rightly obsessed with operational security. In the Oval Office earlier in the week, the President had admonished Zbig, Jody, the Vice President, and me to carry out our regular schedules and not do anything out of the ordinary that would arouse suspicion. "And above all, don't tell anyone—not anyone, do you understand? I know that you all have devoted secretaries who know everything about your work, but I don't want them to know about this!"

I went through the motions that morning of a regular schedule, but Eleanor knew that something was up. "Are you OK?" she asked a couple of times. "Are you feeling all right?"

I got word during the morning that the foreign policy group would have a meeting on the rescue effort, and a little before twelve the President asked me to come to the Oval Office. "I got a disturbing call that a couple of our helicopters are down."

"Do you have any details?"

"No, but Harold may have something more to tell us at lunch. That's not the reason I wanted to see you." He paused. "Cy is going to resign."

I was stunned. Helicopters down, Cy resigning—it was too much to absorb.

"I don't want you to tell anyone about it. I just told Mondale but no one else knows. Think about what we can do."

He rose and we walked into the Cabinet Room, where the Vice President, Vance, Brzezinski, and Jody were waiting. We sat down and began eating sandwiches. Brown reported that only six helicopters were proceeding to Desert One. We all asked questions, and Harold calmly responded that the orders were to maintain radio silence. All he knew was that two helicopters were down. On the positive side, he added that if there were no signs of any military alert, they could just as easily be down due to mechanical problems and the raid could proceed on course with just six.

Helicopters down—that could mean deaths or exposure of the mission and harm to the Delta Force. When we finished lunch, Mondale and I walked down to his office, where we tried to reassure each other. He was as troubled about the report as I was.

Our regular campaign meeting was scheduled for that afternoon at 4:30 in the Treaty Room, which was on the same floor as the First Family's living quarters. We were just getting into the discussion when the phone rang. It was answered by Phil Wise, who called the President to the phone. I watched Carter and read his face. He said nothing, then put the phone down. "Y'all continue. I've got to run to the Oval Office for a minute." With that he was gone.

We continued our meeting, and in about ten minutes the phone rang again. "The President for you, Mr. Jordan," the operator said.

"Ham, I want you to get Fritz and Jody and come to the Oval Office at once. Try not to arouse suspicion."

I turned to the group. "Mr. Vice President, Jody, we got another ultimatum from Iran that the President's got to respond to. He wants us to go over it with him. Bob [Strauss], the President suggested that you carry on." As we walked to the Oval Office, I told Jody and the Vice President that I had no idea what the President's call was about, but it couldn't be anything good.

When we entered his private study, he was standing behind his desk, his coat off, sleeves rolled up and his hands on his hips. Zbig was with him. "I've got some bad news . . . I had to abort the rescue mission."

We stood there silently for a long second. My first reaction was not to believe what I had heard. Then the President recounted what had happened. "Two of our helicopters never reached Desert One—that left us six. The Delta team was boarding the six helicopters when they found out that one of them had a mechanical problem and couldn't go on."

"What did Beckwith think?" I blurted out.

"I asked Colonel Beckwith, General Jones, and Harold [Brown] for their recommendations. They all recommended that we abort."

So even Beckwith—the man I knew had believed passionately in the mission and who would never give up—had concluded they had to come back. Helicopters. Damn helicopters! That's what America's supposed to do best—mechanical things. The most difficult part of the mission was supposed to be getting into Iran undetected. We pulled that off, only to have a "mechanical problem." I wondered what that meant . . . a loose bolt, a missing part, or someone somewhere who didn't go through his checklist before sending the helicopters off?

Brown and Vance soon joined us in the small office. "At least there were no American casualties and no innocent Iranians hurt," the President said gently.

He's rationalizing, I thought. *He's as devastated as we are.*

There was silence in the room as Carter leaned back in his chair. Each of us was thinking his own thoughts, wondering where this left us. When the phone rang, the President sat up straight in his chair as he took another call from General Jones, on duty at the Pentagon and in direct contact with Delta.

"Yes, Dave . . ."

The President closed his eyes. His jaw dropped and his face turned ashen. I knew right away that something terrible had happened. He swallowed hard. "Are there any dead?" A few more seconds passed. "I understand . . ." He slowly hung up. In an even voice, he informed us that during the withdrawal, a helicopter had crashed into the C-130 loaded with the Delta team members. There were casualties and probably some dead.

No one said a word. The harsh reality of the failed mission and the tragic deaths began to sink in. Cy's voice broke the stillness. "Mr. President, I'm very, very sorry. . . ."

The President and Brown made several more calls, trying to get details.

Soon the President's small office was crowded, and we moved to the Cabinet Room, where we waited anxiously for the news that the Delta team had gotten out of Iran safely. We discussed how and when to notify our allies, the families of the hostages, Congressional leaders, and the American people.

I began to think more and more about the soldiers lying dead on a faraway desert. It was hard for me to accept that the careful plan had gone awry, that people had actually been killed. I thought about terrible telephone calls that night to the wives and parents of the men. I began to feel dizzy, and, after steadying myself on the arm of my chair, got up and left the Cabinet Room, hoping that no one had noticed. I could almost imagine the stench of the charred bodies. I first walked through the deserted Oval Office and out the door to the South Lawn, but the muggy night air was stifling, so I entered the West Wing. I wandered to my office, then back toward the Oval Office, hoping to clear my head. A tremendous wave of nausea gripped me. I ducked into the President's private bathroom and vomited my guts out. But I didn't feel any better.

When I returned to the Cabinet Room, President Carter was asking the Secretary of Defense, "Harold, what are the plans for notifying the families of the men killed on the mission?"

"Mr. President, we will handle them in the normal way, the service secretaries will—"

"Harold," he interrupted, "I would like to make those calls myself."

"Mr. President, these were military professionals who volunteered for a dangerous mission and were killed in the line of duty. I appreciate your willingness to make the calls, but it is something that has always been done by the service secretaries. Because of the unusual nature of this mission, I'll make some calls myself."

"Very well. But convey to the families that I consider each member of the Delta team a hero."

My God, I thought, *did Carter think he could atone for this by making those terrible calls himself?*

Once it was confirmed that Delta had cleared Iranian airspace, and after we had made plans to inform our allies, Congress, and the families of the hostages and the Delta team, Jody turned the discussion to what President Carter would tell the American people. "Mr. President," he said, lighting one cigarette from another, "what you have got to do in the morning is give the American people a rationale for the mission: why we did it and why we did it now."

Carter nodded and turned to look at Cy with the trace of a smile. "Cy," he said to his old friend, "perhaps you can draft a statement for me presenting a rationale for the mission."

Vance, caught off guard and clearly uncomfortable, looked down at the table. The President's attempt at humor was his strange way of acknowledging that Cy's reservations about the mission had proven to be wise. But, if you had examined Vance's demeanor through the long night, you wouldn't have suspected that he was any less responsible for the disaster than the rest of us. Given the kind of man he was he would never have said, "I told you so."

The President asked Jody to get him a copy of the speech that President Kennedy had made after the failure of the Bay of Pigs invasion.

He then walked over to his large chair, picked up the phone mounted under the table, and asked the operator to get the First Lady, who was out on the road campaigning in Austin, Texas. The President told Rosalynn she should cancel her schedule and make plans to come home early in the morning. He kept saying, "I can't tell you any more now, but you should just come home." It was obvious that she knew something had gone wrong with the rescue mission, but she didn't know what.

On my way home at about 3:30 that morning, my driver, who had heard the news at the garage, said, "The Boss had real guts to try that rescue, Mr. Jordan, real guts! It makes me proud!"

"Yeah, Sergeant—he would have been a hero if it had worked, but now we're going to catch hell for it." Our critics would be sure to say that the failure confirmed Carter's ineptness and demonstrated American impotence. Some in Congress would say the President had violated the War Powers Act by not officially informing them before attempting the rescue. If the mission had succeeded, Jimmy Carter would have been praised for his courage and foresight. Because it didn't, there would be speeches bitterly condemning our plan, Congressional hearings, and, who knows, possibly attempts to impeach the President.

The Sergeant interrupted these gloomy thoughts when we arrived at my apartment. "Would it have worked if they hadn't lost the helicopters, Mr. Jordan—would it have worked?"

He wanted badly to believe that it would have, and so did I.

"Yes, Sergeant, it would have worked. I'm sure it would have."

April 25, 1980 (Friday)

I had been lying awake in bed for about an hour when my White House line rang at about four o'clock.

"Mr. Jordan, please," I heard a strange voice say. "Excuse my English," the voice said haltingly, "I am the interpreter, calling for your Iranian friend."

I had forgotten that I had given him my straight-line number at our first meeting.

I waited, heard a lot of chattering in another language in the background, then the familiar voice on the phone. "Mr. Jordan?"

"Yes."

"What is going on?"

"We tried to rescue our people tonight, but it failed," I said quietly, ashamed of our failure. "It was not a military strike and no Iranians were hurt. It was simply an effort to free the hostages."

"How stupid!" he almost shouted. "How *stupid* of your country to try this. You are going to get the hostages killed!"

I couldn't control myself any longer. "Stupid? The stupid thing is your government holding innocent Americans! The mission that failed tonight should be a lesson to your country. We are losing our patience—and let me warn you that if any harm comes to a single one of our hostages, Iran will pay—and pay dearly!"

He slammed the phone down, and I never spoke with him again.

I arrived at the White House a few minutes before the President went on television to tell the nation about the catastrophe. He looked exhausted and careworn, sitting behind the big wooden desk in the Oval Office as he spoke. "It was my decision to attempt the rescue operation. It was my decision to cancel it when problems developed. . . . The responsibility is fully my own."

The mood at the senior staff meeting was somber and awkward. I sensed that we were all uncomfortable, like when a loved one dies and friends don't quite know what to say.

I sat down at the head of the table and looked slowly around the room at my friends. "Of course, I lied to you two days ago about the rescue mission. I apologize for having to do it, but I believe if you had been in my position and had known that the mission was under way, you would have done the same."

The staff looked shell-shocked. Stu Eizenstat was staring down at the table. Anne Wexler was shaking her head slowly. Was it because she felt sorry for the President or was she angry because I had lied to them all?

After the meeting, I wandered around the White House, feeling like a zombie, lightheaded from no sleep and emotionally drained. My thoughts kept returning to the bodies in the desert. *And the hostages—what will happen to them now? Will they suffer because we failed? And what will Bourguet and Villalon think? Will they feel betrayed?*

I phoned Stephanie and asked her to call the two intermediaries and say I was sorry that I hadn't been able to tell them about the raid, that it wasn't a punitive military strike, but an attempt at a peaceful resolution. "Tell them, Stephie, that the aborted mission has embarrassed the President and our country—and that if anything happens to our people in Tehran, there will be war."

Stephanie called me back to report that she had reached Bourguet. "Christian was shocked but doesn't feel betrayed. He and Hector believe you were against it but that 'radical elements in the Pentagon' convinced the President to attempt it."

"Stephanie," I said, "you should call them back and let them know that I was involved in the planning of the raid and supported it. It was the best way to resolve the crisis."

She relayed that to them and reported back. "They were surprised at your involvement, Hamilton, but said that it was important for you to maintain your credibility with the Iranians, so they will tell them that 'radical American generals have gained the upper hand' in the American government and that this crazy raid was an example of how desperate the American people have become."

I smiled as I heard the message my friends sent back. Always scheming and planning for the future, and never giving up.

April 26, 1980 (Saturday)

I stepped into the Oval Office just as Zbig, Stan Turner, General Vaught, David Jones, and Harold Brown were leaving. "What was that all about?" I asked.

"A postmortem on the rescue mission," the President answered. "Harold thought it would be a good idea so I'd have a clear understanding of what happened."

"That must not have been very pleasant."

"No, it wasn't, but it made me feel better. Everybody will be looking for scapegoats and second-guessing the mission. But we had bad luck—a violent sandstorm caused one of the helicopter's to turn back and one to go down, and then the damn hydraulic failed on the third one. Maybe I'm just rationalizing our failure, but I'll always believe that if Beckwith and the Delta team had been able to go on, they would have been successful."

Months after the Carter Presidency was over, I asked Harold Brown what he had thought about the mission and its chances. He told me that "six or seven times out of ten" it would have worked. "The mission was well planned, well organized and well led," Harold Brown said. "We just had some bad luck."

And then I got my own postmortem straight from Colonel Beckwith. "My big concern all along was operational security," Beckwith recalled. "I felt good about it when we left for Egypt Sunday morning. The pilot who was going to fly us walked out to me and said, 'The way you are acting, you must be in charge.' I said, 'I'm the foreman of this here ranch, what's the question?' He said, 'How much fuel should I put on board?' I asked him, 'Do you know where you're going?' He said that he didn't and that he got his instructions on where to fly to at a certain time and altitude bearing. That made me feel real good. General Jones was doing his part to keep the lid on."

In Egypt, the ninety-seven-man Delta team went on the schedule that would be kept in Iran, sleeping during the day and working at night. Thursday morning, they prepared to leave for Desert One, Iran, hardly looking like crack paramilitary men. "We wore Levi's and nonpolished boots, Army field jackets that had been dyed black and had an American flag on the shoulder, covered with tape. (We'd pull the tape off when we went over the wall in Tehran.) Every man had a Navy watch cap on, and a flannel shirt, any color he wanted as long as it was dark. Some of the men had beards and long hair. If we got in a crack in Iran, a man could throw that jacket away and had a chance of not being too noticeable. Dressing up in a fancy camouflage outfit is a big bunch of shit. It's like wearing a prophylactic."

Before they boarded the C-130s to take them to Oman on the way to Desert One, Beckwith assembled the Delta Force in the hangar and had a major ("a religious sort of fella but not afraid to pull the trigger") read over the roar of the plane's engines a passage from the scriptures. "Chargin' Charlie" then led the group in singing "God Bless America." A psychologist who had worked with the unit said to Beckwith, "God, you guys are up!"

"That had been one of my problems," Beckwith remembered, "getting our guys up one more time. We were only human. We'd sit there at Bragg and read the papers and all the bullshit about negotiations and think, *Well, this time they are going to have to send us in.* Or there'd be a signal from the Pentagon to get ready. There must've been seven or eight times when we were convinced we were going. You know, Bear Bryant wouldn't win many bowl games if he had to tell his players over and over again that the game had been postponed. But after that prayer and singing 'God Bless America,' we were up! God, were we up! You could feel the fucking vibrations!"

The flight in was quiet; the quarters were so tight that the men were sitting or standing in every inch of the plane. A Delta Force intelligence officer told me, "I thought it was just another exercise and we were being jerked around again. Then we started going down, the plane banked for its landing, and I said to myself, *Hell, this is for real!*"

Once on the ground, Beckwith scouted the area, walking a hundred yards down the road. When they saw headlights coming, they fired shots and stopped a busload of bewildered Iranians, whom they unloaded off to the side. "I wasn't worried," Beckwith said. "One of the officers ran up to me and said, 'What do you think?' I told him that I didn't think anything. We had practiced for an encounter with a vehicle. We stopped the bus, and I wasn't going to worry until we stopped ten buses. Then, we'd have a parking problem."

The other four Delta planes brought in the rest of the men and fuel for the helicopters. As soon as they landed, they were covered with camouflage nets. Everything was right on schedule; the men were waiting to move by helicopter to a site near the mountains under cover of dark.

After forty-five minutes, Beckwith radioed General Vaught, in Egypt, on his secure communications. "I need some choppers!"

Beckwith said. Vaught told him that one was seven minutes away; but it took another forty-five minutes before six were there. They would not arrive at the next site until daybreak, which meant risking discovery, but Beckwith made a decision: "Hell, I didn't come this far to turn back. We're going on!"

At this point, Beckwith was not even aware that two helicopters hadn't made it to Desert One at all. "I didn't know then and didn't care," he told me. "All I needed was six choppers, and there were six of 'em there." Beckwith ran from one to another, loading his men and checking that everything was set.

Suddenly, one of the pilots said, "The skipper said to tell you that we've only got five flyable helicopters."

"Dammit man," Beckwith barked, "I've got to get moving. You guys talk special flying language to one another. Go find out what's happening and let me know. I've got to go!" Beckwith went about loading his men. Colonel Kyle, the skipper of the helicopter pilots, came up to him. "Charlie, two choppers didn't make it, and the hydraulic's down in one chopper. It's unsafe and can't go."

"You telling me that you've only got five choppers?" Beckwith barked.

"That's right, Charlie."

"Well, you tell me which one of those planes you want us to get on, because me and my boys are loading up and going home."

Kyle reported their misfortune to Vaught, who called Beckwith and asked if he would consider going on with five helicopters. "Shit no," Beckwith said. (I asked Beckwith what he would have done if he had received a message from the President: "You will go with five." He told me, "I'd have said, 'I can't hear you, we're coming out.'")

Then a disappointed Beckwith set about aborting the mission. He told me, "I started loading my people on the 130s and then Kyle called me back over and said, 'Charlie, what do we do with the helicopters?' And I said, 'If they're flyable, fly them back to the carrier—they cost Sam money.'"

The helicopter pilot who had been the first to arrive at Desert One was worried about having enough fuel to make it back to the carrier. Beckwith advised him to refuel off one of the C-130s. "He lifted up, to move toward the plane, and stirred up a godawful amount of dust. He hit the front of the plane, and the whole thing exploded like a goddamn ball of fire. It was just a plain old accident."

April 27, 1980 (Sunday)

I went to the White House because I didn't want to be alone at my apartment. The offices were deserted and I spent the morning reading the newspaper accounts of the rescue mission.

Hawks were charging that the White House had interfered with the mission, and already liberals were bemoaning the very idea of a military operation. But the reaction of the American people was different. One man-on-the-street interview summed it up: "After months and months of doing nothing, thank God Carter tried something!"

Wait till the other shoe drops, I thought. *When Cy Vance announces his resignation. That's going to rock this city and the world.*

The President and the First Lady went to church that morning and, I learned later, Zbig had arranged for Carter to meet early in the afternoon with Colonel Beckwith and the members of the Delta team. No one was told about the meeting, and the President left by helicopter with Zbig, Harold Brown, and General Jones for his rendezvous with the men.

I was waiting in the Oval Office when he returned. I was surprised to see the big smile on his face.

"Ham, you should have seen them—God, it made me proud! When I got off the helicopter, Colonel Beckwith had his men in formation. And these guys weren't in fancy uniform, they were wearing civilian clothes, some had beards, and a few were banged up. Beckwith walked up to me and saluted. His lips were quivering and he was fighting back tears. He said in a shaky voice, 'Mr. President, on behalf of myself and the Delta team, I want to apologize to you and to the country for our failure to complete our mission.' When he said that, I almost broke down. I shook his hand, he grabbed my arm, and we ended up hugging each other.

"I had expected his men to be big and bulky like Beckwith, but most of them were small and lean and tough-looking. I told the men how proud I was of them, that although their mission hadn't been completed, we all owed them our thanks for their willingness to sacrifice their lives for their countrymen. Then I walked with Beckwith up and down the formation line, stopping to shake hands with each man and say a few words. They were all a little nervous about facing me, but every one of the men, Ham, either said he was sorry for their failure or asked me to let them go back and try again.

"The last few days have been plain hell for me, thinking about those poor men who died on the desert, knowing that we had failed, and that the hostages are stuck in Iran. But that visit today lifted me. At least now I'll always know that we gave it our best try."

Jody and Mondale joined us, and the President reported that Cy had called and was ready to proceed with his resignation. The President said he was inclined to ask Senator Muskie to be Secretary of State. I argued for Warren Christopher, but conceded that Muskie would be a popular public and political choice. Mondale argued strongly for Muskie and Jody agreed.

By late afternoon, stories had begun to leak out about Cy's resignation. Jody urged the President to accelerate his decision to leave as little time as possible between news of the resignation and the announcement of his replacement. The President tracked Muskie down in Nashville, Tennessee, and asked him point-blank to be his Secretary of State. Muskie asked for time to think about it, but Carter was certain that he would accept.

April 28, 1980 (Monday)

I was waiting in the President's outer office when Vance walked out. Gracious as always, he paused to thank Nell Yates, who sat at the desk by the door and managed the Oval Office traffic. Cy was wearing a gray suit, as usual. The smile he gave me seemed strained. He moved slowly, his hand tightly gripping the wooden cane he used because of his recent gout attack. "Zbig bit him on the foot," Rafshoon said irreverently later that day.

The last thing Cy would ever want was pity. As I saw him leaving the office for the last time, any anger I felt toward him was washed away. Cyrus Vance had been in and out of government for most of his life. And this was probably the end. There would be articles and editorials and accolades for his act of principle. But this was not the way he would have wanted to complete his service. He hobbled over to me. "Ham, good luck. Take care of the Boss," he said quietly, shaking my hand.

Words were hard. "Mr. Secretary, don't forget about us here. Stay in touch. We'll all miss you."

He squeezed my hand for an extra second, turned, and walked out to the South Lawn, where his car was parked so he could avoid the press. I stood at the door and watched the gray head bobbing atop the gray suit as he shuffled toward the waiting limousine. Each step seemed painful. I remembered hearing of the wiry young Vance who had played hockey at Yale and had been nicknamed "Spider." Time and events had slowed and crushed Spider Vance, but his honor was intact.

Watching him leave, I felt confused. I was irritated by his sudden departure and the problem it created for the President and the country, but I also admired his having acted out of principle. At the time, it struck me as terribly self-indulgent to put his personal honor and integrity above the interests of the country and his duty to the President. Yet, as the days and weeks passed, my feelings softened. I recognized that if Vance had continued as Secretary of State, he would have had to appear before the press and face endless, hostile Congressional committees and publicly support the failed mission. It would have meant lying—and that was not possible for him.

I feel now that his obligation to the President should have kept him in the Administration for several weeks until Carter could quietly pick his successor and the country had had time to recover from the shock of the failed mission. Then he could have done his duty to himself. After all, Cy Vance had always done his duty.

The President called me into his office right after Cy left.

"Was it difficult?" I asked.

"No, not really. The difficult time for me and Cy was last week, when we both realized that he was leaving. I was just disappointed with him at first. Then after the mission failed, I became angry, really mad at him—you know, the idea that he would walk out on me right in the middle of a crisis. But once I accepted the fact that he was leaving and thought about Ed Muskie, I relaxed. Now I'm sure that his leaving is best for me and for Cy. You know, he hasn't been happy for a while. I'll miss him, but it's for the best."

We began to make plans to announce Muskie's appointment as Secretary of State. President Carter had the unpleasant chore of calling Warren Christopher to tell him that Muskie had been chosen to replace Cy. No one knew Muskie was a contender, and the press reported and widely assumed Christopher to be the front-runner.

April 29, 1980 (Tuesday)

"How did he take it?" I asked the President after he had made the dreaded call to Christopher.

"Just as you'd think. He spoke highly of Ed, thanked me for the honor of being considered, and pledged his support to Ed in the transition. I pushed him to continue as Deputy, but he said that Ed should be free to choose his own Deputy."

I thought about Warren Christopher's career in public service: number-two man at the Justice Department in the Johnson Administration, number-two man at the State Department under Vance, and now maybe number-two man under Muskie. "Always a bridesmaid," I said, thinking out loud.

"He'll be a bride in the second term," the President responded.

"I hope so, Mr. President. He'd be great on the Supreme Court or anywhere else for that matter. As I've told you many times before, Chris is the single most capable person I have met in Washington."

But the President was right to choose Ed Muskie. Warren's talents were not known outside the Administration, whereas Muskie was a large and reassuring public figure coming into a big job right on the heels of the catastrophe on the desert. "You could almost feel the sigh of relief on Capitol Hill," Frank Moore reported, "when we started making the notification calls on Muskie." Press and foreign reaction were equally favorable.

I bumped into Hal Saunders, who was one of Vance's closest friends at the State Department. He was disappointed for Chris but happy about the Muskie appointment. "The President has honored us through this appointment," Hal said simply.

Thank God for Ed Muskie, I thought. *What would we have done without him?* His willingness to serve as Secretary of State was an important political signal that the President, under attack within his own party and down in the polls, could still attract a man like Muskie to give up his safe seat in the Senate for a position in his Administration. It was a strong vote of confidence in Jimmy Carter's political future.

We had been talking about it among ourselves for a couple of days, and Mondale finally brought it up at the regular 10:00 meeting.

"Mr. President," he said, "I don't know if you want to hear this now, but I feel you just have to get out of the White House and talk to the American people. I understand your promise not to

leave the White House until the hostages are released, but nobody dreamed that they would be held for months! We've got a
lot of problems on our plate—the hostages, the economy, a tough
re-election campaign—and the American people need to hear
your voice."

"Fritz, I agree, but I don't know how to get out of here without
breaking my promise."

"Hell, you just do it, Mr. President," Jody chimed in, "and
take the heat for a couple of days."

"What about it, Ham?"

"Mr. President, I agree. It's going to be rough, but you might
as well get it over with."

"See," Mondale continued. "I think that the American people
want you out there badly enough that they won't worry too much
about your pledge not to campaign."

The President smiled. "Fritz and Rosalynn just want me out
there so they won't have to keep campaigning."

Mondale smiled, then said seriously, "I don't know what
Rosalynn thinks, but let me tell you my experience. The first couple of months I explained that you were back at the White House
trying to deal with the hostage crisis and all our other problems,
and people would respond warmly and sympathetically. In the
last couple of months, they just aren't buying that anymore.
They're tired of seeing me pinch-hitting; they want to see their
President."

"Let's do it," Carter said. "It'll be a relief for me to be able to
get out and stop being coy about it. What's the best way, Jody?"

"You'll probably get a question at your press conference
tonight. And just to be sure, I'll try to plant one with somebody
in the White House press corps."

But the press conference was dominated by questions about
Cy's departure and Muskie's taking over, and the question that
we wanted never came. The President was disappointed, because
once he made a decision, he wanted to implement it. Jody and I
looked for another way to announce the change in our posture.

April 30, 1980 (Wednesday)

Carter was having a meeting, open to the press, with community leaders from around the country. Jody and Anne Wexler prompted Chuck Manatt, treasurer of the Democratic National Committee, to ask the President when he would campaign again.

Eleanor and I sat in my office listening to Carter on the White House closed-circuit TV. The President said he had decided to end his self-imposed ban on travel because the problems facing the country were "manageable enough." Eleanor winced. "'Manageable enough.' What does *that* mean?"

"We'll catch hell for that," I said. "They'll show film clips of the President saying back in January that he wasn't going to travel as long as the hostages were being held, and then flash to the meeting today with his comment that the country's problems are manageable. I don't know what he was thinking."

I wandered down to the Oval Office just as the President and Jody were returning from the meeting. One thing about Jimmy Carter—when he screwed up badly, he acknowledged it. Smiling wryly, he said, "Poor choice of words, huh?"

"I'm afraid so, Mr. President," I replied.

"We'll just have to hunker down," said Jody, who would have to bear the brunt of explaining to the media.

"At least I'm free," the President said.

There had been many times during the past four years when I thought the press gave us hell unfairly. Now we were going to catch it—and deserved to. The President had made an unconditional pledge not to campaign until the hostages were released. Contrary to what most people believed, the original decision not to take to the hustings was not political—all of Carter's political advisers had opposed his withdrawal from active campaigning. Yet, we had benefited the same way Presidents usually do in a crisis, as the American people rallied to support their Commander-in-Chief.

Now, several months later, we were reversing course: the rationale presented by the President—that the problems facing the country were manageable—was completely bogus. Much to my surprise, the media reaction to the switch was moderate and understated. Maybe there was simply too much else going on—the failed rescue mission, the Vance resignation, and the Muskie appointment.

May 1, 1980 (Thursday)

Criticism of the rescue mission was growing. Congressional committees announced that they would hold hearings to determine why it failed and whether the President and the White House had "interfered" by not giving the military the necessary support. And was Carter's decision to abort made over the objection of the Delta Force commanders?

The President and Harold Brown decided that Colonel Beckwith should hold a press conference to set the record straight. Beckwith resisted, thinking that he was being made the scapegoat for the failed mission and worried that public exposure would destroy his quiet role as leader of the Pentagon's elite counterterrorist unit. But he reluctantly honored their request and met with the press, insisting that no pictures be taken. The tough, grizzled soldier told the Pentagon press how he had cried when he realized that the mission couldn't go on and had to recommend it be aborted. To the charge that he was so upset by the President and the Pentagon that he planned to resign from the Army, Beckwith replied, "That's pure *bull*, sir!" Later, when asked if it was true that he and the other commanders had wanted to continue the mission but that President Carter would not allow it, he said, "Sir, I hope that I am brave, but I know that I am not stupid. I was not about to risk the lives of those brave men by continuing without enough helicopters."

Charlie Beckwith's appearance before the press ended the

rumors and wild stories that were circulating around the Pentagon and Congress. As he predicted, it also ended his job, which he described as the "best in the Army," and his military career.

After the press conference, Beckwith, slightly uncomfortable, went to the Oval Office to meet with the President, who thanked him for "going public." Beckwith asked if he could tell Carter something.

"Of course, Colonel."

"Mr. President, me and my boys think that you are as tough as a woodpecker's lips."

The two men talked for ten minutes about South Georgia, mutual acquaintances, and hunting. "Mr. President," Beckwith said, "someday I hope me and you can go hunting behind the same bird dog."

May 9, 1980 (Friday)

We spent some time at the foreign policy breakfast talking about the hostages. The elections for the Iranian Parliament were being held that day, and it was widely expected that the religious hardliners would win firm control of the government, further undermining the influence of the group in Iran that wanted to resolve the hostage crisis, particularly Bani-Sadr and Ghotbzadeh.

Bourguet and Villalon had worked to return the bodies of the dead American soldiers to the United States. Then they met in Zurich with the Swiss and Hal Saunders to assess the alternatives for negotiating the release of the hostages. One possibility was that a group of Socialist leaders might go to Iran. Another was an initiative by Islamic countries that had good relations with Iran.

Attending his second foreign policy breakfast as the new Secretary of State, Ed Muskie summarized the situation. "Our people at State think that we are going to have to just sit back and let this thing work its way through Iran's political system. We'll pursue other possibilities, Mr. President, but we're not kidding ourselves. The Iranians are going to have to ultimately see how holding the hostages is hurting their Revolution."

I agreed. "Hector and Christian are going to continue trying, but they think that we are just going to have to sit quietly on the sidelines and wait for the Iranians to come to their senses."

The President peered over his glasses and said, "That could be years."

But there was nothing more we could do. We had felt impotent from the outset and were impotent now. We had tried diplomatic pressures, economic sanctions, negotiations, and finally military action. Our options appeared to be exhausted. The sense of helplessness that weighed on us was relieved only by the knowledge that we had tried everything.

Later, when we were about to leave for the memorial service at Arlington for the eight Delta Force members who were killed in Iran, President Carter stood behind his desk, thumbing through correspondence in his "in" box. "I wonder how the families really feel about the mission—and about me," he said sadly.

Sitting in the amphitheater at Arlington, I could see the President flanked on one side by the families of the dead men—little boys and girls all dressed up, teary-eyed young women, and sad-looking older couples, parents of the men.

On the other side, with the Pentagon brass, Colonel Beckwith sat erect, proud, wearing the same confident look I had noticed that night in the Situation Room. General Vaught, the overall commander of the mission, was tense; the failure seemed to be etched on his face. As the speeches ended, a squadron of jets in full formation flew low over the amphitheater. One of them peeled off, leaving a gap in the tight formation. I glanced over at the President; his eyes were following the path of the squadron.

On the way to the car to join the Presidential motorcade, I saw Harold Brown. He was wiping his face with a handkerchief and seemed a bit embarrassed that I had caught him crying.

"Harold, it was a beautiful ceremony."

"It was, and I'll always feel that we did the right thing," he said, walking briskly to his car.

At the White House, the President told Jody and me what had happened before the ceremony.

"They took us into a large room to meet the families. I think they knew how uncomfortable I felt, because the minute Rosalynn and I walked in, all the wives and parents and children just surrounded us and hugged us and made us feel like one of them," Carter said quietly. "It was so difficult to see those pretty young wives all dressed up, and the children in their best clothes, and to realize that their fathers would never see them again. It was emotionally wrenching, but it was also a wonderful experience. They're all so proud of what those men did."

"The ceremony was touching," I said, "particularly the planes."

The President smiled. "I thought I was going to be able to make it through the ceremony all right, but when I looked up and saw the single jet break formation, it was just too much."

May 21, 1980 (Wednesday)

I couldn't help but worry about what would happen to the campaign. I was prepared for the worst, but somehow the political sky did not fall in on us. Tuesday after Tuesday we stumbled on toward final victory over Kennedy.

We survived politically, but the victories felt hollow to me every time I thought of the dead men—and of the hostages still in Iran.

I had been the point man in the negotiations with the Iranians, and we had failed. I had been a strong advocate of the rescue mission, and it had failed. I had failed before, but never had the consequences seemed so enormous.

May 28, 1980 (Wednesday)

Steve Pollak and Henry Ruth called to say that the special prosecutor's office had informed them that a public announcement on my case was imminent.

"What's their decision?" I asked nervously.

"We don't know. Just relax," Henry responded. "We'll be right on over."

I reminded myself I was innocent, but couldn't help thinking that I might not be believed. I remembered the sad letter H. R. Haldeman had sent me from prison in hopes that I might help him. *Hell*, I thought, *he believed he was innocent too*. (The bond between Chiefs of Staff isn't that strong, and I forwarded his letter to the legal counsel's office without replying.)

Ruth and Pollak came to my office and began phoning around trying to confirm reports that I had been cleared. Finally a wire service reporter called to get a reaction.

"A reaction to what?" Ruth asked. He smiled at me, covered the phone, and said, "They have a report from their New York desk that you've been cleared. You can relax."

The grand jury had voted unanimously not to indict me, and Christy made a strong statement saying that "there is no evidence whatsoever" that I had used drugs.

News spread, staff members were dropping by to congratulate me, and eventually the President strolled in, which was quite an unusual gesture. One of the only other times that he had been to my office was when the special prosecutor was named in my case. He shook hands with Ruth and Pollak, thanked them for their good work, put his arm on my shoulder, and said, "I'm sorry you had to go through this." Someone produced a bottle of cheap champagne and plastic cups, the cork was popped, and soon everyone was celebrating. The festive air seemed strange to me. I was not a hero. All I had done was beat a bum rap.

Jody came in to ask if I wanted to make a statement to the press. I told him that I would prefer to release a simple statement and be done with it.

Later, I met with Ruth and Pollak to discuss my bill. We had agreed at the outset that they would charge me their normal rates. They didn't want to appear to be ingratiating themselves with the White House or doing me any special favors. I owed them a lot of money, but they had earned every penny of it. When I told Eleanor the amount, her response was simple. "How will you ever pay it back?"

"Very, very slowly," I said with a chuckle. "You know, Ellie, maybe I should have hired them to defend me against the gossip columnists."

She laughed, but I wasn't completely kidding.

May 30, 1980 (Friday)

Several days before the last round of primaries, I got a call from a casual friend who worked in our 1976 campaign effort. The friend was now supporting Kennedy. "I've got an important member of the Senator's inner circle who wants to talk to you privately on the condition that it be kept absolutely confidential."

"What about?" I asked skeptically, not sure if I was being sent a message or whether this person wanted to defect.

"About how to get Kennedy out."

"Does your friend want to help, or is he switching sides, or what?"

"I'm not sure. I'd just urge you to meet with him. And I promised him that you'd tell no one. It's worth your while."

We met the next night at my apartment. The campaign worker seemed uneasy as I showed him in and offered a beer.

"I'm going to tell you some things," he said, "but only on the condition that you treat all this confidentially."

He said he realized that the campaign was over and had been for weeks, but that the Senator was now on a kamikaze mission that would destroy the party and ruin Kennedy's future.

"You won't get any argument from me on that," I said.

He smiled. "Some of the people the Senator is listening to now don't care about the party or about him. They're convinced that Carter is such a bad man that he has to be defeated even if it means a Reagan Presidency."

"Is that what *you* think?" I asked abruptly, annoyed by both the arrogance and the illogic of the thinking in the Kennedy camp.

"No," he said quietly, "I don't think the President is a bad man." He paused and then looked me straight in the eye. "But I do think he's been a poor President."

His direct and obviously sincere response gave me a jolt. I could tell that he took no joy in expressing his negative feelings about the President to my face. "Our personal feelings are not that important," I said. "What are we going to do?"

"For the sake of the Senator's ego and his own future, and for the sake of the party, we have to find an honorable way for him to get out of the race after Tuesday," he said.

"I agree. How?"

"You must modify your position on some of the key issues," he quickly responded. "Or . . . or," he repeated, "you must debate the Senator, give him the forum that he deserves to express his differences with the Administration."

"That's impossible," I said strongly. "Even if it were possible to get Carter to swallow Kennedy's positions, do you realize how it would look for him to reverse course just to get the Senator out of the race?"

"I understand. But I think what we're really talking about is an honorable way for the Senator to drop out and also claim that he's made a difference in policy."

"That's acceptable to a point if you are talking about face-saving gestures for the Senator, but—"

"No, I'm talking about a real change in the President's policy."

"It'll never happen," I replied.

We went on for a while, argued a bit, had a few more beers, and began to feel relaxed with each other. It was a comfort to me to know that at least he was personally committed to Kennedy and believed in his issues and was not just trying to ingratiate himself with the Administration.

"What is it about the President that the Senator finds so distasteful?" I asked.

"I think the best way to describe it would be a general lack of respect for Jimmy Carter as a political leader."

We agreed to talk again after the primaries. "I'll call you late Tuesday," he said as we stood at the door to my apartment. I slept better that night. At least there was someone in the Kennedy camp to talk to now.

June 3, 1980 (Tuesday)

I went over to campaign headquarters to watch the returns from "Super Tuesday" with the staff. Waiting for the results, I remembered the 1976 primaries. Ex-Governor Jimmy Carter had started off red-hot, winning Iowa, New Hampshire, Florida, and Pennsylvania. But as the contest dragged on and Carter emerged as the front-runner, his opponents ganged up on him, the scrutiny of the press increased, and the party establishment tried to stop him. Averell Harriman articulated the feelings of the Washington establishment when someone in the press asked him what he thought about Carter as the party's nominee. "Carter? How can Carter be nominated? I don't know him and don't know anyone who does!"

And the American people, at first fascinated by the grinning Carter who had slain all of the political giants, began to tire of seeing him on television every week claiming victory in another primary. He was frequently defeated in the late primaries by Jerry Brown and Frank Church, but we had amassed an insurmountable delegate lead.

We had prevailed, but were badly tattered by the time it was over.

On Super Tuesday 1980 Kennedy won five of the eight primaries, but more important we had won 2123 delegates by the end of the day, more than enough to lock up the nomination. I felt like the long-distance runner who falls across the tape to victory.

June 4, 1980 (Wednesday)

Caddell and Rafshoon were at my office. "Pat and I have been thinking about this for a while," Jerry said. "We think you should leave the White House and work full-time on the campaign."

I was shocked. "I can't leave here . . . of course, nobody's indispensable, but if I don't sit on things here, who will? This damn government is one huge time bomb that can go off at any moment. The best place for me to be is here trying to anticipate and head off problems."

"I disagree strongly," Pat said, obviously unshakable in his belief. "You can't run the campaign from the White House, but maybe you *can* run the government from the campaign!"

"Pat, that's not realistic. There are so many damn moving parts to this government that we can't even run it from the White House, much less from the campaign."

Rafshoon was more convincing. "Too many campaign decisions are either not being made or being made incorrectly because people can't get you to pay attention to them. Basically, it's a question of whether or not someone here at the White House can do what you do. No one else at the campaign can or wants to make these decisions."

And the more I thought about the move, the more attractive it became. Leaving the White House meant freedom to me. I would no longer be a "government official." I had a nightmare of hearing Reagan say, "I promise you that if I am elected President, I will surround myself with staff people who will look and play the role of experienced advisers." The Republicans would have more trouble making such a charge if I were over at campaign headquarters instead of a dozen steps from the Oval Office.

I had already made up my mind to leave the White House in November after the election, and had even accepted a position with Emory University. I hadn't told Carter, partly because there had been no need to bother him and partly because I didn't look forward to having him try to talk me out of it. I sat down at my typewriter and pecked out the memo that presented the arguments for and against my leaving soon. I first noted my plan to resign after November, then wrote: "Quite frankly, Mr. President, I am worn out emotionally and intellectually and have no desire to continue working at the White House. As a practical matter, I couldn't afford to continue working here even if I wanted, as I have a huge legal bill that I have to pay."

I went on to say that whether I should stay at the White House or go to the campaign was largely a matter of measuring what there was to be done at the campaign as opposed to what some other person—either staff director Al McDonald or Jack Watson—could do here in my place. Both men, I mentioned, were stronger than I on administrative details.

After the President read my memo, he called me in. "I talked to Kirbo and Rosalynn and thought about it a good bit. I think you should go on over to the campaign. We haven't really paid that much attention to it the past few months. Once we won the first batch of primaries and mounted a delegate lead, the campaign staff has had to kick and scream to get our attention. We are going to have a tough damn time in the fall the way Kennedy is behaving and the way the economy looks."

The President made no reference to my plan to leave Washington in November. I wondered if he just accepted the idea or whether he would try to talk me out of it after the election. In any case, I was glad not to have to discuss it then. Perhaps he thought that after the campaign it would be best for him if I moved on. I never did find that out.

In the evening the phone rang at my apartment.

"I'm sorry I didn't call you last night," the Kennedy contact said, "but a lot is going on."

"I understand," I replied, in an effort to be gracious. I added, "You guys did pretty well yesterday."

"That's one of the problems. Everybody here is up. The Senator has been in meetings all day today with staff and advisers and on the phone talking around the country. Everybody is telling him how great he did Tuesday—"

"And?"

"Well, Hamilton, I don't think we're going to get out. Forty-eight hours ago, we didn't have a reason to continue the race, but after the primaries yesterday, a lot of people think we should stay in and continue to fight to change some of your policies. If we drop out now, we'll be saying to the people who worked for us and voted for us yesterday that it was all for nothing."

I was disappointed. His tune had changed totally in the several days since I had seen him. "Don't you realize that we've won the nomination and will control the platform proceedings and the convention?" I argued back. "We are not going to change our policy. All you guys are going to do is divide the party and give Reagan the White House. Does that bother you?"

"Hell, yes, it bothers me! But, as I told you the other night, there are a lot of people in the campaign who think that Carter is as bad as Reagan."

"Aw, come on," I said, trying to control my anger. "I don't think the Senator believes there is no difference between the President and Reagan. But I *am* starting to think that some of you Kennedy people are so bitter that you just don't care who wins!"

He was silent.

Sighing, I asked, "Where do we go from here?"

"I'm not sure. The Senator is going to see the President tomorrow. Things could change overnight, but my strong hunch is that he'll tell the President that, unless he agrees to debate the issues or makes some basic change in economic policy, the Senator plans to continue his fight."

"I'm sorry to hear that." I paused for a second. "Well, let's stay in touch. You know how to reach me. I'll talk to you any time. I hope you'll think about what you're doing." I remembered his metaphor. "I think you guys are on a kamikaze mission that will prove absolutely nothing and could be fatal to us both."

"Kamikazes can make a point," he responded quickly. "In fact, they usually altered the course of the ship they were trying to hit."

I chuckled. "OK, you win—but we're going to shoot you down before you have a chance to sink our ship."

"Touché," he replied. We both laughed and hung up.

I was prepared for the worst now, because it looked as if Ted Kennedy was going to fight us all the way to the convention. I remembered what Kirbo had said about how hard it could be to call it quits, particularly for a Kennedy. A lot of people in the party were going to be calling for Ted Kennedy to drop out. Maybe after a couple of days they would change their minds and I would hear again from the Kennedy contact.

He never called.

June 5, 1980 (Thursday)

After Senator Kennedy met with the President, I waited for Carter to call me in and give me a report. When he didn't, I assumed the meeting hadn't gone well. I couldn't contain my curiosity, so I walked down to the Oval Office.

The President looked irritated when I asked, "What happened?"

"Nothing good," he snapped. "He was nervous and kept rambling on about wanting to debate me, and that I should change my policies and stimulate the economy, and that he felt a special responsibility to his voters and the party. Finally I said, 'Ted, are you going to get out or not?' He said that he wouldn't and that was that." The President paused. The frustration that he had undoubtedly disguised during his meeting with Kennedy was all coming out now. "I think he's going to fight us right through the convention, and I wouldn't bet on his support for the ticket in the general election. I don't think he cares about the party or who wins in November. Deep down, I suspect he'd rather see Reagan elected than me."

"I'm not even sure if that feeling is deep down, Mr. President," I said.

We agreed to continue being publicly gracious to Kennedy but to stick to our guns about the budget and economic policy. The President summed up his feelings: "The only thing worse than having him fight us all the way to the convention would be for it to appear to the American people that I am buying him out of the race by changing my policies."

June 9, 1980 (Monday)

If I was going over to the campaign, it was essential that Bob Strauss support the move. I went to campaign headquarters, located on five floors of a rundown office building directly over a topless bar. Loud music poured out into the dingy lobby where I waited for the poky elevator to arrive.

It was amusing to see the elegant Strauss in these crowded, shabby surroundings. He welcomed me warmly. I told him that I had been thinking of working full-time on the campaign, but that I didn't want to do so if it created any problems for him or if he thought my efforts were needed more at the White House.

Strauss paused. I could see the wheels in his head spinning. "I've been thinking the same thing for a while," he said, rolling a little piece of paper up tightly between his fingers and sticking it into his mouth. "This damn thing here has too many moving parts for me to keep up with it all and have time to do what I do best— raise money, deal with the press, and work with the party and the Hill."

Bob didn't say it, but I could tell that he was worried about how it would be perceived. He wanted me there, but not in a way that diminished his own role. And I didn't want to do that, as Bob Strauss had skills and contacts to deal with the press and political community that no one else in the Democratic community had. "Bob, we won't even consider this unless you think it's necessary and will work. If I come, I want to do it in a way that helps you and the campaign and frees you for bigger problems. My title," I said, "should be deputy chairman."

"Hell, yes!" he said. "Come on over and let's do it soon." Then, smiling, he added sarcastically, "Mr. Jordan, if I am going to be captain of the *Titanic*, I want to have your ass over here. Because when we hit the iceberg and start to go down, I am going to turn and point the finger at the navigator—*you*," he said with a roar. I laughed but sensed he wasn't entirely kidding.

June 11, 1980 (Wednesday)

Jody made the announcement that I was leaving and that Jack Watson would replace me as Chief of Staff. I tried to persuade Eleanor to stay at the White House. I didn't want a move to the campaign to jeopardize her longevity with the government or to "politicize her" in a way that might prevent her from continuing to work at the White House after the election. But she was determined to take those risks, and for selfish reasons I was glad she was.

The day of the announcement Eleanor and I went over to look at our new quarters. I was assigned two small offices that looked out onto an alley. The toilet on our floor didn't work. We would no longer have people falling all over us, eager to meet our every need. It was just the two of us. "You might say it isn't the White House," Eleanor said playfully.

"That's why I like it," I told her.

We loaded my personal files and boxes into my car. As I drove out of the White House gates, I realized that this was my farewell to government.

I had one last challenge before me, and it invigorated me to know that in six months it would all be over. During Jimmy Carter's political career, we had defeated George Wallace, Scoop Jackson, Morris Udall, Birch Bayh, Jerry Brown, Frank Church, President Gerald Ford, and Teddy Kennedy. It would feel good to have Ronald Reagan's scalp too—and then I could go home to Georgia.

June 12, 1980 (Thursday)

"I expect to be running against Reagan," the President had told
me one day in October 1979, and he cautioned, "It would be a
mistake to underestimate him. After years and years on the radio
and traveling around the country, speaking to Republican au-
diences, he's got a hard-core following that is unshakable in its
support."

I disagreed. I thought that Reagan's very strength—his hold on
the right wing of the Republican Party—was also his vulnerability, and I thought that the primaries would expose it. But
Jimmy Carter's expectation proved to be true.

Tim Kraft and Les Francis arranged for a group of prominent
Democrats from California to come to Washington and spend the
day talking about Reagan. Our goal was to learn about this man
from the people who knew him best. Among the visitors was "Big
Daddy" Jesse Unruh, former Speaker of the California House and
current State Treasurer, who had run for Governor against Reagan and lost. At a conference table in the Hay-Adams Hotel, Jesse
shook his massive finger in my face and said, "Hamilton, don't
make the same mistake that every person in this room has made
at one time or another and underestimate Ronald Reagan. You
may think he's too old or too much of a right-winger or just a
grade-B movie actor. He's all of those things, but above everything else Ronald Reagan is an excellent communicator. You can
argue with him or debate and think you've got him cornered,
then he'll say something folksy, shrug his shoulders, and he's
gone."

Later, I highlighted what we had learned in a memorandum to
the President.

People tend to underestimate Reagan. While he may not
have a first-class mind or be a deep thinker, he is not
dumb. "Shrewd" is the word used by these men who have
known him for so long.

He does have a strongly held conservative philosophy which often leads him to simplistic, black and white judgments about complex issues.

People who know him and work with him like him. I believe he enjoys the public perception of being a "nice man."

He does not work hard. Regardless of what was pending in the Governor's office or before the Legislature, Reagan would always head home around three or four. He paces himself.

He has few close friends in politics or government. Most of his close personal friends are from the entertainment business. He is also close to a group of conservative businessmen who have "sponsored" his political career.

Reagan has a bad temper, but has been generally successful over the years in controlling it in public. Jesse Unruh said that there was a mean side to him, and if he ever got piqued publicly, it could really hurt him.

Although they have attempted to downplay it, his wife Nancy has a strong influence on his political thinking and decisions.

All major decisions are made in consultation with a group of advisers who have been with Reagan a long time. In this sense, you can't think of Reagan as an individual but as part of a group of people who make decisions. It would be unheard of for Reagan to make a major decision without extended consultation with his kitchen cabinet. The people who made this observation added that there are very bright political minds in his group of advisers.

Above all, Ronald Reagan is a very effective "communicator." They say that he just has an uncanny ability to say things in a way that appeals to a broad spectrum of the voters. True, it is almost always simplistic and sometimes wrong, but people hear him, like him and believe him. For this reason, our California friends predict that he will do well in any debate setting.

Performance as Governor of California. Our California friends, much to my surprise, said that for a Republican,

Reagan had not been a bad Governor. They said that he made some good appointments to key positions and had pursued a more moderate policy generally than was perceived by either the media or the political community. They said that his conservative rhetoric always exceeded his actions and decisions as Governor of California. Still, he was a Republican and approached problems from the basic assumption that government was too big, basically bad and that it worked against the interests of capitalism and the free enterprise system.

Still, Reagan is vulnerable on a number of specific issues which have come to light in the course of our research. The consensus (of the California group) was that what Reagan had said would be more damaging than what he had done. I believe that this is particularly true in the area of foreign policy, where his political rhetoric has been simplistic and extreme.

I reviewed my memo before sending it in. I had written it to convey to the President what we had learned about Ronald Reagan and to make sure that we didn't underestimate the man. But I had ended up convincing myself that the re-election campaign was not going to be easy.

Week of June 16–20, 1980

A rash of national polls confirmed publicly what Pat Caddell had been telling us privately—that Reagan had pulled ahead of the President.

The Kennedy forces, who were being defeated on the issues as the Democrats met in Washington and began to draft a platform, were heartened by the evidence of Carter's vulnerability and switched their political efforts to try to change the vote of the Carter delegates. The device they chose was a rule that would be voted on first at the convention; it provided that each delegate was bound to vote for the candidate to whom he or she was pledged.

Talk of an "open convention" swept Washington. "Calling it an open convention is a slight misnomer," Jody said sarcastically in an interview. "It's an obvious, blatant attempt to dump the President, to change the rules after the game has been won, and, most important, to ignore the wishes of the millions of people who voted in the primaries."

We redoubled our effort to "stroke" our delegates, planning special mailings, regular telephone calls, and briefings for them in Washington.

It looked like it was going to be a long, hot summer.

June 25, 1980 (Wednesday)

After moving to the campaign and having a couple of weeks to settle in, I knew that it was time for me to do once again what I had done as long as I had known Jimmy Carter—go off and think about the upcoming campaign and put my thoughts down on paper. So my typewriter and I headed for the eastern shore of Maryland for a few days.

For the first time in months, I was able to sleep late every morning and relax beside the quiet waters. I also read several books about Presidential elections. During the warm afternoons, as the breeze blew steadily off the water, I sat on the screened porch, typing out my thoughts.

Eyes Only

TO: President Carter
FROM: Hamilton Jordan

Overview

I would like to present at the outset a summary of my

own thoughts and an analysis of the problems that we must overcome for you to win re-election as President.

1. <u>The Kennedy challenge hurt us very badly, not only within the Democratic Party but with the electorate as a whole.</u> Some of the ways that he hurt us are obvious, and others more subtle, but all are important:

   A. Kennedy engaged us in a protracted campaign that placed you in a political posture for an extended period of time and undermined your image.

      Serious and sustained media speculation about a possible Kennedy candidacy began last June. The result is that the campaign for the Democratic nomination has lasted for over a year, putting you in the continuing posture of being both an incumbent President and a political candidate over a very long period of time. This long campaign and the extensive coverage that it has received (and continues to receive) is beyond the tolerance of most people. As a result, the American people today are sick of the process and tired of the candidates.

      The American people have had a double dose of you as both a candidate and as a President constantly involved and embroiled in controversial issues and problems.

   B. Because of the extended campaign, the exhaustive coverage by the media, and the continuing irresponsible attacks by Senator Kennedy, almost everything that you have done over the past year— even when unpopular and controversial—has been presented to the American people by the news media in a political/campaign context.

      The most costly consequence is that support for you based on your being a likable, well-intentioned, compassionate, and at times atypical politician has eroded badly. The Kennedy attacks, reinforced by the media's natural tendency to see everything in the context of the campaign, have made you seem more like the manipulative politician bent on re-election at all costs than the man and the President that you are.

C. Kennedy's sustained and exaggerated attacks on your record and his unrealistic promises have alienated key groups in the Democratic Party by obscuring the solid record we have.

As a result, key elements of the Democratic Party are unappreciative of what we have done when measured against Kennedy's rhetoric.

D. Kennedy's attacks have hurt us badly with liberals. As a result, liberals are today providing a financial and political base for a candidate whose record does not deserve their support (Anderson) against an incumbent President whose record on issues of symbolic importance to liberal ideologues is deserving of their support.

E. The tough primary campaigns and his harsh, paid media in certain states—Pennsylvania and New York, for example—have left state parties divided and many Democratic and independent voters alienated.

For all of the reasons presented here, we have come out of this primary year and the unsuccessful Kennedy challenge not enhanced or strengthened by the contest, but damaged severely.

2. A growing number of people in this country do not believe that it makes a real difference who is elected President of the United States. This feeling, however unfortunate and invalid, works against your re-election in ways both obvious and subtle.

3. Despite the critical nature of the problems which face our country at home and abroad, there is no evident feeling that the 1980 election is particularly significant.

4. A significant number of people believe that there is

no difference between you and Ronald Reagan.

5. You will not be elected President unless we succeed partially in dispelling the notion that it doesn't matter who the President is, unless we convince the American people that this is a critical election in the life of our country and that there are real and substantial differences between you and Ronald Reagan.

If the perception persists and grows that there are no real differences between you and Reagan, the electoral consequences will be severe for us:

—The Democratic coalition will never coalesce.

—Minority voters will stay home in record numbers.

—Liberals will defect and/or sit home.

—The Anderson candidacy will flourish, making our "wasted vote/spoiler" theme invalid.

—The natural tendency for disenchanted voters to favor a change will be a strong and significant factor in voting decisions.

—When no differences are perceived between candidates, the voting decisions are increasingly oriented toward personal qualities and characteristics. Based on Pat's recent figures, this would work to our disadvantage.*

6. As Pat Caddell often says, the candidate who is successful in "defining" the election is usually the winner. If we are able to accurately define the 1980 election as an important election in the history of our country and present the American people with a vision of our country's future, you will be re-elected.

We must be successful in putting this election in a historical context, explaining the past four years, the Administration's successes, failures, and attempts to

---

*This is the first time that "personal qualities" are not a basic strength of ours. This has to be recovered.

confront the real problems which face our people.
This campaign will not be won if we become mired
down in a defense of the Consumer Price Index and
the unemployment figures. It can only be won by
painting the American people an accurate picture of
where we are as a nation and a people, what our
problems and opportunities are, what we have done
the past four years, and what we propose to do over
the next four years.

7. For us to be successful in presenting to the American
people a vision of our country's future, you must tell
us what your vision, your plans and hopes are for our
people and nation. I know that you have such a vision, but it must be communicated to us if we are to
be able to develop a credible rationale for the re-election of Jimmy Carter and Walter Mondale.

I wrote him several pages called "Lessons from the Past,"
which drew on the 1976 campaign. One "lesson" was a reminder
that he had damaged his own cause with his tactics against Ford.

You were at times strident and personal in your attacks
on President Ford. Because Ford was widely perceived as
being a "good man," rhetoric directed at Ford that seemed
personal and harsh hurt us. I believe that we will find ourselves in a similar posture in the fall campaign when anything that smacks of a personal attack on Reagan will be
counterproductive.

I went on in the memorandum to address and dissect every
problem and obstacle to re-election. But time and again, I got
back to the basic theme: we could win re-election only by clearly
showing the American people "the differences" between a Carter
Presidency and a Reagan Presidency.

I was troubled by the insinuation of my own analysis that we couldn't just run on our record. (And as the campaign approached, there were some who thought that the Carter record should be the basis for the re-election effort.) For the things that we had done that I was most proud of—energy legislation, the Panama Canal Treaties, the Camp David peace treaties, SALT II, and our China policy—were all political losers. We would try to make the argument in the fall campaign that Jimmy Carter had tackled the tough issues, but that wasn't going to be enough.

When I returned to Washington, I gave the President my memorandum. He agreed with my analysis, signed off on a series of questions I had raised, and instructed that it be circulated to Mondale, Strauss, Kirbo, Powell, Caddell, and Rafshoon for their reactions.

July 16, 1980 (Wednesday)

I watched the Republican convention in my apartment with a couple of friends. I was chilled when I heard Walter Cronkite interviewing former President Gerald Ford about the possibility of his being Vice President on the Reagan ticket. An earnest-sounding Ford said, "If I go to Washington—and I'm not saying that I am accepting—I have to go there with the belief that I will play a meaningful role across the board."

"My God," I exclaimed. "They're serious about this thing!"

"They could run as the 'nice' ticket," someone joked. I didn't find it very funny.

"Reagan and Ford would be strong medicine," I said, thinking that together they could dominate the right and center of the political spectrum, plus carry their home states of California and Michigan.

Around ten o'clock, CBS News reported unequivocally that Gerald Ford had agreed to be Reagan's running mate. This was followed by interviews with friends of both Reagan and Ford talking about the negotiations and the "deal" that was shaping up between them. Gerald Ford was asking for day-to-day control over the budget process and foreign policy.

"What else is there?" someone asked with a hoot.

I realized that Reagan and Ford were actually discussing the sharing of the Presidency. The very thing that made it a strong ticket was its major weakness: the basic question of "who's in charge?" I relaxed and enjoyed watching them mired down in a public debate that demonstrated Ronald Reagan's lack of understanding of the power, the structure, and the traditions of the American Presidency. Whether or not Ford joined the ticket, the public spectacle of Reagan bartering away the powers of his Presidency to get the popular former President on his ticket was at significant cost to the image that he surely had hoped to achieve at the convention.

Ronald Reagan, however, was reportedly sitting in his hotel watching television and seeing the same messy situation develop. After a couple of hours of stories and speculation, it was announced that he was headed to the convention hall to address the delegates. And I was impressed with the decisive way that he dropped the idea, marched over to the hall, and announced his selection of George Bush, his former opponent and a man unacceptable to many of his right-wing supporters as his running mate. Reagan had seized the moment and the initiative in a deft way that confirmed what we had heard from the Californians.

"He may be an ideologue," I said to Caddell, "but he's a pragmatist, and choosing Bush proves that he is not going to help us paint him as a right-wing conservative."

Reagan got a boost out of the convention, but it looked as if the reporters and columnists might still have a field day with the "Ford-Reagan" deal, which might prove to be damning evidence that Ronald Reagan did not understand the scope and magnitude of the job he wanted.

July 25, 1980 (Friday)

I was lying on the beach enjoying the Puerto Rican sun when the Billy Carter story exploded. I had spoken to a party fund-raiser, taken a few days off, and left word with Eleanor not to disturb me unless it was an emergency. *The San Juan Star* kept me up-to-date on the news in the States. The stories of Billy Carter's "Libyan connection" had moved quickly to the front page, with headlines about subpoenas and Congressional hearings.

"It's starting to smell like Watergate," I said to a friend.

When the press began calling it "Billygate," I realized that my self-imposed isolation had ended, and I phoned Jody.

"Of course nothing is wrong," Jody said calmly, "but it looks godawful and it's like a tar baby—everybody here that's touched the damn thing looks bad: the President, Zbig, Rosalynn, and now Attorney General Civiletti."

I had never resented Billy Carter's making capital of his brother's success—after all, it had disrupted his own life in Plains. What I could not understand was that, while speaking all over the country as "the President's brother," Billy never accepted any responsibility for the trouble his actions caused the President. I never thought his remarks were deliberately malicious, but they had the same effect.

Time and again over the four years, friends of the President who were not comfortable talking to him about his brother would pull me aside and say, "Can't the President do something about Billy? Can't the President shut him up?"

They never understood that if the President had tried to "change" Billy, it would have only reinforced Billy's resentment and made things worse. And now, in the summer of 1980, it made little sense for the President to get mad at the sober Billy for what the drinking Billy had said and done.

I stayed in Puerto Rico for two more days, but Billygate had pretty much spoiled my vacation. So much for our hopes that the President could keep a low profile until the convention. And it was inevitable that the image of the President, mired down again in controversy, Senate committee hearings, and depositions would give comfort to those trying to steal the nomination from us.

July 29, 1980 (Tuesday)

Eleanor came into my office carrying a wire story. "Have you seen this?"

I read it: an ABC-Harris poll showed that 77 percent of the American people disapproved of the President's handling of his job, the worst rating of any American President in the history of polling, and worse even than Nixon at the height of Watergate.

"What do you think?" asked Eleanor.

"I can't think anymore." I called Caddell for reassurance.

"You know," Pat explained, "it's not like our ratings have been good or anything, but the President's approval rating has hung around 35 percent. But in the last ten days, our polls show that his approval rating has dropped 12 percent. That's an unbelievable drop! This damn Billy Carter stuff is killing us!"

We're in worse shape than Nixon, I thought. *Is it possible that Billy Carter's shenanigans with the Libyans have hurt Carter more than the Watergate burglary hurt Nixon?*

July 31, 1980 (Thursday)

I had taken a memo to the President about plans for the convention and started discussing our latest delegate count, but he wanted to talk about the Shah, who had died in Egypt on July 27. Tehran radio rejoiced: "The bloodsucker of the century has died at last."

"Maybe this will give the Iranians an excuse to end the crisis," he reasoned. "We'll try to use the Shah's death as a pretext to get negotiations started again."

I didn't say anything.

"Think about all that has happened to the Shah since I first saw him in seventy-seven," the President mused. "He lost his throne, his country, and finally his life. He tolerated a lot of bad things in order to stay in power over the years, but in spite of all the stories about Savak and torture and murders, when he was under attack from the Khomeini forces, he didn't use military force to try to stay in power."

"And regretted it," I added, remembering my conversations with the Shah at Lackland; how he said he was sorry he hadn't cracked down on his opponents.

"I don't know," the President said. "That may have just been his way to rationalize what happened to him."

"But he blamed you totally, Mr. President, for his downfall," I added.

"Khomeini blames me for keeping the Shah in power, and the Shah blamed me for bringing him down." He sighed, then smiled and said, "But that's what Presidents are for."

Several people on the campaign staff gathered in my office to watch the evening news coverage of the bizarre scene of independent candidate John Anderson visiting Ted Kennedy at his Senate office and the two of them posing for pictures and trading compliments.

"I think he's one of the distinguished leaders of the Democratic Party," the bespectacled Anderson said, smiling warmly at the Senator.

"I admire the efforts he has made to reach a responsible solution to the concerns of millions of Americans," Kennedy said in return.

Anderson also hinted that he would "consider" dropping his independent candidacy if the Democrats awarded Kennedy the nomination.

NBC described them as the political "odd couple." "They're a picture of innocence, aren't they?" someone commented.

"Innocence, hell," I said. "They're like two hookers at a Shriners' convention."

Everyone laughed, but I was really angry. Here were two men who had been defeated all over the country, yet they had both managed to get on the evening news by appearing together. I never really resented Kennedy's challenge to us, for, at the time he decided to run, it seemed that he had good prospects for winning. Later, as it became mathematically impossible for him to be nominated, I developed an enormous resentment of what his continuing in the race would do to our chances of beating Reagan.

And I never had any strong personal feelings against Governor Reagan. He believed deeply in certain things, things that scared the hell out of me, but I knew he was sincere in his beliefs.

John Anderson was another matter altogether. The only other person I had ever seen in my own political experience who was so consumed by his image of himself was Lester Maddox. Both men had a habit of referring to themselves in the third person, as if they were on the outside talking about someone other than themselves.

John Anderson was a political aberration, largely a product of the media's accurate contention that neither Carter nor Reagan was a highly popular choice. Consequently, as speculation grew about how a third-party effort would affect the general election, the press played a big part, willing or not, in increasing Anderson's recognition and stature by drawing attention to his candidacy. The ten-term congressman had failed to win a single primary, and, in fact, had even been trounced by Reagan in his own home-state primary in Illinois.

I wondered what he believed in. It was hard to tell by looking at either his voting record as a congressman or his statements as a Presidential candidate. Rejected within his own party, he had adopted policies and rhetoric that were designed to appeal to liberal voters. He had gone from being a conservative Republican to being the darling of the doctrinaire liberals. The only thing that I was sure about was that John Anderson believed most of all in himself and his own ambitions.

To see Anderson and Kennedy using each other disgusted me; their appearance together should hurt them both. Kennedy was demonstrating how little he cared for the Democratic Party with his public flirtation with Anderson, and Anderson's lofty appeal was reduced to his blatant effort to appear on the evening news. It irritated me even more that they had pulled it off, getting national attention for their strange meeting, which produced nothing more than the coverage of it.

August 1, 1980 (Friday)

"We've got a full-fledged revolt on our hands," I said to Eleanor as I read the papers, which were filled with Billygate and stories of possible defections from President Carter.

"The Democrats in Congress are really kicking the President, now that he's down," she said.

"Hell, they kicked us when we were up!" (A later study showed that 75 percent of the public criticism of President Carter in his first year in office had come from Democrats.)

There were a lot of reasons for the rocky relationship between the Democratic President and the Democratic Congress, but it was primarily a consequence of the new direction in which Jimmy Carter was trying to lead the party and the nation.

Carter arrived in Washington with few allies, and was met by a deep resentment of his victory over the Democratic establishment. He also arrived with a sense of what he wanted to do. *But he lacked a unifying political philosophy that had been affirmed through his election.* To the extent it is possible to attach a label to the amalgam of Carter's beliefs, that tag would have to be "moderate"; his approach to his Presidency and the country's problems was nonideological.

For example, he did not believe that the solution to the nation's energy shortage was to be found in either liberal or conservative political theory. To deal with the problem, he reasoned, the United States had to reduce oil imports, produce and conserve more energy here at home, and develop new forms of energy.

Thus, President Carter made a series of ad hoc decisions that he believed to be in the best interests of the country, but which were made at the expense of a consensus in his own party.

The absence of a unifying political philosophy reinforced the special-interests dynamics of Washington and further fragmented the Democratic Party. As Frank Moore put it, "Dealing with the modern Congress is like a floating crap game. One day we would be working with a coalition of conservative Democrats and Republicans trying to increase the defense budget, and the next day we would be working with liberal Democrats and moderate Republicans trying to pass environmental legislation or kill the B-1 bomber."

The nonideological approach was as valid as the traditional "philosophy" offered by either party, but it failed to create a consensus and resulted in merely transient coalitions and friendships with the Congress. Politically, it left the President straddling the middle—Republicans were against him simply because he was a Democrat, and many Democrats were against him because he was trying to lead the party in a different direction.

The Democrats came along kicking and screaming. They argued that Carter had won no "mandate" to abandon the party's traditional approach. To make things worse, we gave the Congress plenty of tough issues to vote on—"the kind you have to hold your nose when you vote," as one member put it—but we gave the Democrats little to take home and brag about. Consequently, when the economy turned bad, the Democrats in Congress hadn't much to fall back on, and had no way to change the subject. They couldn't argue, "Sure, I know inflation is bad and interest rates are high, but we passed the Panama Canal Treaties and energy legislation that raised the cost of your gasoline." Democrats in Congress had to either defend the President's policies or join the chorus of critics. And Billygate was certainly going to increase enrollment in the choir.

August 4, 1980 (Monday)

I watched the President's "Billy Carter" press conference with
the campaign staff. As even Carter's critics would admit afterward, it was a stellar performance. He released a ninety-two-page
report that refuted every charge and rumor and presented a convincing argument that neither he nor anyone else had done anything wrong. At the same time, he conveyed the essence of his
relationship with Billy. "I love Billy," the President said quietly,
"but I cannot control him."

The phones started jingling the minute the conference ended.
People who had been whining or nervous about "Billygate" were
back on board, praising the President's performance. The White
House call-in line reported 84 percent of the calls were pleased
with the press conference. For the first time in weeks, our campaign workers were smiling and laughing. It was as though we
had won a big primary instead of putting an end to a political
wound that had been hemorrhaging for weeks. Some people even
considered the whole thing a plus. I didn't. It had cost us time we
badly needed to give the American people a break from a badly
overexposed President.

Later, I talked with Tim Kraft and a jubilant Bob Strauss, who
had been out front fighting the Billy Carter charges. "Maybe
going through all this Billy Carter thing and coming out on top
will strengthen the President," Kraft said.

Strauss stopped laughing. "Krafty, you are trying to make
chicken salad out of chicken shit. Don't kid yourself. Billy Carter
hurt us badly. The best thing that can happen to us now is for
people to forget about it."

August 5, 1980 (Tuesday)

I met for the third time with the Kennedy camp on "neutral ground" at the Capitol Hilton to try to work out a convention schedule satisfactory to both sides. We had an almost two-to-one lead in delegates, but we needed to win the nomination in a way that would let millions of American voters watching on television see a united party.

Although the Carter delegates had prevailed in drafting the Democratic platform in June, the Kennedy forces had introduced a large number of "minority reports," some reflecting the real differences between the two men, but most of them frivolous. If all the Kennedy reports were debated at the convention, the major speeches (including the President's acceptance) would be delayed until the middle of the night.

The Kennedy supporters were going to use the threat of disrupting the convention schedule as leverage for concessions on issues. Mondale's chief of staff, Dick Moe, Carter convention coordinator Tom Donilon, and I began to meet with the Kennedy forces—political director Paul Kirk, New York political operative Jack English, and convention managers Karl Wagner and Harold Ickes—to see if we could agree on a convention schedule. The Kennedy strategy was obvious. The vote on the critical "open convention" rule would come Monday night. They offered to withdraw most of their minority reports if we moved the vote to the second night of the convention, obviously wanting more time to lobby among the delegates, hoping to start a stampede away from the President.

That was unacceptable to us, and at both the first and second meetings we made little progress and were coy about our different motives. At our third meeting, I said bluntly to Kirk, "Look—we've got the nomination, but even if you managed to take it away from us, you would have the same interest as we do in having a good convention for the American people to see. You want the rules vote moved beyond Monday and a forum for the

Senator to address the convention. We want the rules vote to take
place Monday night and for you to withdraw a lot of your minority
reports to protect the convention schedule." Looking him straight
in the eye, I said, "Let's quit playing games with each other,
Paul. We are not going to allow the rules vote to be delayed. We
have a majority of the delegates, they are holding firm, and we
are not going to change. We will allow the Senator to address the
convention any time he wants to after the rules vote."

They finally gave in, agreed to withdraw many of their minority
reports in exchange for our commitment to allow Kennedy to
speak and for them to have additional floor passes and other goodies. A handshake was not sufficient. "Let's put it in writing," said
Kirk.

I asked for a statement in our agreement that the Senator
would support the ticket in the general election. "I am not authorized to say that now," Kirk responded.

"He's not going to support the President," Donilon whispered
in my ear.

We worked for five hours hammering out the agreement and
putting it in writing; it was then typed up and Kirk and I signed
it.

Although I respected Kirk personally, the "signing ceremony"
was about as friendly as an estranged couple signing a divorce
agreement.

August 10, 1980 (Sunday)

It was not easy returning to the same city, the same hotel, and
even the same room where I had stayed in 1976, when Jimmy
Carter won the Democratic nomination. We had arrived in New
York in '76 like a band of guerrillas who had come out of nowhere
and beaten the big names in a series of lightning maneuvers all
over the country. I was the general of that ragtag army from
Georgia—some called me the "mastermind" of Carter's victory.

People strained to see us and touch us. I couldn't get used to hearing people whisper and sometimes yell out, "There's Jody Powell!" or, "Isn't that Jordan?"

In New York in 1976, Jimmy Carter had a 23-point lead in the polls, Democrats were ecstatic about their new hero, talking about winning big majorities in Congress on the Carter coattails, and, for the first time in eight years, tasting the White House. That gathering wasn't a convention—it was a political love-in.

People still noticed me, but now, as often as not, it was to stare or sometimes snicker. We were veterans this time around, here to fight a rearguard action. The main challenge was to hang on to our delegates. I had told our convention team for the past two months that we had to treat our Carter delegates like they were the only people on the earth. We had secured vital information about each delegate—ranging from employment and age, to the political issues that mattered most, to hobbies and recreation and friends and foes within the delegation—and put it all into the computer. We were able to have an instant print-out, for example, of all the female Carter delegates under thirty-five from Midwestern states who were against abortion. More important was the human contact. We had sent them numerous mailings, had desk people at the campaign responsible for staying in touch by phone with certain delegates. Our delegates were brought to Washington earlier in the summer, briefed by campaign officials about convention issues and procedures, then taken to the White House for presentations by Eizenstat and Brzezinski on domestic and foreign policy and a reception with the President and First Lady.

I remember a woman at one of those briefings standing up and asking, "Mr. Jordan, twenty years from now, how would you like President Carter to be remembered?" I paused for a second. "Twenty years from now I'd like President Carter to be remembered as a two-term President." The Carter delegates stood up and cheered.

One of my worries starting in 1978 was whether the re-election campaign of an incumbent President could attract the enthusiasm of young people. (In 1976, at the age of thirty-two, I was about the oldest paid staffer, but most of the critical work was done by twenty-two- and twenty-three-year-old men and women.) That worry was allayed in early 1979, when another bright group of young people came into the Carter campaign, led this time by a pudgy, lovable Irish hack, Tom Donilon, a twenty-two-year-old politico who had worked on Frank Moore's Congressional staff.

Several days before the convention, Donilon and company laid out for the President how the Carter forces in New York would function, the whip system, and how communication with our delegates and each other would proceed.

At the convention, we had a Carter "whip" for each ten Carter delegates in each state delegation. The whips were supposed to pamper their delegates.

When they finished their impressive presentation, Strauss observed, "Mr. President, the good news is that Tom and his crowd have done an excellent job of getting ready. The bad news is that none of these people planning for the convention have ever attended one!"

August 11, 1980 (Monday)

All of our efforts to please and hold our delegates were aimed at winning the rules fight Monday night. We spent all day going from hotel to hotel, attending state caucuses, arguing over and over again the merits of our case on the rules, and constantly forwarding phone calls to Camp David, where the President and Rosalynn were calling individual delegates while he worked on his acceptance speech.

Our numbers looked firm, but there was always the chance that a break in the ranks could start a stampede away from Carter. Oddly enough, Ted Kennedy had become an asset: lukewarm as some of the Carter delegates were about the fall campaign and the President's "electability," few thought that Kennedy, after defeats all over the country, would fare any better.

Strauss, Rafshoon, Jody, and I gathered in the Carter VIP trailer—one of a group of trailers off the convention floor, set in a circle like a wagon train, that served as our operations center. In another trailer were the "gerbils," the young people in phone contact with the Carter whips on the floor. The whips wore green-and-white vests and hats for easy recognition. The VIP trailer had three television sets (so we could monitor all the major networks at once), a large telephone console, a small bar, and a constant flow of people.

A Democratic convention was Bob Strauss's idea of heaven: thousands of politicians, officeholders, and press people—most of whom knew and liked him. Here, Strauss, the extrovert, could exercise his considerable skills. And watching him was fun: phones at both ears, he would loudly berate a wavering delegate by reminding him of those football tickets or of that lunch at the White House, then quietly tell another that the President and the country are counting on him. "Look at him," Jody cackled. "Strauss is like a pig in shit."

Carter delegates were holding firm but they were under a lot of pressure, and rumors of defections floated throughout the day. One of the biggest problems was Illinois, where Chicago Mayor Jane Byrne, up to her old tricks, had threatened and cajoled the Carter delegates; but in midafternoon, Tom Donilon told me to "relax," he had "bought off" one of the leaders who was threatening to bolt. "What in the hell did you promise," I asked, amused, "a federal judgeship or an ambassadorship?" "No, this guy had a lot of family and friends in for the convention. I gave him a handful of VIP passes." I laughed. Byrne was no match for Tom Donilon.

Strauss, Jody, Rafshoon, and I watched in the trailer with tally sheets, marking each state's vote. Every now and then, one of the gerbils would phone or run in with a request, usually for Strauss to call a wavering delegate.

At one point we received a report that the Maine delegation was about to leave Carter as part of a scheme to draft Ed Muskie. I thought about calling the Secretary myself, but decided it was too critical and the President should express his concern directly.

Within minutes, he had called Muskie, who in turn called the Maine delegation on the floor and insisted that they not draft him or embarrass the President he served.

The Carter delegates held firm, the vote totals mounted, and the final results on the rule were 1,936 to 1,390 in favor of our position. A cheer went up from the Carter trailers. The President called from Camp David and said kiddingly, "Ham, can I take Rosalynn off the phone now?"

After talking with Strauss and Jody, he called the gerbils and thanked Donilon and his crew for the big victory. A few minutes later, he called back to say that Kennedy had phoned to congratulate him and to tell him that he planned to withdraw from the nomination fight. I asked the President if Kennedy gave any indication of whether he would appear with him at the convention or how active he would be in support of the Carter-Mondale ticket. "I didn't press him, Ham. We didn't talk but a couple of minutes. It was an uncomfortable call for him. I'm not sure what he'll do Thursday or in the fall."

The battle was obviously not over.

August 12, 1980 (Tuesday)

Jody, Jerry, Pat, Kirbo, Democratic Party chairman John White, and I met at Strauss's suite at the hotel at 9:00 A.M. to talk about the platform fight that night. Three economic issues representing the distinct approaches of Carter and Kennedy were at stake: a plank that called for wage and price controls, which the President had always opposed; a $12 billion "stimulus" package, which the President considered excessive; and another plank that gave fighting unemployment priority over the other components of our plan. The three together represented a repudiation of our economic policy. "These are apple-pie issues," Strauss said. "They sound good, people can vote for 'em and go back home and don't have any responsibility for the consequences."

Strauss, Donilon, and I had reports from whips and delegates that some labor delegates were nervous about voting against the stimulus package when a lot of their members were out of work. And some, after saying no over and over again to the Kennedy forces on the rules vote, looked upon the platform vote as a way to make peace with the Kennedy supporters in their own delegations.

I called Carter. "Mr. President, the vote tonight on the economic planks looks tough." Strauss picked up the other phone and added, "We're going to take a pasting!"

"I understand, Bob," Carter snapped, "but what in the hell would you have me do? The idea of a convention trying to second-guess decisions that I have already made and will not change is ludicrous! Y'all hold firm on our issues. I'd rather lose 'em than have the American people see me trying to buy Ted Kennedy's support."

We worked hard through the day, arguing—in caucuses, hotel rooms, and hallways—that, like them or not, repudiating the President's policies on national television made no sense. Few Carter delegates told us to our face that they were defecting, but their lukewarm support worried me.

Ted Kennedy's speech that night would be followed by the platform vote. The Carter whips gathered in the Carter compound, a sea of green-and-white surrounded by the trailers. I stood on a chair. "The President understands that we face a tough fight," I shouted, trying to be heard over the din of the convention and the speeches from the podium, "but he expects us to fight hard and try to win." Some of the whips shouted agreement, others just listened. "It'll be bad if we lose, but even worse if we lie down and don't fight."

Strauss spoke next, said basically the same thing, and got the same halfhearted response. When he stepped down, he pulled me aside. "We're going to lose this vote tonight."

Strauss, Jody, Rafshoon, and I watched Kennedy's speech in triplicate on the stack of television sets in one corner of the trailer. Just months ago, before his bumbling interview with Roger Mudd, he was looked upon as a winner. Tonight, looking cool and assured, the eloquent Kennedy was clearly a loser. *He's come a long way*, I thought—

—And so have I. I was remembering the first Kennedy, Jack, who inspired my own interest in politics when I was in high school. Now here I was helping to orchestrate the final round of the struggle against the last Kennedy brother for the heart and soul of the Democratic Party.

For a long year, Ted Kennedy had been the enemy. Throughout the campaign, I had been able to separate him from the Kennedy legacy, but it was difficult for me to see him in the convention setting without thinking of his family and its tragedies, of Bobby Kennedy's emotional appearance at the 1964 convention, when he stood looking sad while the Democrats cheered and cried for half an hour. Ted Kennedy's words triggered open the floodgates of memories: Camelot, magic rhetoric, and the shock of assassinations.

Standing tall in a dark-blue suit, leaning forward on the podium, his eyes swept the delegates and his voice boomed out over them as he pleaded, "I have come here tonight not to argue as a candidate but to affirm a cause. . . . I speak out of a deep sense of urgency about the anguish and anxiety I have seen across America. . . . We cannot let the great purposes of the Democratic Party become the bygone passages of history."

With a huge smile and in a scornful tone, eliciting delighted cheers, Kennedy repeated statements Reagan had made: "'Social Security should be voluntary,'" he said and the delegates laughed gleefully and shouted, "No, no, no!" He continued, "'Eighty percent of air pollution comes from plants and trees!'" The convention roared. And when he quoted, "'Unemployment insurance is a prepaid vacation plan for freeloaders,'" the crowd went wild.

He closed with language crafted only for a Kennedy: "My golden friends across the land: for me, a few hours ago, this campaign came to an end. But for all those whose cares have been our concern, the work goes on, the cause endures, the hope still lives, and the dream shall never die."

For several eerie seconds the convention hall was silent—as if everyone, friend or foe, knew that great words had been uttered.

Then, applause resounded through the hall, Kennedy blue banners were hoisted everywhere, and television cameras zoomed in on cheering, teary-eyed Carter and Kennedy delegates.

The Carter trailers were quiet, but I could feel my own emotions tugging against my better sense.

"Great speech," Strauss said simply, shaking his head. "Great speech."

Chairman John White and Speaker O'Neill, co-presiding over the session, banged their gavels over and over, trying to bring the convention to order so the voting on the platform could begin. They finally gave up, smiling, as the demonstration for Kennedy continued.

Moments later, Donilon asked me to come to his trailer immediately. I ran over to where the gerbils, answering jingling phones, sat at long tables that stretched the length of the trailer. The reports streamed in. "Pennsylvania called and said we didn't have ten votes on the economic planks." "Ohio called and said they can't hold their votes."

I asked Donilon to check his vote totals, to see if there was any chance of winning any of the three votes. Kennedy operative Karl Wagner called me in the gerbils' trailer. We had agreed to a roll-call vote on the wage-and-price-controls plank and a voice vote on the other two. Wagner had a new offer. "We'll agree to have voice votes on all three planks if you agree to concede the wage-and-price issue," he said cockily. After months of being on the losing end, he was on top and seemed determined to make the most of it.

"Do you think, Karl, that we're going to just roll over on the wage-and-price controls? Go to hell!" I yelled and hung up the phone.

Donilon was standing by.

"I shouldn't have done that," I said. "We're going to need those guys for November. But I couldn't help it."

In a couple of minutes, White and O'Neill called our trailer. The Kennedy forces, they said, offered to concede the wage-and-price controls to us on a voice vote if we would concede the other two economic planks the same way. The other two issues were surely lost anyway. It made no sense now to have a roll-call vote on the wage-and-price plank, which we would likely lose, since the protracted roll call would only document our defeat and irritate the convention. Strauss and I agreed we should get it over with. He called Tip O'Neill, who tried to quiet the convention, then called for voice votes on the three issues, and, ignoring the sentiment of the convention favoring the wage-and-price plank, declared that Kennedy's minority position had prevailed on the two planks and that we had won on the wage-and-price issue.

I sat in the trailer for a while, watching it all on television, reflecting on what had just happened to us. It was crazy: a Democratic national convention in which a majority of the delegates were pledged to an incumbent President had just passed resolutions to force drastic changes in his policies.

The various reforms of the party in 1972 had taken the selection of its nominees away from the bosses, out of the smoke-filled rooms, and given it to the voters. These reforms made it possible for an unknown like Jimmy Carter to win the big prize. But, after he was elected, the special interest groups spawned by the same reforms made it more difficult for him to govern effectively—or to be re-elected.

And the party itself had changed. The Democratic Party was like a phony façade on a Hollywood set. Thirty years ago, it was a collection of several groups of reliable voters: the big-city ethnics of the Northeast and Midwest, working people, Jews, liberals, and white Southerners. The base of the party was the big-city machines, which, corrupt or not, provided certain practical services for the people.

Those party machines also educated and informed citizens about issues and candidates. And both parties stood for something. If you called yourself a Democrat, it meant you believed in certain things. But times changed. As the children and grandchildren of traditional Democratic voters began to obtain better jobs and more education, they left their old neighborhoods, moved to the suburbs, and many began to vote Republican. Their historical base eroding, the party machines began to crumble as they lost their patronage and their ability to help citizens and influence their votes.

Largely as a result of the evolution of television during this same period, the ideas that both parties stood for became diffused; the distinctions between Democrats and Republicans blurred. And in large part, the enormous political void left by the demise of the party was filled by television. Through its skillful use, candidates could appeal directly to the voters over the heads of the precinct captains. Media advisers became adept at using television to emphasize different aspects of a candidate's background and beliefs in order to appeal to different types of voters, obscuring even further the differences between the parties.

The Democratic Party, in an effort that was well-intentioned if not well thought out, carried its "reforms" to the extreme. After getting rid of the bosses, the Democrats glorified the individual, the organization, the special interest group, that strove to do what the party organization had once done. In 1972, party rules mandated that the process include people by sex and race. But "affirmative action" exploded to include the handicapped, Indians, gays, senior citizens, and so on. It seemed as though the only persons not guaranteed a voice in the party were the ordinary voter and elected officials who had to run on the Democratic ticket.

So, when one walked out on the floor of the convention, it was not the many faces of American life that one saw, but instead the many faces and representatives of special interest groups. "Our party can't survive the way it's going," the President said later, back in Washington after the convention, "if we don't figure out some way to nominate a convention that also represents the mainstream of American life in this country."

That was another of those things we were going to try to do in "the second term."

I circulated among our people, trying to calm them. "Kennedy had his night," I assured them over and over. "We'll have ours next."

Finally Speaker O'Neill read a terse statement from Kennedy to the convention. "I congratulate President Carter on his renomination. . . . I will support and work for the re-election of President Carter. It is imperative that we defeat Ronald Reagan in 1980. I urge all Democrats to join in that effort."

The session was adjourned. We may have won the nomination, but Ted Kennedy had won their hearts.

August 14, 1980 (Thursday)

Thursday was the big night. Millions of people would be watching the last session of the convention and Carter's acceptance speech. We had spent hundreds of hours and many thousands of dollars trying to orchestrate events that last night to take maximum advantage of the huge audience. We had commissioned a special film, had carefully picked the speakers to make specific points in their support of the President and their attack on Reagan. They had seen enough fighting in the past three days. "Tonight should be a love-in," Caddell admonished.

Mondale spoke first. Preparing for his speech, he had remarked that he was "free at last." For the past year, while the President was in the White House, Mondale had been the point man in the effort against the Kennedy forces. There was no love lost between Kennedy and Mondale, but the fight for the nomination was very much a family quarrel, and it often pitted Mondale against political groups and individuals who had been longtime friends and allies. He made a highly partisan speech which attacked Reagan, and talked about the "stark differences" between Reagan and Carter.

Mondale seemed unleashed as he led the charge against Reagan, attacking the Republicans and their nominee with great relish, and soon he had the convention crowd with him, answering his questions about which candidate cared for peace, social justice, and everything else with the refrain, "but not Ronald Reagan!"

We followed with a film produced by Rafshoon to "introduce" the President. We had carefully prompted all of the speakers, but the only sure way to say what we wanted to was through this film. At the 1976 convention, Rafshoon had produced a film that captured the very essence of Jimmy Carter and the promise that he held for the party and the nation. Some critics said that it was the single most powerful and effective political film they had ever seen. But his film for 1980 was as different as the circumstances that faced America and Jimmy Carter. It showed Carter in the Oval Office, dealing with the enormous complexities of the Presidency. The not-so-subtle message was, "Can you imagine Ronald Reagan sitting in that office, dealing with these problems and decisions?" Rafshoon's film was effective for making that point, but it lacked the emotional wallop of his '76 film. Just as Carter's candidacy did.

To avoid the press, I sat in the audience with friends in the New Hampshire delegation, waiting nervously for the President's speech. We had undergone the usual battle over what kind of speech it would be. Some wanted it to be thematic—a spelling out of his vision of America's future. Others wanted it to be a laundry list of accomplishments and new promises that paid lip service to every special interest group. I had learned early in the Administration that the persons who control the President's rhetoric exert an enormous influence over his actions and policies. For when a President says something, it moves pending issues, policies, and thinking in one direction or another and often defines the terms on which the battle, in Congress or among the voters, will be fought. The press, political figures, and people everywhere hang on every word a President utters, analyzing and dissecting every comment. The battles over a President's words are really struggles over the heart and soul of his Presidency.

In 1976, Jimmy Carter had won the Democratic nomination and the Presidency not on a given set of issues but on the general impression of an honest, intelligent man who was going to Washington to take a different approach to the country's problems. His message had been thematic.

Once he had been elected and was faced with energy shortages and a sick economy, that thematic approach was more difficult to sustain and often not credible. Increasingly, the President approached his speeches like an engineer; he regarded them as vehicles for making logical arguments. If the speech contained enough facts to support a contention or a policy, then it was "successful." This approach to his rhetoric was reinforced by Stu Eizenstat, Jack Watson, Anne Wexler, and others on the front line who dealt with the special interest groups.

What better proof of the special interest groups' clout than the mention or acknowledgment of their organization or their issue in a major speech? Consequently, whenever an important address was being crafted, the questions and pressures began. "It's a good speech, but the President didn't mention the Equal Rights Amendment." Or, "The President didn't say anything about the labor movement." Or, "What about the minorities and environmentalists and the need for a Department of Education?"

Rafshoon once said that he wished he had a way to do a commercial at the end of each speech: "President Carter's speech was brought to you by the supporters of the Equal Rights Amendment, the American labor movement (with the exception of the Teamsters), the consumer movement, the friends of Israel, and some white Southerners."

Rafshoon's film had helped to rev up the crowd. The President mounted the podium to the strains of "Hail to the Chief" and moved from side to side, waving to the delegates, who were either dutifully swinging their green-and-white Carter-Mondale placards back and forth or sitting quietly in their chairs with their blue-and-white "Kennedy '80" buttons. President Carter was smiling as he raised his hands for quiet and began what Rafshoon and Caddell had called "the most important speech of his political career."

It seemed that the President lacked confidence as he began, speaking in broken phrases without any rhythm or cadence. (Later I learned that there was a problem with the teleprompter and he couldn't see his speech text.) He seemed to settle down once he got into the meat of his talk, but I was still nervous because I knew that the impression I had sitting in the audience could be quite different from that projected through the television to millions of viewers.

Perhaps he sensed that many in his audience were not really

with him and that the speech of an incumbent President which addressed America's "hard choices" was likely to be compared unfavorably to the fiery, emotional speech that Kennedy had delivered the night before. I was glad when he was finished, and I had no illusions about how it would be received. It was a solid defense and explanation of his policies and Presidency, appealing to their heads—but Kennedy had already captured their feelings.

The audience applauded, the band played "Happy Days Are Here Again" over and over, and I looked up at the large net stretched over the convention hall, stuffed with colorful balloons. Someone was tugging on a cord to release them onto the convention floor, but nothing happened. *That's not a good omen,* I thought. *We can't get the balloons out any better than we can get the hostages out. . . .*

The Vice President and Mrs. Mondale joined the President and Mrs. Carter on stage, where, arms wrapped around one another, they moved from one side of the podium to the other, waving constantly to the delegates on the floor. Bob Strauss played political ringmaster and began to call Democratic celebrities onto the podium. He started with the big names, Senators, Governors, party officials, the Carter Cabinet and staff. When he introduced Brzezinski, a loud boo went up from the floor. I winced, feeling bad for the proud man, but he smiled hard and waved. But before a second had passed, Strauss, like a vaudeville stage manager with a long hook, had jerked him back into the crowd on the podium and called someone else up. Strauss soon ran out of both celebrities and adjectives. He raised and lowered his voice for emphasis, and soon his introductions took on a singsong quality as he introduced minor officials and politicians whom no one knew.

It was obvious that what everyone was waiting to see was the coming together of the party: Carter and Kennedy standing on the podium with their arms upraised, signifying the end of the long battle and the beginning of a united effort against the Republicans.

I waited for a couple of minutes, thinking that the suspense would make Kennedy's appearance all the more dramatic and the crowd reaction more enthusiastic. Finally I grabbed the New

Hampshire phone that was connected to the podium and called Bob Keefe, who was managing things there. "Where in the hell is Kennedy?"

"He's en route, but it's taking him a long damn time!" Keefe told me.

We sat and waited and waited as Strauss resorted to calling persons even I hardly knew onto the podium. "There are more people on the podium than there are in the audience," I joked to a New Hampshire man sitting behind me. I started to look at my watch. It was one thing to sit there in the middle of the convention audience, but a minute is a long time on television and I wondered how long we could wait before millions of people started to turn their sets off or to switch to local channels looking for old movies, possibly starring our Republican opponent.

I called the podium again and was given the same message, "He's on the way."

It was a full fifteen minutes before Kennedy arrived. He skipped up the steps, shaking hands along the way, and went over to the President for a handshake and a few words. Both men looked ill at ease, but the crowd cheered. Carter put his hand on Kennedy's big shoulder, and Kennedy then turned and began to shake hands with others on the podium. As Kennedy moved around among the VIPs, the President's eyes followed him. As a result, Kennedy—not the President—was the focal point of attention. Kennedy moved back to the President, shook hands, walked to the side of the podium, waved to the crowd, and was gone. Chants of "we want Teddy" brought him back. He walked over to the President, waved to the crowd, and circulated briefly on the podium. By then, the President had turned around, appearing to be clapping for him, but also wanting more than Kennedy was ready to give. The arms raised together—the symbol of a united party—never came.

August 15–31, 1980

After the convention, the President talked with Kennedy and planned a joint appearance in Boston. "Kennedy is really anxious to help," Carter said and told me to get in touch with Steve Smith, Kennedy's campaign manager and brother-in-law, to discuss how we could work together.

I knew that gestures were important to the Kennedys, so I called Smith and asked if I could come see him. He suggested that we meet several days later. I sat waiting in the outer room of Kennedy's Senate office, being stared at politely or being thrown disdainful glances, and finally was shown into a large office where Steve Smith and Rick Burke, Kennedy's administrative assistant, were waiting. Smith, smaller than I had expected, was wearing a shiny, light-gray suit that looked as if it had to be polished every couple of days; he looked more like an overdressed used-car dealer than the financial wizard of the Kennedy empire.

We shook hands and exchanged pleasantries. "We appreciate your willingness to get together and talk about the fall campaign," I began.

"Yes, the Senator is ready to put all that happened in the past behind him and really help the President in the campaign," Smith said.

"That's very generous." I was pleasantly surprised by his forthcoming manner. "It's going to be tough. The very people we need to get back in the fold are the people who support the Senator."

"I think that's right," Smith replied. "What exactly do you need the Senator to do?"

"Appearances in key states, mostly," I explained. "What I'd like to do is work out a master schedule for the campaign that takes full advantage of the time you'll give us. We might start off with a joint campaign appearance by the President and the Senator and then let him work some specific states for us."

"That's reasonable," Smith said. "Let me tell you how you can help us. We're eager to campaign extensively on behalf of the ticket, but we have a sizable debt from the primaries."

"I'm not surprised," I replied. "We ended up owing about six or seven hundred thousand ourselves."

"For the Senator to give you the time you need from him to campaign, we are going to need some help getting rid of this debt, because if we have to raise it ourselves, it won't leave us any time to help the ticket," Smith said, smiling.

You bastard, I thought, returning his grin. *You're blackmailing us. You'll campaign for us if we help you eliminate your campaign debt. I wish we didn't need Kennedy so badly. It would really feel nice to stand up, say go to hell, and walk out.*

"Steve, we've got our own campaign debt to work on," I protested.

"But you've got the White House," he replied quickly.

"That doesn't make the fund-raising as easy as you think."

After a while we decided that there was some joint fund-raising we could do. But Smith again made the point that before any appearances would be scheduled, they'd want us to come up with a fund-raising plan and have a written agreement committing both camps to the effort.

I was mad as hell when I returned to the White House, and the President was furious about having to raise money for Kennedy. "He's blackmailing us," he said as I stood before his desk and reported on my meeting with Smith. He particularly resented the idea of a written agreement, and I couldn't resist repeating his words to him: "Kennedy is really anxious to help us."

Carter glared at me, and I left.

Eleanor, whose first job at the White House had been with John F. Kennedy, laughed as I reported on my meeting. "I would have liked to be a fly on the wall," she said, "and seen that meeting between you and Smith: the Southern Baptist and the Northern Catholic. It must have been like Appomattox in reverse— General Grant giving his sword to General Lee," she said chuckling.

"And charging him for it," I added.

The President making an early-morning statement to the press
in response to Bani-Sadr's speech *(April 1, 1980)*.

Dr. Brzezinski and General Jones in the Cabinet Room
the night of the aborted rescue mission.

Colonel
"Chargin' Charlie" Beckwith.
Newsweek—LARRY DOWNING

Memorial ceremony at Arlington Cemetery honoring the eight
Delta Force members who died at Desert One (*May 9, 1980*).

Last minutes: the President, Rosalynn Carter, Sick, Jordan, Pat Caddell, and Cutler *(January 20, 1981).*

Carter greeting the former hostages in Wiesbaden (*January 22, 1981*).

"To freedom": Jordan, Carter, and staff
on the flight back from Wiesbaden (*January 22, 1981*).

We spent two weeks getting ready for the campaign kickoff on Labor Day.

Our basic strategy was to have Mondale and the Cabinet lead the attack against Reagan, pointing out the flaws in our opponent's candidacy and platform. Our goal was to keep the President above the fray, looking "Presidential," talking about the "stark differences" between Democrats and Republicans and about the "different futures" they represented. We would mix substantive events at the White House with campaign trips, which would increase as Election Day drew near. Some called our plan a "limited Rose Garden strategy" after the tactic that Gerald Ford used so effectively against us in 1976.

To win the nomination of either party, a candidate had to prevail week after week in the ongoing skirmishes that took place across the country; personal appearances could greatly influence a candidate's success in a single state. But the dynamics are much different in a general election: fifty separate contests held on the same day in fifty states that have varying interests, needs, and political traditions. With the historical structure of both parties in shambles, the only way to reach millions of voters was through television—either paid political advertisement or news. And as television was being used more and more, the credibility of political advertising diminished considerably, particularly when what was being said on behalf of the candidates in the advertising was in conflict with what was being shown on news programs.

By the summer of 1976, we had spent four years thinking, working, and planning to win the nomination, but had given very little thought to the general election. Consequently, when the campaign against Ford began, we resorted to what we had done during the primaries—racing around the country, trying to squeeze as many speeches and appearances as possible into each day. And while Jimmy Carter looked as if he was running for sheriff in fifty states, President Ford stayed in the White House, making pronouncements about national problems and issues, and, in a word, looking Presidential. Our lead shrank and almost disappeared by Election Day, until we just squeaked by Ford. Only the debates, and the aura of acceptability that Jimmy Carter gained by standing toe-to-toe with an incumbent President, won that election for us.

So, while I would go into the campaign office every day, and worry about the endorsement of a labor leader or a former Kennedy activist who was sitting on his hands, or figure some way to get an extra $10,000 for phone banks in a key state, I was not kidding myself. Those things might help if the election were a cliff-hanger, but I knew that it would be won or lost on the evening news. What mattered was the cumulative feelings about the candidates and the issues that were conveyed into the living rooms of millions and millions of American voters as night after night they heard Walter Cronkite, or Frank Reynolds, or John Chancellor talk about what Reagan, Carter, and Anderson had said and done that day.

The Reagan campaign did not wait for the "official" beginning of the campaign on Labor Day. He was already actively campaigning across the country—and putting his foot in his mouth: stating that the Vietnam war was a "noble cause," expressing his personal doubts about the theory of evolution, voicing pro-Taiwan views that threatened relations with the People's Republic of China, and describing the economic dilemma facing the country as a "severe depression."

For two weeks it was delicious, watching Reagan on the news each night stumble from one controversy to another, doing what we had thought we'd have to do—making him, not the President, the issue. But I wasn't sure that it would last.

One day a woman introduced herself to me on an elevator at my apartment building as an employee of the Republican National Committee. Smiling, I asked her what the mood was at her office. "Not so good, with all of these self-inflicted wounds."

I tried to reassure her. "The last time I saw anyone get off to such a bad start was Jimmy Carter in 1976. Do you remember the *Playboy* interview and the comments about Clarence Kelley? Don't worry," I said, "it'll be our turn soon to say or do something stupid."

I was being nice, but really didn't think we'd have to go on the defensive. We had a grip on things inside the government, an active speakers' bureau which had fanned out all over the country telling our story, and plenty of surrogates making the points against Reagan that I had outlined in my campaign plan.

September 1, 1980 (Monday)

The President opened his general election campaign in Tuscumbia, Alabama. The South was our political base in 1976 and had to be our base again in 1980 if we were to reach the winning number of electoral votes.

Pat Caddell called me at campaign headquarters in the middle of the day, so excited he could hardly talk. "Did you hear what Reagan said?" I told him I hadn't. Opening his campaign in New Jersey, Reagan charged that the President chose to open his campaign for re-election in "the birthplace of the Ku Klux Klan." Not only was this remark about Tuscumbia untrue, but it implied that Carter's presence in Alabama was linked in some way to support for the Klan. "Can you believe he said that?" Caddell exclaimed.

We discussed how to exploit it. Our Southern coordinator, Jim Free, was already lining up Southern Governors and politicians to call on Reagan to apologize for his insult.

Caddell had a bank of telephones for conducting polls on a continuing basis in crucial states. "If Reagan keeps putting his foot in his mouth for another week or so, we can close down campaign headquarters," he quipped. "Doubts about him are growing, his lead is shrinking, and more and more people are wondering whether he's up to the job. If this impression hardens, he'll be out of the race."

"Is it that bad?" I asked hopefully.

"Yes, Ham, I really think it is."

Won't it be wonderful if Reagan just self-destructs, I thought.

—And maybe he would have if the "meanness issue" hadn't moved his faux pas off the front pages.

September 9, 1980 (Tuesday)

The possibility of Presidential debates dominated the political news. It was commonly believed that Nixon's gruff, unshaven look in the 1960 debates had cost him the Presidency, and that Gerald Ford's gaffe about Eastern Europe in the '76 debates had disrupted his momentum and allowed Jimmy Carter to edge him out. Political wisdom had it that, in another tight election, debates could be the decisive factor.

The League of Women Voters had sponsored the 1976 Presidential debates and had done a good job producing them. With that success still fresh in their minds, they felt they owned the debates—and they proved to be more difficult for us to negotiate with than the Iranians.

The President's position had been that we would be willing to debate other candidates after he had had a chance for a one-on-one debate with the Republican nominee. The League, pressured by Anderson and excessively concerned about its image, set an arbitrary criterion for Anderson: he would be included in the debate if he had 15 percent of the support in national public opinion polls. We never doubted that the leadership of the League—which was at least half Republican and a few other "good government" types—would combine to insist that John Anderson be heard.

The League went ahead and issued invitations to a three-way debate. Anderson and Reagan accepted immediately, while Strauss told the press that the President would not agree to such a debate unless it were preceded by a Carter-Reagan debate.

The next day, League President Ruth Hinerfeld said that President Carter might be represented at the debate by an "empty chair." An exasperated Jody complained, "It's like on the sixth day of the Creation, the Lord had commanded, 'Let there be Presidential debates—sponsored and controlled by the League of Women Voters.'"

The first debate—without Jimmy Carter—would take place in Baltimore on September 21.

September 12, 1980 (Friday)

I was riding with the President to campaign headquarters, where he was to give a pep talk to the campaign staff. As he waved to the crowd standing along the route of his motorcade, he said, "Ham, don't say a thing about it, but I think we have finally got a chance to resolve the hostage thing."

The West German government, he said, had been contacted by an Iranian related to Khomeini who wanted to meet secretly with someone representing "the American government." "We've been burned so many times that I was naturally skeptical, so I asked that they furnish us some kind of proof that this was authentic. They came back immediately and told us to listen to a speech that Khomeini would make today which would list four conditions for the release of the hostages that would be basically acceptable to us. They told us exactly what he would say about the four conditions. Well, the people over at State monitored his speech, which had all the usual crap about me and the U.S., but tucked right in the middle of it was this precise language."

"Jesus," I said, "that's really something. It looks like we've made contact with Khomeini."

The President turned to smile. "Or at least with his speechwriter."

He told me that he had met with Christopher and Muskie that morning and that Christopher would probably go to meet secretly with Khomeini's relative.

I had not allowed myself to hope that the hostages would be home before the election, but now it looked as if it was really happening. This was the first time we had solid evidence of Khomeini's personal involvement. It would sure make our job of winning re-election easier.

September 15, 1980 (Monday)

An ABC-Harris poll confirmed that Reagan's blunders were really hurting him: by a margin of 82 to 15 percent, the persons surveyed agreed that Ronald Reagan "seems to make too many off-the-cuff remarks which he has trouble explaining or has had to apologize for making."

But that was not enough. For, despite Reagan's problems, it was obvious after the first two weeks of the campaign that our early strategy was not working. When the President was on the campaign trail, he was receiving good coverage, but when he was back at the White House, the media were not giving serious attention to the contrived events—like meetings with special interest groups—we were trying to get on the evening news. Nor were they paying any attention to Mondale or our surrogates. They had covered Mondale through the long primary campaign and were tired of him. "I'd have to set my hair on fire to get on the news," he complained after the second week out on the trail with only puny mention of his biting attacks on Reagan.

The media, sensing that we were trying to manipulate them as Ford had done in 1976, refused to give thoughtful treatment to White House events, and we were forced to resort to more campaign trips by the President than we had originally planned.

We worried that Carter was a bit rusty on his political rhetoric, but he was loaded with facts and figures that we had fed him about Ronald Reagan and was determined to show the American people the differences between the two candidates and their parties.

September 16, 1980 (Tuesday)

I was doing some paperwork at the White House and listening to the evening news when Rafshoon called. "Did you see it?"

"You mean the CBS-New York Times poll?" I said. "It's great. They've got us ahead of Reagan!"

"No, no—the story about the President in Atlanta calling Reagan a racist."

"He didn't say that, Jerry."

"I know, but that's the way they made it sound. He's got to be careful. It's that old Carter hyperbole. He just can't help himself sometimes."

I ordered a transcript of what Carter had said in Atlanta. Speaking without notes at Ebenezer Church, the home church of Martin Luther King, Jr., to an audience of black preachers and civil rights leaders from all over the South, the President had said, "You've seen in this campaign the stirrings of hate and the rebirth of code words like 'states rights,' and a campaign reference to the Ku Klux Klan relating to the South. This is a message that creates a cloud on the political horizon. Racism has no place in this country."

In the days to follow, the Republicans jumped all over the Atlanta statement. "I'm appalled at the ugly, mean little remark Jimmy Carter made," George Bush announced.

"His intemperate and totally misleading statements demean the office of the Presidency," Gerald Ford criticized.

At Carter's Thursday news conference, four of the twelve questions asked by the press addressed the "tone" of the campaign and the remarks in Atlanta. Television correspondents and commentators probed time and again: "Is Jimmy Carter mean?"

Rafshoon was right—it was the old Carter hyperbole.

Jimmy Carter's tendency toward overstatement sometimes got him in trouble.

I always thought that it had resulted from his growing up in a little town in south Georgia, where everything that happened "in town" was "the biggest" or "the best" or "the greatest."

I wrote him a memo in early 1977 about his use of exaggerated language, arguing that even if there were a "perfect" solution to a problem, or if we passed an "excellent" piece of legislation, it simply was not credible to attach those adjectives to our own work.

On the way to the Bonn economic summit in July 1978, Jerry, Jody, and I were talking with the President about his need to communicate more effectively with the American people. He seemed receptive, and when he asked what he could do, Jerry told him one thing was tone down his rhetoric. In Germany, the President went directly to a difficult meeting with Chancellor Helmut Schmidt. After they finished, Schmidt and Carter faced the press corps and Carter began, "I want to thank Chancellor Schmidt for the superb welcome they've given us. I've never met any other world leader who has been of more assistance . . ." Rafshoon and I looked at each other and started laughing. Jerry's lesson had lasted only a couple of hours. Carter saw us laughing and smiled as if to say, "I can't help it."

When the President returned from Atlanta, Jerry, Jody, Pat, and I talked with him about the ad lib comments that had created such a firestorm there. "Mr. President," I said, "you've just got to be careful what you say."

"Dammit," he said, "I'm just trying to point out the differences like you guys said I should."

"Maybe you just shouldn't try so hard," Rafshoon added.

September 18, 1980 (Thursday)

I was headed for Jack Watson's office when I bumped into Warren Christopher in the parking lot, just back from his secret meeting in Germany with the Iranian and on his way to report to the

President. "Ham, I think we have something," he said excitedly. "The man I met with was realistic and obviously ready to resolve this thing."

I wanted to hear all about it, but Warren had to rush to see Carter. He told me that his contact would return to Iran in a few days to pursue the release of the hostages.

For the methodical, cautious Christopher to be optimistic was really something. *Maybe the hostages will be home before Election Day after all*, I thought.

I didn't think Christopher was authorized to tell me that, and I didn't feel comfortable raising the subject with the President myself. After all, I was off the government payroll and no longer privy to secret information.

Then the President called and asked me to come over. He repeated in some detail what Christopher had told me, and said that we might be only days away from having the hostages home. "Ham, I want you to help me think about how to welcome them home in a way that is dignified and takes into account that we are in the middle of the campaign. God knows, after what they have been through, I want to honor them properly. But if we go overboard, Reagan and the press will say that we are using their return improperly."

"What I would like to do, Mr. President, is use their return improperly and not be blamed for it."

He laughed.

I went to Phil Wise's small office off the Oval Office and typed out a three-page memorandum. First I suggested we implement the standing plan to send the hostages to Germany and allow them time there with the medical team to "decompress" before the emotionally difficult encounter with their families. Since Cy Vance was their leader at the time they were captured, I suggested that he be designated as the President's representative to greet them in Germany, and I argued strongly that the President wait to greet the hostages in the States, as going to Germany to see them might seem to be reaching too much.

My second suggestion was to recognize that many of the hostages probably had no idea of what had been done to gain their release, nor did they have any sense of the outpouring of love for them from the American people. I proposed the State Department put together a brief "documentary" of news clips that showed what was happening in America throughout the crisis. I wrote, "We can tell them that we cared deeply for them every day they have been gone, but a film of the type I am suggesting would show them." Finally, I said that whatever welcome we gave them here be dignified and Presidential and take into account the reality of the ongoing campaign. To ensure bipartisan support and protect us against charges of "politicizing" their welcome, I suggested that Reagan be invited to greet the hostages with the President.

I put the memo in an envelope and left it on his desk, hoping that it would be needed soon.

September 21, 1980 (Sunday)

Watching the Reagan-Anderson debate at Rafshoon's home, I had mixed feelings. I was bothered by the insinuation that Carter feared either man, but I was sure that we had been right to refuse the three-man debate, which would have provided John Anderson with a national audience of 90 to 100 million people as well as with an aura of respectability and authenticity. Also, there was a damn good chance that Reagan and Anderson would gang up on the President for an hour, and our message to the American people and the "stark differences" between Reagan and Carter would be lost along the way. So I had no favorite in this debate; I didn't want either man to win. We needed Anderson's candidacy to shrink and go away, but I hoped he would bloody up Reagan a bit first.

"The best outcome would be for Reagan to say something dumb and for Anderson to agree with him," Rafshoon said.

On the issues, sharp differences existed between the two men, but they united to attack Carter. When it was over, I didn't feel very good. Reagan hadn't made any big mistakes and Anderson had handled himself well. Still, I knew that it would have been a mistake for the President to be there.

A reported 50 to 55 million people watched the event, which the President described as a "debate between two Republicans."

September 22, 1980 (Monday)

I stopped by Zbig's office in the morning to get some news on the fighting between Iran and Iraq which had erupted Sunday.

"What will it mean for the hostages, Zbig?"

"One of two things," he said. "It could be a pressure on Iran to release the hostages quickly so they can get the military spare parts that we have withheld. Or the outbreak of war could prove a distraction to the Iranians that makes the release impossible."

His second prediction proved to be right. The next day the Iranian Parliament announced that it was "freezing" the hostage negotiations because of the war against Iraq, and officials in Tehran began to blame "the devil Carter" for inspiring the Iraqis to attack Iran. Once again the hostages were pushed to the back burner.

Speaking to an AFL-CIO convention in California, the President said that the American people on Election Day would be faced with a choice to determine "whether we will have war or peace." Reagan responded quickly, charging that Carter was guilty of "smear tactics."

"Can you believe he said that?" Rafshoon asked.

"He's discouraged, Jerry," I told him. "Here you've got two guys who disagree on every issue and on the approach to the country's problems, and the Boss feels like no one is pointing it out. He can't get a man-to-man debate with Reagan so he's just doing it himself."

But the President had given the press a story that would only grow. I had seen it happen many times before. Once the press is conditioned to a certain perception, or senses the vulnerability of a political figure, particularly a Presidential candidate, reporters and columnists begin to look for other stories that confirm and embellish that perception. After Gerald Ford had stumbled a couple of times in public, and bumped his head, the media quickly turned out stories that symbolically linked these minor mishaps with policy errors. Now Carter was getting the same treatment. Reports of his "mean streak" were served up regularly. We would have to be careful to keep it from becoming a major campaign issue.

September 25, 1980 (Thursday)

Finally, after John Anderson's decline in the polls and, presumably, after realizing that our position on the debates would not change, the League of Women Voters issued an invitation for a Carter-Reagan debate, to be followed by a three-way debate including John Anderson.

We accepted immediately. The next day Reagan refused to participate with only Carter, stating, "it's unfair" to exclude John Anderson.

October 2, 1980 (Thursday)

The Senate committee's investigation of "Billygate" concluded that while there were no violations of law, the President was "ill-advised" to try to involve his brother in efforts to influence Iran through the Libyans and that brother Billy merited "severe criticism."

Interviewed on the evening news, Billy said, "I'm not apologizing for a damn thing."

October 5, 1980 (Sunday)

The National Organization for Women (NOW) met in national convention. They condemned Reagan for his "medieval stance" on feminist issues, endorsed the Democratic platform, but refused to endorse the President.

NOW had worked for Kennedy against Carter, but with a choice between Carter and Reagan, it wouldn't make a decision to support either candidate.

October 7, 1980 (Tuesday)

In a speech in Chicago yesterday, the President said that the election of Ronald Reagan would divide the country, "black from white, Jew from Christian, North from South, rural from urban." Reagan, responding on television, shook his head and said, with a well-rehearsed tone of sadness in his voice, "The President is reaching the point of hysteria and owes the country an apology."

I felt sick as Jerry, Pat, and I met to discuss the President's latest, ill-advised charge. "We have a major problem on our hands," I argued, "and we are going to have to eat a little crow to put this 'meanness' thing behind us."

We agreed to take advantage of an interview the President already had scheduled with Barbara Walters for him to do a "mea culpa," taking his share of the blame for the "tone" of the campaign. Carter didn't like the implication that he was at fault.

Her first question was on the "meanness" issue. "Mr. President," she probed, "in recent days you have been characterized as mean, vindictive, hysterical, and on the point of desperation."

The President seemed a bit taken aback by the edge to her question, forced a smile, and responded, "Well, those characterizations are not accurate, Barbara. I think it's true that when Mr.

Reagan says I'm desperate or vindictive or hysterical he shares part of the blame that I have assumed. The tone of the campaign has departed from the way it ought to be between two candidates for the highest office in this land."

"Are you saying, Mr. President, that you've made some mistakes in personally attacking Mr. Reagan, and that now in the next few weeks you have to get back on the track again?"

"Yes," the President replied, "I'd say that. But there's enough blame to go around, and I think that the press sometimes has failed to cover major issues. Mr. Reagan has made some comments about me that probably are ill-advised."

"No more name-calling?" Walters asked, like a teacher chiding a naughty student.

"I'll do my best," replied the President.

The President had come close to "apologizing." I was sure that he didn't mean it.

Partisan attacks against Presidents are expected and tolerated, particularly during a campaign, but the American people want their President to stay a bit above the battle; they don't want to see him in the political trenches. So, when a President makes a personal attack on his opponent, in the eyes of many Americans it diminishes the office itself.

Jimmy Carter, stung by some of the false and even insulting statements made about him by Reagan, and frustrated by our own inability to demonstrate the differences between him and his opponent, didn't understand that the standards that apply to a President don't necessarily apply to the men who want his job.

October 10, 1980 (Friday)

In a television interview in Florida the President said, "Reagan is not a good man to trust with the affairs of this nation."

Rafshoon called, frustrated nearly to the point of anger. "I might as well just pull all our television ads. As long as the President is running around the country saying all this crap, it doesn't matter what we're running on the tube. I don't know what he's thinking. How many times do we have to tell him?"

The press jumped on the new comment, but didn't play it nearly as big as his "war and peace" remark or the Chicago charge that the election of Reagan would "divide the nation." Maybe they didn't have to—the "meanness issue" had already sunk in.

Several reporters came to my office, and I tried to talk about the "differences" and give them an upbeat line on our prospects. There were no takers—all they wanted to talk about was "meanness." Conceding that the President's campaign rhetoric had been exaggerated at times, I challenged them to cite a single instance of Jimmy Carter's "meanness" affecting a policy decision or personal action while he had been President. (Ironically, many of the columnists who charged that the President was "mean" were the same ones who had criticized him earlier for not "using the stick" on his opponents and creating respect out of fear.) No one could come up with a specific, concrete example.

For it was Jimmy Carter's words as a candidate, not his actions as President, that had gotten us in trouble. When I thought about all that was at stake in this election—the real differences between Carter and Reagan on energy, economic policy, the environment, and arms control—I realized just how bogus the "meanness" issue really was.

October 13, 1980 (Monday)

An ABC-Louis Harris poll showed that twice as many people as a year ago thought that "President Carter is not a man of high integrity."

October 14, 1980 (Tuesday)

In a speech to the National Press Club the President charged that Reagan's plan to drastically cut taxes and sharply increase the defense budget could result in a $140-billion budget deficit by 1983, leaving only a bloated defense budget and a few uncuttable programs like Social Security.

In his interview with Barbara Walters the next day, Reagan responded, saying that every economist who had studied his program believed the federal government would have a budget surplus by 1983 that would provide for additional tax cuts. As for Carter's charge that a Reagan Presidency would be bad for the country, Reagan flashed a smile, shook his head sadly, and said, "Well, he's kind of an authority on people who are not good Presidents."

The Gallup survey showed Reagan's lead over Carter had shrunk from 45 to 42, with John Anderson dropping from 15 to 8 percent. This conformed with the trends that Caddell had been finding for several days.

October 17, 1980 (Friday)

Linda Peek, the campaign press secretary, rushed into my office with a wire story: Reagan had decided to debate without John Anderson. To me, this was a clear sign that Reagan and company realized that we were closing in on them.

"He must think he's going to lose," I said. "His people would never let him debate if they were ahead."

Caddell called, frantic. "Is there any way we can avoid debating him?"

"I don't see any way out."

Pat's position all along had been that we had everything to lose and very little to gain in a debate. Recognizing that the President was committed to a two-man debate, he had been steadfast all along in opposing such a contest. But now it couldn't be avoided.

Pat talked about stalling the negotiations, but I replied that it wouldn't work. Resigned, Caddell said, "If we're going to debate him, it's damn important that we get rules that increase the possibility that he'll say something dumb or screw up."

I agreed.

We had spent months planning for campaign personnel, deciding budgets for each state, making millions of telephone calls to potential voters, and now all that would fade to nothing compared with the importance of a debate.

But I was ready for it. While in the abstract I understood Pat's concern, I had never feared a debate with Reagan nor questioned how the President would fare up against an elderly former actor.

One consolation was seeing John Anderson fussing and whining about being left out of the debate and trying to blame it on "the White House."

Strauss, Powell, and Rafshoon began the debate negotiations, with Caddell feeding in his ideas from the sideline. Caddell felt that the debate had become everything and that the election would be "frozen" until undecided voters and wavering Democrats and Republicans had made up their minds.

October 20, 1980 (Monday)

As part of our "agreement" with Kennedy, Jack English, a respected Kennedy partisan, joined our staff as overall liaison and also to prod us on our efforts for the Kennedy campaign debt, which we hoped to accomplish at a big fund-raising dinner featuring the President and the Senator.

Several weeks before the event, Jack poked his head in my office and reported that tickets for the dinner were selling poorly and that the Kennedy staffers thought we were not living up to our end of the bargain. We were asking Kennedy to campaign extensively during the last two weeks before the election, and English's assessment was that he might refuse if the dinner was a failure.

I turned to the White House and campaign staffs to contribute. None of them took my plea very seriously, so I went to the bank, arranged a loan, and wrote a check for $1,000 to "The Kennedy Campaign," copied it, and waved it around. Others joined in reluctantly.

The dinner was a success after all—thanks in large part to the money I had squeezed out of the young people at the campaign and the White House. Someone had obviously told Kennedy about my efforts, so he tore himself away from his wife, Jean and Steve Smith, the other Kennedy family members, and all of the "beautiful people," and came over to thank me. I accepted his words of appreciation, gritting my teeth as I shook hands with him. I deeply resented Ted Kennedy and his millions, coercing all of us to pay off his debt.

October 28, 1980 (Tuesday)

For almost a week, nothing had happened in the campaign. Pat Caddell's polls showed that people had quit making up their minds. It was as if the entire election had been put on hold, waiting for the debate.

I was surprised to find the President in a foul mood the day of the debate. His afternoon was to have been reserved for relaxation and a final practice session, but he had been interrupted by matters only he could see to. He tried to assure me that he was relaxed, but I could see tension written on his face.

I chose not to watch the debate from the special VIP seats in the auditorium. I wanted to see it the way millions and millions of Americans would—on the tube. Twenty or thirty people—including Stu, Jody, Jerry, and Pat, some of the advance staff, and several Secret Service agents—assembled in a large, rectangular room over the auditorium, lined with tables of cookies and punch. A couple of dozen folding chairs in the middle of the room surrounded several television sets.

Everyone was very quiet. Jody seemed destined to set a smoking record that night. The images of Reagan and Carter appeared on the screen. I didn't like what I saw: Reagan looking relaxed, smiling, robust; the President, erect, lips tight, looking like a coiled spring, ready to pounce, an overtrained boxer, too ready for the bout.

We had won an earlier flip of the coin and chose to let Reagan go first, thinking that the early pressure might unnerve him. Reagan didn't do badly but neither did he gain any advantage. Then it was the President's turn. He hesitated, then nervously over-answered the question. I remembered his first debate in 1976 with President Ford, when our candidate, known for his great confidence and composure under fire, was visibly shaken; afterward he explained that he was not psychologically prepared to find himself standing toe-to-toe with the President of the United States. I had hoped that this time around the tables would be turned.

I tried to put out of my mind what I heard Rafshoon say so many times: "It's not so much what you say but how you say it, and what kind of overall impression you convey."

The questions continued, and Carter seemed to unwind—but none of us in that room did. In fact, after almost every question, one of us would get up, and go over to another viewer, and ask, "What do you think?" or, "How's it going?" Stu Eizenstat would sit up in his chair when the President made a point, or he would lean forward, look down at the floor, and shake his head when he failed to take advantage of an opportunity. Several times Stu or Pat spoke out in frustration: "Why did he say that?" or, "He didn't use the answer we gave him!"

Suddenly we heard Carter describe how he had asked Amy, "What is the most important issue?" and she had responded, "Nuclear weaponry and the control of nuclear arms."

Jody winced. Rafshoon stood up and clapped his hand to his

head. "Oh my *God*—not that!" The President had told us in his debate practice that afternoon about his conversation with Amy, saying that the response of a little girl was a way to personalize the real concern of the American people about nuclear war. Maybe he should work it into the debate? We had all argued against it, perhaps not as bluntly as we should have. Most people, we tried to impress on him, saw Amy as a freckled-faced little girl growing up in the White House. They didn't know how smart she was, and quoting her on nuclear war sounded contrived. I had completely forgotten about it until now. "Cartoon artists all over the country are sharpening their pencils," said Rafshoon. Then, with a slightly sour smile he added, "It's so bad that it's funny."

But the debate then settled down. The President was carefully following Pat's game plan, mentioning the issues and problems and sounding the code words and phrases intended to appeal to the diverse groups in the Democratic constituency. Reagan seemed not to have a tactical plan but to be intent instead on appearing to be relaxed, avoiding mistakes, and shying away from rhetoric that might sound extreme or belligerent.

I had been waiting for Reagan to mention the Misery Index—a term we had invented to use against President Ford in 1976. It meant the total of the rates of inflation and unemployment, which—we contended—measured the human misery and suffering of the American people under Republican economic policy. The Misery Index was 13 points in 1976 and at least 21 points throughout 1980.

But little did I know that Reagan would use it in his closing statement. Looking straight into the television camera with an almost pained look, he asked, "Are you better off than you were four years ago? Is it easier for you to go and buy things in the store than it was four years ago? Is there less unemployment than there was four years ago? Is America as respected throughout the world as it was? Do you feel that our security is as safe, that we're as strong as we were four years ago?

"If you answer all of those questions yes, why, then, I think your choice is very obvious. If you *don't* agree, if you *don't* think that this course we've been on for the last four years is what you would like to see us follow for the next four, then I could suggest another choice that you have."

"He's a goddamn actor," someone said.

"And a good one," I added.

"Are you better off?" What a narrow and selfish premise, I thought, *asking people to choose their President based solely on their present condition.* Nevertheless, it was our idea, and now Reagan had turned it against us. And if somehow he managed to win, some Democrat would be firing the same question at him four years from now. Looking ahead to the future and to the complex problems and scarcities that face our nation and the world, the answer to that question—Are you better off?—could very well be no, time and again for the balance of the century and beyond. Would that mean if we have twenty difficult years ahead as a nation, we would have five different Presidents, none able to serve long enough to deal with the problems?

The debate was over.

Pat said everything was OK. Jody thought that "the Boss did good." We reinforced each other's hopes and beliefs that we had won. We all had to act upbeat—the press would be looking for clues of disappointment. We rushed downstairs and greeted the President and Rosalynn as they came offstage.

"How did I do?"

Grasping his hand, I exclaimed, "You won, Mr. President! You did it!" I actually believed it.

"Really?"

"You did a lot better than Reagan," Rafshoon added.

Rosalynn was beaming, and he gave her a big kiss before they left the hall and walked back to their hotel.

Whether it's football or politics, the American people like a winner. So the first task after the debate was to persuade the press and the public that we had "won." Rafshoon, Caddell, Jody, and I put on our biggest smiles, tried to seem confident, and fanned out through the crowd of press people, telling them that "of course" we had won. We could see the Reagan team doing the same thing.

Then ABC News began to broadcast the results of their poll,

which showed Reagan the clear winner. Caddell was screaming and yelling about the technical flaws in their phone-in survey, but the poll was the first suggestion that there was, in fact, a clear "winner." I was confused. The President had followed our strategy, avoided big mistakes, and sent the right signals to Democrats and interest groups.

I decided to call my brother, who lived in Georgia. He was a Carter supporter—and a realist. "What'd you think, Lawton?"

"My boy, the Gipper did well. After the last few weeks, I was sure that Reagan would say something stupid or make a mistake like Ford did in 1976. But overall Reagan looked good." He paused. "He did better than Carter."

I was afraid he was right. Pat Caddell had said all along that our best hope of defeating Reagan would be to keep people from being able to seriously consider him as President. Pat had said, "We've got to keep him from reaching the 'plausibility threshold.'" It looked as if Reagan had marched across it tonight in Cleveland.

October 30, 1980 (Thursday)

Deputy Secretary of State Warren Christopher called me Thursday and told me that the Iranian Parliament was going to meet Sunday morning, November 2, and that the Swiss and other "sources" in Tehran expected it would produce "a specific proposal" for ending the crisis.

"Could the hostages be released before Tuesday?" I pressed.

"They could, Ham, but I doubt it and sure don't count on it."

He went on to say that he was concerned about the President's response to whatever the Parliament said or did and wanted to be certain he had time to carefully weigh his response. I looked at the campaign schedule. "Chris, the President will be in Chicago Saturday night, making his last stop of the campaign in Illinois—a state we'll have to have if we're going to win."

"It's a tough call, Ham. If the Boss cancels his campaign trip and comes back to the White House, it focuses attention on the hostages and raises expectations. If he brings his foreign policy team out to meet him on the campaign trail, it looks as if the campaign is more important than the hostages."

Finally, Christopher suggested that I fly out to Chicago Saturday and be with the President when the message from the Parliament came in. We could decide on the spot what would be the best way for him to respond.

"Right down to the wire," I told Eleanor. "This damn hostage thing is going to surface right when the voters are making up their minds." If they voted the hostage release Sunday, was there a chance the hostages could be on their way home by Tuesday? And how would the American people react? They would be over-joyed, but there would be charges that the President had manipulated their release. The Reagan strategists had been talking about an "October surprise" for weeks, implying that Carter could bring the hostages home when he wanted to and conditioning the American people for a slick political maneuver if and when it happened.

And some people would simply resent its happening so close to the election, feeling that the Iranians were trying to manipulate our election, trying to re-elect Carter because they feared Reagan. It was too much even to contemplate the impact of the hostages on the election. We had to get them out—whenever we could.

October 31, 1980 (Friday)

Rosalynn didn't usually call me unless she had a specific idea or suggestion or some problem she didn't want to bother the President with. When she phoned my apartment around ten o'clock on Friday night, it was for reassurance.

"I've been in Texas today," she reported. "Everybody is excited and the crowds are going wild."

Hearing that made me feel good, because Rosalynn had keen

political antennae. But I also remembered that in the last week or ten days of the McGovern campaign in 1972, the crowds were so wildly enthusiastic that McGovern's people started to disbelieve their own polls, which showed them way behind, and to think they were on the verge of a miracle. They were right—a McGovern victory would have been a miracle, as the ticket went down to historic defeat.

"But I'm still very worried," Rosalynn said. "What do *you* think?"

"There's no doubt that Reagan helped himself in the debate. Pat's polls showed Reagan moving ahead, but he thinks that things are settling down now. A disproportionate number of undecided voters and the 'soft' Anderson voters are Democrats. These people should come home," I said.

"What impact will all this speculation on the hostages have?" she asked.

"Rosalynn, I honestly don't know."

After we hung up, I thought, *She called me to get encouragement, and I'm as worried about the election as she is.* But I was optimistic. Polls showed Reagan ahead, but not by much, and there was plenty of evidence that it was tight going into the homestretch, with a lot of people undecided. We had to try to convince those people that it was better to cast a "safe" vote for an experienced incumbent than to take a chance on a new President. That was what the race with Gerald Ford had come down to in 1976. Were the voters sufficiently unhappy with Ford to take a chance on an unknown, a former Governor of Georgia? The voters in 1976 had favored the challenger. We had to figure out some way in four short days to have them resolve that same question in favor of Carter.

Maybe the hostages would do it. The sweet possibility that something would happen over the weekend excited me. I, of all people, shouldn't have allowed myself to become hopeful that the Iranians would meet our campaign schedule. *But it could happen, I thought, it really could happen. . . .*

November 1-2, 1980 (Saturday-Sunday)

I spent the day at campaign headquarters, making calls and last-minute decisions. But I wasn't kidding myself. The key to the election of an American President was now in the hands of unpredictable fanatics halfway around the world, revolutionaries who hated the United States and its Chief Executive. If something dramatic happened Monday—like the release of the hostages—it would probably allow us to nose Reagan out; a bad signal from the Iranian Parliament Sunday would probably mean Reagan's election.

Pat's weekend polls showed the contenders neck and neck.

I took a commercial flight out to Chicago Saturday afternoon, went straight to the airport hotel, and waited in the President's spacious suite. He, Jody, and Phil Wise came in about 11:30, exhausted from a long day of campaigning but pleased with the crowds. He was surprised to see me and I explained why I was there. (The only times I had ever left headquarters in the 1976 or 1980 campaigns were to be with him at his debates.)

He went on to bed. Chris called me at 3:45 A.M. The Majlis had set four conditions that probably could be met, but there was a lot of rhetoric which was being translated. In Chris's opinion, the President needed to be able to sit down with his advisers and formulate a response.

I walked down to the President's suite. By the time I got there, he was on the phone with Christopher. When he hung up, I said, "Mr. President, I think you should go back."

He listened, but did not respond. Instead he picked up the phone and placed calls to Mondale and Muskie. He talked briefly with both men, who advised the same. Jody and Phil had arrived by this time, and Carter said he wanted to leave as soon as possible. Jody rushed to wake the press.

We left Chicago at 5:30 A.M. Air Force One cut through the thick morning clouds; a brilliant golden sunrise shimmered against the horizon. The President went up to the cockpit and spent several minutes admiring the view.

When he returned, Jody and I joined him in his compartment and had eggs and bacon. I couldn't help but be optimistic. We'd had a lot of bad luck this year, maybe it was time for it to change.

"You know," Jody said, "I always worried that if the hostages came home a month or six weeks before the election, there'd be an initial outpouring of support for getting 'em back alive, followed by weeks of partisan attacks and second-guessing. The Republicans have done a good job of preparing the American people for an 'October surprise,' but they won't know how to handle a 'November surprise.'"

"It's a hell of a note," the President said, "being the President of the United States and going into the homestretch of a close race that will be decided not in Michigan or Pennsylvania or New York—but in Iran."

Back in Washington, the President went directly to the Cabinet Room to confer with his foreign policy team. He scanned the translation of the official text from the Majlis, pulled his glasses off and said, "These are the same four conditions that Khomeini approved in September, wrapped in a bunch of political rhetoric. This should bring our people home . . . eventually."

No one said anything, but every single person in that room knew at that moment that the hostages would not be free by Election Day.

We spent the rest of the day deciding how to respond to the Majlis's statement. We had to play it down the middle to avoid the press charge we were using the crisis for election purposes. I tried to discourage Rafshoon and Caddell from coming over just so the President's "political advisers" wouldn't be seen running in and out of the White House, but they managed to get in without being noticed, anyway.

That afternoon the President took a break from the meeting in the Cabinet Room to ask Kennedy to fill in for him at rallies in Detroit and Philadelphia. Kennedy quickly agreed.

While Jody, Strauss, Caddell, and I were meeting in my old office, staff director Al McDonald came in. The former Marine officer was visibly angry. "I don't know what the Boss is going to say, but let me tell you that I'm mad—and the American people are mad—at the notion that the Iranians are trying to manipulate our election."

"What would you suggest?" asked Jody.

McDonald smiled. "I'd tell 'em to shove it!"

But the President didn't, and later in the day, he made a statement to the American people, calling the Majlis action a "significant development" and adding, "We are within two days of an important national election. Let me assure you that my decisions on this crucial matter will not be affected by the calendar."

The hostages wouldn't be home by Tuesday, but I believed that his statesmanlike response to the Majlis was still a political plus.

November 3, 1980 (Monday)

Jody, Jerry, Pat Caddell, and I gathered in the Oval Office in the morning for a few minutes with the President before he left for what he described as "my last day as a political candidate." He seemed relaxed and confident as we talked about what points he should stress on the eve of the election.

"Mr. President," Caddell said, "there is still an incredible number of undecideds—particularly blue-collar Democrats—who are tempted by Reagan and liberal Democrats and independents who are leaning toward Anderson. I think you should make a plea this last day for Democrats to come home and a direct appeal to Anderson voters."

We all agreed. President Carter shook hands with Rafshoon, Caddell, and me and walked out the door. We stood at the window, watching him and Jody walk to the waiting helicopter. "Just think," Rafshoon mused, "with all the exit polls, the next time we see him, we'll probably know whether he won or lost."

My own feelings were confused. I glanced over at the President's desk. I couldn't imagine the American people putting Ronald Reagan there. But with the economy in bad shape and the hostages still being held, our political problems were enormous. What would be the impact of the last-minute hostage news? Perhaps it would make people imagine Reagan sitting here in the Oval Office, faced with all the problems, and conclude that he wasn't up to it. Even the polls gave us different stories. *The Washington Post* showed the President 3 points ahead, while a Gallup poll gave Reagan a single point. *It's going to be another cliff-hanger*, I thought. *Just like 1976, when we stayed up all night in the hotel suite in Atlanta waiting to hear that Jimmy Carter had edged Gerald Ford out.*

We gathered in Bob Strauss's office at the campaign headquarters to watch the evening news, our last chance to show the large mass of undecided voters the "stark differences" between Carter and Reagan. We hooked up a couple of sets so we could watch all three major networks at once.

None of them led with the traditional last-night story from the campaign trail. All carried the latest news flash from Iran: the militants had met with the Ayatollah Khomeini and told him that they were ready to turn over the American "spies" to the government.

Following that flash story from Iran were stories from the campaign trail, with Carter and Reagan trying to avoid questions on the possible release of the hostages.

All three networks concluded not with stories about the Presidential election the next day but with a commemoration of the anniversary of the captivity. CBS showed film clips of the President's early pronouncements on the embassy takeover, his early-morning announcement of the failed rescue mission, the Vance resignation, and the outrage of the American people. All three networks took their viewers on an emotionally wrenching review of the past year.

Rather than drawing the contrasts between the two men who wanted to be President, the news was a strong reminder of our inability after a long year to win an honorable release of the hostages or to avenge the wrong done us by the Iranians.

Bob Strauss put his hands over his face in horror, shook his head, and said, "The news tonight was bad, bad, bad for us. We needed a lift tonight, an upbeat story, pictures of people clapping and smiling and a confident President shaking hands. . . . Instead we got this hostage stuff. It's bad, Hamilton, bad."

Tim Kraft agreed. I was so shell-shocked that I didn't know

what to feel. "Maybe it's not that bad," I countered. "At least it looks like the Iranians may be getting ready to negotiate seriously."

"Mr. Jordan," Strauss said sarcastically, "the American people have quit believing us on the hostages. Do you think they're going to pay any attention to what those bastards over there say?"

I didn't argue with Strauss; I knew the minute he said it that he was right.

We sat around for a couple of hours, making last-minute calls to key states, phoning a number of people who had worked hard to thank them in advance, and preparing for any voting irregularities that might crop up. Finally, about ten o'clock, I went home.

November 4, 1980 (Tuesday)

Hostages, was my initial reaction as I woke up suddenly and answered the phone at about 2:00 A.M. The White House operator apologized for calling so late but said, "Mr. Caddell insists on talking with you." Then I remembered it was election eve and that Pat Caddell had promised to let me know the results of his telephone survey conducted after the evening news.

My stomach knotted as I waited for him to come on, knowing he might already have the outcome of the election.

"Ham!" Caddell said excitedly.

Reading his voice, I thought to myself, *It must be good—please let it be good.* "Ham," he repeated, "it's all over—it's gone!"

"Gone!" I almost yelled. "What do you mean it's gone?"

"The sky has fallen in. We are getting murdered. All the people that have been waiting and holding out for some reason to vote Democratic have left us. I've never seen anything like it in polling. Here we are neck and neck with Reagan up until the very end and everything breaks against us. It's the hostage thing."

"What do you mean, 'breaks against us'?"

"It's going to be a big Reagan victory, Ham, in the range of eight to ten points."

I was silent.

"All these last-minute developments about the hostages and all the anniversary stuff just served as a strong reminder that those people were still over there and Jimmy Carter hasn't been able to do anything about it. The hostage crisis symbolizes our impotence. Ronald Reagan's message is, 'Elect me and you won't have to take that anymore.'"

I didn't have the heart or energy to talk about why we had lost, and wasn't ready yet to accept it. Caddell was always right—but I wasn't ready to buy it. *Besides,* I thought, *all across the nation not a single person has voted.* I simply said, "Well, let's talk about what to do."

"Should we call the Boss?" Pat asked.

"Pat, if you're sure of it, hell yes, we should call him. He's got every right to know what we know." I paused and said softly, "That won't be an easy call to make."

"Hamilton, I am sure. I wish I wasn't, but I am."

I told Pat that he and Rafshoon should meet me at the White House, in my old office, at 3:15 A.M.

When Rafshoon walked in, I was leaning back in my old chair, my feet propped on the desk. For once the wisecracking Rafshoon was subdued, shaking his head and slumping down in the chair across from me. "It's hard to believe, isn't it?"

I nodded. Caddell walked in, wearing blue jeans and looking more rumpled than usual. He looked devastated. But always the professional, he was set on understanding what had happened and lapsed into a detailed explanation in the past tense of an election that hadn't even begun.

"It was unbelievable, like nothing I've ever seen. Here we were rocking along in a classic close race, the lead shifting back and forth, and then kaboom," he said, throwing his arms up in the air. "An electoral explosion."

Rafshoon leaned forward. "Are you absolutely sure, Pat? Are you sure of your figures?"

"I'm afraid so," Caddell said quietly. "Jerry, I wouldn't be so sure if it were two points or even three or four points, but it looks to me like Reagan is going to win by eight or ten points."

Rafshoon gave out a low whistle, then mumbled, "A landslide!"

"What can we do, Pat?" I asked.

"We can try to save some of the Democratic candidates if the President would make an impassioned statement to scare the hell out of some of these Democrats who are staying home or voting for Anderson."

We finally agreed that the best course of action was to give the President the bad news and encourage him to make a statement when he voted at Plains that might increase the Democratic vote. We reached Jody in Seattle on Air Force One, where he often waited when the President made a quick stop for a rally. This was the last stop of their trip before they headed back east to Georgia. "Jody," I said, "brace yourself. Because it looks like it's gone. And it could be bad."

Pat picked up the extension and gave Jody the details. And I said, "If we could lose by five points instead of ten, it would be a lot better. We could save some Congressional seats." The minute I said it I thought to myself how desperate we had become— talking about reducing our margin of defeat to 5 points!

Jody was shocked. He just muttered "jeez!" and "good Lord!"

He said the President was about to begin his last speech of the campaign to an airport rally of Carter partisans, and he would break the news to him as soon as Carter returned to the plane.

After we hung up, Rafshoon said, "God, I feel bad for Jimmy." It was strange to hear him called that, as we had addressed him as "Mr. President" for four years now. It was as though he had already lost the title.

"I feel bad for Jody," I countered. "How would you like to tell Jimmy Carter that this race we always thought we would pull out was gone?"

Later, Jody told me how he had handled it. He poured himself a big drink and walked out into the hangar. "It was such a strange feeling," he said. "Most everyone there in the crowd and even the press thought that Carter had a good chance of winning.

Some always thought that we ultimately would win, particularly the President himself. And here I am watching what was likely the last campaign speech of his life with the sure knowledge that we would be defeated. It was eerie.

"It was a good speech," Jody recalled. "You know, typical come-home Democrats and Anderson voters with a nice remembrance of what being a Democrat had meant to him growing up in the South during the Depression. You have to do so many of those damn things that they often don't have feeling, but this speech did. It was like the President knew that for better or worse this was it, and he did a good job with it. There was one of those cold Northwestern drizzles, but the crowd enthusiastically responded to the speech. Finally, when it was over, he began to work the crowd, shaking hands. Then one of the advance men played a tape of our 1976 campaign song, 'Why Not the Best?' over the PA system. I caught Carter's eye as he walked back to the plane, elated by the crowd's reaction and touched by the song. His eyes were blinking like he was fighting back a tear or two."

After his return to the plane, the President sat down with the traveling press, and Jody was unable to get him alone to give him the bad news. Finally, while the impromptu meeting with the press was coming to an end, Pat and I called again from Jack's office to see if Jody had broken it to him. Jody told us that he hadn't been alone with him long enough to tell him. Just as he was saying this, Carter walked in, took the phone, and said in a happy voice, "What's happening, Patrick?"

I could hear Pat take a deep breath and then say, "Mr. President, I am afraid that it's gone."

There was silence on the other end. Pat paused, waited for the response that never came, then went on with his analysis. He had told the story enough times so that now it was a smooth and convincing spiel: how the hostage crisis seemed to trigger people's pent-up feelings and frustrations about the Administration and the economy. "We're losing the undecided voters overwhelmingly, and a lot of working Democrats are going to wake up tomorrow and for the first time in their lives vote Republican."

In a voice notable only for its lack of emotion, the President said, "Well, you guys get with Jody and try to draft something that I can say in Plains that might help. Don't say anything yet to Rosalynn. Let me tell her. I'm going to try to get some sleep. Good night."

"Yes, sir," I said.

He put Jody back on the phone and he and Pat discussed what Carter might say to dramatize the risk facing the Democratic Party. Pat was suggesting drastic rhetoric, while Jody was insistent that whatever the President said had to be responsible and couldn't appear desperate or it would be counterproductive. When Pat hung up, the three of us sat for a few minutes without saying much to each other, stunned and saddened.

Finally, Pat pulled his chair up to my old globe and began moving his finger across it. "You know what?" he said. "The Boss is flying from Washington State to Plains and he will not fly over a single state that we will carry."

It was past four o'clock. There was nothing else we could do, so I walked to the parking lot to get my car. In the lobby, one of the guards stopped me and asked, "Is the Boss going to win, Mr. Jordan? I've got a couple of bets around here. What do you think?"

"Sergeant, it's hard to tell—but you guys all be sure to vote!"

"Oh, we will. A couple of guys around here will vote Republican, but most of 'em are going to stick with the President."

It was the kind of tidbit I usually relished on election eve, but tonight I knew it was different. *What a funny feeling,* I thought. *Not a single person in the country has voted and we already know we've been defeated. Modern technology takes a lot of the honest emotion out of politics.*

As I drove out of the front gate, I stopped and looked back on the magnificent white building, awash with lights, glowing in the dark. *In a few months the White House will be off limits to me. . . .*

I got an early wake-up call and flicked the television set back and forth between the morning shows until I caught a picture of the President and Rosalynn voting and then speaking to the crowd assembled at the railroad depot in Plains. Four years earlier, at that same spot, candidate Jimmy Carter had returned to the small town in the early-morning hours, stood on those same steps, spoken to his townspeople, broken down, and almost cried. I had seen it on television and had shed a happy tear with him.

His remarks this morning were not right at first. He listed some of the issues that we had worked on that had hurt us politically. I realized that he was trying one last time to do what we had failed to do during the fall campaign: establish a credible rationale for his re-election as President. After stumbling around, he spoke from the heart. "Many people from Plains, from Americus . . . from around this area have gone all over the nation to speak for me and shake hands with people, to tell them that you have confidence in me and that I would not disappoint them if I became President. I've tried to honor my commitment—" His voice broke. I edged forward on my bed, pulling for him to regain his composure. He paused, looked down, and added, "—to you. God bless you. Thank you. Don't forget to vote, everybody!"

Pat had wanted him to scare Democrats to the polls. But this was the sad speech of a proud and defeated man.

I went into the campaign office early and tried to wear a smile for all the young people who were working so hard to get out the vote. But I was a zombie that day, taking calls, encouraging people, and most of all trying to hide my own fear of a landslide.

By midday, I had moved over to the White House. The President and Rosalynn arrived back. They met a crowd of staff members who had gathered on the South Lawn to greet them, then went to the Residence and left word with Phil Wise that they were going to get a couple of hours of sleep before the returns started coming in.

By midafternoon, the networks had started getting results in, and word began to spread. Gloom settled in over the West Wing.

At about 4:30, the President called. "What's happening, Ham?"

Not wanting to get into it on the phone, I replied, "Nothing very good, Mr. President."

He told me to gather Pat, Jerry, Jody, Bob Strauss, Kraft, and Kirbo and meet him in the Oval Office at 5:30.

I rounded up the others and we walked quietly down to the Oval Office. I had delivered a lot of bad news to him over the years, but never had I been as apprehensive about taking those dozen steps. I remembered Carter's other defeat, at the hands of Lester Maddox in 1966, and how he had packed up his family and driven off into the night without thanking his campaign workers. I wondered how he would take this one, which would undoubtedly be interpreted as a repudiation of his Presidency.

He and Rosalynn, dressed casually, were standing behind his large desk. He walked around to the front of the desk and gave each of us a smile and a firm handshake. Up close, I could see that his fair and sensitive complexion was a deep pink, almost red. Had he been crying?

We sat in a semicircle around the front of his desk, where we could all be close to him.

In a gesture that had become familiar from many election nights, he turned to Caddell, smiled, and said, "Pat, tell us what happened."

Happened, I thought. *He's already accepted that it's over.*

The usually glib Caddell squirmed on the sofa as he "read" the election: "Mr. President, we went into the weekend neck and neck with Reagan," he began. He went on through the nearly hourly ups and downs since then. "Then last night we did a telephone poll after the evening news—and we saw the thing explode!"

Strauss's head bobbed up and down as Pat talked.

Finally Pat said, "A lot of people who were undecided got up mad Tuesday morning, said that they had had enough of this, and went out and voted against us."

"Or against me," the President said quietly. "How bad is it going to be, Pat? Jody was talking about five points this morning."

"Mr. President, Reagan is going to win by close to ten points."

Carter winced. There was a quiet moment, and then he said, "Well, at least we won't have to stay up all night the way we did in seventy-six."

I thought about that long night four years before. The entire Carter family and all of us were sitting in the suite at the Omni Hotel in Atlanta when the networks gave Mississippi to Carter and projected, "James Earl Carter of Georgia has been elected the thirty-ninth President of the United States." From that moment, we stopped calling him "Governor" or "Jimmy." It had been "Mr. President" ever since. That seemed like fifty years ago.

The President was questioning Caddell about the meaning of the election. I didn't want Pat to have the whole burden of bearing the bad news.

"Mr. President," I said, "when you spread a ten-point margin out all over the country, it means that Reagan will have an electoral landslide."

The President said nothing. Rosalynn frowned.

"And a lot of Democrats are going to get defeated," Pat added.

I jumped in again. "Ironically, probably many of the liberals who criticized you for abandoning the traditional approach of the Democratic Party."

The President was doing a good job of disguising the hurt I knew he felt. This night he was a good actor. Finally he said, "Well, let's look to the future. I'll never forgive Ford for his harsh personal attacks on me during that campaign, but I'll never forget how gracious he and his people were to us during the transition. I'd like to be just as gracious to Governor Reagan and his team. I want to have the best transition between Administrations that there has ever been."

I sneaked a glance at Rafshoon, who grinned back at me. The Carter hyperbole was present in defeat as it was in victory.

I thought fast. I had no desire to get caught up in passing the torch to the new crowd. As far as I was concerned, I would leave for Georgia that night if I could. "Mr. President, Jack Watson did such a good job of heading the transition in 1976 that I would recommend him to head your transition team. You should mention that to Reagan when you call him to extend congratulations."

My transparent attempt to remove myself from the transition was noticed by all, and there were a couple of snickers. "I think you ought to be involved, Ham," Jody said, "since you were involved in seventy-six."

"I'm only good at transitions in—not transitions out."

We stayed in the Oval Office for a while, and Carter's apparent good spirits—real or not—helped everyone to relax.

"When should I concede?" he asked.

Pat and Jody said he should wait until the polls had closed on the West Coast, eleven o'clock our time. The President agreed and asked for suggestions about what he should say.

He came around and sat on the edge of his desk like a school-teacher. "I don't have any regrets about what we tried to do over the past four years or in the campaign. We've had some notable accomplishments, some failures, and more than our share of bad luck. But we were bucking the tide on a lot of issues. I don't want any of you to have any regrets either. The mistakes that were made were mine or were my responsibility. We'll all have a lot of time to reflect on the four years and the election and why we didn't win. But, most of all, I want you all to thank everyone who helped us. And we need to make our best effort to assist the new President and his team. God knows, they are going to need all the help they can get!"

A couple of people mistook Carter's last comment as a joke and chuckled. We rose and filed past the President and Rosalynn on the way out. They both shook our hands. I clenched my jaw as my turn came.

"Thanks, Ham," he said.

I couldn't talk, and didn't want to look him in the eye, so I just nodded. I wanted to get the hell out of there before the tear that I could feel welling up in my eye ran down my cheek.

Pat, Jody, and I then met with the Cabinet and White House staff in the Roosevelt Room and broke the news. Everyone was in a state of shock. Strauss and Muskie made strong statements about being proud of what we had accomplished.

I had just walked in the door to my apartment at 8:30 when Jody called. "The President is going on to the Sheraton in thirty minutes."

"What?" I said. "Why the change?"

"He wants to get it over with. He says he thinks he'll look ungracious if he waits till eleven o'clock. The networks started calling it by eight-fifteen, and he's afraid people will think he's sulking in the White House, bitter in defeat."

"I understand that," I said, "but I still think he ought to wait till the polls close."

"Ham, it won't do any good to argue with me. I agree with you.

I'm just telling you that he's leaving for the hotel in thirty minutes and wants you to round up the staff and Cabinet."

I made the calls and got to the White House in time to ride over to the Sheraton in the motorcade with the President, lights flashing, sirens whirring. Groups of people gathered on the streets along the way, some to wave, others to stare at the defeated President.

When we arrived, the advance team told us that Carter wanted us all on stage with him. *For comfort?* I thought. My gut reaction was to stay off national television, but then I remembered that it no longer mattered. The election was over. I couldn't hurt the President anymore.

The crowd cheered and shouted greetings to us as the staff and Cabinet walked out. I could see some tear-stained faces, but otherwise there was very little evidence that we had lost. At least political tradition allows the loser the comfort of being among friends.

The President and Rosalynn appeared, the band started playing "Happy Days Are Here Again," and the crowd went wild. It was not a greeting for a loser. He held up his hands several times, trying to quiet the crowd, which ignored him and kept on cheering. Finally he stepped up to the podium. With Rosalynn, his children, and grandchildren clustered around him, he pulled out his little note cards, forced a smile, and said, "I promised you four years ago that I would never lie to you, so I can't stand here tonight and say it doesn't hurt."

"No, Jimmy, no!" someone in the crowd yelled.

He didn't stop. "The people of the United States have made their choice, and of course I accept that decision—but I have to admit not with the same enthusiasm that I accepted the decision four years ago." The President expressed good wishes to Reagan, pledged his personal support through the transition, and it was over.

The band struck up a lively tune, the crowd yelled, the President moved back and forth across the stage, his right arm outstretched. I noted how serene he looked. *Even in humiliating defeat,* I thought. *Maybe it's some comfort and relief to know that the awful burdens of the Presidency will soon be off his shoul-*

ders. Then he went down the row of the Cabinet and staff, saying over and over again, "Thank you," "Thank you." When he got to me, he threw his arms around me and said a couple of times, "Don't worry, Ham, don't worry—we did the best we could. You help us be strong."

Then, as was his custom, he jumped down off the stage into the crowd to shake hands. As I watched him, I couldn't help but think that his only other political defeat had come at the hands of Lester Maddox. *How strange,* I thought. *Lester Maddox and Ronald Reagan, two right-wingers—the bookends to his political career.*

I mixed with the crowd for a few minutes and then headed up to several suites we had rented in the hotel for a "victory party." I ran into Jody in the hallway upstairs. "Ham, you and I ought to circulate. These young people are devastated. At least you and I have had the luxury of twenty-four hours to prepare for this."

Jody and I split up and went from suite to suite, where groups of people were standing quietly around television sets watching state after state go to Reagan. In several rooms where members of the White House or campaign staff had assembled, I spoke briefly, saying that we had tackled a lot of tough issues and that sometime soon the American people would come to appreciate what we did and tried to do.

After circulating through several more rooms, thanking people, we settled into a corner suite where most of the campaign brass had assembled. We watched the networks as their projections came in, showing the Carter states in blue and Reagan in red. The map was a sea of red.

We had carried the South in 1976 not on the issues but because Carter was a Southerner. It looked now that the more conservative South was back to voting the issues, as state after state on the electoral map was turning Reagan-red. In fact, Georgia was a lonely island in the South which had not been "called." Then one of the networks carried a report from Georgia. Based on early results, it showed the President "slightly" ahead in his home state. I felt a sick feeling in my stomach. I couldn't stand the thought of Jimmy Carter being repudiated in his home state. *How horrible it would be,* I thought, *to lose Georgia.* I stopped and said a little silent prayer. *We have lost and lost big. Isn't that enough? Please, please—don't let us lose Georgia. . . .*

Finally I ended up with my friends from the campaign—Tim Kraft, Tim Smith, and Tim Finchem—standing around a television set, drinking beer, and thinking out loud. "What could we have done differently that would have won the election?" Finchem wondered.

"I tell you what we could have done," Kraft replied quickly. "We could have taken that twenty-nine million that the government gave us to run the campaign and bought a few more helicopters for the rescue mission."

And Kraft was probably right. By Election Day, we were burdened with the hostages, a party still divided from the Kennedy challenge, and a weak economy. If the mission had worked in April, the hostages would have been free and Kennedy would probably have ended his candidacy. If we had had six months to unify the party, to develop a Democratic consensus on the country's economic problems. *If, if, if . . .*

At last the networks colored Georgia blue for Carter. "Thank God for small favors," I mumbled, picking up another cold beer. We all stayed up late into the night comforting each other.

November-December 1980

Several days after the election, I left with some friends for a vacation we had planned—win or lose—in the Virgin Islands. Pat's analysis that the hostage crisis caused Reagan's victory provided a rationale for the magnitude of our defeat. But, away from Washington, with time to clear my head, I knew that the reasons were not that simple.

I thought back to the memo I had written in June and to our strategy. Our goal was to give the American people a breather from Carter's campaigning by lying low through the summer. Instead, the President was forced to spend the better part of six weeks on the evening news and on the front pages wallowing in "Billygate," fighting the charge that he and his Administration had been involved in a cover-up. And just when the Billy Carter affair began to subside, Americans were treated to a rancorous and devisive Democratic convention.

I had hoped that July and August would afford the President time to restore some of the glow to his image, tarnished through the protracted campaign. Instead, the long, hot Washington summer only embellished the picture of an incumbent Chief Executive who couldn't control either his family or his party.

In the campaign itself, we had failed to clarify the stark differences between the two candidates, their views of the nation's interests and needs. Ronald Reagan began his campaign with enormous baggage: a near majority of Americans had either deep-seated doubts about his ability to lead the country or genuine fear that his right-wing, bellicose view of the world could push the United States into a war. But he had managed to shed that appearance during the campaign, looking less and less like the "mad bomber." We were hoping that the debates would confirm the jingoistic image. It didn't.

Reagan's rocky start smoothed right out when the "meanness issue" turned attention back to Jimmy Carter. Our worst fear all along had been that the race would ultimately become a referendum on Carter's Presidency instead of a choice between him and Reagan. Presidential campaigns historically follow one of two patterns: one candidate starts with a commanding lead, maintains that lead, and wins a lopsided victory, as in LBJ's landslide win over Goldwater in 1964 and Nixon's against McGovern in 1972. More often, Presidential polls show a clear favorite and then the race tightens to a dead heat with one edging the other out, as Kennedy did to Nixon in 1960, Nixon did to Humphrey in 1968, and Carter did to Ford in 1976. What was so unusual about the Carter-Reagan race was that it started far apart: Reagan led Carter by 30 points over the summer. Then the race narrowed: some polls had Carter slightly ahead going into the last ten days, more favored Reagan, but most said it was just too close to call. And finally, the election exploded, with Reagan beating Carter by a solid 10 points.

I felt that many voters were genuinely troubled by the prospect of a Reagan Presidency but unhappy with us. A large number of undecided voters, disproportionately blue-collar Democrats, waited throughout the fall for the President to provide a positive reason for them to vote for Carter or against Reagan. Our message to those voters either was not effective or was obscured by the reality of high interest rates, inflation, and hostages, so that Reagan, through relaxed and careful campaigning, and in the two debates, began to look more and more plausible as a President.

Ultimately, the anniversary of the seizure of the hostages and the demands of the Majlis the Sunday before the Tuesday election served as dramatic reminders to Americans that the President had not been able to resolve the deadlock that had come to epitomize for many not only our Administration but also the frustration that our nation was losing control of its destiny. Many commentators would call it a watershed election, reading implications into the vote that I did not see then and do not accept today. Certainly, the point can be made that any ideological shift in the American electorate over the last decade has been toward conservatism. But what happened in 1980 was not an ideological tidal wave; it was instead an expression of frustration with the Democratic Party and doubt that it could provide the solutions to America's problems.

When I returned to Washington, I was not happy but certainly reconciled to our loss, and I understood the reasons for it. But reaction in Washington disturbed me as much as the defeat itself. For almost four years, the Washington establishment had been like a pack of jackals, lurking near a wounded animal, smelling its blood, but hiding in the bushes and peering out only from time to time. Now that their prey was dead, they descended on the carcass with a vengeance.

Their assessments of Jimmy Carter—as a President and as a human being—were vicious and implacable, and the perverse logic of the press and the political community was quick to equate defeat at the polls with failure as a leader. By their reasoning, it followed that since Jimmy Carter was defeated, he was by definition not a good President; since he lost by a wide margin, he was a terrible one.

It was as though the extent of our defeat had negated all of his achievements; as though the Camp David peace treaties hadn't been signed, as though the energy legislation we had worked for three long years to pass were null and void, as though normalization with China had been withdrawn at the ballot box.

I was perplexed by the enormous divergence between what the President had accomplished and the way he was now being perceived. How much of this misunderstanding was our fault? I wondered. And how much of it was the result of Jimmy Carter's being a complex man who didn't comfortably wear the traditional labels and whose thoughts didn't fit neatly into an ideological box? How much of it was the Administration's inability to explain its goals?

And, finally, how much was a result of changing attitudes within the White House press corps itself?

Even after four years as Governor of Georgia and a long campaign for the Presidency, Jimmy Carter underestimated—as all Presidents do—the aggressiveness and hostility of the White House press, although we did recognize and accept the basic adversarial nature of that relationship, realizing there never had been a President who was pleased with his press coverage. We did not, however, understand or appreciate the extent to which the Washington press corps had changed in the past decade.

I believe that Watergate and Vietnam pushed the American media from wholesome skepticism and doubt into out-and-out cynicism about the American political process generally and the Presidency specifically. Both Vietnam and Watergate had assumed the coloration of a struggle between the press and the President.

President Lyndon Johnson told the American people that national interests and "our national honor" were at stake in the steamy jungles of Southeast Asia, and the Pentagon and its generals provided helpful body counts—sure proof that a great American victory was just around the corner. The press challenged Johnson's claim of national interests and showed the horrors of the war to millions of Americans every night on the evening news.

President Richard Nixon dismissed the Watergate break-in as "just politics" and proclaimed, "I am not a crook." But *The Washington Post* would not be denied, and dug out the truth about the conspiracy and the subsequent cover-up.

So, in less than a decade, the American people had suffered through two traumas: the nation's first military defeat, the result of a flawed policy, which cast doubts on our nation's intentions in the world; and the first resignation of a President, the result of a flawed character, which cast doubts on the integrity of all those involved in politics.

One consequence was a widespread sentiment that in these two great crises, the press was entirely right and the President was entirely wrong. Carried to the extreme, these feelings resulted in the belief that the media are the good guys and the Presidents are the bad guys. It was LBJ versus Walter Cronkite; "Tricky Dick" versus *The Washington Post,* Bob Woodward, and Carl Bernstein. The guys in the white hats were fairly obvious.

The cynicism of the Washington press—born in Vietnam and nurtured in Watergate—seeped into news coverage and into the living rooms of millions of Americans.

Just as the attitudes of the media had changed prior to the Carter Administration, so had the men and women who had chosen reporting as a profession. The old-timers had worn their anonymity as a badge of honor. The dream of the cub reporter was to write the thoughtful column (à la Walter Lippmann) or to file the big story quickly (like Merriman Smith, UPI reporter at the White House). But the role models had changed. The goal now was to be like Dan Rather, who could stand nose-to-nose with the Chief Executive and ask the tough question; or ABC's irreverent Sam Donaldson, who would shout out his questions to any President, any time or any place; or even to be another Bob Woodward, who had brought down a President. The journalist satisfied with a tiny by-line had been replaced by the news personality whose name and face were known throughout America.

Television news presented other problems. Television's greatest strength is its immediacy—its ability to flash stories from anywhere in the world instantaneously to countless viewers. No type to set; no waiting for newsboys to deliver words. Pictures—real pictures—are available at the turn of a knob.

There are of course disadvantages to television's immediacy. The instant reportage of news and events forces quick, glib analysis from men and women who often don't have the background to cover the story. The television news broadcast has very little sense of priorities and proportion. A newspaper can put the big story on page one, the medium-sized story on page five, and trivia on page twenty-five. But television news, limited after commercials to less than twenty-five minutes, has to either cover a story or drop it altogether.

Historically, the political opinions of the American people have been formed slowly, percolating, and building over a period of time. But the immediacy of television causes snap judgments and ready-made opinions. The Presidency is a four-year contract with the American electorate. But with television news, the American people can more easily monitor that contract, being sure every "i" is dotted and every "t" crossed.

It was against this backdrop of subtle but profound change in the media that the Carter Presidency was reported and judged, and any resentment that we felt against the media would have been experienced by any person sitting in the Oval Office in the 1970s.

But that didn't make it any easier to accept their appraisals of our Administration and our President.

I went back to the White House—this time my job was described as "consultant"—but I was torn between actively preparing for my new life in Georgia and wanting to be as helpful to the Reagan crowd as the Ford people had been to us. And although I had been on the sidelines of the hostage negotiations for the past five months, I was determined to do anything I could to help President Carter get the hostages out during his Administration—even though we were very lame ducks.

Several days after my return, I tried through Jack Watson to contact Ed Meese, who was in charge of Reagan's transition. "Tell him," I told Jack, "that I just want to help if I can, to sit and talk about the mistakes we made—not policy or anything like that—but some ideas I have about the structure of the White House and the approach to problems." In a few days, Jack reported that Ed Meese was "anxious" to talk to me, but he never called, and it soon became clear that the new Administration seemed mainly intent on taking exactly the opposite approach to ours in every possible way. "Avoid at all cost doing anything the same way the Carter people did" seemed to be the watchword of the new group, and conferring with Hamilton Jordan would probably have been considered a capital offense.

My plans for the future developed quickly. I rented an apartment in Atlanta, began to think seriously about writing a book, and prepared for my duties with Emory University. There was also the possibility of speaking around the country. I had learned during the four years that when people are overthrown in other countries, they often faced a firing squad. But in America, when the voters rise up and throw you out, you take to the lecture circuit. I contacted some lecture agencies—one promised enormous fees. I saw this as the solution to my gigantic legal bills, but the agent returned sheepishly in a few weeks to report that big fees were not likely.

"Why?" I asked.

"The cocaine business," he said, embarrassed.

"That's a hell of a note," I said to Eleanor. "I need to make some money to pay my legal fees from a bogus charge and can't because of the damage done by the publicity from the allegation."

I spent some time going through our records, separating and filing them for the archivists who would catalog each document. They would end up in the President's library. Most of my life and plans and thoughts were in the future, but whenever I brought my mind back to the remaining time in the White House, I thought about the hostages and tried to keep up with the negotiations.

It was damned important for us to get them out before the new Administration took office. A cocky new Administration, riding the crest of a landslide and determined to avoid doing anything like Carter, would find it politically difficult to show restraint with our opponents and to say and do the things necessary to free our people in Tehran. The signs were not good. As before, the Iranians seemed to have the desire to end the crisis but not the capacity to pull it off.

Warren Christopher had left for Algeria to "pursue aggressively" (the President's words) the conditions spelled out publicly by Khomeini and the Majlis. The Algerians had agreed to serve as "messengers" (their term) in negotiating terms for the release.

By the middle of December, most of my personal plans had been completed, and thanks largely to Eleanor's hard work, my government files were in order. There was really little else for me to do at the White House. I took myself off the regular payroll and arranged to be paid on a daily basis only.

Then, on December 19, the Iranians sent what they described as their "final response" to the U.S. position, saying that the hostages would be released when this country paid Iran $24 billion, an amount that far exceeded the Iranian assets frozen by the President in November 1979. President Carter turned them down flat, saying that we would not be "blackmailed."

I packed my car with papers and clothes and drove home to Georgia, certain that the hostages would not be home while Jimmy Carter was still in the White House.

I spent a melancholy Christmas with my family in south Georgia and went with the President and some of his friends to the Sugar Bowl to watch the University of Georgia win the national football championship.

I returned to Washington the first week in January, not because I had a lot to do, but because I felt that being there with the President and my friends those last several weeks—the "deathwatch," I called it—was part of my responsibility. If I couldn't help anymore on the hostage negotiations, at least I could suffer through the last efforts with the President.

January 7, 1981 (Wednesday)

I asked the President to spend some time talking with me about the future. He agreed, on the condition that politics not be on the agenda.

We went down to the White House mess and spent about an hour discussing what we would do when we were back in Georgia.

"You knew we were going to lose all along—that's why you've been planning to go home for over a year," he said.

I chuckled, knowing he was ribbing me.

He and Rosalynn would go home, he said, and take a vacation first thing. "Do you realize, Ham, that for the last fifteen years, since I ran for Governor in 1966, my life—and Rosalynn's life— has been campaigning, shaking hands, meeting and speaking to groups? And then governing. For fifteen years, I've had to wake up every morning and worry about other people's problems and needs. It is going to be an enormous relief for us to have some time alone, to do what we want and to relax. But eventually I'll get bored with doing nothing, and I'm going to have to find an intellectual outlet. Gerald Ford enjoys being an ex-President and playing golf. Nixon leads a quiet life. I'm not like that. I am going to have to stay active."

In the middle of our luncheon, the man in charge of the mess brought the phone over to our table. "Mr. President, Warren Christopher is calling you from Algiers. Will you take it?"

"Yes," he replied quickly, picking up the phone. He said hello and then mostly listened intently for eight or ten minutes. "Warren, call me any time of the night or day," he said and hung up.

"What's happening?" I asked the second the receiver was in its cradle.

"Chris thinks we may really have something. I'm afraid to get my hopes up, but I've started to get the feeling that maybe Khomeini finally wants to end this damn thing."

January 8–13, 1981 (Thursday–Tuesday)

I spent the next five days dismantling my office at the White House. Eleanor had divided my papers by category, boxed them as prescribed by the archivists, and stacked the brown boxes three or four feet high all around my desk.

I was thumbing through a box of personal memos one day when I heard the door open. I peered over the box, and there were Ed Meese and Jim Baker looking around.

I stood up, walked around the boxes, and extended my hand. "Welcome, gentlemen—I'm Hamilton Jordan."

From the look on Meese's face, you would have thought I was a leper.

"Hello, Ham," Jim Baker said in a friendly tone, shaking my hand. He had managed Ford's 1976 campaign and we had had some contact. I had found him personable and capable.

"Hope we didn't interrupt you," Meese added quickly. "No one was at the desk outside. We didn't know you were here. We're just checking out the offices before we make staff assignments."

"As I remember it," I said, "assigning the offices was more difficult than choosing the Cabinet."

They both smiled.

"You're right," Baker said.

"Well, we need to move on," Meese said.

"By the way," I said, "I told Jack Watson to tell both of you that Dick Cheney [Ford's Chief of Staff] gave me some good advice four years ago that we ignored. I'd be glad to do the same if you'd like."

"Good idea," said Meese. "Why don't we try to get together next week for lunch? I'll check my schedule and call you."

"That would be good. Partisan feelings aside, I'd like to help if I could."

"Great, great," Meese said. "We'll do it next week."

We shook hands and they left.

Eleanor had returned and was enjoying the scene from the doorway. "Should I call his secretary and schedule the lunch?"

"No. I want to help but don't want to push myself on them," I replied.

"It sounded as if they were serious about getting together. They'll call, I'm sure," Eleanor said.

"I'll bet you they won't. They can't even imagine that someone like me might be able to help them in some small way."

They never called.

January 14, 1981 (Wednesday)

The President gave his farewell address at 9:00 P.M. It was a thematic speech: no lists of facts and figures and no mention of special interest groups and bills. Just Jimmy Carter, sitting in the Oval Office, talking quietly about America's future.

"It has now been thirty-five years since the first atomic bomb fell on Hiroshima. The great majority of the world's people cannot remember a time when the nuclear shadow did not hang over the earth. Our minds have adjusted to it, as after a time our eyes adjust to the dark. Yet the risk of a nuclear conflagration has not lessened. It has not happened yet, thank God, but that can give us little comfort, for it only has to happen once.

"The danger is becoming greater. As the arsenals of the super-powers grow in size and sophistication, and as other governments acquire these weapons, it may only be a matter of time before madness, desperation, greed, or miscalculation lets loose this terrible force.

"The shadows that fall across the future are cast not only by the kinds of weapons we've built but also by the kind of world we will either nourish or neglect. There are real and growing dangers to our simple and our most precious possessions: the air we breathe, the water we drink, and the land which sustains us. The rapid depletion of irreplaceable minerals, the erosion of topsoil, the destruction of beauty, the blight of pollution, the demands of increasing billions of people, all combine to create problems which are easy to observe and predict, but difficult to resolve. If we do not act, the world of the year 2000 will be much less able to sustain life than it is now.

"The battle for human rights, at home and abroad, is far from over. We should never be surprised nor discouraged, because our efforts have had, and will always have, varied results. Rather, we should take pride that the ideals which gave birth to our nation still inspire the hopes of oppressed people around the world. We have no cause for self-righteousness or complacency, but we have every reason to persevere, both within our own country and beyond our borders."

In closing, he said, "I will continue, as I have the last fourteen months, to work hard and to pray for the lives and the well-being of the American hostages held in Iran. I can't predict yet what will happen, but I hope you will join me in my constant prayer for their freedom. . . . Again, from the bottom of my heart, I want to express to you the gratitude I feel. Thank you, fellow citizens, and farewell."

There was hardly a dry eye at the White House that night. Rafshoon and Jody both said it was the best speech of his Presidency.

January 15, 1981 (Thursday)

We were at the Metropolitan Club for a farewell dinner in honor of the President and the First Lady. The election defeat was far enough behind for the mood to be upbeat. The staff and Cabinet members were circulating, talking about book contracts, and discussing going on the lecture circuit or returning to law firms and businesses.

We were all among friends, and didn't have to worry about being gracious losers. The good feeling and a few drinks produced a rash of transition horror stories about encounters with Reagan successors. For every anecdote there was someone who could top it: "Wait'll you hear what happened in *my* department!" It was the same kind of thing that people had said about us four years before. But who cared? It was a chance to snicker and laugh together.

Harold Brown talked about the right-wingers coming into the government. "They are putting people in charge of arms control that are *opposed* to arms control!"

"Well, wait till you get a look at this guy Jim Watt," Interior Secretary Cecil Andrus replied. "All the people in the West who've been complaining about our water policy will love us. They're not going to need water in a few years—Watt is going to pave the West!"

Small comfort, I thought. *They're taking our jobs and offices and we're laughing.*

The dinner ended with a series of toasts in honor of President Carter. Harold Brown made a touching toast to the peace that America had enjoyed during the past four years, and Ed Muskie raised his glass and said, "Mr. President, many of my former colleagues in the Senate have treated me like a dead man since the election. 'Poor Ed,' they say behind my back. 'He left a safe seat in the Senate to serve for eight months in the Cabinet.' To those who say it to my face, and even to those who say it behind my back, I respond that the past eight months have been the most exciting and gratifying experience of my life, and if I had to make that decision over again to leave the Senate to serve as your Secretary of State, I would gladly do it."

Everyone applauded. The President smiled and then looked down at the table.

Mondale rose and proposed a toast: "To President and Mrs. Carter: You kept the peace, you obeyed the law, you told the truth, you did your best for the American people."

When the dinner was over, Lloyd Cutler pulled the President off to the side, briefed him on the latest news from Christopher in Algiers, and asked if I would like to go with him to the Treasury Department to check on the financial arrangements for the hostage release. We walked into the office of Robert Carswell, the Deputy Secretary of the Treasury. There, a group in shirtsleeves were gathered around a long wooden table piled high with papers and memos. Their talk was technical and complex, and they referred again and again to their problems in a pessimistic tone. Lloyd wouldn't allow them to be downhearted. "We all sound like lawyers, gentlemen. Let's figure out how to overcome these problems instead of spending all of our time enumerating them."

As I sat in the room listening to the Treasury officials argue about the deal, I got confused and exasperated.

Lloyd walked over once in the meeting and said, "It's something, isn't it, Ham? I suspect that this is the most complex agreement ever negotiated between two nations."

"You're telling me," I replied. "Escrow accounts and special telex codes and central bankers in Algiers and London and Tehran. It's going to be like one of those Willie Mosconi trick pool shots where you have to hit all sides of the table just exactly right, then the ball hits a group of balls which all go into separate pockets."

The silver-haired Cutler smiled. "There's only one difference, Ham."

"What?"

"None of us knows how to play pool."

I went home feeling discouraged. The complex deal might work between friendly nations, but between hostile nations through a third party? *Not likely,* I thought. *Not likely.*

January 17, 1981 (Saturday)

Lloyd Cutler's office had become the nerve center, and Jody and others stayed there most of the day, talking back and forth to the Treasury Department about the transfer of money, to the President at Camp David, and to Warren Christopher, Hal Saunders, and Arnie Raphel, who were working round the clock in Algiers trying to sew up the agreement.

I came in to see what was happening on the hostages and grabbed the phone when I heard it was Chris on the other end. "What in the hell is taking you guys so long?" I demanded without identifying myself.

He laughed. "Hello, Ham—I wish you were here with us."

"We're all just glad that you're there," I said seriously.

"Now I know what you went through," he replied.

"Yeah. I feel like the quarterback who was knocked unconscious in the first quarter of the game, only to wake up in the fourth quarter and see that my replacement is going to win it."

"We're doing our best," Chris said, "but I'm not sure we're going to make it by Tuesday."

I signed off with, "I've got a feeling that Christopher will throw a touchdown to Cutler before this thing is all over."

January 18, 1981 (Sunday)

The President canceled his last weekend at Camp David and rushed back to the White House in the middle of the day to be near the communications center and the various people working on the hostage negotiations. It was touch and go, with increasingly optimistic reports from Deputy Secretary Christopher in Algiers, who was with Algerian officials in direct contact with the Iranians. The nine-and-a-half-hour time difference meant most of the meetings and decisions were being made during the early-morning hours.

Sunday night the President settled into the Oval Office, waiting and waiting for more word from Christopher. He was wearing a beige cardigan sweater and blue pants. He took off his shoes and lay down on one of two sofas that were back-to-back in the office, one facing the fireplace and flanked by two chairs and the other facing his big oak desk. Every now and then he got up to throw another piece of wood on the fire.

Lloyd Cutler, the point man at the White House, in touch with the Treasury Department, the bankers, and Algiers, kept running in and out of the Oval Office with news and tidbits on the negotiations. On one trip, Carter said, "Lloyd, why don't you just relax here with us so you won't have to be going back and forth?" This was more that just a polite gesture; it was a quiet request. On his next-to-last night in the White House, the President wanted the company of this wise man.

January 19, 1981 (Monday)

At about two in the morning, the President ordered blankets from the stewards and lay down on a sofa, indicating that Lloyd take the other one. I sat in a chair on the side, watching them. Lying on the back-to-back sofas, light-blue blankets pulled up around their necks, the President and his counsel looked like two boys at summer camp, stretched out on their cots, talking about the day's activities or sharing secrets about girls.

I remained silent as they chatted, enjoying the unusual and informal scene.

"How do you think Reagan will do, Mr. President?" Cutler asked at one point.

"I'm not sure. I hope he'll do better than I think he will. He's done well in the transition period, but that's almost inevitable with all new Presidents. Everybody wants a new President to succeed, and the press coverage reflects that. But Reagan will have two early tests, one on the domestic front and a couple in foreign policy. Domestically, the big question is what will he do on Kemp-Roth" [the Reagan tax-cut plan].

"It just won't work," Cutler said.

"Yeah, but I think Reagan believes in it. I thought it was just campaign rhetoric, but from everything I can tell, he really believes in Kemp-Roth. If he doesn't moderate or back down from that, he'll wreck the economy. In foreign policy, he'll face one test from a friend, Israel, and one test from an adversary, the Soviet Union. Begin will test Reagan early to see what he's made of," the President said, then, chuckling, he added, "God help Reagan and the United States if Begin thinks he's afraid to stand up to him. The other big test will come on the grain embargo. If Reagan lifts it as he promised the farmers in the campaign, it will send a signal to the Soviets that although he talks tough, he doesn't back up his talk with strong action. I've urged Reagan to hold off lifting it until they've been in office awhile and can take a look at the situation. If he decides to keep the embargo, I'll support him publicly and try to help keep it bipartisan." The President sighed and smiled. "You know, the problems of the country look very different from the Oval Office than they do from the campaign trail."

"I wonder if he'll involve George Bush as you did Fritz," Cutler said.

"They would be smart to. I'll never forget what Kirbo told me down in Plains that month that I was interviewing Vice Presidential candidates. He said that some Presidents, like Johnson, were always worried about the Vice President overshadowing them, but he said that no one could overshadow a President and that what I should do is pick someone to be Vice President whom I could get along with, who could help me with my problems and be President someday if anything happened to me. He was right, and Fritz has been extremely helpful and terribly loyal, even when he disagreed. Kirbo's personal choice was Scoop Jackson, but that wouldn't have worked. I could have handled Scoop, but it wouldn't have been much fun having to remind him every day that I was the President, not he."

Cutler and I laughed.

"How do you think Fritz will do in 1984?"

"It won't be easy for him. But he'll go into the contest with several advantages. He can be a full-time candidate, not burdened by the responsibilities of being a senator. His association with me will hurt him with some groups, but I think he's got the best of both worlds, perceived by the interest groups as being effective in carrying their message but not blamed for my tough political decisions. But it's a tough damn road. I couldn't do it again."

My ears pricked up when I heard that. I hoped it was true.

Things went on this way for a couple of hours, the President and Lloyd doing most of the talking, interrupted occasionally by calls from Algiers. Finally, the call came through from Algiers.

"We have a deal!" Jimmy Carter said proudly, beaming. He shook Lloyd's hand vigorously and thanked him, then placed a call to Rosalynn.

Lloyd ordered a couple of bottles of champagne that he had brought to the White House, and we were soon joined by the First Lady and Lloyd's wife, Louise, who had been asleep on the couch in Lloyd's office and wandered in with her shoes off, wrapped in a baby-blue blanket and looking very much like a squaw. Lloyd popped the champagne, poured several glasses, and turned to the President, who raised his glass high and toasted, "To freedom!"

"To freedom!" we all responded, and began talking excitedly about the trip to Germany to meet the hostages.

At 4:44, the President went to the press briefing room to announce that the United States and Iran, with the good help of the Algerians, had reached an agreement. We refused to discuss the details, saying that claims of "victory" could jeopardize the release. After the announcement, the President returned to the Oval Office to await implementation of the agreement and to prepare for his trip to see the hostages.

Phil Wise had calculated that Carter would have to leave Washington no later than two o'clock Monday afternoon if he wanted to see the hostages in Germany and be back for the Inauguration. "We'll have plenty of time," the President said.

But it didn't work out that way, and as we sat in the Oval Office through the early morning hours and past daybreak, it began to occur to us that the release of the hostages still might not take place while Jimmy Carter was President. Chris reported that although a deal had been struck, the head of the Iranian bank was causing some complications. By late Monday morning, the mood had turned gloomy. It was looking doubtful that the President would see the hostages before he left office. "Maybe we could get the British to loan us the Concorde," I suggested. "You could get over and back in time for the Inauguration."

"I would still be President, and the Concorde wouldn't have the communications that I would need as Commander-in-Chief," Carter answered quietly.

"Do you have to go to the Inauguration?" I asked desperately.

"Ham, it would look terrible if he wasn't there. The Inauguration is a symbol of the continuity of our government," Lloyd said. I knew he was right.

"I just won't get to see them," the President said despondently.

"Surely Reagan will want you to," Cutler offered.

"I doubt it," the President said, "and I certainly would never ask to go."

The two-o'clock deadline went by, and we switched from worrying about seeing the hostages before the Inauguration to worrying that hang-ups in Algiers and Tehran would prevent their release altogether.

The President spent the rest of the afternoon either on the phone with Algiers or waiting for the Iranians to begin to implement the agreement. One of the few breaks was his exchange of gifts with the Vice President: Mondale presented Carter with a beautiful globe; the President gave Mondale a handmade rifle.

The Carters had invited the Mondales and the Kirbos for dinner that last night in the White House. I had to go up to the private dining room several times with messages and found them talking quietly among themselves.

The President, Mondale, and Kirbo came back to the Oval Office at about 8:30 P.M., then Mondale left for a while. Kirbo and the President chatted about old times and the long road to the White House. I remained quiet, feeling like an intruder with these two old friends.

They talked about the Quitman County voting fraud case of 1962 when Jimmy Carter was running for the State Senate and was cheated out of a close election by a powerful county boss. Judge Griffin Bell, then a federal judge and a friend of Carter's, suggested that he hire Charles Kirbo. Kirbo took the case and, in an unusual action, the judge threw out the ballots from the disputed county, making Jimmy Carter the winner. Kirbo said with a chuckle, "If we hadn't won our case, you probably would have never gotten into this mess."

They went on to Carter's 1970 gubernatorial race, the political friends and foes, the headaches caused by Lester Maddox, who was Lieutenant Governor under Carter.

"I'll tell you what has really changed," Kirbo drawled. "The ladies are going to take over the world."

"What do you mean, Charlie?" the President asked.

"Just look at my law firm. It used to be an unusual thing to see a lady lawyer. Anyone you'd see worked for the government or for some big company. In the past several years, we've hired a number of lady lawyers—and they're crackerjacks! Most of them have better work habits than men: they're smart and tough and just damn good lawyers," Kirbo continued.

"You know, Charlie, we had trouble sometimes finding enough women to appoint to the Federal Court because the available pool of female lawyers with five or ten years' experience was relatively small. We still appointed more women to the bench than all previous Presidents combined. Reagan won't have that problem. In the next two or three years there'll be so many more eligible to serve on the bench."

"Yeah," Kirbo responded, "I suspect we'll see a woman on the Court before long."

"I wish I could have done that," mused the President. "Charlie, do you realize that I am the only President in the history of the country who didn't make a single Supreme Court appointment?"

"Mr. President, you always wanted to distinguish yourself," he said.

They both chuckled lightly.

Carter began to clear off his desk, signing pictures for staff members and friends. "I wonder how many pictures I've signed in the last two months. We've had thousands of people at the White House for thank-you receptions since the election. It was nice to do, but it has worn me and Rosalynn out."

"Everybody appreciated it," Kirbo responded.

"Oh, I know. If everybody who came to the White House since the election had voted for us, we'd have won by a landslide!"

January 20, 1981 (Tuesday)

Shortly after midnight (daylight in Algiers and Tehran), activity began to pick up. The United States government opened a special account with the Bank of England. The Federal Reserve Bank was to transfer a portion of the frozen Iranian assets to that account; the Bank of England would then place the money in an escrow account controlled by the National Bank of Algiers, and the Algerians would notify the Iranians that their assets were in Algeria's possession. Once the hostages were on the Algerian plane and out of Iranian air space, the government of Algeria would be notified and the funds would be transferred to the Iranians.

Communications among the three countries would be by telex, with an agreed-upon language and a series of codes.

At 1:50 A.M., Treasury Secretary Bill Miller called the President to say "The machine is burping."

"I can't believe it," Carter exclaimed. "It's finally happening."

In about half an hour Lloyd Cutler walked in from the Treasury Department. "Mr. President, we finally got the message from the Iranians, but it's garbled. It has the wrong code and incorrect figures."

The President was visibly shaken. "They're going to screw around and have to renegotiate this thing with Reagan."

Kirbo listened, shook his head, and broke the serious mood. "No wonder the Shah killed so many of those people—they're crazy!"

I kept thinking about all that was happening and how I wanted to stay awake and savor every moment of it. But I was so damned tired, having been up for two days and nights. I was fighting sleep, and wasn't going to allow it . . . but maybe just a couple of minutes with my eyes closed. No more, just a couple of minutes, was the bargain that I struck with myself . . .

Actually, I was supposed to be sleeping in the Residence last night and tonight. The President had invited me and the Powells, the Rafshoons, the Mondales, and the Kirbos to be his guests during his last days at the White House. Some of the others may have made it to bed, but I never turned the covers down.

I woke up to the sound of voices, opened my eyes, and saw the President standing over the sofa, hands on his hips, looking down at me with a big smile. "You wouldn't believe what's happening, Ham. We've got the agreement! We've got the agreement!"

I sat up slowly. "That's great, Mr. President, that's great!" I mumbled groggily, embarrassed and angry with myself for sleeping through such a rich bit of history.

"No thanks to you, Ham," he shot back. "The agreement was delayed for about thirty minutes because we couldn't hear Christopher on the phone over your snoring."

I tried to smile back, gazed around the room, and saw Jody and Lloyd laughing at me.

I looked at the antique wood clock by the door of the Oval Office. It was 5:45 A.M.

"What's happened?"

Jody briefed me that the cables containing the right words and pledges had finally gone from Tehran to Algiers and from Algiers to the London banks. "The agreement is in place," he explained. "We've got a few loose ends and papers to be signed. Then they ought to let our people go. And you slept through it all."

At 6:32, the President picked up the phone, put his hand over the mouthpiece and said, "It's Christopher." He listened for a few seconds, said, "That's great, Chris," then paused to tell us that Christopher had signed the final papers in Algiers on behalf of the United States at 6:18 A.M., Washington time.

At 6:47, Treasury Secretary Bill Miller called to say that the Bank of England had certified the funds deposited by the United States in the escrow account.

"It's moving," Carter said. "I just hope they release them while I'm still President." He picked up the phone, asked for the First Lady, and gave his wife a report. "I have a foreboding feeling. It looks like it's greased, but we've been disappointed so many times before."

We waited and waited for the next step. Carter considered calling Algiers again, but then said, "No, if I keep calling 'em, I'll be a distraction." Then, around 7:00 A.M., he said quietly, "I'm going to call Reagan and brief him." He asked Phil Wise to phone Blair House.

Wise stepped out and came back in a couple of minutes. "Mr. President, I placed the call, which was intercepted by his aides. They said that he had had a long night, was sleeping, and was not to be disturbed."

"You're kidding."

"No, sir, I'm not."

Smiling, Carter responded, "Well, I suppose he does have a busy day, but I'm going to wake him up later if anything happens, whether he wants to get up or not."

The President sat for a long several minutes without saying anything or making or receiving any calls. I decided to try to cheer him up. "We're not cutting it close enough," I said sarcastically. "We still have five hours before the Inauguration."

He looked at me but still didn't speak.

In a few minutes, he called Rosalynn and asked if she could send over his coat with his comb and the little cross in his pocket. It arrived in a few minutes, and he stood up and tied his red tie and put on his suit coat while talking to Lloyd and Kirbo.

Muskie and Cy Vance arrived. Muskie pointed and said, "Mr. President, your eyes match your tie." Everyone laughed.

The President gave them both a status report, then talked with Cy about his plans to meet the hostages. They agreed that he should go on out to Andrews Air Base and stand by, so that when the hostages left Iran, he would take off for Wiesbaden and be there to greet them when they arrived.

It had been almost an hour since the Bank of England certified the funds, and nothing had happened. At 7:44, the President called Miller again. "What's the holdup, Bill? With the time difference between here and Iran, it's starting to get dark over there. I can just see the Iranians delaying for another day, Reagan becoming President and saying something inflammatory, and our deal going down the drain." Miller checked and called back to say that the Bank of England was having to draw up language to certify that the money was in their possession. As the President covered the phone and repeated Miller's message for those of us around his desk, he said, "The damn bankers can't decide how to word their message certifying that the funds have arrived."

"What about 'It's here'?" Jody said playfully.

Irritated by the delay, but obviously relieved that it represented nothing serious, Carter said, with a twinkle in his eye, "You tell the Bank of England that the President of the United States—Carter, not Reagan—says that they are delaying the release of the hostages."

It was 7:57. The President pulled out the drawer on the left side of his desk. In it was his red secure phone. Our intelligence reported that the Algerian plane which was supposed to carry the hostages to freedom was taxiing onto the runway in Tehran. The President very excitedly reported the news to us. "It's finally happening!"

He had put off having his regular haircut. "I'm shaggy-looking," he had explained earlier in a call to Rosalynn. So the barber came over, and Jimmy Carter, Rosalynn, and the barber went back to his small office, where he sat with a sheet wrapped around him and had his hair cut.

At 8:09 a call came in from Algiers. "That's great, Chris," Carter said. The money had been certified.

In a few minutes he was back in the Oval Office monitoring progress on the red phone when Reagan returned his call.

"Good morning, Governor," the President said, winking at me. "I hope I didn't disturb you." He then gave Reagan a six- or seven-minute detailed report. He listened for a few seconds, then said, "Fine. We'll see you and Mrs. Reagan at the White House in a couple of hours. Good luck."

I was so curious I couldn't contain myself. "What did he say, Mr. President?"

Everybody in the Oval Office gathered around the desk to hear him recount his conversation with his successor. Looking dead serious, Jimmy Carter said, "Well, I briefed him on what was happening to the hostages. He mostly listened. But when I finished, he said, 'What hostages?'" Everybody cracked up.

At 8:39 A.M., we got a report that two Algerian planes—probably carrying the hostages—were on the end of the runway at Tehran airport. Several minutes later word came that an Iranian jet had taken off. "I wonder why?" I mused.

"Probably to serve as an escort for the two Algerian planes," the President responded.

In a few minutes, Jack Watson appeared with some last-minute proclamations for the President to sign. "What are these?" Carter asked, the red phone still pressed to his ear.

"It moves the Inauguration back a couple of hours, Mr. President," Jack quipped.

A few minutes before 9:00, the President received another report on his red phone. "Boy, I bet those hostages' hearts are just pounding, sitting on that plane waiting to fly off," he said, smiling.

Two calls came from Christopher in Algiers. "Mr. President,"

Lloyd reported, "Chris says that he's been told that they will take off 'within your Administration.'"

"Lloyd, I'm not going to count on Iranian promises."

The second call from Christopher came in at 9:55. He recommended, and the President agreed, that there be no public announcement on the departure of the hostages until they had cleared Iranian airspace by at least one hour, just in case someone would use that information to try to shoot the plane down.

The President handed Sick the red phone to monitor and stepped into his private bathroom. When he returned, he looked around the office, by now filled with all of the foreign policy team, plus Rafshoon, Caddell, and an ABC film crew that had been allowed in earlier to film the last hours for historical purposes. "I'll be in the study," he said quietly, and left.

It didn't seem right to turn the Oval Office into a waiting room, so at about ten o'clock, I said, "OK, everybody, let's get out of here and give the President some time alone before he leaves this office." It was altogether fitting that I deliver the bad news, as that had been my job for much of the four years. But no one objected as my words sank in. People began to quietly file out of the office, one by one. The President returned to the Oval Office just as I was starting to leave. "Ham, you and Gary stick around," he said.

With the red phone to his ear again, he said, "God, we have been busy these last few days! I thought our last weekend at Camp David would be nostalgic for Rosalynn and me, and probably difficult, and leaving the office and the White House would be rough, but we've been too busy to think about it. It's probably been a blessing." I felt he was trying to convince himself.

The First Lady called twice to urge him to come get dressed. He glanced at his watch: 10:25. "Well, I better go put on my monkey suit." Finally he put down the phone and admonished Gary and me to call him the minute we heard anything. He walked over to the door that looked out on the South Grounds, opened it, and just stood there staring back into the Oval Office. His eyes swept the room one last time. "Ham, y'all keep me informed."

"Yes, sir."

He turned and walked quickly away. I headed for the Situation Room.

Eleanor was still pleading for me to go.

I remained silent and tried to ignore her. I waited for another couple of minutes.

"Hamilton, you have got to go. The plane will leave you if you don't get there on time."

As usual, she was right. "OK, OK," I said. "Let's go!"

I thanked the intelligence officer on the phone, hurriedly shook hands with the Situation Room professionals, and said goodbye to Captain Gary Sick.

Eleanor, Jerry Rafshoon, and I sprinted off to catch the limousine that would carry us to Andrews. We ran through the White House basement, which is traditionally decorated with informal photographs of the President and the First Family. When I had arrived at the Situation Room forty-five minutes earlier, it was still the Carter White House. But as I rushed out, I was stunned to see pictures of the Reagans—on horseback—smiling at me. The White House had been Reaganized in a matter of minutes.

"Reagan really did get elected, didn't he?" I shouted to Rafshoon.

Eleanor laughed but urged me to be quiet. As we ran out the door toward the car, I could see what looked like an army from Wall Street—clean-scrubbed, smiling Republicans in dark-blue or gray suits, carrying briefcases, were marching toward the White House.

We hopped into the car. The driver didn't seem too happy with the chore of taking me to Andrews. Instead of meeting Messrs. Meese, Deaver, and Baker, he was chauffeuring a has-been to catch a plane back to Georgia.

Rafshoon joked that he could just see the next day's *Washington Post:* "Hamilton Jordan, bitter to the very end, almost had to be evicted from the White House Tuesday afternoon after President Reagan was inaugurated."

I wondered how it would feel in the future to ride by the White House and not have the security guards recognize my car and wave me quickly through the massive iron gates. Washington was going to be a Republican city—a city that no longer belonged to us. But had it ever really belonged to us when we were there?

On the ride to Andrews, I used the car phone to call the Situation Room several times. Still, nothing new.

At Andrews, Air Force One, on loan from President Reagan, was waiting to take Citizen Jimmy Carter, on his way from the Inauguration, home to Georgia.

Several hundred people had turned out to see him off. The White House press corps was roped off in a designated area, straining like trapped animals against the ropes, hoping to shout their questions to the President—had the hostages been freed or not?

We loaded our bags onto the plane and milled around, waiting for the President and Mondale with the crowd of Cabinet members and White House staff.

We asked each other for news on the hostages. Rumors abounded, but no one knew anything. I went aboard Air Force One to call the Situation Room once again. Several of the crew were in the President's lounge, looking at Reagan, on television still at the Inaugural ceremonies.

They seemed embarrassed that I saw them watching Reagan, and after an awkward minute, they dispersed.

I called the Situation Room on the secure communications system to inquire about the hostages. The person who answered the phone asked me to hold on for a minute. He came back on and said he was sorry but the information was not available.

"But I'm calling on a secure phone," I protested.

"That's not the problem, Mr. Jordan. Mr. Carter is no longer President, so classified information is no longer available to you."

Stunned, I mumbled something, hung up, and walked back outside to wait for the President. I understood that when we lost the Presidency, the trappings of power went with it, but I hadn't expected the loss to be so immediate and complete.

The President and Mondale finally arrived in a modest motorcade. Carter seemed renewed by the friendly crowd and sprang out of the car.

They must have taken off, I thought. *He looks happy.*

A military honor guard conducted a farewell ceremony for the retiring President. This final touch was not lost on the Annapolis graduate. Jimmy Carter walked erectly down the long lines, reviewing the troops. He placed his hand over his heart as the band played "The Star-Spangled Banner."

The Cabinet and staff formed lines on both sides of the red carpet leading to the ramp. And, as the military band played lively Sousa marches, the President and the First Lady walked slowly down the lines, thanking the men and women who had been a part of their lives for the past four years.

When Carter reached me, he whispered, "Don't say anything yet, but they've taken off."

"Good," I replied. The instant that he moved on, I felt foolish. It was a time to say something memorable—and all I could come out with was "good."

Rafshoon and I sat together on the plane and looked out at the crowd. "There are our friends in the press," he said sarcastically, pointing to the White House press corps. "Two-thirds of them voted for us, but they're all glad to see us go."

It was a harsh statement, but largely true.

After four years of covering a President, there was a subtle but strong bias among the press corps in favor of the challenger. A new President meant new personalities to cover, new power struggles to analyze, and new controversies and scandals to discover and exploit.

Like an old, used sponge, we had been wrung dry of news.

Air Force One lifted off and turned southward toward Georgia. The captain dipped his wing as we crossed the Potomac, and we strained to get a last look at the White House and the city, partially covered with clouds.

As we had so many times before, Jody Powell; Phil Wise; Jerry Rafshoon; Susan Clough, the President's secretary; and several others gathered in the staff area to talk and relax. The crew had stocked Bloody Marys and champagne for the trip.

But our return was hardly a celebration. For most of us on the plane, the past several days had been a blur of tension and worry about the hostages. We were too numb and tired to celebrate.

As they often did, the President and Rosalynn joined us. Someone asked if there was any news on the hostages.

Carter grinned and said he had received word en route to the airport that the hostages had taken off. "While we're flying home to Georgia, the hostages will be leaving Iranian airspace to be safe and free."

Some staff members clapped; others hugged Rosalynn and shook the President's hand in congratulation. But their reaction, like my own, was subdued. All I could feel at that moment was relief.

Carter said that President Reagan would make the main announcement from Washington that they had cleared Iranian airspace, and that he would make a statement in Plains. "Wouldn't you like to know what's going on in that plane right now?" the President mused.

Then he talked on, as if he needed to vent his own feelings about those last difficult days. He admitted that he was totally exhausted and hadn't even had time to think about what it all had meant.

Then he told us about the arrival of the Reagans.

At the White House that morning, Carter had briefed the new President on everything that had taken place and had given him the latest report: the hostages were on the plane, and the plane had been cleared for takeoff. Carter said Reagan was pleasant and friendly, but seemed totally unaware of the pressure he—Carter—was under as he waited for news of the release. It was almost as if he didn't realize that the hostages were coming home.

As they rode together in the car to the Inaugural ceremonies, Carter said he thought that his successor might talk about the upcoming ceremony or ask about Carter's inaugural address or say something about the hostages. Instead, Ronald Reagan told a couple of corny jokes. Carter said he had to work hard to force a smile.

The Inauguration ceremony had not been difficult, Carter said. It was just a blur of words to him, as all he had been thinking about was whether the hostages had taken off—and whether the message would come.

He went on to say that he thought Reagan's offer for him to take Air Force One and greet the hostages in Wiesbaden was an act of real generosity.

"I'll give Reagan credit for being smart—but not generous," I said. "Those hostages are *your* hostages, Mr. President. Reagan would have caught hell if he hadn't asked you to go greet them."

Carter smiled and said, "Ham, you've grown cynical in your old age."

At Robins Air Force Base, we boarded the Presidential helicopter and choppered to Plains, where our Georgia friends had arranged a welcome. We landed on the red-clay baseball diamond, where Jimmy Carter, citizen; Jimmy Carter, candidate; and Jimmy Carter, President, had played countless games of softball. As we stepped off the helicopter into the chilly drizzle, we were welcomed by thousands of Georgians. A human chain stretched several hundred yards from the ball field to the center of town, where a platform had been erected for the occasion.

The well-wishers shouted greetings and congratulations as we walked along. Someone must have figured out that we had received a lot of flak over the past four years and very little thanks, and the people in the lines had been prompted to say something nice to each of us. "You did a great job," and, "Thanks for all you did for the country," were said over and over again.

The platform, draped in red-white-and-blue bunting, wet and soggy from the rain, with high school bands on both sides of it blaring out barely recognizable songs, made it feel like the Fourth of July in January—except, maybe, for the cold rain.

The President and Rosalynn mounted the platform and waved happily to the cheering crowd, which raised homemade banners and signs, many of them last-minute creations, expressing the hope that the hostages were on their way home.

The President announced: "Just a few moments ago on Air Force One, before we landed at Warner Robins, I received word officially for the first time that the aircraft carrying the fifty-two American hostages has cleared Iranian airspace." Carter continued, "Every one of the fifty-two hostages is alive, well, and free."

The crowd broke into a wild cheer, the country music band burst into song, and the President grabbed Rosalynn's waist and spun her around a few times to the delight of the crowd.

Then it was over. The President and the First Lady waved and left the platform. The crowd pressed around them for a hello or to touch them and then quickly scattered. They had come to Plains to see their hero. Once he had gone, there was nothing else to do in the tiny town.

The President, Rosalynn, and the staff went over to an old wooden barn behind the Carter Warehouse. There, the staff presented the President with a complete woodworking shop, which was already on display. He was genuinely pleased with the gift and thanked us profusely.

What a bizarre day this has been, I thought. *Just hours ago, Jimmy Carter sat in the Oval Office, orchestrating a complex international agreement involving human lives, billions of dollars, and the honor of a great nation. And now, here we are in an old barn in south Georgia, and Carter is poring over drills and saws and screwdrivers.*

We planned to leave early the next morning for Wiesbaden, so I had decided to stay with my mother in Albany, about forty miles away. But I hadn't made any arrangements to get there, since I hadn't had to worry about such details for four years.

Soaking wet, carrying a briefcase and suitcase, trying not to look too conspicuous, I wandered around for about an hour hoping to find someone from Albany who might give me a lift home. I finally called a taxi company from the pay phone at Billy Carter's old service station. I was told that no taxis were available, as they were all busy taking visiting VIPs from Plains to the airport.

I was beginning to feel like a hobo. Finally I bumped into an old friend in the Georgia State Patrol whom I knew from Carter's days as Governor. He found a patrolman driving toward Albany and arranged for me to hitch a ride. *It really is over*, I thought as I loaded my luggage into his trunk, climbed into the front seat, and headed home.

January 21, 1981 (Wednesday)

It was overcast when we arrived at the baseball field and boarded the Presidential helicopter for the flight back to Robins, where Air Force One was waiting to take us to Germany. But then I thought, *It really isn't Air Force One anymore. That designation belonged to the President's plane. Jimmy Carter is no longer President. We're hanging on to Carter's Presidency, with the big plane, the press following us, and all the amenities—but none of the power.*

The President looked as old and tired as I had ever seen him, but he smiled and talked excitedly about seeing the hostages. "Look what I'm bringing!" he exclaimed, holding up the *Americus Times Recorder* and the *Warner Robins Daily Sun*. The headlines read, CARTER EFFORTS BRING FREEDOM TO HOSTAGES and FREE AT LAST—HOSTAGES LEAVE IRAN. "Those headlines are as big as the ones they ran when World War Two ended," he said proudly. "I'm going to show this to the hostages just so they'll have some idea how much they were missed."

He said that he and Rosalynn had eaten dinner with Billy at his brother's home in Buena Vista, a town near Plains, and had been entertained by two poets from Arkansas. "I love Dylan Thomas, but you couldn't believe how good this poetry was."

"What was it about?" I asked.

Smiling broadly, he said, "It was about my Presidency."

The plane that was to take us to Germany had already been to Washington and picked up the group that was going to accompany the President to see the hostages. Mondale, Muskie, Harold Brown, Lloyd Cutler, Bill Miller, speechwriter Rick Hertzberg, and a number of others who had worked on the hostage situation were already on board. Vance had gone ahead to greet the hostages. The flight over was quiet and subdued. Almost all of those on board had been up most, if not all, of the past several days working on the negotiations and now had to be ready before dawn to go on this final trip with the former Chief Executive.

Carter rested on the way over, tried to reconstruct the past several days in writing, and asked Lloyd Cutler and the others to undertake the same exercise. He then spent a half hour with Henry Precht, who had brought along an album with the photographs of the hostages. Precht sat in the President's compartment on the sofa across from Carter, moving his finger from picture to picture, chatting easily about the hostages and their backgrounds and relaying any information as to how they had withstood the ordeal. The President would often nod or mention that he had talked with the wife of this hostage, had received the mother and father of that one in the Oval Office, or had exchanged letters with the family of another. Precht's time with Carter seemed to chill the President with the realization that he would soon be facing these fifty-two Americans. (One of the hostages had been released several months before because of illness.)

A few minutes later, Carter summoned Jody and me to his compartment and we talked as the plane reached the coast and began its long descent into Frankfurt. Looking out the window, Carter said, "You know, this could be unpleasant. Henry tells me that most of the hostages have little or no idea of what we did to obtain their release. They have been told over and over again that they were forgotten by their President and by the American people. I could be dealing with some pretty unhappy people."

I conjured up a horrible vision: the Chief Executive comes all the way to Germany to see the hostages only to be rebuked and possibly embarrassed.

Jody brought up the matter of the press. "Mr. President, this will be our best and only chance to explain the details of the agreement. It's a damn good agreement, but so complicated that there aren't five people in the press who understand it. The first round of stories is that the hostages are out. The second round of stories will ask the question, 'What did we have to do to get them out?' I'd recommend that we let Lloyd and Muskie have a briefing after you see the hostages and explain the deal."

"What will I do while they brief?"

"I'd suggest that you simply return to the plane and wait for them," said Jody.

"That will sure delay our getting back to the States if they have to brief the press and allow them time to file," Carter objected.

"Mr. President, it is our best and last chance to put our spin on the story."

"You're right," he said, gazing out the window. "For the first time in a long while, I don't have any reason to rush."

We touched down on German soil and taxied over to the area where the press and Bundesrepublik officials waited to greet the President. I was overwhelmed by the number of people waving

American flags tied with yellow ribbons. Although it was evening, the airport was bright as day with thousands of flashbulbs and the television lights.

Loud applause and shouts greeted Jimmy Carter as he stepped off Air Force One. I was happy for him. He walked down the ramp, jauntily worked his way through the receiving line of German officials, and went to a small building to meet Chancellor Helmut Schmidt and Foreign Minister Hans Dietrich Genscher.

Soon government officials and press people were scrambling for their cars, as the President's limousine, led by a twin column of motorcycles with screaming sirens, pulled out of the airport and onto the highway the police had cleared.

We pulled up in front of the hospital. Nurses, doctors, and hospital employees crowded the windows, waving flags and clapping. The area in front was filled with German and American citizens with the now-familiar American flags decorated with yellow ribbons. The President stood on the running board and waved to the crowd, which responded with a roar.

"I think those people forgot to vote," he quipped.

"Or maybe you should have run for Chancellor of Germany," I said.

We were met by Sheldon Krys, the State Department official who had been responsible throughout the crisis for liaison with the hostages' families and the preparations for the return. The President, Muskie, Cutler, Vance, and I gathered around Krys and the doctors.

"Mr. President," Krys began, "I am sorry to report to you that the mistreatment and abuse of the hostages was more comprehensive and severe than we had anticipated. All of them were subjected to mental abuse and some of them to physical cruelty, particularly those with military backgrounds and those suspected of having intelligence responsibilities."

Carter winced. I wondered about that later. It seemed strange to me that he might have expected otherwise.

Then Krys and the psychiatrist with him described the attitude of the hostages toward the Chief Executive.

"Mr. President," said Krys, "there is a good bit of hostility among the group toward you. One of the former hostages has even refused to attend this meeting. These people have basically been told over and over, 'The U.S. doesn't care about you, and Carter doesn't care about you, and nothing has been done to win your release.' They have almost no sense of what we did to get them out and no sense of the feeling of the American people toward them. We have tried to convey to them what they have come to represent to America and the world. They may understand it in their heads, but they don't really believe it or know it in their hearts. We have had to remind ourselves time and again what they were told for the past four hundred forty-four days. Mr. President, I do not think that your meeting with them will be easy, but the gesture you make by coming is very important."

"I understand," he said. "Do you have any advice for me or any suggestions that I could convey?"

"We are concerned that they not return quickly to the United States. Some are eager to go right away, but we think they need more time here. It would be helpful if you could find a way to reinforce that."

We took the elevator up to the third floor and walked down the hall. Nurses and doctors stood in the doorways, some smiling and holding out their hands in greeting, or waving. As we approached the door, I could feel my heart pounding as I realized that in a second I would be seeing them. We stepped into a very ordinary-looking room that may have been a converted ward. There were windows along the back wall. Sitting in three circles of folding chairs which faced the center of the room were the former hostages, wearing baggy hospital clothes or, in the case of the Marines, blue robes. One man had on a Penn State football jersey. The Marines, sitting together, had already gotten crew cuts. Some of the hostages were silent, others chatted. When they realized the President had just come in, they all rose and applauded politely. Carter, Vance, and Muskie walked into the center of the circle while the rest of us stood along the rear wall of the room.

With Bruce Laingen, the senior American hostage, Cy Vance and Ed Muskie at his side, the President began to walk around the room, shaking the hand of each hostage and sharing a few words. The third person he spoke with had tears in his eyes, and when Carter held out his hand, the man threw his arms around the Chief Executive and smothered him with a bear hug. Carter, at first surprised, was touched by the gesture and hugged him back. From then on, Laingen would introduce the President, and the former hostage and Carter would lock in an embrace. Some of the embraces seemed reluctant, but many times they were followed by tears. The only sound in the room was the President talking quietly to each hostage: "Your wife has been great," or, "I saw your family in the Oval Office last month," or, "I spoke with your wife and children last week."

Then the President stepped into the center of the room, his lips tightly compressed. He took a deep breath and began in a soft but firm voice, "It is a great honor for me, on behalf of the American people and our new President Reagan, to welcome you back to freedom." He paused and looked around at the faces of the former captives. "I know that you have not been kept informed of either the feelings of the American people or our efforts to win your release. Let me just say that more prayers were offered in the past four hundred forty-four days for your health and safety than at any other time in the history of our country. There is no way for me to describe adequately the feelings of the American people for you or to explain what you have come to represent to our nation."

He then held up the two Georgia newspapers he had brought with him and turned them so everyone could see the front pages.

Smiling, he continued, "Normally, the day after Inauguration, the headlines are devoted to the new President and his address to the nation. You stole the headlines from President Reagan. But he doesn't mind—and he asked me to express to you each his admiration and best wishes."

A few of the former hostages smiled. Others did not. I began to fear that his efforts to reach them were not working.

Turning serious, Carter said, "I know that you have each been through an incredibly difficult emotional and physical ordeal. I came here to welcome you back to freedom and to congratulate you on the way that you conducted yourselves through this ordeal." He looked around the room again. "You are considered heroes by the American people. But let me tell you about a group of people who have also represented you and our country well, and that is your families. They have demonstrated a quiet courage and strength through very difficult and trying times when we did not know where you were or whether or not you were alive. Many of your families have become like members of my family. We have worried, prayed, and endured together, and taken comfort from one another.

"I know that you probably have many questions, and I would like to have an opportunity to answer them. But first let me say that I take full responsibility for the decisions made by our government. I may have made mistakes, but the decisions were made always in what we thought were the best interests of our nation.

"I would be glad to try to answer your questions."

A lean man later identified as Thomas Ahern rose, and, looking straight ahead as if not to even acknowledge the President, spoke in a trembling, angry voice. "Mr. President, why did you let the Shah into the States when the embassy advised against it?"

"That's a good question, and one that you all deserve to understand. When the Shah decided to leave Iran, which we had encouraged, we offered him residence in the United States. He refused that offer, as you know, and traveled to Egypt, Morocco, and finally Mexico. He wanted then to come to the States, but we were trying to make our peace with the Khomeini government and discouraged him from coming. In October, Secretary Vance reported to me that the Shah was critically ill with cancer and needed treatment of a sort that could be obtained only in the United States. Secretary Vance and all my other advisers supported his entry into the United States as a matter of principle. They felt that we could not turn down the humanitarian request of a dying man who also had been an ally of our nation for thirty-seven years. We had also had the experience the previous February when the Iranian government came to the aid of our embassy immediately after it was overrun. With that in mind, I made a reluctant decision to allow the Shah to come in." Pausing, he added, "Unfortunately, you know the rest of the story."

Another man asked, "Why did you attempt the rescue mission?"

"By the middle of April, the prospects for your return were very dim. We had negotiated in good faith with the Iranians, but every time we came close to gaining your release, Khomeini would say or do something that destroyed any chance of it. I had ordered the military at the outset to prepare a rescue mission to be used in case of a dire emergency. In the event, for example, the Iranians had begun to execute or try you. The Joint Chiefs were very discouraging at first about the possibilities of such a mission, but by late March they had devised a plan, practiced it over and over, and felt confident. Also, by this time we had developed good intelligence in and around the compound. It was in that atmosphere of no hope for a negotiated release and confidence in the rescue mission that I ordered it. Of course, it failed. It was bad luck and the lack of a helicopter. Eight brave men gave their lives on the deserts of Iran trying to save you."

There was an awkward silence, as though everyone in the room were thinking about the mission, its failure, the dead men, and the effects on their own lives.

Another man stood up. "Mr. President," he said respectfully, "I am concerned about the honor of our country. Does the agreement which led to our release protect the honor of the United States?"

"Yes. Let me explain to you: First, soon after you were seized, it became obvious to me that the Iranian government was not going to force your captors to release you. I ordered thirteen billion dollars in Iranian assets frozen. Under the terms of the agreement, only three billion dollars have been returned."

Spontaneously and immediately, the former hostages applauded loudly.

Carter was clearly delighted by their response: "I thought you'd like that." He continued. "More important than money, however, is the honor of our country. We never apologized to Iran as they demanded. Nor did we agree to extradite the Shah."

Warming up, with real emotion and anger in his voice, he said, "Iran today is isolated politically and economically in the world, scorned by the world community for condoning an illegal and inhumane act. I sincerely believe that your example and the agreement that led to your release are powerful statements against terrorism in the world. And in a way that you will be able to understand only when you return to the States, this crisis has unified our nation and people in a strange way like nothing in my lifetime since World War Two.

"Well, I don't want to keep you too long. I appreciate very much your service to our country, and I thank you for allowing me to meet with you so soon after your return. Let me ask you one last favor. I've talked with your doctors, and they are pleased with your health but are worried that some of you might want to rush home. Don't be in too great a hurry. Stay here as long as they recommend. If not for your own problems, you should stay here with your colleagues and lend your friendship and support. It's the last request that I'll make of you," the President said, beaming. He then introduced everyone who had come with him. When he got to me, he said, "Ham came closer than you'll probably ever know to getting you out last spring."

The meeting was over, and a more relaxed and friendly atmosphere prevailed. The hostages were chatty as they gathered around Carter to shake his hand and have their pictures taken with him or went next door to phone their loved ones.

The doctor in charge said, "In a word, it was therapeutic for them to have this session. Beyond that, the symbol of the President traveling all the way here just to see them for a few hours is proof that as a nation we care very much for them as people."

By now the hostages began to circulate among the rest of us. Former hostage Mike Holland came up to me and said, "I was held at the Foreign Ministry and know all about your negotiations with the French lawyers."

I was surprised. "How did you know what I did?"

"Ghotbzadeh's office was just down the hall from us and people there kept us informed of your negotiations."

"I'm only sorry that it didn't work."

"But you tried. At least those of us at the Ministry had a radio. We knew that something was going on. Those poor bastards at the compound didn't think anyone cared."

The President went to the phone room, where six or eight of the former hostages were talking to their families in the States.

He stood quietly for a couple of minutes. Then he walked over to one, then another, of the hostages, putting his hand on their shoulders and taking the phone to say, "He looks great," or,

"After a home-cooked meal, he'll be back to normal."

Now it was time to go. "Are you going to fly back with us, Cy?" the President asked.

"No, Mr. President. I am going to stay for another day and try to spend some time with my people."

They shook hands and we departed for the press briefing, which took place at a large room at the airport terminal. Carter left for the plane.

Because it involved the official explanation of the Declaration of Algiers, the briefing was long, involved, and tedious. The news people demanded details of hostage torture. An hour later, we were back at Air Force One, ready to head home.

Usually after a foreign trip there was a general release of pent-up tensions on the journey back to the States. The speechwriters had no more speeches or welcoming remarks or toasts to write, the advance staff could forget about the President's schedule and who would sit where in each meeting, the Secret Service agents could relax and play cards, and, for better or worse, the work of the Chief Executive and his advisers was done. So, when everyone climbed back on Air Force One, there was usually a joyous mood, if not to celebrate the results of the trip, at least to toast its conclusion.

President Carter would usually disappear into his compartment up front and reappear in forty-five minutes or an hour dressed in casual clothes, holding a handful of thank-you letters that he had written for Susan to photocopy and send out. He and Rosalynn would then talk with the staff and sometimes stroll to the rear of the plane to make some comment to the press pool. The crew would serve a hearty meal—often a steak—and, after eating, lights would begin to go off and everyone on the plane would go to sleep, exhausted physically and emotionally from the intense schedule and the enormous pressures on the President that had been transferred to them in bits and pieces during the preceding days.

But on the way home from Wiesbaden, the festive atmosphere never ended.

Jody and I stopped by the President's compartment to report on the briefing. "How'd it go?"

"Lloyd, Ed, and Bill did a good job," Jody reported, "but all the press was interested in was trying to get some details on the treatment of the hostages."

"Those people were barbarians," the President said under his breath.

He spent a few minutes writing a report to Reagan. In it he referred to the Iranian captors as savages, argued that the new Administration should support the agreement that had brought about the release of the hostages because it was "good and honorable," and finally thanked his successor for sending him to Germany. He also wrote personal notes to Omar Torrijos, Christian Bourguet, and Hector Villalon, thanking them for their help. (He also wrote a note to Hal Saunders's children, praising their father as the "hero" of the negotiations, and apologizing for keeping him away from home so much during the year.)

About an hour after takeoff, he summoned me to his compartment. "I've just talked to Chris, Ham, and thought I would pass along something he said. He said that he was thinking about you tonight and how everyone was crediting him for winning the release of the hostages. He said you came so close to getting them out earlier, and that he was just thinking of you."

I was touched by Chris's compliment and slightly embarrassed. "That was nice of him," I said, and tried to change the subject.

"You know, Ham, if we had had a little luck back in March or April and gotten 'em out then, we might be flying back to Washington instead of Plains. But I wonder deep down if I would really want to go back to Washington." He seemed to be thinking out loud as he continued. "You know, Rosalynn and I have talked several times since November about how I really felt about the re-election. There are all these forces that compel an incumbent President to run again. You're surrounded by people who want to continue in their jobs, who want you to run. You get this sense of wanting to consummate what you started in your first term, and not to run would be considered by many as an indication that you don't think you could be re-elected and an acknowledgment of failure. I never seriously considered not running, but I've wondered what my true feelings were. I was disappointed, but I have to admit that I was also relieved."

After a big dinner, the President joined a boisterous group that had gathered in the lounge area, and for several hours we

swapped stories and exchanged toasts. Most of us had slept only
four or five hours in the last two or three days and were operating
on adrenaline and champagne.

"You extended your Presidency longer than anyone else in
American history," Muskie joked.

"I bet it's driving the Reagan folks crazy," Jody added, "being
in the White House and seeing us dominating the news."

"Hell—let's just highjack this plane!" Mondale proposed.

"We already have," I said. "We're going to New Hampshire
tonight and start handing out Jimmy Carter brochures for 1984!"

Everyone laughed.

"That's fine," Fritz retorted. "Just drop me off in Iowa" [the
first state to elect delegates].

The President turned serious, raised his champagne glass high,
and repeated his Oval Office toast: "To freedom!"

"To freedom!" we all shouted back, shaking hands and slapping
one another on the back.

Carter said we should keep the champagne glasses bearing the
Presidential seal as mementos, and the celebration ended. We
returned to our seats to doze or talk quietly for the hour or so that
remained before we landed in Georgia.

I wandered up to the cockpit, as I often did on Air Force One,
and sat in the jump seat behind the Captain. *What are my own
feelings?* I thought, gazing out at the beautiful dark sky, the
brightness of the stars blurred and shaded by the soft clouds.
Mostly relief, I decided. I was glad to be going home and leaving
Washington. *It will be nice to wake up tomorrow morning and
not have to worry about the inflation rate or polls or criticism of
me*. I thought about the President's physical appearance. The
boyish look of his early forties had disappeared. The formerly
sandy hair was gray, and wrinkles were creeping across his face.

I wondered how much I had changed. I had gone to Washington as a hero, described by many in the media as a "genius." I
was returning to Georgia a loser.

Then I began to imagine how Jimmy Carter would respond to
his defeat. The challenge of working to liberate the hostages had
probably insulated him from facing the question of what a former
President does with his life. I hoped he'd never run again for that
office. Politically, it didn't seem to be in the cards—but stranger

things had happened. For selfish reasons I dreaded the thought of that call and could just hear him saying, "Let's get you and Jody and Rafshoon and Kirbo together and talk about the future." Or, "Ham, why don't you put your thoughts down on paper about 1984?"

"Yes, sir," I would certainly say—after gulping. Out of loyalty and affection I would unquestionably help him again. But I hoped that would never happen. I'd had a once-in-a-lifetime experience, but I had no desire to repeat it.

My private nightmare was interrupted by the Captain, who reported that we were beginning our descent.

As the plane cut through the gray Georgia clouds, I looked out on the unmistakable flat green farmland, sliced by red clay roads and sprinkled with houses and barns.

After so many voyages and so many memories, my long odyssey with the man from Plains was finally coming to an end.

This would surely be my last flight on Air Force One, which had carried me all over the world. *But I won't miss this plane*, I thought, *or the White House or Washington. I will miss these people who have been so much a part of my life for the past decade*.

After we had landed, I strolled back to the cabin to say goodbye to those who were continuing on to Washington. I spent a few minutes bidding farewell to Ed Muskie, Fritz Mondale, and Harold Brown. We all said the same thing. We'd have to stay in touch; get together regularly. As I heard myself speaking those words I knew that the intention was good, but without the glue of the Carter White House we'd go our separate ways.

Jody approached me and said, "Doctor, it's been something, hasn't it?"

"It has," I muttered. "It really has . . ." I grabbed his hand.

Jimmy Carter came back and circulated as I had seen him do thousands of times in pursuit of the Presidency and thousands of times after his election. But now it was different.

The brief exchanges were filled with emotion. He moved from person to person, firmly grasping the hands of each friend. Some mumbled their thoughts; others remained silent—words were not necessary. The President said his thank yous and goodbyes quietly.

Finally he said farewell to Fritz Mondale, a man very different from him, but one who had been his loyal friend through good times and bad. I couldn't help thinking of Mondale's own ambitions to be President—or wondering why, after seeing what four years had done to Carter, he would want the job.

Jimmy Carter disappeared into his compartment and emerged in his tan topcoat, briefcase in hand. He walked back down the aisle, where Jody and I were waiting. Knowing it was going to be difficult, he tried to lighten the moment. "You clowns don't forget about me down in Plains. We've been through too much together not to stay close."

I couldn't bring myself to say anything. I attempted a smile, nodded, and shook his hand.

He held my hand an extra second, then turned and stepped out the door.

Mondale and I walked out onto the ramp and watched Jimmy Carter skip down the steps, pausing at the bottom to wave to the military families from the base who had gathered to greet him. He walked quickly over to the borrowed Presidential helicopter that would carry him home to Plains. Jody, cigarette in one hand, briefcase in the other, hurried to catch up with him.

The President paused to give a quick salute to the Marine standing at attention by the door of the helicopter, then climbed aboard. Marine One hovered several feet above the ground. We could see the President through his window. He saw Fritz and me standing on the ramp and waved. He was not smiling.

The green bird turned west toward Plains, lifted quickly into the dark sky, and was gone.

Index

424